List of Etonians who fought in the great war, 1914-1919

Edward Littleton Vaughan, Eton College

Nabu Public Domain Reprints:

You are holding a reproduction of an original work published before 1923 that is in the public domain in the United States of America, and possibly other countries. You may freely copy and distribute this work as no entity (individual or corporate) has a copyright on the body of the work. This book may contain prior copyright references, and library stamps (as most of these works were scanned from library copies). These have been scanned and retained as part of the historical artifact.

This book may have occasional imperfections such as missing or blurred pages, poor pictures, errant marks, etc. that were either part of the original artifact, or were introduced by the scanning process. We believe this work is culturally important, and despite the imperfections, have elected to bring it back into print as part of our continuing commitment to the preservation of printed works worldwide. We appreciate your understanding of the imperfections in the preservation process, and hope you enjoy this valuable book.

LIST OF ETONIANS WHO FOUGHT IN THE GREAT WAR MCMXIV-MCMXIX

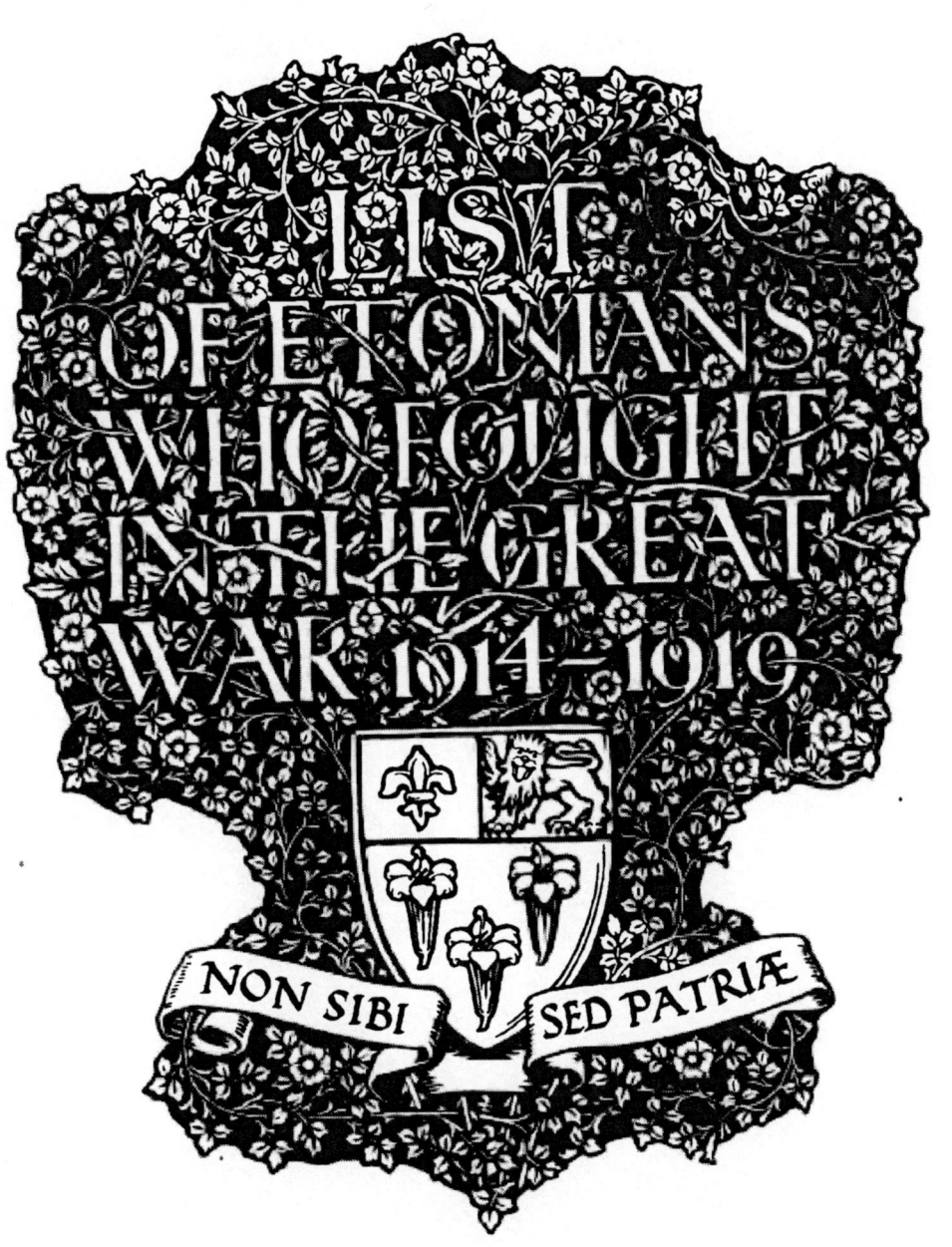

THIS BOOK IS DEDICATED
TO THOSE ETONIANS WHO GAVE
THEIR LIVES IN THE GREAT WAR
MCMXIV - MCMXIX

INTO BATTLE

THE naked earth is warm with Spring,
    And with green grass and bursting trees
    Leans to the sun's gaze glorying
  And quivers in the sunny breeze;
And Life is Colour and Warmth and Light,
  And a striving evermore for these;
And he is dead who will not fight;
  And who dies fighting has increase.

The fighting man shall from the sun
  Take warmth, and life from the glowing earth;
Speed with the light-foot winds to run,
  And with the trees to newer birth;
And find, when fighting shall be done,
  Great rest, and fullness after dearth.

All the bright company of Heaven
  Hold him in their high comradeship,
The Dog-Star, and the Sisters Seven,
  Orion's Belt and sworded hip.

The woodland trees that stand together,
  They stand to him each one a friend;
They gently speak in the windy weather
  They guide to valley and ridges' end.

The kestrel hovering by day,
  And the little owls that call by night,
Bid him be swift and keen as they,
  As keen of ear, as swift of sight.

The blackbird sings to him, "Brother, brother,
   If this be the last song you shall sing,
Sing well, for you may not sing another;
   Brother, sing."

In dreary doubtful waiting hours,
   Before the brazen frenzy starts,
The horses show him nobler powers;
   O patient eyes, courageous hearts!

And when the burning moment breaks,
   And all things else are out of mind,
And only Joy-of-Battle takes
   Him by the throat, and makes him blind.

Through joy and blindness he shall know,
   Not caring much to know, that still
Nor lead nor steel shall reach him, so
   That it be not the Destined Will.

The thundering line of battle stands,
   And in the air Death moans and sings;
But Day shall clasp him with strong hands,
   And Night shall fold him in soft wings.

JULIAN GRENFELL.

Flanders, April 1915.

PREFATORY NOTE

THIS is the Final Edition of the List of Etonians who served in the Great War between 4 August 1914 and 28 June 1919, or in the Baltic or Russia during the next few months. The rule made is that no one is included whose name was not in the Navy, Army, or Air Force Lists during some part at any rate of that period, with the exception of those serving overseas without military rank in such units as the Red Cross, whose names are added in an appendix. The service which entitles to inclusion in the List is supposed to be whole-time service, and therefore Officers of the O.T.C. are, as a rule, excluded, as well as some others. After the appendix are also placed the names of seven Etonians, imprisoned at Ruhleben, who would otherwise probably have served in the War.

The name of Field-Marshal Earl Roberts is included, as he died, 14 November 1914, aged 82, on a visit to the Indian Contingent in France, of illness due to his refusal, when he was reviewing troops who were without their greatcoats, to wear his own.

The names of those whose deaths are directly attributable to the war are rubricated. The number is 1,157.

Temporary, as well as substantive, but not acting rank, is given, and no distinction is made between Regulars and others.

The rank mentioned is that given in the Army List for July 1919 or in the last issue in which the name occurs, but Honours conferred and mentions in dispatches for services before July 1919 are counted up to the last Gazette in 1920. No deaths occurring after 1920 are noted.

In the case of Brigade Commanders and Officers of superior rank, the name of their original Regiment or other unit is added in brackets.

The term R.H.A. is not employed, but R.F.A. or R.G.A., and in the case of some who served only on the Staff, R.A.

Those Chaplains to the Forces only are included who served overseas.

Mentions in Dispatches for actual operations are alone given.

Where a Theatre of War is not mentioned, there was no service overseas, and the duties of D.C.O. are not reckoned as such service. In several cases, the subsequent home service of officers invalided from the front is not given. Service overseas after the armistice is not counted, except that in the Baltic and Russia. Belgium as a Theatre of War is included in France, and Salonica in the Balkans. The terms Palestine and Egypt include respectively the Syrian Campaign, and the campaigns in Sinai and against the Senussi.

The dates on the left of the entries denote the year of leaving Eton, and the initials on the right the Eton House or Houses.

Honours gained previous to the war are printed in smaller Capitals, with the exception of the V.C., which was won in the Great War by Capt. A. H. H. Batten-Pooll, Lt.-Col. A. D. Borton, Lt. G. A. Boyd-Rochfort, Brig.-Gen. J. V. Campbell, †Bt. Maj. W. La T. Congreve, Lt.-Cr. G. H. Drummond, †Lt. J. S. Dunville, †Lt.-Col. N. B. Elliott-Cooper, Lt.-Col. L. P. Evans, Capt. J. R. N. Graham, †Capt. F. O. Grenfell, †Capt. J. R. Gribble, Maj. P. H. Hansen.

A Summary of the Casualties, of the units of Service, and of Honours gained is added at the end of the book.

With regard to almost all doubtful points, the advice has been sought of Lieut.-Gen. The Earl of Cavan (O.E.), or of the Committee, consisting of the Provost, the Vice-Provost, the Head Master, and the Lower Master, appointed by the War Memorial Council to co-operate with the Compiler, who desires to express his thanks to them, and to many others who have given assistance. Among these may be specially mentioned Lieut.-Gen. Sir P. W. Chetwode, Bart. (O.E.), Military Secretary 1919-1920, Lieut.-Gen. Sir F. J. Davies (O.E.), Military Secretary 1916-1919, Vice-Admiral Sir W. C. Pakenham (O.E.), Col. M. D. Graham, C.B., C.M.G., C.V.O., Deputy Military Secretary, Col. W. B. Capper, C.V.O., of the Casualty Department of the War Office, Lt.-Col. S. G. Menzies (O.E.) of the Military Intelligence Department of the War Office, and Maj. B. E. Sutton (O.E.) of the Air Ministry.

Mr. Clay, Assistant Secretary of the O.E.A., and Mr. Barrand, both Lay-clerks of the College, also deserve recognition for their help.

Inaccuracies are inevitable in a long list, and in some cases may be attributable to the fact that a few of those who served have not returned, or have returned too late, the Forms which were sent to them to be filled up and corrected.

The title-page is designed by Mr. Graily Hewitt and reproduced by Mr. Emery Walker, F.S.A. and his craftsmen, and it may be interesting to note that the Greek motto from Simonides was written out specially for this book on the model of a MS. of Hellanicus of the Second Century by Professor F. C. Burkitt, D.D. To all these, and to Lord Desborough, who has allowed the poem of his son, the late Capt. Julian Grenfell, to be here printed, the compiler is under great obligation.

A copy of this book will be written on vellum by Mr. Graily Hewitt, and deposited at Eton, to be kept and seen there.

ABBREVIATIONS

w. = wounded.   d. = died.   d.w. = died of wounds.   k. = killed.
p. = prisoner.   (F) = a foreign decoration, or foreign decorations.
I.A. = Indian Army.   I.A.R. = Indian Army Reserve.   E.F. = Expeditionary Force.
F.F. = Field Force or Frontier Force.   I.W.T. = Inland Water Transport.
m. = mentioned in dispatches.   sp. = special.   t. = temporary.

COLLEGE, DAMES AND HOUSE-MASTERS

K.S.	= College	260	H.S.S.S.	= H. S. S. Salt	2
D.	= Miss Drury	1	R.C.R.	= Rev. R. C. Radcliffe	141
de R.	= Baroness de Rosen	1	F.D.	= F. Drew	9
E.	= Miss Edgar	1	H.G.W.	= H. G. Wintle	30
G.	= Miss Gulliver	7	H.B.	= H. Broadbent	159
R.	= Mrs. Roberts	1	E.L.V.	= E. L. Vaughan	177
W.E.	= W. Evans	27	P.H.C.	= Dr. P. H. Carpenter	12
J.M.E.	= Miss Evans	209	S.A.D.	= Rev. S. A. Donaldson	111
T.H.S.	= T. H. Stevens	3	P.W.	= P. Williams	151
F.F.V.	= Rev. F. F. Vidal	17	S.R.J.	= Rev. S. R. James	54
F.E.D.	= Rev. F. E. Durnford	19	C.L.	= C. Lowry	39
E.B.	= Rev. E. Balston	1	E.I.	= E. Impey	179
J.E.Y.	= Rev. J. E. Yonge	3	C.H.A.	= C. H. Allcock	107
J.L.J.	= Rev. J. L. Joynes	7	A.C.B.	= A. C. Benson	70
W.B.M.	= Rev. W. B. Marriott	8	A.A.S.	= A. A. Somerville	155
J.W.H.	= Rev. J. W. Hawtrey	5	J.H.M.H.	= J. H. M. Hare	144
C.W.D.	= Rev. C. Wolley Dod	15	T.C.P.	= Dr. T. C. Porter	68
R.D.	= Rev. R. Day	4	F.J.T.	= Rev. F. J. Tuck	5
E.H.	= Rev. E. Hale	76	R.W.W.-T.	= R. W. White-Thomson	72
W.W.	= Rev. W. Wayte	10	H.F.W.T.	= H. F. W. Tatham	88
C.C.J.	= Rev. C. C. James	22	H.M.	= H. Macnaghten	115
E.D.S.	= Rev. E. D. Stone	1	H.Br.	= H. Brinton	122
H.S.	= Rev. H. Snow (Dr. Kynaston)	9	A.C.G.H.	= A. C. G. Heygate	104
F. St. J. T.	= Rev. F. St. J. Thackeray	2	H.T.B.	= Rev. H. T. Bowlby	77
G.R.D.	= Rev. G. R. Dupuis	7	L.F.	= Rev. L. Ford	5
E.W.	= Rev. E. Warre	52	R.P.L.B.	= R. P. L. Booker	107
O.B.	= O. Browning	13	J.M.D.	= J. M. Dyer	66
F.W.C.	= F. Warre Cornish	68	R.S.K.	= R. S. Kindersley	95
E.P.R.	= E. P. Rouse	3	R. S. de H.	= R. S. de Havilland	91
T.D.	= Rev. T. Dalton	77	A.M.G.	= A. M. Goodhart	66
E.C.A.L.	= E. C. Austen Leigh	163	L.S.R.B.	= L. S. R. Byrne	88
A.C.A.	= A. C. Ainger	121	E.W.S.	= E. W. Stone	77
H.W.M.	= H. W. Mozley	73	P.V.B.	= P. V. Broke	52
A.C.J.	= A. C. James	137	C.M.W.	= C. M. Wells	47
H.E.L.	= H. E. Luxmoore	111	E.L.C.	= E. L. Churchill	70
F.T.	= F. Tarver	72	W.D.E.	= W. D. Eggar	1
G.E.M.	= G. E. Marindin	62	A.B.R.	= A. B. Ramsay	55
R.A.H.M.	= R. A. H. Mitchell	127	M.D.H.	= M. D. Hill	53
J.P.C.	= J. P. Carter	99	C.H.K.M.	= C. H. K. Marten	43
C.L.L.-C.	= Rev. C. L. Lovett-Cameron	18	H. de H.	= H. de Havilland	36
A.C.	= A. Cockshott	16	S.G.L.	= S. G. Lubbock	23
W.D.	= W. Durnford	126	A.E.C.	= A. E. Conybeare	25
H.D.	= Rev. H. Daman	86	V. Le N.F.	= V. Le Neve Foster	24
C.H.E.	= C. H. Everard	68	A.C.R.-W.	= A. C. Rayner-Wood	9
J.B.L.	= Rev. J. B. Lock	2	F.E.R.	= F. E. Robeson	9
J.C.	= J. Cole	37	T.F.C.	= T. F. Cattley	1
E.S.S.	= E. S. Shuckburgh	10	R. H. de M.	= R. H. de Montmorency	1
J.H.M.	= Rev. J. H. Merriott	9	L.T.	= L. Todd	
F.H.R.	= F. H. Rawlins	142	F.W.D.	= F. W. Dobbs	
			Home		7

In cases where anyone was in two or more Houses, the first only is counted in the above enumeration.

The numerals denote the number in College and in each House who served.

ΤΩΝΔΕ ΔΙ ΑΝΘΡΩΠΩΝ ΑΡΕΤΑΝ

ETON WAR LIST

Please fill in below and forward at once to
E. L. Vaughan, Esq.
The Marches, Willowbrook,
Eton,
any corrections for the Libro d'oro, which will be placed in Eton College.

Rank or Unit of Service

Honours

Other information

2

THE RECORD OF SERVICE

1916 Abbey, N. R., Lt. Grenadier Gds. France (k. 12.4.18)   A.A.S.
1886 Abercorn, Duke of (Lord Paisley and then Marquess of Hamilton at Eton), Capt. 1st Life Gds., att. N. Irish Horse   W.D.
1903 Abercromby, Sir G. W., Bart., D.S.O., Lt.-Col. Black Watch, m. 2. France   A.C.B.
1913 Abercromby, R. A., M.C., Lt. Scots Gds., w., m. France   A.M.G.
1898 Abercromby, R. O., Capt. Gordon Highlanders, late empld. R.A.F., w., m. France   H.D.
1915 Abraham, P. S., Lt. (t. Capt.) R.A., and Staff. France   K.S.
1910 Ackerley, R. H., Lt. R. Welch Fusiliers. France (k. 16.5.15)   K.S.
1914 Ackerley, R. O., M.C., Lt. S. Wales Borderers, w. 4. France   K.S.
1901 Ackers, C. P., Capt. R.A.S.C., M.T., w., m. 2. France   J.P.C., A.C.G.H.
1915 Acland, A. W., M.C., Lt. Grenadier Gds., w. 2. France   E.L.C.
1906 Acland, W. H. D., M.C., A.F.C. (F) Capt. R. 1st Devon Yeomanry, late Major R.A.F., w., m. France   S.A.D., P.V.B.
1877 Acland-Hood, A. Fuller-, empld. Lt.-Col. Cheshire Regt., and Staff, m. Egypt, Gallipoli   E.W.
1915 Acland-Hood, C. A. J., Midshipman R.N. Home waters (k. 31.5.16)   H.Br.
1913 Acland-Hood, F. P., M.C., Capt. Coldstream Gds., and Staff. France   H.T.B., S.G.L.
1895 Acland-Troyte, G. J., C.M.G., D.S.O., Lt.-Col. K.R.R.C., and Staff, m. 6. France   S.A.D.
1889 Acland-Troyte, H. L., Lt.-Col. Devonshire Regt., and Staff. France, Italy, Mesopotamia (k. 17.4.18)   E.W., S.A.D.

1899	Acland-Troyte, H. W., M.C., Capt. (t. Maj.) R. 1st Devon Yeomanry, and Staff Australian Artillery, m. France	S.A.D.
1877	Adam, Sir C. E., Bart., V.D., Lt., Staff, late A.B., R.N.V.R. France	O B., W.D.
1914	Adams, W. McM., Capt. R.E. France	A.M.G.
1889	Adamson, M. C., Lt. Rifle Bde. France	H.D.
1872	Adderley, Hon. H. A., Capt. Warwickshire Yeomanry	E.
1904	Adderley, H. B. A., Capt. Scots Gds., att. M.G.C. and Staff. Gallipoli	H.T.B.
1902	Addington, Lord, O.B.E., T.D.(Mr. Hubbard at Eton), Capt. (t. Maj.) Oxfordshire and Bucks L.I., m. N. Russia	A.C.J., H.T.B.
1889	Adlercron, R. L., C.M.G., D.S.O. and Bar (F) Brig.-Gen. (Cameron Highlanders), m. 5. France	J.C.
1914	Agar-Robartes, Hon. A. G., M.C., Lt. Grenadier Gds., and Staff, w. France	M.D.H.
1906	Agar-Robartes, Hon. A. V., M.C., Lt. Grenadier Gds., w. 3. France	J.M.E.
1911	Agar-Robartes, Hon. C. E., Lt. Rifle Bde., att. Tank Corps. France	J.M.E., M.D.H.
1899	Agar-Robartes, Hon. T. C. R., M.P., Capt. Coldstream Gds., late Capt. Buckinghamshire Yeomanry, w., m. France (d.w. 30.9.15)	J.M.E.
1912	Agnew, E. S., Lt. 5th Lancers, and Staff, m. France, Egypt	H.Br.
1883	Aikenhead, F., Lt.-Col. R.A. France, Egypt	J.P.C.
1901	Ainger, T. E., 2nd Lt. Berks Yeomanry. Gallipoli (k. ..8.15)	K.S.
	Ainsworth, I. S., Lt 11th Hussars, m. France (k. 13.10.14)	R.W.W.-T., C.M.W.
1904	Ainsworth, T., Lt. 11th Hussars, and Staff. France, Balkans	R.W.W.-T.
1915	Aird, J. R., M.C., Lt. Grenadier Gds., att. Gds. M.G. Regt. France	A.M.G.
1911	Airlie, Earl of, M.C., Capt. 10th R. Hussars, w., m. France	R.P.L.B.

1897 Akers-Douglas, Hon. G. A., Bt. Lt.-Col. R. Fusiliers, and
Staff, m. 2. France R.A.H.M.
1916 Akroyd, G., Lt. R. Scots Greys. France A.C.R.-W.
1897 Akroyd, P. B., Bt. Maj. R. Fusiliers, empld. Lt.-Col.
Graves Commn., m. 3. France W.D.
1901 Akroyd, R., Lt. 9th Lancers, att. M.G.Cav. France J.H.M.H.
1905 Albright, M. C., Maj. Worcestershire Yeomanry, and
Staff. Egypt, Gallipoli, Palestine (d.w. 8.11.17) E.L.V.
1907 Aldersey, H., Capt. Cheshire Yeomanry, att. Shropshire L.I. Egypt, Palestine (k. 10.3.18) H.F.W.T.
1915 Aldersey, M., 2nd Lt. Cheshire Regt. France (k. 1.11.17) V.LeN.F.
1888 Alexander, C. J., Capt. Hampshire Yeomanry E.H.
1908 Alexander, D. H. W., 2nd Lt. R.A.F., late Pte. Worcestershire Regt. Egypt J.M.E., H.F.W.T.
1904 Alexander, G., Lt. 10th R. Hussars, w., m. France A.C.G.H.
1914 Alexander, J., 2nd Lt. Res. Regt. of Cav., att. 16th Lancers C.H.K.M.
1914 Alexander, J. C. St. L., Lt. Coldstream Gds., and Staff.
France H.B.
1904 Alexander, J. U. F. C., O.B.E. (F) Capt. Coldstream
Gds., att. Bimbashi Egyptian Army, and Staff, m.
France, Egypt H.B.
1907 Alexander, M., M.C., Bt. Maj. Rifle Bde., and Staff, w.,
m. 2. France A.C.G.H.
1902 Alexander, P. R. M., Capt. R. Fusiliers, and Staff. France E.I.
1886 Alexander, R., Lt.-Col. Rifle Bde. France (d.w. 29.12.14) J.H.M
1905 Alexander, W. J., Capt. Devonshire Regt., and Staff. France P.W.
1914 Alington, Lord (Mr. Sturt at Eton), Lt. R.A.F. A.E.C.
1905 Alington, G. H., 2nd Lt. I.A.R., att. Indian Infantry.
Mesopotamia (k. 23.2.17) J.M.F.
1915 Allan, H., Flight-Sub-Lt. R.N.A.S., late 2nd Lt. Canadian Black Watch. France (k. 6.7.17) M.D.H.
1893 Allcard, H., D.S.O., Lt.-Col. R.F.A., w. France C.H.E.
1893 Allcard, R., O.B.E., Capt. R.E., m. France T.C.P.
1896 Allen, J. H. S., Lt. I.A., empld. Lt.-Col. Remount
Service. France, India F.H.R

1914	Allen, R. C., Lt. R.F.A., att. R.A.F., w. France	R.P.L.B.
1913	Allen, R. L. B., Lt. R.F.A. Egypt (d. 26.12.18)	C.H.A.
1898	Alleyne, C. F., O.B.E., Lt.-Col. R.A.S.C., and Staff. France	W.D.
1900	Allfrey, A. M. St. C., Lt. (t. Capt.) R.A.S.C.	R.A.H.M.
1916	Allfrey, B. H., Lt. 9th Lancers. France	T.D.
1891	Allgood, B., Capt. R. Irish Rifles. France (k. 6.12.14)	R.C.R.
1887	Allgood, W. H. L., C.M.G., D.S.O. (F) Brig.-Gen. (K.R.R.C.), m. 6. France	R.C.R.
1914	Allhusen, D., Capt. K.R.R.C., w. 2. France, Balkans, N. Russia	A.C.G.H.
1907	Allhusen, O., Maj. R.F.A. France, Egypt, Palestine	J.M.E., A.B.R.
1912	Allhusen, R., Capt. R.F.A., w. France, Balkans	A.C.G.H.
1891	Allix, C. I. L., Lt. Coldstream Gds. France	R.A.H.M.
1896	Allix, J. P., Capt. (t. Maj.) Yorkshire Hussars, and Staff, m. 2. France	R.A.H.M.
1902	Allport, C. J., L/ce-Cpl. R.A.M.C. Egypt	E.L.V.
1880	Allsopp, Hon. A. P., Capt. Intell. Corps, and Staff. France	C.W.D., H.D.
1917	Allsopp, S. R., 2nd Lt. Labour Corps. France	A.E.C.
1896	Alston, F. G., D.S.O. (F) Bt. Lt.-Col. Scots Gds., and Staff, m. 5. France	H.W.M.
1904	Alston, R. A., M.B.E., Capt. Northamptonshire Regt. France	J.M.E.
1915	Altamont, Earl of, Lt. R. Scots Greys. France	C.H.K.M.
1916	Ames, W. A. R., Lt. Oxfordshire and Bucks L.I., w., m. France	A.B.R.
1887	Ames, W. H., T.D., Lt.-Col. Oxfordshire and Bucks L.I. France	J.C.
1888	Amory, H. W. L. Heathcoat, Lt.-Col. Somerset L.I.	J.M.E.
1913	Amory, J. Heathcoat, Capt. Devonshire Regt., and Staff, w., m. Mesopotamia, S. Russia	R.S. de H.
1900	Amory, L. Heathcoat, Capt. R. 1st Devon Yeomanry, att. R.A., Staff, m. France (k. 25.8.18)	J.M.E.
1888	Ampthill, Lord, G.C.S.I., G.C.I.E., Bt. Col. Bedfordshire Regt., att. Leicestershire Regt. and Wiltshire Regt., and Staff, m. 2. France	G.E.M., W.D.

1886 Ancaster, Earl of, T.D. (Mr. Willoughby at Eton),
Lt.-Col. Lincolnshire Yeomanry, and Staff R.A.H.M.
1905 Anderson, A. E. D., D.S.O., M.C., Capt. (t. Lt.-Col.)
K.O.S.B., and Staff, late Pte. London Scottish, w., m.3.
France E.I.
1885 Anderson, A.T., C.M.G. (F) Brig.-Gen. (R.A.), w., m.6.
France K.S.
1900 Anderson, G. D., Lt. (t. Maj.) R.F.A. Balkans, Palestine E.C.A.L.
1908 Anderson, G. R. L., 2nd Lt. Cheshire Regt., m. France
(k. 8.11.14) F.I.
1878 Anderson, R. D., O.B.E., Maj. R.A.F. W.E.
1909 Anderson, R. G., Lt. Gloucestershire Yeomanry, w.
Egypt, Palestine (k. 12.11.17) J.M.E., A.B.R.
1902 Anglesey, Marquess of (F) (Paget at Eton), Capt.
R.H.G., and Staff. France, Egypt, Gallipoli H.E.L., R.S.K.
1898 Annesley, Earl (Visct. Glerawly at Eton), Sub-Lt.
R.N.V.R., att. R.N.A.S. France (k. 5.11.14) E.L.V.
1897 Annesley, Hon. A., Capt. 10th R. Hussars. France (k. 15.11.14) W.D.
1900 Annesley, Hon. C. A. J., Capt. 1st R. Dragoons. France
W.D., R.W.W.-T.
1907 Ansdell, R. C., Capt. 7th Dragoon Gds., w. France J.M.E., M.D.H.
1909 Ansdell, T. A., L/ce-Cpl. R.A.M.C. France R.P.L.B.
1914 Anson, A., Lt. Grenadier Gds. France (k. 8.10.15) C.H.K.M.
1914 Anson, F., M.C., Lt. Grenadier Gds., w. 2. France C.H.K.M.
1907 Anson, G. H., M.C., Capt. Staffordshire Yeomanry, m.
Egypt, Palestine E.L.V.
1915 Anson, N. F. E., M.C., 2nd Lt. K.R.R.C., w. 2. France
(k. 10.7.17) E.L.V., A.C.R.-W.
1880 Anstice, J. C. A., Maj. 6th (Inniskilling) Dragoons, and Staff A.C.J.
1915 Anstice, J. H., Lt. 6th (Inniskilling) Dragoons. France R.S.K.
1912 Anstice, J. S. R., Lt. R. Fusiliers, m. Gallipoli (k. 2.5.15) H.B.
1909 Anstruther, D. T., Lt. Highland Cyclist Bn., and Staff.
France A.M.G.
1904 Anstruther, J. A. St. C., Lt. 6th Dragoon Gds. (Carabiniers),
att. 2nd Life Gds. France (k. 30.10.14) P.W.

1891	Anstruther, P. G. (F) Maj. (t. Lt.-Col.) Seaforth Highlanders, w. 2, m. 2. France, Egypt, Mesopotamia	H.G.W., S R.J.
1908	Anstruther, R. E., M.C., Maj. (t. Lt.-Col.) Black Watch, and Staff, w. 2, m. France	E.I.
1875	Anstruther, Sir R. W., Bart., T.D. (F) Lt.-Col. R.E.	O.B.
	Antrobus, E., Lt. Grenadier Gds. France (k. 24.10.14)	E.I
1895	Antrobus, P. H., M.C., Capt. Irish Gds., w. 2, m. France	P.W.
1914	Apsley, Lord, D.S.O., M.C., Capt. Gloucestershire Yeomanry, w., m. 2. Egypt, Palestine	E.I., T.F.C.
	Arbuthnot, A. H., Capt. London Regt., w. France (d.w. 15.5.15)	S.A.D
1900	Arbuthnot, F. S., Capt. Suffolk Yeomanry, and Staff, m. 2. France, Italy	F.H.R.
1899	Arbuthnot, H. A., Capt. Tank Corps, late Lt. R.F.C., 2nd Lt. Res. Regt. of Cav., and Trooper 19th Hussars. France	E.I.
1892	Arbuthnot, J. B., M.V.O., Maj. Scots Gds., and Staff, m. 2. France, Balkans, Italy, Palestine	W.D.
1878	Arbuthnot, L. C., Capt. (t. Lt.-Col.) Suffolk Regt., w. France	F.E.D.
1905	Arbuthnot, M. A., M.C. (F) Capt. 16th Lancers, and Staff, m. 2. France (d. 14.10.18)	F.L.V.
	Arbuthnot, R. G. U., Lt. 16th Lancers, att. M.G.C. and R.A.F., late Trooper 19th Hussars, w. France (k. 3.12.18)	F.W.S.
1908	Arbuthnot, R. W. M., M.C. (F) Capt. R.F.A., and Staff, w. France	J.H.M.H.
1892	Arbuthnot, W. F., Capt. Seaforth Highlanders, att. R. Scots. Egypt	T.D.
1913	Archdale, O. A., Lt. Rifle Bde., and Staff, w. France	P.V.B.
1910	Archdale, R. M., M.C., Lt. 19th Hussars, late 2nd Lt. Interpreter, att. Indian E.F., w. France	P.V.B.
1895	Archer, F. J. E., Maj. Norfolk Regt., empld. Lt.-Col. Nigeria Regt., W. African F.F., w. France, W. Africa	H.D.
1896	Arkwright, B. H. G., Capt. Derbyshire Yeomanry, and Staff, m. Balkans, Egypt	E.I.

1899	Arkwright, E. F. W., M.C., Maj. Scots Gds., and Staff, m. 2. France	A.C.J.
1897	Arkwright, E. H., Lt.-Col. R.A. France, Mesopotamia	E.I.
1904	Arkwright, F. G. A., Capt. 11th Hussars, att. R.F.C., w. France (k. accid. 14.10.15)	J.M.E.
1902	Arkwright, R. A., Capt. Coldstream Gds.	J.M.E.
1912	Armstrong, A. H., Lt. Somerset L. I., att. M.G.C. Mesopotamia	K.S.
1911	Armstrong, E. W., 2nd Lt. Rifle Bde. France (d.w. 11.7.15)	K S
1914	Armstrong, G. C., 2nd Lt. Coldstream Gds. France (k. 25.1.15)	E.L.C.
1907	Armstrong, W. M., M.C., Capt. 10th R. Hussars, and Staff, m. 4. France, Gallipoli (k. 23.5.17)	J.M.E. J H.M.H.
1904	Arnott, J., M.C., Capt. 15th Hussars, and Staff, m. 2. France (k. 30.3.18)	A.C.J . L.F. R.P.L.B.
1914	Arnott, R. J., Lt. K.R.R.C. France, Balkans	J.H.M.H.
1917	Arnott, T. J., 2nd Lt. 15th Hussars	J.H.M.H.
1886	Arran, Earl of, K.P., P.C. (Mr. Gore at Eton), Bt. Maj. R.H.G.	J.M.E.
1917	Arthur, E. S., 2nd Lt. R. Scots Greys	R.S.de H.
1876	Arthur, Sir G. C. A., Bart., M.V.O. (F) Capt. Staff. France, Italy	G.E.M.
1908	Arthur, J., Maj. R.A.F., late Lt. R.N.V.R. France (k. 6.6.18)	L.S.R.B.
1902	Arthur, Hon. J. C., Lt. Ayrshire Yeomanry, and Staff. France	H.E.L.
1912	Arthur, T. A., Lt. 2nd Life Gds., late Lt. Ayrshire Yeomanry. France, Egypt, Gallipoli	R.S.de H.
1914	Ashburner, G. C., Lt. K.R.R.C., and Staff, w. France	J.H.M.H.
1882	Ashburton, Lord (Mr. Baring at Eton), Maj. Hampshire Yeomanry	E.W.
1889	Ashmore, E. B., C.B., C.M.G.. M.V.O. (F) Maj.-Gen. (R.A.) att. R.A.F., m. 5. France	W.D.
1892	Ashmore, G. W. P., Lt. R.E. (drowned 4.5.17)	W D
1886	Ashton, F. E., D.S.O., Maj. (t. Lt.-Col.) York & Lancaster Regt., m. France, Balkans, Palestine	H D

1892	Ashton, H. C. S., Capt. 2nd Life Gds., p. France	W.D.
1898	Ashton, J. A. (F) Capt. (t. Maj.) Lancashire Hussars, and Staff. France	W.D.
1898	Ashworth, M. O., Maj. The King's Own (R. Lancaster Regt.), and Staff, m. Egypt, Gallipoli, Mesopotamia	A.C.J.
1904	Ashworth, P. H. (F) Lt. (t. Capt.) Grenadier Gds., and Staff	H.E.L., L.S.R.B.
1890	Aspinall, A. E., C.M.G., A.B., R.N.V.R.	H.E.L.
1899	Aspinall, C. L. R., Lt. R.N.V.R., att. R.N.A.S., and Staff. France	S.A.D.
1903	Aspinall, G., Capt. Lancashire Hussars. France, Egypt	S.A.D.
1894	Aspinall, J. R., Capt. Lancashire Hussars, att. R.G.A. France	E.I.
—	Aspinall, R. L., D.S.O., Maj. Yorkshire Regt., empld. Lt.-Col. Cheshire Regt. France (k. 3.7.16)	H.E.L.
1913	Assheton, R. T., Maj. Cambridgeshire Regt., empld. Maj. M.G.C., w. France	E.L.C.
1900	Astley, Hon. C. M., Capt. Northumberland Yeomanry, and Staff. France	W.D.
1900	Astley, Hon. J. J., Coy. Sergt.-Maj. Sherwood Foresters, late Squadron Sergt.-Maj. Mounted Rifles. France, S.W. Africa (k. 26.9.17)	W.D., H.B.
1913	Astley, P. R., M.C., Lt. 12th Lancers, att. M.G. Cav. France	C.M.W.
1901	Astley-Corbett, J. D. P., Maj. Scots Gds., and Staff, w. France	E.I.
1903	Aston, H. W., Capt. Surrey Yeomanry. France, Balkans	J.P.C., A.C.G.H.
1905	Astor, Hon. J. J. (F) Capt. 1st Life Gds., att. R.G.A., w. 2. France	A.C.A., R.S.de H.
1898	Astor, Viscount (Astor at Eton), Maj. Staff	A.C.A.
1905	Atherton-Brown, C. H., Lt. 1st Life Gds. France	R.S.de H.
1908	Atherton-Brown, F., Lt. 1st R. Dragoons and M.G.C. France	R.S.de H.
1892	Athlone, Earl of, G.C.B., G.C.V.O., C.M.G., D.S.O. (F) Brig.-Gen. (2nd Life Gds.), m. 3. France	E.C.A.L.

1890 Atholl, Duke of, K.T., C.B., M.V.O., D.S.O. (F) (Marquess of Tullibardine at Eton), Brig.-Gen. (R.H.G. and Scottish Horse), m. 2. Egypt, Gallipoli   J.M.E.

1915 Atkinson, A. F. C., Lt. R.E. France, Italy (k. accid. 22.1.19)   K.S.

1884 Atkinson, F. B., Capt. Durham L.I., att. W. Yorkshire Regt., and Staff   J.P.C.

1900 Atkinson, W. H. J. St. L., Capt. 1st R. Dragoons, m. France (k. 12.5.15)   H.D., J.P.C., R.P.L.B.

1901 Atkinson-Clark, H. F., M.V.O., O.B.E., Capt. (t. Maj.) Scots Gds., and Staff. France   A.C.B.

1906 Aubrey-Fletcher, H. L., M.V.O., D.S.O. (F) (Fletcher at Eton), Capt. and Bt. Maj. Grenadier Gds., and Staff, w. 2, m. 3. France   R.P.L.B.

1917 Aubrey-Smith, P. Y. H., Midshipman R.N. Home Waters, S. America, N. Russia   A.M.G.

1876 Auckland, Lord, the late (Mr. Eden at Eton), Maj. Dorsetshire Regt. (d. in England, 31.7.17)   G.E.M.

1912 Austen-Cartmell, A. J., Lt. K.R.R.C., and Staff. France (k. 1.6.16)   H.M.

1914 Austen-Cartmell, G. H., Lt. H.L.I., w. France (k. 13.11.16)   H.M.

1877 Aylmer, E. K. G., C.B., Col. Res. Regt. of Cav.   C.C.J.

1906 Ayrton, B. F., Capt. London Regt., att. R.A.F., w. France   J.M.D.

1916 Ayscough, H. C., Lt. 18th Hussars. France   A.M.G.

1908 Babington, G., M.C., Capt., late Pte., Fife and Forfar Yeomanry, att. R.A.F., and Staff, w., m. France   R.W.W.-T., C.M.W.

1913 Babington, P., M.C., A.F.C., Maj. (t. Lt.-Col.) R.A.F., late Capt. Hampshire Regt., w., m. 3. France   E.L.C.

1916 Babington, R. V., 2nd Lt. Coldstream Gds. France (k. 9.10.17)   V.Le N.F., L.T.

1897	Backhouse, M. R. C., D.S.O. and Bar, Maj. Northumberland Yeomanry, empld. Lt.-Col. Somerset Yeomanry and Yorkshire Regt., m. 4. France, Italy	H.W.M.
	Backus, A. P., M.C., Capt. Rifle Bde., w. 2. France	H.M.
	... F. ... nd Lt. Durham L.I. France (d.w. 1.11.17)	K.S.
1884	Bacon, R. C., Capt. R. Defence Corps	F.W.C.
1914	Baddeley, E. L. O., Capt. Middlesex Regt., att. Northumberland Fusiliers, Durham L.I., and T.M.B., w., m. France, N. Russia	H.Br.
1915	Baden-Powell, D. F. W., 2nd Lt. Rifle Bde., late Flight-Sub-Lt. R.N.A.S., w. France	A.A.S.
1911	Baerlein, O. F., M.C., Capt. R.A.S.C. France	J.M.D., V.LeN.F.
1906	Baggallay, M. E. C., Lt. 11th Hussars, and Staff, m. France	E.C.A.L., E.W.S.
1894	Bagge, Sir A. W. F., Bart., Lt. (t. Capt.) Norfolk Regt. France	F.D., C.H.A.
1898	Bagge, H. P., M.C., Capt. Yorkshire Regt., att. Durham L.I., w. France	C.H.A.
1903	Bagnell, R. A. (F) Capt. 3rd Hussars, w. France	H.M.
1904	Bagnell, W. G., Capt. 3rd Dragoon Gds., att. 15th Hussars, w., m. France	H.M.
1913	Bagot, Sir A. D., Bart., Lt. R.H.G., att. 12th Lancers, and Staff. France	S.G.L.
	Bagot, F. L. H., 2nd Lt. Welsh Gds. France (k. 10.9.16)	R.S.deH.
1880	Bagot, Hon. W. L., D.S.O., Maj. Grenadier Gds., and Staff. France	J.C.
1887	Bailey, Hon. A., Capt. E. African Mounted Rifles. E. Africa	W.D.
	Bailey, A. Y., 2nd Lt. K.R.R.C. France (k. 27.7.16)	H.Br.
1902	Bailey, F. H., Lt. Shropshire Yeomanry, att. Imp. Camel Corps. Egypt	F.H.R.
	Bailey, Hon. C. S., 2nd Lt. Grenadier Gds., late Lt. King's African Rifles, Nairobi F.F. France. E. Africa	F.I.
1889	Bailey, Hon. H. C., Lt. Sp. List	W.D.

1896 Bailey, Hon. J. L., Capt. S. Wales Borderers. Aden
    (d. 26.10.18)   W.D.
1901 Bailey, R. N. M., Lt. E. Riding of Yorkshire Yeomanry.
    Egypt, Palestine (d.w. 1.12.17)   K.S.
1885 Bailey, Hon. W., Maj. (t. Lt.-Col.) Welsh Horse, and
    Staff. France, Egypt, Gallipoli   W.D.
1909 Bailey, Hon. W. R., D.S.O. and Bar (F) Bt. Maj. (t. Lt.-
    Col.) Grenadier Gds., w., m. 5. France   E.I.
1907 Bailey-Hawkins, A. G., Capt. Durham L.I.   J.H.M.H.
1902 Bailie, T. M. D., Maj. Irish Gds., m. France (k. 15.9.16)   H.F.W.T.
1914 Baillie, Hon. A. M. A., Lt. R.F.A. and Staff. France,
    Egypt   R.S.de H.
1916 Baillie, Sir A. W. M., Bart., Lt. R. Scots Greys. France   H.M.
1912 Baillie, Hon. G. E. M., M.C., Capt. R.F.A., m. Palestine   R.S.de H.
1911 Baillie, Sir G. G. S., Bart., 2nd Lt. R. Scots Greys, w.
    France (k. 7.9.14)   H.M.
1873 Baillie, J. E. B., M.V.O., V.D., Maj. R.F.A. France, Egypt   W.E.
1897 Baillie-Hamilton, W. S. (F) Capt. Intell. Dept. Staff. France   P.W.
1900 Bailward, J., Capt. 19th Hussars, att. Leicestershire
    Yeomanry. France   R.C.R.
1908 Bainbrigge, P. G., 2nd Lt. Lancashire Fusiliers, att.
    Welsh Regt. France (k. 18.9.18)   K.S.
1895 Baird, A. W. F., C.M.G., C.B., D.S.O. (F) Brig.-Gen.
    (Gordon Highlanders), Australian Imp. Force, w. 2,
    m. 6. France   R.C.R.
1912 Baird, C. E., Capt. Seaforth Highlanders, w. 2. France
    (k. 2.7.16)   H.F.W.T., A.E.C.
1910 Baird, D. M., Lt. Gordon Highlanders, att. R.F.C.
    France   J.H.M.H.
1883 Baird, E. W. D., C.B.E., Brig.-Gen. (Suffolk Yeo-
    manry), m. France   W.D.
1900 Baird, J. H. G., M.C., Capt. (t. Maj.) Bedfordshire Regt.,
    late Cpl. King Edward's Horse, w., m. France, Egypt   A.C.J.
1891 Baird, Sir J. L., Bart., M.P., C.M.G., D.S.O. (F) Maj.
    Scottish Horse, and Staff, m. France   R.C.R.

1912 Baird, R. I., Capt. Gordon Highlanders, w. France, Italy — J.H.M.H.

Baird, W. F. G., Capt. Bedfordshire Regt., att. Lincolnshire Regt. France (k. 5.11.14) — A.C.J., H.M.

1913 Baker, H. A., M.C. and Bar, Capt. R.F.A., w. France — A.B.R.

1894 Baker, R. L., O.B.E., Capt. R.F.A., w. France — T.D.

1902 Baker, W. H. Benson, Maj. R.G.A., m. France — H.F.W.T.

1890 Bald, E. H. C., M.C. (F) Capt. (t. Maj.) 15th Hussars, empld. R.A.F., w. 2, m. 3. France, Egypt — W.D.

1915 Baldwin, O. R., Lt. Irish Gds. France — H.M.

1897 Balfour, A. E., Capt. Gordon Highlanders, att. R.A.O.C. France — C.L.

1874 Balfour, Sir A. G., C.B., K.B.E. (F) Brig.-Gen. (H.L.I.) — F.F.V.

1907 Balfour, C. J. (F) Capt. Scots Gds., w. 3. France — A.M.G.

1910 Balfour, D., 2nd Lt. Lothians and Border Horse, late Pte. London Regt., and Staff. France — A.M.G.

1902 Balfour, E. W. S., D.S.O., O.B.E., M.C., Maj. 5th Dragoon Gds., and Staff, m. 2. France — W.D., H.M.

1902 Balfour, F. C. C., C.I.E., M.C. (F) Capt. (t. Lt.-Col.) Northumberland Fusiliers, m. Egypt, Mesopotamia — R.W.W.-T.

1913 Balfour, J., M.C., Capt. Scots Gds., m. France (k. 21.3.18) — A.B.R.

1880 Balfour, J. E. H., C.M.G., D.S.O., Lt.-Col. 11th Hussars, m. 2. France — C.H.E.

1880 Balfour, K. R., Maj. Res. Regt. of Cav., and Staff. France — C.H.E.

1905 Balfour, L., Lt. R.A.F., late R.N.A.S. Home Waters, Mediterranean — H.B.

1897 Balfour, M., M.C., Capt. R.F.A., late 2nd Lt. Interpreter att. I.A. France — S.R.J.

1888 Balfour, N. H., O.B.E., Maj. (t. Lt.-Col.) R.A.S.C., M.T., m. France, Egypt — A.C.J.

Balfour, R. F., Capt. Scots Gds., and Staff. France (k. 2.10.14) — W.D., H.M.

1872 Balguy, J. H., Brig.-Gen. (R.A.) — F.T.

1905	Ballance, A. C., Surgeon R.N., att. R.N.D. France, Gallipoli, Home Waters, N. Russia	H.Br.
1907	Ballance, L. A., Capt. K.R.R.C. France (k. 27.9.16)	H.Br.
1895	Ballard, J. A., Maj. Oxfordshire and Bucks L.I., empld. Lt.-Col. R. Welch Fusiliers, w., m. France	P.W.
1890	Balston, C. H., Capt. (t. Lt.-Col.) R. E. Kent Yeomanry. France, Egypt, Gallipoli, Palestine	C.H.E.
1898	Balston, F. W., Capt. R.A.S.C. France	F.T., T.C.P.
1897	Balston, G. R., D.S.O., Maj. R.F.A., w., m. 2. France	F.T., T.C.P.
1903	Balston, H., Trooper Australian Imp. Forces, w. Egypt	A.C.G.H.
1906	Balston, M., Lt. R.F.A., att. R.A.F. France, Egypt	A.C.G.H.
1902	Balston, T., O.B.E., M.C., Maj. Gloucestershire Regt., and Staff, m. 2. France	K.S.
1911	Bambridge, G. L. St. C., M.C. (F) Lt. Irish Gds., w. 2, m. France	P.W.
1896	Banbury, C. E., Maj. (t. Lt.-Col.) Res. Regt. of Cav., and Staff, m. France	A.C.A.
1895	Banbury, C. W., Capt. Coldstream Gds. France (d.w. 16.9.14)	C.H.A., J.M.E.
1898	Banbury, R. E., Capt. R. Fusiliers, w. France	A.C.A.
1901	Banbury, W. M., Capt. Rifle Bde. France (k. 17.8.17)	J.M.E.
1905	Bankes, R. W., Capt. Montgomeryshire Yeomanry, att. R. Welch Fusiliers, and Staff, m. Egypt, Palestine	P.V.B.
1902	Bannatyne, J. F., Capt. 11th Hussars, empld. Maj. Manchester Regt. France (d.w. 14.5.16)	H.B.
1906	Barber, N. E., Maj. K.R.R.C., p. France	H.M.
1894	Barber, T. P., D.S.O., Maj. (t. Lt.-Col.) S. Notts Hussars, w., m. 2. Balkans, Gallipoli, Palestine	J.P.C.
1900	Barber, W. D., M.C., Bt. Lt.-Col. K.R.R.C., and Staff, w. 2, m. 3. France	J.P.C., F.H.R.
1885	Barclay, C., Capt. (t. Maj.) 10th R. Hussars. France	F.W.C.
1915	Barclay, C. G., M.C., Lt. Coldstream Gds., w. France	H.Br.
1914	Barclay, D. S., Lt. Scots Gds., w. France (d.w. 24.4.17)	P.V.B.
1900	Barclay, E. H., Lt. Scots Gds., late Capt. R. Glasgow Yeomanry. Egypt, Gallipoli	S.A.D.

1895	Barclay, G. W., M.C., Maj. Rifle Bde., w., m. France (k. 28.7.16)	R.W.W.-T., C.M.W.
1875	Barclay, H. D., Maj. K.R.R.C.	T.D.
1900	Barclay, Rev. H. G., M.C., C.F., m. 3. France	H.B.
1876	Barclay, H. T., Maj. Leicestershire Yeomanry	T.D.
1901	Barclay, J. F., Maj. (t. Lt.-Col.) Norfolk Yeomanry, att. Norfolk Regt. France, Egypt, Gallipoli, Palestine	H.B.
1905	Barclay, M. E. (F) Maj. Norfolk Yeomanry, att. Norfolk Regt., w. 2, m. 2. France, Egypt, Gallipoli, Palestine	R.W.W.-T.
1907	Barclay-Harvey, C. M., Capt. Gordon Highlanders, and Staff	H.B.
1914	Bardsley, E. W. S., Capt. The King's Own (R. Lancaster Regt.), w. France, E. Africa	R.S.K.
1903	Bardwell, T. B., Capt. Montgomeryshire Yeomanry, att. R. Welch Fusiliers. France, Egypt, Palestine	C.H.A.
1902	Bardwell, T. G. N., T.D., Maj. E. Riding of Yorkshire Yeomanry, att. Bimbashi Camel Corps, Egyptian Army. Egypt	C.H.A.
1916	Baring, Hon. A. F. St. V., Lt. R. Scots Greys. France	E.I., T.F.C.
1914	Baring, C. C., Lt. Coldstream Gds., w. France	C.H.K.M.
1897	Baring, Hon. C. D., Capt., Staff. France	A.C.J.
1883	Baring, Hon. E., C.V.O., C.B.E., Brig.-Gen. (10th R. Hussars)	E.W.
1910	Baring, E. B., Lt. Hampshire Regt. E. Russia	A.M.G.
1884	Baring, Hon. F. A., Capt. Hampshire Yeomanry	E.W.
1891	Baring, Hon. G. V., M.P., Lt.-Col. Coldstream Gds., m. 2. France (k. 15.9.16)	A.C.J.
1894	Baring, Hon. H., O.B.E., Capt. att. 10th R. Hussars, and Staff, w., m. 2. France, Italy, Siberia	W.D.
1889	Baring, Hon. M., O.B.E. (F) Maj. R.A.F., m. France	W.D.
1900	Baring, T. E., O.B.E., Maj. Rifle Bde., att. M.G.C., Tank Corps, and Staff, m. France, Siberia	A.C.A.
1898	Baring, Hon. W., Lt. R.N.V.R. Home Waters	W.D.
1901	Barker, A. P. (F) Lt. R.A.S.C., M.T., att. Serbian Army, m. Balkans	J.P.C., R.P.L.B.

1897 Barker, D., Capt. R.A.S.C., m. France, Balkans, Egypt, Gallipoli   J.M.E.
1885 Barker, F. G., C.B.E., Lt.-Col. R. Berkshire Regt., and Staff. France   J.P.C., S.A.D.
1907 Barker, F. W., Capt. Westminster Dragoons, and Staff, m. Egypt, Palestine   R.W.W.-T., C.M.W.
1914 Barker, G. C., Lt. 16th Lancers. France, Palestine   H.deH.
1886 Barker, G. E., Lt.-Col. Middlesex Regt.   A.C.A.
1915 Barker, H. A., Lt. Rifle Bde., late Pte. R.A.M.C., w. France   E.W.S.
1903 Barker, H. R., Capt. Yorkshire Regt.   C.H.A.
1916 Barker, R. G., M.C., Lt. Scots Gds., w. France   P.W., F.E.R.
1875 Barlow, H. S., Lt.-Col. Seaforth Highlanders   A.C.J.
1877 Barlow, Sir H. W. W., Bart., C.B., C.M.G., Col. Sp. List   C.C.J.
1881 Barnard, E. W., Maj. Wiltshire Regt.   R.A.H.M.
1906 Barnard, Lord, M.C. (Mr. Vane at Eton), Maj. Westmorland and Cumberland Yeomanry, att. Border Regt., w. 2. France   R.P.L.B.
1916 Barnard, T. T., M.C., Lt. Coldstream Gds. France   A.M.G.
1891 Barne, M., D.S.O., Maj. Suffolk Yeomanry, att. Scots Gds., m. France (d.w. from accid. 17.9.17)   F.C.A.J.
1903 Barne, S., M.C., Capt. 20th Hussars, and Staff, att. R.F.C., w., m. France (k. 23.4.17)   F.C.A.J.
1891 Barneby, W. T., Lt. (t. Capt.) Shropshire Yeomanry   F.H.R.
1909 Barnes, A. C., D.S.O. and Bar, Lt.-Col. Yorkshire Regt., att. Durham L.I., m. 3. France, Italy   A.M.G.
1908 Barnes, J. S. (F) Capt. R.A.F., late R.H.G., w. France, Italy   E.W.S.
1899 Barnes, L. H., Lt. (t. Capt.) Grenadier Gds., att. Gds. M.G. Regt. France   H.D
1906 Barnes, R. G., Capt. Canadian Engineers, p., w. France   A.C.B., A.M.G.
1914 Barnes, T. H., Lt. R.F.A., att. Sherwood Foresters, w. France   C.H.K.M.
1906 Barnes, W. G., Pte. H.A.C.   A.C.A., J.M.D.

	... P......, C. F. P., 2nd Lt. Gloucestershire Regt. France	
		F.T., C.H.A.
1883	Barnett, E. G., Capt. Northumberland Yeomanry, empld. Capt. Remount Service. Egypt	E.H.
1886	Barnett, F. P., Capt. Northumberland Yeomanry. France	E.H.
1912	Barnett, J. C. L., M.C., Capt. Oxfordshire and Bucks L.I., att. R.A.F., and Staff. France	H.T.B., S.G.L.
	Barrett, C. J. C., Capt. R. Scots Fusiliers, m. France (...)	H.D.
	Barrington-Kennett, B. H., Bt. Maj. Grenadier Gds., R.F.C., m. France (k. 13.5.15)	J.M.F.
	Barrington-Kennett, V. A., Maj. R.F.C. m. France (...)	K.S.
1903	Barrington-White, I. B., Capt. Grenadier Gds., att. R.A.F., and Staff. France	A.C.G.H.
1897	Barron, C. A., O.B.E., Lt.-Col. R.A.S.C., m. 2. France	F.T., T.C.P.
1896	Barron, O., Capt. W. Yorkshire Regt., att. E. Yorkshire Regt. France	F.T., R.S.de H.
1893	Barrow, C. D., Lt.-Col. R. W. Kent Regt.	J.P.C.
1914	Barry, G., M.C., Capt. Coldstream Gds., w. 2. France	A.M.G.
1881	Barry, L. E., Maj. 1st Life Gds., and Staff, m. France	E.C.A.L.
	Barttelot, Sir W. B., Bart., D.S.O. (F) Bt. Lt.-Col. Coldstream Gds., and Staff, w., m. 4. France, Gallipoli, Mesopotamia (d. 23.10.18)	R.C.R.
1878	Basing, Lord, the late, C.B. (Mr. Sclater-Booth at Eton), Brig.-Gen. (1st R. Dragoons). (d. 8.4.19)	G.E.M.
1909	Basing, Lord (Mr. Sclater-Booth at Eton), Capt. 1st R. Dragoons, att. Cav. Signal Service. France	R.W.W.-T., C.M.W.
1917	Basset, R. L., 2nd Lt. R. Scots Greys. France	A.C.R.-W.
1894	Bassett, P. R., Lt. Devonshire Regt., late Lt. Suffolk Regt. France	C.H.E.
1897	Bastard, R., D.S.O. and Bar, Maj. (t. Lt.-Col.) Lincolnshire Regt., and Staff, w., p., m. 3. France	A.C.A.
	Batchelor, G. A., L.-Cpl. Princess Patricia's Canadian L.I. France (k. 27...15)	C.H.A

1912	Bate, A. C. L., the late, Capt. R.G.A. (d. 25.10.18)	J.H.M.H.
1906	Bate, L. R. A., Capt. K.R.R.C., and Staff, w. France	T.C.P., E.L.C.
1879	Bates, Sir C. L., K.C.M.G., C.B., D.S.O. (F) Brig.-Gen. (1st Dragoon Gds.), Director of Remounts, m. 4. France, Balkans, Egypt, Palestine	F.F.V.
1894	Bath, H., Lt. The Queen's, and Labour Corps, late Sub-Lt. R.N.V.R. France	J.P.C.
1883	Bathurst, Earl, C.M.G. (Lord Apsley at Eton), Lt.-Col. Gloucestershire Regt., and Staff. France	E.C.A.L.
1890	Bathurst, Hon. A. B., M.P., Lt.-Col. Gloucestershire Regt.	E.C.A.L.
1909	V.C. Batten-Pooll, A. H. H., M.C., Capt. R. Munster Fusiliers, att. N. Russian Rifles, and Staff, w., p., m. France, N. Russia	E.L.C.
1907	Batten-Pooll, J. A., D.S.O., M.C., Capt. 5th Lancers, w. 2., m. 2. France	J.H.M.H.
1901	Batten-Pooll, W. S., Capt. N. Somerset Yeomanry, and Staff. France, Italy	J.H.M.H.
1886	Battye, L. R. J. S., Capt. 13th Hussars	E.H.
1902	Baxendale, G. V., Capt. R.F.A.	H.F.W.T.
1895	Baxendale, J. F. N., Lt.-Col. Hampshire Yeomanry, w., m. France	H.D.
1906	Baxter, E. H., Capt. Northumberland Fusiliers, and Staff, w. France	C.H.A., A.B.R.
1885	Baxter, F., C.P.O., R.N.V.R.	T.D.
1899	Baxter, G. L., D.S.O., Capt. Cameron Highlanders, empld. Lt.-Col. King's African Rifles, att. Staff Nyasaland F. F., m. 3. E. Africa	C.H.A.
1902	Baxter, H. H., M.C., Maj. R.F.A., w. 4. France, Egypt, Palestine	A.C.G.H.
1898	Baxter, N. E., Maj. Hampshire Regt., w., p., m. France, N. Russia	S.R.J., H.F.W.T.
1914	Baxter, R. P., Lt. R.F.A., w., m. 2. France	H. d. H.
1890	Bayford, E. H., D.S.O., Capt. 18th Hussars, and Staff. m. France	C.H.E.

1899	Bayley, E. C., Capt. City of London Yeomanry. Balkans, Gallipoli	H.B.
1893	Bayley-Worthington, A. B., Maj. S. Nottinghamshire Hussars, and Staff, France	F.T.
1893	Bazley-White, J., M.C., Lt. W. Yorkshire Regt., w. France	E.L.V.
1902	Bazley-White, R. B. L., D.S.O. (F) Capt. R. W. Kent Regt., att. Bimbashi Egyptian Army, and Staff, m 4. Egypt, Palestine	R.C.R.
1886	Beale-Browne, D. J. E., D.S.O., Brig.-Gen. (9th Lancers), m. 2. France	A.C.A.
1912	Beasley-Robinson, A. C., Lt. R.F.A., w. Mesopotamia, Palestine	E.L.C.
1915	Beauchamp, B. C., 2nd Lt. 1st Life Gds. France	C.H.K.M.
1908	Beauchamp, E. A., Lt. Coldstream Gds., w. France (d.w. 22.12.14)	P.W.
1886	Beauclerk, G. M. de V., Capt. K.R.R.C. France	J.C.
1892	Beauclerk, Lord O. de V., Capt. Staff, m. France	C.H.E.
1901	Beauford, F. S., Capt., late Pte., R. Fusiliers. France	C.H.A.
1891	Beaumont, D. J., Lt. Gloucestershire Regt. France, W. Africa	W.D.
1878	Beaumont, Hon. E. de G., Maj. Remount Service, att. Lancashire Hussars. France	G.E.M.
1881	Beaumont, H. R., Capt. R. Berkshire Regt.	G.E.M.
1909	Beaumont, Hon. W. H. C., M.C., Capt. 2nd Life Gds. France	A.C.G.H.
1911	Beaumont-Nesbitt, F. G., M.C., Capt. Grenadier Gds., and Staff, m. 2. France	E.I.
1882	Beckett, Hon. W. G., M.P. (Denison at Eton), Capt. Yorkshire Hussars, and Staff	G.E.M.
1896	Beckwith, W. M., D.S.O. (F) Maj. (t. Lt.-Col.) Coldstream Gds., and Staff, m. 3. France, Italy	R.C.R.
1909	Beckwith-Smith, M. B., D.S.O., M.C. (F) Capt. (t. Maj.) Coldstream Gds., and Staff, w., m. 3. France	R.S. de H.
1901	Beddington, E. H. L., C.M.G., D.S.O., M.C. (F) Bt. Lt.-Col. 16th Lancers, and Staff, m. 5. France	J.M.E.

1914	Beddington, H. L. V., Lt. R.F.A. France	C.M.W.
1918	Beddington, T. A. H., Driver H.A.C.	L.S.R.B.
1912	Beddington, W. R., Lt. 2nd Dragoon Gds. (Queen's Bays), late 2nd Lt. Westminster Dragoons, w. France, Balkans, Egypt, Gallipoli	C.M.W.
1890	Beebee, M. J. L., P.O., R.N.V.R.	K.S.
1908	Beech, D. C. M., M.C., Capt. 20th Hussars, and Staff. France, Egypt, Palestine	F.H.R., H.de H.
1906	Beech, R. A. J., Lt. 16th Lancers, m. France (k. 21.2.15)	F.H.R
1914	Beech, R. C., Capt. Rifle Bde. France (k. 18.10.16)	A.B.R.
1916	Beit, T. H., 2nd Lt. 1st R. Dragoons. (d. 27.1.17)	H B . R.H.de M
1914	Beith, J. A., Lt. 19th Hussars, w. France	E.L.C.
1905	Belfield, S. St. G. C., Capt. (t. Maj.) R.A.F., late Cpl. King Edward's Horse and Lt. R.N.A.S. France, E. Africa	P.W.
1898	Belfour, A. O., Cpl. R.E. Signals, w., p. France	A.C.A.
1899	Belhaven, Master of (Hon. R. G. A. Hamilton) (F) Lt.-Col. R.F.A., m. 2. France (k. 31.3.18)	E.C.A.L.
1893	Bell, A. S., Capt. Derbyshire Yeomanry	H.D.
1907	Bell, C. W., M.C., Lt. (t. Capt.) Intell. Corps, Staff, m. France	R.S.de H.
1911	Bell, J. G. A., Lt. 7th Hussars. Mesopotamia	J.M.D., V.Le N.F.
1914	Bell, J. W., Lt. R.F.A., and Staff, w., m. France	P.V.B.
1889	Bell, M. G. E., O.B.E. (F) Lt.-Col. Rifle Bde., and Staff. France	J.M.E.
1889	Bell, M. H. L., C.M.G., T.D., Lt.-Col. Yorkshire Regt. m. 2. France	J.M.E.
1898	Bell, W. A. J., Maj. R.A.S.C. France	A.A.S.
1895	Bellville, G. E., Capt. 16th Lancers, w., p. France	E.H., A.A.S.
1911	Benett-Stanford, V., M.C., Maj. R.F.A., w. 2., m. France	C.H.K.M.
1913	Benjamin, C. M., Lt. R.A.F., late K.O.Y.L.I. France	J.M.D., V.Le N.F.
1911	Benjamin, R. N., M.C., Capt. R. Fusiliers, w. 3. France	J.M.D., V. Le N.F.

1912	Bennett, D. W., Lt. The King's Own (R. Lancaster Regt.), and Staff, w. 2. France, Balkans	J.H.M.H.
1901	Bennett, R. A., Capt. Gloucestershire Yeomanry	J.M.E.
1913	Benson, C. E., D.S.O., Lt. Grenadier Gds., late Lt. W. Kent Yeomanry, w., m. France, Egypt, Gallipoli	E.I.
1907	Benson, G. H., Capt. W. Kent Yeomanry, att. 9th Lancers. France, Gallipoli	E.I.
1905	Benson, G. R., Maj. R.F.A. France	A.C.B., A.M.G.
	Benson, H. C., Lt. Rifle Bde. France (k. 22.6.15)	F.H.R.
1873	Benson, H. W., D.S.O., Maj. (t. Lt.-Col.) Welch Regt.	J.H.M.
1900	Benson, R., D.S.O., Maj. R.F.A., and Staff, w., m. 2. France, N. Russia	S.A.D.
	Benson, R. E., Lt.-Col. E. Yorkshire Regt. France (d.w. 27.9.14)	C.H.E.
1908	Benson, R. L., D.S.O., M.C. (F) Maj. 9th Lancers, and Staff, w. 2, m. 4. France	E.I.
	Bentall, E. H., 2nd Lt. K.R.R.C. France (k. 3.10.15)	H.de H.
1912	Benthall, E. C., Capt. Devonshire Regt., att. Intell. Corps, and Staff, w. Mesopotamia	K.S.
1904	Bentinck, A. W. D., Capt. Coldstream Gds., att. Egyptian Army, w. France, Egypt	J.M.E.
1900	Benyon, H. A., Capt. Berks Yeomanry, att. Remount Service. France, Egypt	A.A.S.
1902	Beresford-Ash, D. (Beresford at Eton), Capt. R. Fusiliers, empld. Maj. M.G.C., w., m. France, Balkans, S. Russia	H.E.
1876	Beresford-Ash, W. R. H. (Beresford at Eton), Bt. Col. R. Welch Fusiliers, empld. S. Wales Borderers, w. France	G R.D., A.C.J.
1909	Beresford-Peirse, A. C. P. de la P., M.B.E., Capt. Durham L. I., and Staff, w. France	R.S.de H.
1895	Beresford-Peirse, E. F. de la P., Capt. Yorkshire Regt. France	E.I.
1911	Beresford-Peirse, R. W. de la P., Lt. 2nd Life Gds. France	R.S.de H.

1903	Berg, A. W., Capt. Welsh Gds. France, N. Russia	H.Br.
1900	Bernard, A. C., Lt. Gloucestershire Regt. France	K.S.
1901	Bernard, D. J. C. K., C.M.G., D.S.O. (F) Bt. Lt.-Col. Rifle Bde., and Staff, w., m. 5. France, Balkans, Egypt, Gallipoli	C.L., R.P.L.B.
1893	Bernard, R. P. H., Bt. Lt.-Col. Rifle Bde., att. R.E. Signal Service, and Staff, m.	A.C.J.
1912	Berners, G. H., Lt. Norfolk Regt., w. Mesopotamia	E.I.
1899	Berners, H. H., Capt. Irish Gds. France (k. 14.9.14)	H.D.
1886	Berners, J. A., O.B.E., Lt. Sp. List	W.D.
1889	Berners, R. A., D.S.O., Brig.-Gen. (R. Welch Fusiliers), m. 4. France, Afghanistan	W.D.
1901	Bernton-Benjamin, H. E., Lt. R.A.S.C., M.T., late Lt. R.N.V.R. France	A.C.G.H.
1913	Berridge, W. E., 2nd Lt. Somerset L.I. France (d.w. 20.8.16)	K.S.
1884	Berry, R. A. J., Capt. Northumberland Fusiliers, w. France	A.C.
1909	Bertie, A. W., M.C., Capt. R.A., and Staff, late Pte. London Regt., m. 2. France	F.H.R., H.de H.
1906	Bertie, S. M., Lt. S. Nottinghamshire Hussars, empld. Remount Service. France, Balkans, Palestine	F.H.R.
1877	Best, T. G., Maj. R.F.A.	A.C.A.
1907	Best, T. W., Maj. Leicestershire Yeomanry, att. R.A.F., w. France	H.T.B.
1892	Best, W., Capt. R. Welch Fusiliers	S.A.D.
1911	Bethell, D. J., M.C. and Bar, Capt. Scots Gds., late Lt. K.O.Y.L.I., m. France	E.L.V.
1897	Bethell, Hon. R., Capt. Scots Gds., w. France	R.C.R.
1907	Bethell, W. A. V., Capt. 2nd Life Gds., w. France	H.Br.
1911	Bevan, D. R., Lt. R.A.S.C., M.T. France	E.I.
1911	Bevan, F. H., Lt. Intell. Corps, Staff, w., p. France	H.M.
1913	Bevan, J. H., M.C., Capt. Hertfordshire Regt., and Staff, m. 3. France	H.M.
1887	Bevan, O. C., M.C., Maj. R.F.A., and Staff, w., m. 2. France	R.C.R.
1909	Bevan, T. R., Lt. Hertfordshire Regt., and Staff. France, Italy	H.M.

1914	Bevir, A., Lt. The King's (Liverpool Regt.), m. 2. France	K.S.
1894	Bevis, C. B., O.B.E. (Pape at Eton), Lt.-Col., Staff, m.	E.L.V.
1910	Bewicke-Copley, R. G. W., M.C. (F) Lt. (t. Maj.) K.R.R.C., att. M.G.C., w., m. France, Balkans, S. Russia	C.M.W.
1905	Bewicke-Copley, R. L. C., Capt. Coldstream Gds., w. France (k. 21.12.16)	R W.W.-T., C.M.W.
1910	Bibby, F. B. F., Capt. 1st Life Gds., m. France	M.D.H.
1914	Bibby, F. S., 2nd Lt. Cameronians (Scottish Rifles). France (k. 20.7.16)	P.V.B.
1913	Bibby, H. P., Pte. The King's (Liverpool Regt.), w. France	H.B.
1909	Bibby, J. D., Lt. 4th Hussars, w., p. France	P.V.B.
1914	Bibby, J. E. H., Lt. R. Welch Fusiliers, att. R.A.F. France	J.H.M.H.
1911	Bibby, J. Patrick, Lt. Cameronians (Scottish Rifles). France (k. 10.3.15)	P.V.B.
1908	Bibby, J. Pengelly, Lt. Grenadier Gds., late 2nd Lt. R. Fusiliers. France (k. 12.10.17)	E.L.C.
1908	Bickersteth, E. R., Lt. R.G.A.	E.L.V.
1881	Bickersteth, R. A., Maj. R.A.M.C. France	H.E.L.
1879	Bicknell, M. B., Lt.-Col. R.A., Staff	H.E.L.
1900	Biddulph, A. L. N., Maj. R.A.S.C. France	A.C.J., A.C.G.H.
1915	Biddulph, M. W. J., 2nd Lt. Coldstream Gds., w. 2. France	A.M.G.
1907	Bigge, H. J., Lt. 19th Hussars. France	H.M.
1904	Bigge, Hon. J. N., Capt. K.R.R.C., and Staff. France (k. 15.5.15)	F.H.R.
1906	Bigge, W. E., Capt. Northumberland Yeomanry, att. 13th Hussars, and Staff, m. France, Mesopotamia	H.M.
1891	Bigham, Hon. C. C., C.M.G., C.B.E. (F) Bt. Maj. (t. Lt.-Col.) Grenadier Gds., and Staff, w., m. Egypt, Gallipoli	K.S.
1891	Bill, C. F., Capt. N. Staffordshire Regt., w. France	R.A.H.M.
1916	Billson, R. A. L., 2nd Lt. R. Fusiliers, and Staff, w. France	H. de H.

1916	Bingham, Lord, M.C., Lt. Coldstream Gds., w. France	A.M.G.
1904	Bingham, D. C., Lt. Coldstream Gds. France (k. 14.9.14)	S.A.D
1901	Bingham, R. C., D.S.O. (F) Bt. Maj. (t. Lt.-Col.) Coldstream Gds., w., m. 3. France	S.A.D.
1910	Bingley, H. J., Capt. R.F.A. Palestine	E.I.
1916	Binney, R. C. C. J., Lt. R. W. Kent Regt. France	K.S.
1875	Binning, Lord, C.B., M.V.O., Brig.-Gen. (Lothians and Border Horse). France (d. 12.1.17)	O.B.
1908	Birch, F. L., O.B.E., Lt.-Cr. R.N.V.R. Home Waters, Atlantic, Dardanelles	E.L.V.
1910	Birch-Reynardson, H. T., Capt. Oxfordshire and Bucks L.I., w. Mesopotamia	A.C.G.H.
1896	Birchall, A. P., Capt. R. Fusiliers, empld. Lt.-Col. Canadian Infantry, m. France (k. 23.4.15)	T.D., J.H.M.H.
1903	Birchall, E. V. D., D.S.O., Capt. Oxfordshire and Bucks L.I., m. France (d.w. 10.8.16)	A.A S
1894	Birchall, J. D., M.P., Maj. Gloucestershire Yeomanry, empld. Labour Corps. France	T.D.
1896	Bircham, B. O., M.C., Capt. Hampshire Regt., late L/ce-Cpl. Middlesex Regt., w. 2. France, Gallipoli	J.M.E.
1896	Bircham, F. R. S., Capt. R.N.V.R., and Staff	J.M.E.
1893	Bircham, H. F. W., D.S.O., Lt.-Col. K.R.R.C., m. 4. France (d.w. 23.7.16)	J M.E.
1903	Birchenough, R. P. (F) Maj. Derbyshire Yeomanry, m. Balkans, Egypt	E.I.
1904	Birkbeck, B., D.S.O., M.C., Maj. Coldstream Gds., m. 2. France	H.T.B.
1913	Birkbeck, G., Lt. Norfolk Yeomanry (d. 19.2.15)	P.V.B.
1905	Birkbeck, G. W., Capt. Norfolk Regt., m. Egypt, Gallipoli, Palestine (k. 19.4.17)	S.A.D., P.V.B
1904	Birkbeck, H. A., M.C., Maj. Norfolk Yeomanry, att. Norfolk Regt., w. France, Egypt, Gallipoli, Palestine	S.A.D.
1911	Birkbeck, O., Lt. Shropshire L.I., late 2nd Lt. 1st R. Dragoons. France, Balkans, Black Sea	P.V.B.
1876	Bishop, C. W., Maj. Res. Regt. of Cav.	H.W.M.

1915	Bishop, G. C., Lt. 9th Lancers, w. France	C.M.W.
1916	Bishop, H. F., Lt. Devonshire Regt., empld. Capt. Sp. List. France, Italy, N. Russia	K.S.
1893	Blaauw, H. T. G., Lt., late Pte., R. Fusiliers, w. France	E.L.V.
1896	Black, C. M., Lt. K.R.R.C. France	E.H., T.C.P.
1916	Black, F. R. J., Lt. H.L.I., w. France, N. Russia	E.W.S.
1884	Blackburn, A., Cpl. Forestry Corps, Canadian E.F. France	E.H.
1871	Blackburn, H., Maj. A. and S. Highlanders	E.H.
1867	Blackburn, J. E., C.B., Col. Chief Engineer Northern Command	D.
1914	Blacker, C. P., M.C., Capt. Coldstream Gds., w., m. 2. France	H. de H.
1915	Blacker, J. R., 2nd Lt. Coldstream Gds. France (k. 29.9.15)	H. de H.
1905	Blackett, B. J. (F) Lt., late Cpl., Australian Imp. Forces, att. R.A.F., and Staff, w. 2. France, Gallipoli, New Guinea	H.T.B.
1891	Blackett, Sir H. D., Bart., Capt. Northumberland Yeomanry, att. Middlesex Regt.	E.H.
1903	Blackett-Ord, J. R., Maj. Northumberland Fusiliers	J.H.M.H.
1907	Blackett-Ord, M., Capt. Northumberland Fusiliers	H.Br.
1913	Blacklock, A. H., 2nd Lt. A. and S. Highlanders. France (k. 21.10.14)	H.B.
1896	Blacklock, C. A., C.B., C.M.G., D.S.O. and Bar, Maj.-Gen., w., m. 8. France	A.C.J.
1896	Blacklock, G. H., Lt. (t. Lt.-Col.) Shropshire Yeomanry, and Staff, m. France	F.T., H.B.
1897	Blackwood, A. P., D.S.O. (F) Brig.-Gen. (Border Regt.) France, Balkans, S. Russia	E.I.
1911	Blackwood, H. S., Lt. London Regt. France (d.w. 1.5.17)	H.B
1872	Blagrove, H. J., C.B., C.B.E., Bt. Col., Staff	C.C.J.
1893	Blaine, G., M.C., Capt. Somerset L.I. France	H.W.M.
1901	Blake, C. R., Capt. K.R.R.C. France (k. 4.4.17)	J.M.E.
1900	Blake, M. F., Lt. K.R.R.C. France (k. 14.9.14)	J M.E.
1915	Blakiston-Houston, J. M., Lt. 11th Hussars, att. Tank Corps. France	R.P.L.B.
1880	Blakiston-Houston, R., Capt. Rifle Bde.	E.H.

1918	Bland, J. E. M., 2nd Lt. Scots Gds.	K.S.
1915	Blandford, Marquess of, Lt. 1st Life Gds. France	E.I., T.F.C.
1914	Blandy, G. K., Capt. R.A.F., late Sub-Lt. R.N.A.S. and 2nd Lt. E. Surrey Regt., w., p., m. Balkans, Mediterranean	R.S.de H.
1911	Blane, M. G. S., Lt. Cameron Highlanders. France (k. 25.9.15)	E.I.
1883	Bledisloe, Lord, K.B.E., M.P. (Bathurst at Eton), Capt. R. Monmouthshire R.E., and Staff	A.C.A.
1872	Blencowe, R. C., Lt. R. Defence Corps	W.E.
1877	Blewitt, A., Maj. (t. Lt.-Col.), K.R.R.C., empld. Labour Corps. France (d.w. 4.9.17)	C.L.L.-C.
1907	Bligh, A. S., Pte. R. Fusiliers. France	R.S.K.
1910	Bligh, J. F., M.C., Capt. R.F.A., w. 2. France (k. 1.7.17)	R.S.K.
1906	Bligh, Hon. N.G., D.S.O., Lt.-Col. Rifle Bde., w., m. 2. France	H.T.B.
1900	Bliss, H. J. W., Capt. R.A.S.C., M.T. France	H.D., H.T.B.
1903	Bliss, P. W., Capt. R.E., m. 3. France	K.S.
1908	Blofeld, F. D'A., 2nd Lt. 2nd Life Gds., late Pte. Gloucestershire Yeomanry. France (k. 12.5.15)	T.C.P., E.L.C.
1894	Blofeld, J. C., the late, Capt. Norfolk Regt. (d. 8.9.20)	P.W., S.R.J.
1903	Blomfield, F., Pte. R.A.S.C., M.T., w. 4. France	R.S.de H.
1896	Blundell-Hollinshead-Blundell, C. L., O.B.E., Maj. Grenadier Gds., and Staff. France	F.W.C., J.H.M.H.
1888	Blyth, J., C.B.E., Lt.-Col. Oxfordshire and Bucks L.I. France	R.C.R.
1914	Blyth, J. C., 2nd Lt. K.R.R.C. France (k. 13.4.17)	C.M.W.
1896	Blyth, Hon. R. A., Capt. Essex Yeomanry, and Staff, m. France, Egypt, Gallipoli	E.H., T.C.P.
1887	Blythswood, Lord, M.V.O. (F) (Campbell at Eton) Maj. Scots Gds., and Staff	F.H.R.
1890	Boden, A. D., Maj. Rifle Bde. France (k. 25.9.14)	J.M.E.
1912	Boden, A. P., M.C. (F) Capt. 12th Lancers, att. R.E. Signal Service, m. 2. France	E.L.C.
1912	Bodley, J. R. C., M.C., Capt. K.R.R.C., and Staff, w., m. France	H.Br.

1910	Bodley, R. V. C., M.C. (F) Maj. K.R.R.C., and Staff, w. France	H.Br.
1915	Bogle Smith, J. A., Lt. 1st (King's) Dragoon Gds. France, Afghanistan	A.E.C.
1878	Bogle Smith, S., C.B., C.B.E., Col. Remount Service, m.	T.D.
1886	Boileau, R. F., Maj. Labour Corps, late Maj. R. Fusiliers and R.G.A., m. France	C.H.E.
1915	Bolckow, H. C. R., Lt. 7th Dragoon Gds., w. France	H.B., R.H.deM.
1904	Boles, D. C., Capt. 17th Lancers, and Staff. France	P.W.
1914	Boles, H. F., 2nd Lt. 17th Lancers, att. R.F.C. France (d.w. 24.5.15)	P.W., F.E.R
1907	Bolton, I. F. C., Capt. A. and S. Highlanders, w., m. France	L.S.R.B.
1879	Bolton, R. G. I., Lt.-Col. Scots Gds., p. France	H.W.M.
1892	Bond, K. D., Capt. S. Staffordshire Regt., and Staff, late Pte. R. Fusiliers, w. France	S.R.J.
1897	Bond, W. de G., Lt. R.A.S.C., M.T., m. France	S.R.J.
1892	Bonham, E. H., M.V.O. (F) Maj. R. Scots Greys, and Staff, m. France	J.M.E.
1895	Bonham-Carter, A. E., Capt. K.R.R.C.	E.I.
1898	Bonham-Carter, F. H., Capt. R.G.A. Egypt, Gallipoli, Palestine	J.P.C.
1902	Bonn, W. B. L., D.S.O., M.C., Maj. Leicestershire Yeomanry, att. Welsh Gds., w. 2, m. France	C.L., R.S.K.
1901	Bonsor, A. C. (F) Maj. W. Kent Yeomanry, att. M.G.C. France, Egypt, Gallipoli, Palestine	R.A.H.M.
1897	Bonsor, M. C., Capt. Norfolk Yeomanry, att. Norfolk Regt. Egypt, Gallipoli, Palestine (k. 10.3.18)	R.A.H.M.
1898	Bonsor, R., Maj. Surrey Yeomanry, att. The Queen's. France, Egypt, Gallipoli, Italy	R.A.H.M.
1899	Bonsor, R. C., M.C., Lt. Welsh Gds. France	R.A.H.M.
1914	Bonvalot, A. C., Capt. Coldstream Gds., att. T.M.B., and Staff. France	A.E.C.
1910	Bonvalot, E. St. L., 2nd Lt. Coldstream Gds. France (d.w. 9.10.15)	H.F.W.T., A.E.C.

1911	Booker, G. H., Lt. Sp. List	J.H.M.H.
1904	Booth, C. Z. M., Lt. Leicestershire Yeomanry, late Lt. R.N.D. France, Egypt, Gallipoli	H.F.W.T.
1913	Booth, J. L., Maj. R.E., att. R.A.F., w. France, Egypt	A.C.G.H.
1908	Borrett, P. R., Lt. Scots Gds., w. France	L.S.R.B.
1900	V.C. Borton, A. D., C.M.G., D.S.O. (F) Lt.-Col. K.R.R.C., empld. London Regt., w., m. 4. France, Balkans, Gallipoli, Palestine, N. Russia	A.C.A.
1903	Borton, A. E., C.M.G., D.S.O., A.F.C. (F) Brig.-Gen. (Black Watch), Group-Cr. R.A.F., w., m. 5. France, Palestine, Sinai	A.C.A., R.S.de H.
1897	Borwick, G., Capt. Bedfordshire Regt., att. R.F.C. France	H.B.
1903	Borwick, R. G., Lt. (t. Capt.) R.F.A., late Capt. Hertfordshire Regt., w. France	H.B.
1909	Bosanquet, A. R., M.C., Lt. The King's Own (R. Lancaster Regt.), w. France	E.I.
1896	Bosanquet, B. J. T., Lt. R.A.F.	R.A.H.M.
1883	Bosanquet, H. P., Lt. Bedfordshire Regt., late Lt. R. W. Kent Regt. India	T.D.
1885	Bosanquet, W. C., Bt. Maj. (t. Lt.-Col.) R.A.M.C. India	K.S.
1911	Bosanquet, W. S. B., D.S.O., Capt. Coldstream Gds., and Staff, w., m. France	E.L.C.
1905	Boscawen, Hon. G. E., D.S.O., Maj. R.A., and Staff, m. 5. France (d.w. 27.5.18)	R.W.W.-T.
1910	Boscawen, Hon. M. T., D.S.O., M.C., Capt. Rifle Bde., empld. Lt.-Col. London Regt., and Staff, m 2. France, N. Russia	R.W.W.-T., C.M.W.
1909	Boscawen, Hon. V. D., 2nd Lt. Coldstream Gds. France (k. 1.11.14)	R.W.W.-T., C.M.W.
1911	Boswell, W. G. K., Capt. Rifle Bde., m. France (d.w. 28.7.16)	K.S.
1915	Boughton-Leigh, E., Capt. Rifle Bde., and Staff, w., m. France	A.A.S.

1895	Boughton-Leigh, H. A. W., Lt. (t. Capt.) R.F.A., w.2. France	H.W.M.
1898	Boulter, C. S. C., Capt. R.F.A. France	C.L.
1892	Boulter, R. S. L., Capt., R.A.S.C., and Staff. France.	S.R.J.
1902	Boulter, S. J., Lt. R.A.S.C. Balkans, S. Russia	C.H.A.
1902	Bourke, N. E. J., Maj. Manchester Regt. France	H.Br.
1881	Bourne, G. C., Maj., Gen. List, late Maj. Worcestershire Regt.	F.W.C.
1907	Bourne, R. C., Capt. Herefordshire Regt., and Staff, w. France, Gallipoli	R.P.L.B.
1900	Bouwens, B. G., Lt. R.A.S.C., M.T., w. France	J.M.E.
1906	Bovill, A. C. S., M.C. (F) Capt. 9th Lancers, m. France	H.M.
1901	Bovill, C., O.B.E. (F) Lt.-Col. R.A.F., late Maj. R.G.A. m. 4. France, Egypt	E.L.V.
1906	Bovill, M. W., Capt. R.A.F. France	E.L.V.
1880	Bowen, G. W. H., Lt. R. Defence Corps	W.D.
1875	Bower, E. T. C., Capt. Staff	G.E.M.
1916	Bower, L. T., Lt. Coldstream Gds. France	P.V.B.
1917	Bowes-Lyon, A. P., 2nd Lt. Grenadier Gds.	C.M.W.
1903	Bowes-Lyon, C. L. C., Lt. Black Watch. France (k. 23.10.14)	R.W.W.-T.
1901	Bowes-Lyon, Hon. F., Capt. Black Watch. France (k. 25.9.15)	R.W.W.-T., C.M.W.
1904	Bowes-Lyon, G. F., Capt. Black Watch, and Staff, w. France	R.W.W.-T.
1914	Bowes-Lyon, G. P., Lt. Grenadier Gds. France (k.27.11.17)	C.M.W.
1904	Bowes-Lyon, Hon. J. H., 2nd Lt. Black Watch, w. France	R.W.W.-T.
1892	Bowes-Lyon, Hon. M., Maj. 2nd Life Gds., w., m. France, Mesopotamia	R.A.H.M.
1912	Bowes-Lyon, Hon. M. C. H., Capt. R. Scots, p. France	C.M.W.
1901	Bowlby, G. V. S., Capt. R.H.G., m. France (k.13.5.15)	C.L., H.T.B.
1909	Bowlby, H. R., Lt. R.N.V.R., Staff, late Capt. Rifle Bde. w. France	S.A.D., H.M.
1911	Bowlby, H. S., M.C., Maj. R. Sussex Regt. France	H.M.

1910 Bowlby, L. H. S., Lt. R. Scots Greys, w. France
(k. 4.6.19) H.T.B., S.G.L.

1909 Bowlby, R. F., Lt. London Regt. France P.W.

1900 Bowman, A. W., L/ce-Cpl. London Regt., p. France
(d.w. 17.4.18) R.P.L.B.

1902 Bowman, C. F., M.C., Maj. R.A.S.C., m. France J.P.C., R.P.L.B.

1898 Bowman, H. E., C.B.E., Capt. R. Fusiliers, and Staff.
France, Mesopotamia J.P.C.

1885 Bowring, J. F. E., Capt. Lancashire Fusiliers, empld.
Maj. Labour Corps, m. France, Balkans R.C.R.

1904 Bowyer, G. E. W., M.C., Capt. Oxfordshire and Bucks
L. I., and Staff, w., m. 2. France A.A.S.

1901 Boxall, A. P., T.D., Lt.-Col. R.F.A., w., m. 2. France R.W.W.-T.

1906 Boxall, C. L., Capt. Hampshire Regt. Gallipoli (d.w. 27.4.15) H.M

1912 Boyd, C. L., Capt. A. and S. Highlanders, att. Gordon
Highlanders, and R. Welch Fusiliers, and Staff, w. 2.
France H.F.W.T., A.E.C.

1903 Boyd-Rochfort, C. C. (F.) Maj. Scots Gds., att. R.A.F.,
and Staff, w. France E.C.A.L.

1897 V.C. Boyd-Rochfort, G. A., Lt. (t. Capt.) Scots Gds. France H.W.M.

1897 Boyd-Rochfort, H., D.S.O., M.C., Bt. Lt.-Col. 21st
Lancers, att. Tank Corps, and Staff, m. 4. France H.W.M.

1865 Boyle, C. J., Maj. R. Defence Corps F.E.D.

1912 Boyle, G. F., Capt. R. Scots Fusiliers. France, Balkans A.M.G.

1898 Boyle, G. H. P., the late, (F) Maj. Seaforth Highlanders,
empld. Lt.-Col. R.E. Signal Service, m. 4. Gallipoli
(d. 16.10.19) A.A.S.

1900 Brabourne, Lord (Mr. Knatchbull-Hugessen at Eton),
Lt. Grenadier Gds. France (k. 11.3.15) H.M.

1906 Brace, H. F., D.S.O., M.C., Capt. 15th Hussars, w. 2.,
m. 3. France H.M.

1895 Bradford, E. A., D.S.O., Bt. Lt.-Col. K.R.R.C., and
Staff, m. 2. France W.D.

1885 Bradford, Sir E. R., Bart., Lt.-Col. Seaforth Highlanders, m. France (k. 14.9.14) W.D.

1878	Bradford-Atkinson, T. H. H., Maj. Grenadier Gds.	F.W.C.
1913	Bradish-Ellames, J. E. M., Lt. 8th Hussars. France	A.B.R.
1892	Bradshaw, C. P., Maj. 2nd Dragoon Gds. (Queen's Bays), and Staff. France	F.W.C.
1914	Bradshaw, R. E. K., Lt. London Regt. France (k. 1.7.16)	H.Br.
1914	Bradshaw, V. C. I., Lt. 15th Hussars. France	A.C.G.H.
1915	Bradshaw, W. D., 2nd Lt. R.F.A. France (k. 31.10.16)	H.Br.
1914	Bradshaw, W. P. A., D.S.O., Capt. Scots Gds., m. France	M.D.H.
1905	Braithwaite, G. G., Capt. The Queen's, att. R.A.F., and Staff	A.C.G.H.
1888	Bramwell, H. D., Lt.-Col. 15th Hussars, late N. Somerset Yeomanry, w., m. France	J.M.E.
1905	Brand, H. A. T., Capt. 12th Lancers, att. R.E. Signal Service, m. France	L.S.R.B.
1903	Brand, J. C., D.S.O., M.C. (F) Bt. Maj. (t. Lt.-Col.) Coldstream Gds., and Staff, w., m. 4. France, Egypt, Gallipoli	E.C.A.L.
1887	Brand, W. J. H., the late, Bt. Maj. London Regt., and Staff (d. 24.1.20)	J.H.M.
1914	Brandford-Griffith, W., Lt. The Buffs, and Staff, w. 2. France	A.A.S.
1904	Brass, W., Capt. Surrey Yeomanry, att. R.A.F. France, Egypt, Italy	J.M.E.
1882	Brassey, Earl, T.D. (Brassey at Eton), Lt.-Col. W. Kent Yeomanry, and Staff. Italy	F.T.
1914	Brassey, C. H., Lt. 1st Life Gds. France	A.B.R.
1897	Brassey, E. H., M.V.O., Lt.-Col. 1st Life Gds., w., m. 3. France	F.D., C.H.A.
1900	Brassey, E. P., D.S.O., M.C., Capt. (t. Lt.-Col.) 7th Hussars, att. R.H.G. and Coldstream Gds., w. 2, m. France	A.A.S.
1917	Brassey, G. C., 2nd Lt. Coldstream Gds. France (k. 27.8.18)	A.B.R.
1894	Brassey, H. E., Lt.-Col. R.H.G., empld. Lt.-Col. S. Lancashire Regt., m. France (k. 16.7.16)	F.D., C.H.A

1887	Brassey, H. L. C., M.P., Maj. Northamptonshire Yeomanry	R.A.H.M.
1893	Brassey, R. B., Capt. Res. Regt. of Cav. and Staff	R.A.H.M.
1900	Brett, Hon. M. V. B., M.V.O., O.B.E. (F) Lt.-Col. Black Watch, and Staff, m. 4. France	A.C.A.
1898	Brett, Hon. O. S. B., M.B.E., Capt. London Regt., and Staff	A.C.A.
1907	Brett, R. J., D.S.O., Bt.-Maj. (t. Lt.-Col.) Oxfordshire and Bucks L.I., att. R. Fusiliers, empld. Lt.-Col. R. Berkshire Regt., w. 3, m. 4. France, Egypt	J.M.D.
1914	Bridge, A. D., M.C., Lt. (t. Capt.) Coldstream Gds. France	A.C.G.H.
1916	Bridgeman, G. J. O., M.C., Lt. R.F.A. Egypt, Palestine	R.P.L.B.
1915	Bridgeman, R. C., M.C., Lt. Rifle Bde., w. 2. France	R.P.L.B.
1911	Bridges, E. E., M.C., Capt. Oxfordshire and Bucks L.I., w. France, Italy	L.S.R.B.
1902	Bridges, J. W. W., Capt. Coldstream Gds., late 2nd Life Gds., att. R.F.A., w. 2. France	H.D., A.C.G.H.
1884	Brierley, A. P., Trooper Res. Regt. of Cav., att. Labour Corps. France	H.D.
1914	Brierly, H. J. R., M.C. (F) Lt. Coldstream Gds., and Staff. France	H.M.
1889	Brigstocke, W. P., Capt. Staff. France	F.T.
1915	Brinckman, T. E. W., Lt. 1st Life Gds. France	A.E.C.
1880	Brinckman, Sir T. F., Bart., C.B., empld. Lt.-Col. London Regt. France	C.W.D., H.D.
1882	Briscoe, H. A. W., Maj. K.R.R.C., att. Rifle Bde.	A.C.A.
1911	Briscoe, R. G., M.C., Lt. Grenadier Gds., late L/ce-Cpl. 7th Dragoon Gds. France	R.S.K.
1906	Bristowe, L. G., Lt. R.F.A., att. R.A.F., w. France, Gallipoli	J.H.M.H.
1911	Bristowe, O. C., Lt. R.E., late Pte. H.A.C. France	E.I.
1911	Britten, C. R., M.C., Capt. Grenadier Gds., w. 2. France	E.W.S.

1871	Brittlebank, H., Pte. Pioneers, E. African F.F. E. Africa	W.B.M.
1867	Brittlebank, W., Lt. E. African Transport Corps. E. Africa	W.B.M.
1903	Broadbent, J. C., Sergt. A.V.C. Balkans, Egypt, Palestine	R.P.L.B.
1916	Broadbent, J. G., Lt. K.R.R.C., w. France	E.L.C.
1911	Brocklebank, C. G., M.C. (F) Capt., late Sergt., R.E., m. France	P.V.B.
1916	Brocklebank, D. R., Sub-Lt. R.N. Home Waters	E.L.C.
1906	Brocklebank, H. A., Capt. The King's Own (R. Lancaster Regt.), p. France	P.W.
1893	Brocklebank, J. J., D.S.O., Maj. Scottish Horse. Egypt, Gallipoli	E.H.
1889	Brocklebank, R. E. R., Lt. (t. Maj.) The King's (Liverpool Regt.)	F.W.C.
1899	Brocklebank, R. H. R., D.S.O., Maj. (t. Lt.-Col.) 9th Lancers, att. M.G.C., m. France, Egypt, Gallipoli	T.C.P.
1915	Brocklebank, R. R., 2nd Lt. R. Welch Fusiliers. France (d.w. 16.5.17)	E.L.C.
1901	Brocklebank, T. G., Capt. R.F.A. France (k. 5.8.16)	P.W.
1904	Brocklehurst, G. E. D., Lt. Gloucestershire Yeomanry	R.C.R.
1905	Brocklehurst, H. C., Capt. 10th R. Hussars, att. R.A.F., w. France, E. Africa, Arabia, Palestine, N. Russia	J.M.D.
1901	Brocklehurst, J. H., Maj. Coldstream Gds., att. Bimbashi Egyptian Army, w. 2. France, Egypt	R.C.R.
1901	Brocklehurst, Sir P. L., Bart., Maj. Derbyshire Yeomanry, att. 1st Life Gds., w. France	J.M.D.
1907	Brodie, B. C., M.C. and Bar, Lt. (t. Capt.) Surrey Yeomanry, att. Gordon Highlanders, and Staff, m. France, Gallipoli	J.H.M.H.
1896	Brodie, D. R., M.C., Lt. (t. Capt.) Scots Gds., late Pte. London Regt., w. 2. France	H.E.L.
1914	Brodie, E. M., Capt. Black Watch. France	C.H.K.M.
1887	Brodie of Brodie, I. A. M., D.S.O., M.C., Capt. Lovat's Scouts, and Staff, m. Egypt, Gallipoli, Palestine	H.E.L.

1885	Brodrick, Hon. A. G., T.D., Col. The Queen's, m. 2. Mesopotamia	E.W., S.A.D.
1896	Bromley, H. A., Lt. British Columbia Regt., Canadian E.F., w. France (k. 24.4.15)	H B
1885	Bromley-Davenport, A. H., Lt. Staffordshire Yeomanry. Egypt	A.C.J.
1889	Bromley-Davenport, H. R., O.B.E., Lt. R.E., I.W.T., m. France	G.E.M., P.H.C.
1880	Bromley-Davenport, W., C.M.G., C.B.E., D.S.O., T.D. (F) Lt.-Col. Staffordshire Yeomanry, and Staff, m. France, Egypt, Italy	G.E.M.
1885	Bromley-Martin, E. G., Maj. Worcestershire Yeomanry, att. R. Fusiliers, and Staff. France	J.M.E.
1890	Bromley-Wilson, Sir M., Bart. (Bromley at Eton), 2nd Lt. Suffolk Regt., late Maj. S. Nottinghamshire Hussars	H.B.
1899	Brooke, Lord, C.M.G., M.V.O. (F) Brig.-Gen. (1st Life Gds.), att. Canadian E.F., w., m. 3. France	S.A.D.
1915	Brooke, E. H., M.C., Lt. 19th Hussars, w. France	H.B., R.H.de M.
1912	Brooke, F. N., Lt. K.O.Y.L.I., and Staff. France, Balkans, Egypt	H.B.
1879	Brooke, F. W., Capt. Suffolk Regt., att. Labour Corps. France	C.W.D., H.D.
1893	Brooke, G., Lt. Irish Gds. France (d.w. 9.10.14)	S.R.J.
1901	Brooke, J. A., Capt. 6th (Inniskilling) Dragoons, att. R.A., and Staff, m. France	H.W.M., H.M.
1907	Brooke, Sir R. C., Bart., Lt. Scots Gds.	J.M.E., M.D.H.
1894	Brooke, W. J., Maj. Shropshire L.I., att. Middlesex Regt., w. France (k. 9.4.18)	W.D.
1914	Brooks, N. B., M.C., Lt. Cheshire Yeomanry, w. France, Egypt, Palestine	S.G.L.
1911	Brooks, T. M., M.C. (F) Capt. Cheshire Yeomanry, att. Shropshire L.I., w. France, Egypt, Palestine	H.T.B., S.G.L.
1903	Brooksbank, E. Y., Capt. 5th Lancers. France	H.T.B.
1905	Brooksbank, S., Capt. Yorkshire Regt. France (k. 25.9.15)	H.T.B

1900	Brooman-White, C. J., C.B.E., Maj. A. and S. Highlanders, late Maj. Rifle Bde. France	H.Br.
1900	Brooman-White, R. G., 2nd Lt. R. Inniskilling Fusiliers. France (k. 15.5.15)	H.T B.
1901	Brougham, Hon. H., Capt. Coldstream Gds.	H.M.
1911	Broughton-Adderley, A. R., Lt. Scots Gds., late 2nd Lt. Staffordshire Yeomanry. France	E.W.S.
1914	Broughton-Adderley, E. R., Pte. Canadian E.F. France	R.P.L.B.
1910	Broughton-Adderley, P. H., M.C., 2nd Lt. Scots Gds., late Sub-Lt. R.N.A.S., w. France (d.w. 16.10.18)	E.W.S.
1892	Brown, A. L. (F) Capt. (t. Maj.) 12th Lancers, and Staff, m. France	H.E.L.
1893	Brown, G. A. C., Pte. Canadian E.F., att. T.M.B. and R.E., w. France	J.P.C.
1898	Brown, G. Hargreaves, Capt. Coldstream Gds., w. France (k. 29.10.14)	P.W.
1915	Brown, T. R., 2nd Lt. R.F.A., w. France	K.S.
1913	Brown, W. N. S., Lt. Somerset L.I., att. Worcestershire Regt., w. France	H.Br.
1915	Browne, A. H. M., 2nd Lt. R.F.A. France, India	C.M.W.
1884	Browne, A. S., Maj. R. N. Devon Yeomanry	H.D.
1914	Browne, A. S. C., Lt. 12th Lancers. France	C.M.W.
1881	Browne, D. S., Capt. R. Scots Fusiliers, and Staff	J.C.
1912	Browne, J. B., Lt. 16th Lancers, w. France	E.L.V., A.C.R.-W.
1888	Browne, M., Maj. Northumberland Yeomanry, att. Labour Corps, and Staff. France	E.H.
1913	Browne, O. L., Lt. Cheshire Regt., att. M.G.C., w., m. Egypt, Gallipoli, Palestine	H.F.W.T., A.E.C.
1912	Browne, W. P., M.C., Capt. 1st R. Dragoons, and Staff, w., m. France	E.L.V., A.C.R.-W.
1897	Browning, C. H., Capt. R.F.A. France (k. 26.8.14)	K.S.
1914	Browning, F. A. M., D.S.O. (F) Lt. Grenadier Gds., and Staff, m. France	A.A.S.
1901	Browning, H. B., Lt. R.G.A., late Cpl. R.E. France	C.L., J.M.D.

1895	Browning, J. A., Maj. 2nd Dragoon Gds. (Queen's Bays), m. France (k. 31.10.14)	J.P.C.
1883	Brownlow, Hon. J. R. (F) Bt. Col. K.R.R.C.	H.W.M.
1906	Bruce, Hon. D. (F) Bt. Maj. (t. Lt.-Col.) Seaforth Highlanders, w. 3, m. France	H.E.L., R.S.K.
1891	Bruce, Sir H. R., Bart. (F) Maj. R. Irish Rifles	H.G.W., S.R.J.
1898	Bruce, K. H., D.S.O., Bt. Lt.-Col. Gordon Highlanders, and Staff, w., m. 2. France, Palestine	H.E.L.
1901	Bruce, Hon. R., Bt. Maj. Res. Regt. of Cav., and Staff	H.E.L.
1916	Bruce, R. C., M.C., Lt. Grenadier Gds. France	C.M.W.
1905	Bruce, R. J., Lt. R.A.O.D., late L/ce-Sergt. R.A.S.C.	C.H.A.
1903	Bruce, T. R., Capt. 14th Hussars. Mesopotamia (d. 8.2.17)	C.H.A.
1915	Bruce, Hon. V. A., Lt. 11th Hussars, and Staff. France	R.S.K.
1913	Bruce-Gardyne, I. M., M.C., Lt. (t. Capt.) Black Watch, w., m. France	P.V.B.
1905	Bruen, H. A., Capt. 15th Hussars	H.T.B.
1917	Bruxner, G. M., 2nd Lt. Scots Gds. France	R.S.K.
1891	Bryant, H. G., D.S.O., Capt. Shropshire L.I., m. France (d.w. 1.5.15)	J.M.E.
1897	Buchanan-Riddell, W. R., Capt. Hampshire Regt., late Pte. R. Fusiliers. Siberia	J.M.E.
1893	Buck, B. F., Lt. Sherwood Foresters. France (k. 3.9.16)	H.B.
1914	Buckland, D. H., Lt. K.R.R.C., m. France	A.E.C.
1880	Buckland, Sir R. U. H., K.C.M.G., C.B. (F) Maj.-Gen. (R.E.), m. 5. France	E.H.
1911	Buckland, T. A., Lt. Norfolk Regt., late Pte. London Regt., w., m. France (d.w. 19.10.15)	H.F.W.T., A.E.C.
1909	Buckley, Hon. B. B., Lt. London Regt.	K.S.
1877	Buckley, E. D. H., O.B.E., Maj. R.G.A.	H.W.M.
1911	Buckley, E. G. M., Capt. Northumberland Fusiliers, and Staff, w., m. France, Gallipoli	J.H.M.H.
1913	Buckley, R. M., M.C., Capt. K.R.R.C., late Capt. M.G.C. France	A.B.R.
1891	Bucknall, L. C., D.S.O. (F) Maj. Northamptonshire Yeomanry, and Staff, m. 2. France, Italy	H.G.W.

1892 Bucknall, R. E., O.B.E., Capt. Remount Service, m. France   H.B.
1900 Buckston, G. M., Capt. Derbyshire Yeomanry. Balkans, Egypt   T.D., J.H.M.H.
1910 Buckworth, T. R., Lt. R.E., w. 2. France   F.H.R., H.de H.
1912 Buddicom. W. D.. M.C.. Lt. 4th Hussars. France (d. from accid. 6.6.18)   E.I.
1897 Budgett, H. M., Lt. Sp. List, att. R.A.M.C. France   R.W.W.-T.
1901 Bulkeley, C. I. R., Capt. Scots Gds., late Capt. Shropshire L. I., att. K.R.R.C., w. France (k. 16.5.15)   C.H.A.
1898 Bulkeley, F. R., Capt. Oxfordshire and Bucks L.I., att. R.F.A. and Remount Service. France   H.D.
1895 Bulkeley, T. H. R., C.M.G., M.V.O., Capt. Scots Gds. France (k. 22.10.14)   F.T., P.H.C., C.H.A.
1909 Bulkeley-Johnson, V. F., Capt. Rifle Bde., w. France   R.S.K.
1908 Bull, R. E. B., Lt. Oxfordshire and Bucks L.I. France (k. 16.5.15)   W.D.E.
1910 Buller, F. E., Trooper King's African Rifles. E. Africa (k. 25.9.14)   A.C.G.H.
1902 Buller, H. A., Lt. R.A.S.C., M.T., late Pte. Manchester Regt. France   H.T.B.
1898 Buller, H. C., D.S.O., Lt.-Col. Rifle Bde., empld. Lt.-Col. Princess Patricia's Canadian L.I., and Staff, m. 2. France (k. 2.6.16)   J.M.E.
1895 Buller, J. D., C.M.G., D.S.O., Maj. R.A.S.C., and Staff, m. 2. France, Gallipoli   J.M.E.
1904 Buller, L. M., Capt. Lincolnshire Regt. France (k. 24.8.14)   J.M.E.
1897 Buller, N. M., Lt. Irish Gds., w. 2. France   S.R.J.
1905 Bullough, I., M.C., Capt. Coldstream Gds., late Maj. Scottish Horse, m. 2. France   H.F.W.T.
1908 Bulteel, J. C., D.S.O., M.C., Capt. (t. Maj.) Buckinghamshire Yeomanry, m. 2. France, Egypt, Gallipoli, Palestine   R.S.de H.
1913 Bulteel, M. C., Capt. R. Scots, att. R.A.F., w. 2. France, Balkans   A.M.G.

1914	Bulteel, R., Lt. Res. Regt. of Cav., att. 17th Lancers, late 2nd Lt. Buckinghamshire Yeomany. France	A.M.G.
1904	Bunbury, C. H. N., Lt. Coldstream Gds., late Lt. R. Wiltshire Yeomanry. France	A.C.G.H.
1904	Bunbury, H. W., Capt. Suffolk Regt., att. R.A.F., w., m. France	L.S.R.B.
1901	Burbury, B. T., M.C., Maj. Yorkshire Regt., and Staff, m. 3. France	C.L., H.T.B.
1912	Burbury, J. F., 2nd Lt. The Queen's Own (R. W. Kent Regt.). France (d.w. 23.2.15)	R.S.K
1913	Burdett, A. St. G., Lt. R.A.S.C., M.T., late Leinster Regt. France, Balkans, Egypt	A.E.C.
1888	Burdett, Sir F., Bart., Capt. 17th Lancers, and Staff. France	F.W.C.
1911	Burdon, R., Capt., Durham L.I., att. Northumberland Yeomanry and R.F.C. France (k. accid. 10.1.17)	J.H.M.H.
1907	Burdon, W. W., Capt. Northumberland Yeomanry, w. France	J.H.M.H.
1907	Burdon-Muller, R., 2nd Lt. Sp. List. France	J.M.E., A.B.R.
1882	Burford-Hancock, H. di S. B., Lt.-Col. Hampshire Regt. Afghanistan	H.D.
1874	Burges, W. E. P., O.B.E., Col. Gloucestershire Regt.	C.C.J.
1915	Burgess, G. H., Lt. R.F.A., and Staff, w. 2. France	R.S.de H.
1908	Burgess, R. E., Lt. R.F.A.	R.S.de H.
1900	Burleigh, Master of (Hon. G. J. G. Bruce) (F) Bt. Maj. Intell. Corps, Staff, late Interpreter I.E.F., w., m. 4. France	J.H.M.H.
1897	Burleigh, Master of (Hon. R. Bruce), Capt. A. and S. Highlanders. France (k. 26.8.14)	J.H.M.H.
1894	Burmester, H. L., Sergt. Ottawa Bn., Canadian E.F. France	F.T.
1909	Burn, A. H. R., 2nd Lt. 1st R. Dragoons. France (k. 30.10.14)	F.L.C.
1876	Burn-Murdoch, J. F., C.B., C.M.G., C.B.E., Maj.-Gen. (1st. R. Dragoons)	C.L.L.-C.

1894	Burnell, C. D., D.S.O., Capt. (t. Lt.-Col.) London Rifle Bde., w., m. 2. France	E.H.
1907	Burness, A. R., Lt. Seaforth Highlanders. France (d.w. 25.4.15)	J.H.M H.
1911	Burnet, J. R., Lt. R. Fusiliers, empld. Imp. Recruits Depot, Nova Scotia	A.A S.
1905	Burney, E., M.C. (F) Lt. R.A.F., late Lt. Intell. Corps, and Staff. France, S. Russia	H. Br.
1874	Burney, H. H., C.B., Brig.-Gen. (Gordon Highlanders) France	A.C.A.
1904	Burnham, G. le R., Bt. Maj. 6th (Inniskilling) Dragoons, and Staff. France, Egypt, Palestine	J.H.M.H.
1916	Burns, Hon. J. A., Lt. Scots Gds., w. France	A.B.R.
1914	Burnside, E. B. C., Capt. The Buffs. France (k. 12.10.17)	J.H.M.H
1901	Burrell, L. S. T., Maj. R.A.M.C. France	E.I.
1895	Burrell, Sir M. R., Bart., C.B.E., Lt.-Col. Remount Service	A.C.J.
1908	Burrell, R. F. T., 2nd Lt. The Queen's Own (R. W. Kent Regt.). France (k. 26.9.15)	E.I.
1893	Burroughes, C. F., Capt. Leicestershire Yeomanry	S.R.J.
1896	Burroughes, H. N., D.S.O. (F) Lt.-Col. R.A.M.C., m. 2. France	S.R.J.
1913	Burrows, M. B., D.S.O., M.C., Lt. 5th Dragoon Gds., w., p. France, N. Russia	L.S.R.B.
1912	Burrows, R. F. G., Capt. Manchester Regt., w., p. France	L.S.R.B.
1869	Burton, B., C.B., C.M.G., Maj.-Gen. (R.A.)	F.E.D.
1909	Burton, B. L. E., Maj. R.A.S.C., M.T., and Staff, m. 2. France	A.C.G.H.
1908	Burton, G. E. E., Lt. Suffolk Regt. France (k. 16.7.16)	A.C.G.H.
1899	Bury, Visc., M.C., Maj. Scots Gds., att. Hood Bn. R.N.D. France	W.D., C.L.
1910	Bury, E. L., M.C., Capt. R.E., and Staff, late Sergt. R.E., m. France (d. 9.11.18)	R.S.K.
1903	Bury, E. W., Capt. K.R.R.C. France (k. 4.12.15)	E.C.A.L.
1907	Bury, H. S. E., 2nd Lt. Grenadier Gds., att. Scots Gds. France (k. 25.1.15)	E.C.A.L., E.W.S.

1914 Bury, J., Lt. 17th Lancers, late Lt. R. Sussex Regt., and Staff, m. France — P.V.B.
1901 Bury, L. E., C.B.E. (F) Maj. R.E., m. 2. Egypt — E.C.A.L.
1909 Bush, H. G. de L., M.C., Lt. Gloucestershire Regt., att. Welch Regt., m. France (d.w. 17.1.17) — J.M.D
1915 Bush, R. H., Lt. R.F.A., w. Balkans — A.M.G.
1882 Bushby, H. N. G., Capt. R. Defence Corps — F.W.C.
1908 Busk, J., Capt. Dorset Yeomanry, att. R.F.A. France, Egypt — H.Br.
1910 Busk, W. R., Capt. R. Fusiliers, late Capt. 7th Dragoon Gds. France, Balkans, Black Sea — H.Br.
1910 Butcher, W. G. D., Capt. London Regt. France (k. 16.8.17) — K.S
1876 Butler, A. H., Maj. Gloucestershire Yeomanry — E.W.
1917 Butler, A. S., 2nd Lt. Coldstream Gds. France — A.C.R.-W.
1871 Butler, F. J. P., Lt.-Col. Remount Service — E.W.
1892 Butler, G. L., Maj. R.F.A., m. France, Balkans, Egypt, Italy — H.E.L.
1875 Butler, L. W. G., Lt.-Col. Staff — E.W.
1901 Butler, W. M., Maj. R.E. France (d. 5.3.19) — E.L.V.
1903 Butler-Henderson, Hon. E. B. (Henderson at Eton), Capt. Berks Yeomanry, w. Egypt, Gallipoli — E.I.
1892 Butler-Stoney, T. (Stoney at Eton), Lt. Irish Gds.; late 2nd Lt. R. Dublin Fusiliers, w. France (d.w. 30.9.17) — C.H F.
1889 Butter, A. E., C.M.G., Capt. Scottish Horse, and Staff — E.L.V.
1904 Butterworth, G. S. K., M.C., Lt. Durham L.I., late Pte. D. of Cornwall's L.I. France (k. 5.8.16) — K.S
1892 Butterworth, R. F. A., C.M.G., D.S.O. and Bar, Col. R.E., and Staff, m. 5. France — A.C.A.
1911 Buxton, C. E. V., M.C., Maj. R.F.A., and Staff m. 3. France — H.M.
1915 Buxton, Hon. D. B. S., 2nd Lt. Coldstream Gds. France (k. 9.10.17) — C.M W.
1916 Buxton, D. G., Lt. K.R.R.C. France — P.V.B.
1897 Buxton, G. C., Capt. (t. Maj.) Coldstream Gds., att. King's African Rifles, and Staff. France, E. Africa, Egypt — R.C.R.

1900	Buxton, H. F., Lt. Rifle Bde., late 2nd Lt. King Edward's Horse. France (d.w. 3.11.16)	H.E.L.
1903	Buxton, I., D.S.O., Maj. Norfolk Yeomanry, and Staff, w., m. 3. France, Egypt, Palestine	R.C.R.
1896	Buxton, J. L., C.M.G., D.S.O., Bt. Lt.-Col. Rifle Bde., and Staff, m. 5. France	J.M.E.
1916	Buxton, M. V., the late, M.C., Lt. (t. Capt.) Coldstream Gds. France (d. 8.8.19)	H.M.
1905	Buxton, R. G., Capt. Norfolk Yeomanry. France	J.H.M.H.
1902	Buxton, R. V., D.S.O. (F) Capt. W. Kent Yeomanry, empld. Lt.-Col. Imp. Camel Corps, and Staff, m. Arabia, Egypt, Gallipoli	H.E.L.
1908	Buxton, Sir T. F., Bart., Lt. Essex Yeomanry, and Staff, m. France	K.S.
1898	Byam-Grounds, N. B. C., Maj. (t. Lt.-Col.) The King's (Liverpool Regt.), att. Manchester Regt. and R. Warwickshire Regt., w. France	H.D.
1894	Byles, C. M. B., Lt. London Regt., and Staff, w. France	J.P.C.
1892	Byles, H. V. B., Capt. (t. Maj.) W. Yorkshire Regt., late Maj. Leicestershire Regt., and Staff. France	J.P.C.
1878	Byng, Lord, G.C.B., K.C.M.G., M.V.O. (F) (Mr. Byng at Eton), Gen. (3rd Hussars), Comm. Third Army, m. 9. France, Gallipoli	H.W.M.
1916	Byrne, R. R., Lt. R.A.F., m. France, Egypt, Palestine	C.H.K.M.
1917	Byron, R. G. G., 2nd Lt. 4th Dragoon Gds.	J.H.M.H.
1899	Cadogan, Hon. E. C. G., Capt. Suffolk Yeomanry, empld. Maj. Suffolk Regt., and Staff, m. Egypt, Gallipoli, Palestine	A.C.B.
1897	Cadogan, Hon. W. G. S., M.V.O., Maj. 10th R. Hussars, m. France (k. 12.11.14)	A.C.B.
1889	Cahen d'Anvers, R. (Cahen at Eton), Capt. 42me Régt. d'Infanterie, French Army. France	F.T.
1894	Cairnes, A. B., Maj. R. Irish Rifles. France (k. 9.9.16)	F.T.

1913	Caldwell, J. H., Lt. Cameron Highlanders, att. R.F.C. Mesopotamia (k. 24.1.18)	L.S R.B.
1887	Caldwell, J. S., Lt. A. and S. Highlanders	R.C.R.
1885	Caldwell, Rev. W. H. McK., C.F. Palestine	F.F.V., E.S.S., A.C.
1903	Caledon, Earl of, Capt. (t. Maj.) 1st Life Gds., w. France	A.C.J., A.C.G.H.
1912	Callander, G. D., Capt. 16th Lancers, m. France	H.de H.
1917	Calrow, G., 2nd Lt. 2nd Dragoon Gds. Palestine	A.C.G.H.
1891	Calvert, C. A., D.S.O., Bt. Lt.-Col. Surrey Yeomanry, w., m. France, Balkans, Palestine	F.H.R.
1911	Calvert, F. W. A., Capt. R.E., m. France	F.H.R., H. de H.
1878	Calvert, H. H., Lt.-Col. Gloucestershire Yeomanry	A.C.A.
1905	Calvert, H. M., Capt. Gloucestershire Yeomanry, att. Australian Imp. Forces. France	A.C.G.H.
1912	Calvert, R. D., Lt. R.A.S.C., M.T., late Pte. London Regt. France	R.S.K.
1890	Camden, Marquess, T.D., Maj. W. Kent Yeomanry. Gallipoli	T.D.
1898	Cameron, A. G., Capt. Cameron Highlanders. France (k. 25.9.14)	F.H.R.
1896	Cameron, E. C., Maj. Lovat's Scouts, and Staff	F.H.R.
1896	Campbell, A., 2nd Lt. R.A.F. France	F.H.R.
1914	Campbell, A. D., Lt. 9th Lancers, late Surrey Yeomanry. France	C.H.K.M.
1904	Campbell, A. H. G., Lt. A. and S. Highlanders, late 2nd Lt. Australian Imp. Forces, late Pte. Ceylon Planters' Corps, w. France, Balkans, Egypt, Mesopotamia	C.H.A.
1890	Campbell, A. M. M., Capt. R. Scots Fusiliers, w. France	A.C.A.
1903	Campbell, A. W. G., Lt. Coldstream Gds. France (d.w. 20.9.14)	A.A.S.
1906	Campbell, B. A., Capt. Scottish Horse, and Staff. Gallipoli	S.A.D., J.H.M.H.
1889	Campbell, C. G. P., Lt.-Col. R.F.A.	H.G.W.
1906	Campbell, C. H., Lt. R.F.A., w. 2. France, Balkans	K.S.

1893	Campbell, C. L. K., C.B., C.M.G., Brig.-Gen. (16th Lancers), w. 2, m. 4. France (d. 31.3.18)	J.C.
1898	Campbell, Sir C. R., Bart., Maj. 2nd Life Gds., att. Tank Corps, and Staff. France	E.I.
1882	Campbell, D., C.B., Brig.-Gen. (Seaforth Highlanders), m. 2. France	E.H.
1914	Campbell, D., Lt. Coldstream Gds., w. France (k. 19.7.16)	R S de H
1910	Campbell, D. S., M.C., Capt. W. Kent Yeomanry, att. The Buffs, and Staff. France, Egypt, Gallipoli, Palestine	R.C.R., C.H.K.M.
1912	Campbell, E. F., D.S.O., Capt. K.R.R.C., late R.A.F., w., m. France	C.M.W.
1904	Campbell, Hon. E. O., D.S.O. and Bar, Lt.-Col. Seaforth Highlanders, w. 2, m. 3. France (d. 4.6.18)	R.C.R
1906	Campbell, E. R. (F) Capt. R. Sussex Regt., w., m. 3. Egypt, Gallipoli, Palestine	R.C.R.
1902	Campbell, E. W., Lt. Irish Gds., w. France	C.H.A.
1904	Campbell, G., Paymaster Lt. R.N.R. Home Waters, N. Russia (d. 25.11.18)	C.H.A.
1903	Campbell, G. A., Lt. Coldstream Gds., m. France (k. 29.10.14)	A.C.B.
1904	Campbell, G. C., Maj. K.R.R.C., and Staff, w. France	R.W.W.-T.
1902	Campbell, G. V., M.C., Capt. Rifle Bde., m. France	C.H.A.
1914	Campbell, H. B., 2nd Lt. A. and S. Highlanders. France (k. 23.2.15)	P W., F E.R.
1899	Campbell, H. D. C., Lt. Oxfordshire and Bucks L.I., att. Cheshire Regt., late Pte. H.A.C. France, Italy	H.D.
1909	Campbell, H. F., Bt. Maj. Rifle Bde., empld. Maj. M.G.C., w., m. 3. France, Mesopotamia	E.I.
1875	Campbell, Hon. I., the late, Capt. Staff (d. 16.3.17)	C.L.L.-C.
1908	Campbell, I., 2nd Lt. A. and S. Highlanders, att. Seaforth Highlanders. France, Mesopotamia (d.w. 8.1.16)	H.Br.
1902	Campbell, Hon. I. M., D.S.O., Maj. Lovat's Scouts, empld. Lt.-Col. E. Lancashire Regt., m. France, Egypt, Gallipoli	R.C.R.

1915	Campbell, J. A., Lt. K.R.R.C., and Staff. France	C.M.W.
1882	Campbell, Hon. J. B., D.S.O., Capt. Coldstream Gds., m. France (k. 25.1.15)	F.W.
1909	Campbell, J. H. D. M., Capt. R.A.F., late R.N.A.S., and Staff. France	P.W.
1916	Campbell, J. L., Lt. Grenadier Gds., w. France	E.L.C.
1894	V.C. Campbell, J. V., C.M.G., D.S.O. (F) Brig.-Gen. (Coldstream Gds.), m. 4. France	R.C.R.
1910	Campbell, K. A., D.S.O., Lt. Grenadier Gds., late Lt. Scottish Horse, w. 3, m. France, Gallipoli	H.Br.
1895	Campbell, M. I. M., M.C., Maj. Connaught Rangers, att. Welch Regt., m. France (d.w. 4.9.16)	A.C.B
1895	Campbell, N. D. H., Maj. 7th Dragoon Gds., and Staff. France	S.R.J.
1897	Campbell, R., D.S.O. and Bar, Maj. (t. Lt.-Col.) Cameron Highlanders, m. 2. France	R.C.R.
1895	Campbell, Hon. R. A., C.B.E. (F) Bt. Lt.-Col. Lovat's Scouts	R.C.R.
1892	Campbell, R. C., Capt. R. Defence Corps	E.L.V.
1892	Campbell, V. L. A., D.S.O. and Bar, O.B.E., Cr. R.N., late Cr. Drake Bn., R.N.D., m. France, Gallipoli, Home Waters, N. Russia	S.R.J.
1893	Campbell, W. F., Capt. R. Sussex Regt. France	F.H.R.
1914	Campbell, W. H. E., A.F.C., Capt. R.A.F., late R.N.A.S., m. France	C.M.W.
1874	Campbell, Sir W. P., K.C.B., Lt.-Gen. (H.L.I.) G.O.C. Western, late Southern, Command	C.W.D.
1897	Campbell, W. R., D.S.O., Maj. 14th Hussars, att. 10th R. Hussars and N. Somerset Yeomanry. France (k. 13.5.15)	E.I.
1899	Campbell-Douglas, Rev. L. C. H. D., C.F. France, Egypt, Palestine	F.H.R.
1916	Campbell-Jones, H., 2nd Lt. R.F.A. France	K.S.
1882	Campbell-Orde, Sir A. J., Bart., Maj. Lovat's Scouts, att. Cameron Highlanders	A.C.J.

1884 Campbell-Preston, R. W. P. C., Bt. Lt.-Col. Black Watch, att. Labour Corps, m. France F.W.C.
1890 Campion, E., Maj. Seaforth Highlanders, m. France (d. of gas poisoning, 25.2.16) T.D.
1891 Campion, Rev. F. H., C.F. Gallipoli R.A.H.M.
1888 Campion, W. R., M.P., D.S.O., T.D., Lt.-Col. R. Sussex Regt., w., m. 3 France, Gallipoli. R.A.H.M.
1901 Cane, M., 2nd Lt. R.F.A., late Canadian N.R. France (k. 4.8.17) C.L., H.T.B.
1900 Cantrell-Hubbersty, G. A. J., D.S.O., Maj. S. Nottinghamshire Hussars, att. M.G.C., w., m. France, Balkans, Egypt, Palestine E.L.V.
1895 Cantrell-Hubbersty, W. P. C., O.B.E., Maj. 15th Hussars, att. Remount Service, m. 2. France R.A.H.M.
1900 Carill-Worsley, P. E. Tindal-, (Frank at Eton), Capt. Shropshire Yeomanry, att. R.E. A.C.J., A.C.G.H.
1908 Carlton, Visc., Capt. 2nd Life Gds., and Staff. France A.A.S.
1911 Carnegie, Lord, Capt. Scots Gds. H.T.B., S.G.L.
1886 Carnegie, Hon. R. F., Bt. Maj. Gordon Highlanders, att. E. African F.F. E. Africa A.C.A.
1916 Carr, A. M., M.C., Lt. Coldstream Gds., p. France J.H.M.H.
1908 Carr, E. G., t. Capt. Cheshire Regt., w. France J.H.M.H.
1895 Carr, R., Capt. (t. Maj.) King's African Rifles. E. Africa E.H.
1899 Carr, R. H., Maj. Staff K.S.
1896 Carr-Gomm, H. W. C., M.P., Capt. London Regt. France, Balkans F.T., H.B.
1900 Carr-Gomm, M. C., Lt. R.E., late Lt. Middlesex Hussars. France, W. Africa H.B.
1903 Carr-Saunders, A. M., Capt. R.A.S.C., late Pte. London Regt. France, Egypt C.H.A.
1883 Carre-Smith, M., Maj., att. E. Surrey Regt. and Rifle Bde. H.E.L.
1897 Carrington, C. R. B., D.S.O., Bt. Lt.-Col. R.F.A., and Staff, m. 7. France E.L.V.
1873 Carter, A. H., C.M.G., Bt. Col. R.F.A., m. 2. France W.B.M., A.C.J.

1899	Carter, G. V., O.B.E. (F) Maj. Dorset Yeomanry, and Staff, m. 2. Balkans, Gallipoli, Mesopotamia	H.D.
1899	Carter, J. S., 2nd Lt. Grenadier Gds. France (k. 27.9.18)	J.P.C
1912	Carter, R. T., M.C., Capt. R.G.A., and Staff, m. France (d.w. 18.8.18)	K.S.
1917	Carter-Campbell, G. L., 2nd Lt. Scots Gds.	A.E.C.
1913	Carton de Wiart, M. L., Lt. Welsh Gds., late 2nd Lt. Lancashire Fusiliers, w. 2. France, Egypt, Gallipoli, Palestine	H.B.
1904	Cartwright, A. R. A., Lt. Coldstream Gds., att. King's African Rifles, late Trooper E. African Mounted Rifles. E. Africa	F.H.R.
1908	Cartwright, G. H. G. M., Lt. Coldstream Gds., att. Gds. M.G. Regt., w., m. France	A.C.G.H.
1874	Cartwright, H. A., Lt.-Col. Staff. France	F.W.C.
1897	Cartwright, R. A. T., Capt. R.A.S.C.	S.A.D.
1911	Carver, R. B., Capt. E. Yorkshire Regt., att. Yorkshire Hussars and Camel Corps. France, Egypt	E.W.S.
1914	Cary, Hon. P. P., Lt. Grenadier Gds., w. 2. France	R.S.de H.
1915	Casey, D. A., M.C., Lt. R.F.A. France	V.Le N.F.
1900	Cassavetti, D. J. (F) Lt. Staff. France	K.S., L.F.
1890	Cassillis, Earl of, Maj. R. Scots Fusiliers, and Staff, m. France	H.D.
1917	Castéja, Comte C. de, Canonnier Artillerie, att. État Majeur, French Army. France	V.Le N.F., L.T.
1893	Cathcart, A. E., Capt. K.R.R.C. France (k. 14.9.14)	E.C.A.L.
1891	Cathcart, F. A., Maj. R. Scots Fusiliers	E.C.A.L.
1893	Cator, A. B. E., C.B., D.S.O. (F) Maj.-Gen. (Scots Gds.), m. 10. France	E.C.A.L.
1898	Cator, C. A. M., M.C., Capt. Scots Gds., w. 3. France	E.C.A.L.
1914	Cator, H. J., M.C., Lt. R. Scots Greys. France	R.P.L.B.
1906	Cattley, C. F., M.C., Maj. The Buffs, m. France (k. 30.11.17)	F.H.R.
1909	Cattley, H. P., Pte. Middlesex Regt., att. Manchester Regt. France (k. 14.3.17)	P.W.
1884	Cavan, Earl of, K.P., G.C.M.G., K.C.B., M.V.O. (F) (Mr. Lambart at Eton), Lieut.-Gen. (Grenadier Gds.), G.O.C. British Forces in Italy, m. 8. France, Italy	H.E.L.

1883	Cave, A. S., Maj. R. Berkshire Regt.	A.C.J.
1912	Cave, E. C., Lt. Somerset L.I., w. France	A.M.G.
1884	Cavendish, Lord J. S., D.S.O., Maj. 1st Life Gds. France (k. 9.10.14)	J.M.E.
1889	Cavendish, Lord R. F., P.C., C.M.G., C.B., Lt.-Col. The King's Own (R. Lancaster Regt.), w. France	J.M.E.
1905	Cavendish, R. H. V., M.V.O., Capt. Grenadier Gds., m. France	J.M.D.
1887	Cavendish-Bentinck, Lord C, D.S.O., Bt. Maj. (t. Lt.-Col.) 9th Lancers, and Staff, w., m. 3. France, Egypt, Gallipoli	E.C.A.L.
1904	Cavendish-Bentinck, F. W., Capt. K.R.R.C., w. France	S.A.D.
1881	Cavendish-Bentinck, Lord H., M.P., T.D., Lt.-Col. Derbyshire Yeomanry. Gallipoli	E.C.A.L.
1914	Cayley, D. C., Capt. K.O.S.B., att. M.G.C. France, Egypt, Gallipoli	A.G.G.H.
1879	Cayley, Sir G. E. A., Bart., Capt. R. Defence Corps (d. 15.11.17)	C.H.E.
1911	Cazalet, E., 2nd Lt. Welsh Gds. France (k. 10.9.16)	R.P.L.B.
1915	Cazalet, V. A., M.C., Capt. 1st Life Gds., late Lt. W. Kent Yeomanry, and Staff. France, Siberia	R.P.L.B.
1915	Cazenove, A. de L., Lt. Coldstream Gds., m. France	J.H.M.H.
1892	Cazenove, P., O.B.E., Maj. Herts Yeomanry, and Staff, m. 3. France	A.C.J.
1910	Cazenove, R. de L., Lt. Northamptonshire Yeomanry. France	J.M.D.
1884	Cecil, Lord Hugh, Lt. R.A.F. France	G.E.M.
1905	Cecil, Hon. T. J. A., Capt. K.R.R.C., w. France	R.A.H.M., T.C.P., E.L.C.
1901	Cecil, Hon. W. A., M.C., Capt. Grenadier Gds., m. France (k. 16.9.14)	R.A.H.M
1913	Chace, G. P., Lt. R. Berkshire Regt., late Cpl. London Regt., m. France	J.M.D., V.Le N.F.
1915	Chadwyck-Healey, E. R., M.C. (F) Lt. R.F.A., and Staff, m. France	R.S.de H.

1891	Chadwyck-Healey, G. E., C.B.E. (F) Lt. R.N.V.R. Home Waters	F.H.R.
1906	Chadwyck-Healey, H. P., Capt. E. Surrey Regt., att. Norfolk Regt. Mesopotamia	F.H.R.
1905	Chadwyck-Healey, O. N., Maj. R. Berkshire Regt., and Staff, m. France	F.H.R.
1901	Chalmer, F. G., D.S.O., M.C., Bt. Maj. Black Watch, empld. Lt.-Col. M.G.C., and Staff, w. 2, m. 4. France, Palestine	A.A.S.
1901	Chalmers, C. H. L., Lt., late Pte., Gordon Highlanders. France	H.B.
1906	Chalmers, I. P. H., Capt. Seaforth Highlanders, and Staff, w. 2. France, Balkans	H.B.
1898	Chalmers-Hunt, N. G., Capt. R.A.S.C., M.T. France	E.L.V.
1897	Chaloner, R. G. H., Capt. 16th Lancers, att. Wiltshire Regt., and Staff. France (k. accid. 3.4.17)	J.H.M H.
1903	Chaloner, Hon. T. W. P. L., Capt. Yorkshire Regt., att. R.A.F., p. France, Egypt	C.H.A.
1902	Chamberlain, N. G., Lt. Grenadier Gds., late Capt. R. Warwickshire Regt. France (k. 1.12.17)	F.I.
1900	Chamberlayne, E. T., D.S.O., T.D., Maj. Warwickshire Yeomanry, m. Egypt, Gallipoli	R.A.H.M.
1910	Chamberlayne, T., Lt. H.L.I., w. Egypt, Gallipoli	T.C.P., E.L.C.
1881	Chambers, C. E., V.D., Bt. Col. R.F.A. France	H.E.L.
1871	Chamier, A. C., Maj. Sp. List	J.W.H., E.H., C.C.J.
1917	Chance, E. G. St. C., 2nd Lt. Coldstream Gds. France (k. 27.9.17)	H.Br.
1912	Chance, G. H. B., Maj. M.G.C. Balkans, Egypt, Gallipoli, Palestine	L.S.R.B.
1910	Chance, G. O. de P., Lt. R. Welch Fusiliers. France (k. 19.10.14)	A.C.G.H
1899	Chance, N. R. L., M.C., Maj. R.F.A., and Staff, att. Sherwood Foresters, m. France	F.H.R.
1898	Chance, O. K., C.M.G., D.S.O., Brig.-Gen. (5th Lancers), m. 4. France	H.B.

1912	Chance, R. J. F., M.C., Capt. Rifle Bde., late Capt. 4th Dragoon Gds., w. 2, m. 2. France	H. Br.
1914	Chance, W. H. S., Lt. Worcestershire Regt., att. R.A.F., p. France	H. Br.
1915	Chancellor, G. E., 2nd Lt. The Queen's Own (R. W. Surrey Regt.), att. R.F.C. France (k. 9.7.16)	V Le N.F
1902	Chancellor, R. E., Lt. Australian Imp. Forces. France	P.W.
1913	Chandor, H. H., Capt. Lovat's Scouts, att. K.O.S.B., and Staff. France	A.B.R.
1891	Chandos-Pole-Gell, H. A., C.B.E., Brig.-Gen. (Coldstream Gds.), w. France	F.H.R.
1910	Chanler, L. S., Maj. F.A., American Army France	H.M.
1892	Chaplin, Rev. A., C.F. France, Gallipoli	S.R.J.
1878	Chaplin, C. S., Lt.-Col. K.R.R.C. France (k. 30.7.15)	H.E.L.
1874	Chapman, A. G., Lt. Middlesex Regt., late Lt. Sussex Regt. (d. 5.5.17)	C.C.J
1900	Chapman, A. H. D., Capt. 1st R. Dragoons, m. France (k. 27.9.15)	E.I.
1910	Chapman, D. A. J., 2nd Lt. Scots Gds., late 2nd Lt. 19th Hussars. France (k. 15.9.16)	E.L.C.
1893	Chapman, E. H., Capt. (t. Maj.) Yorkshire Regt., and Staff, m. France	E.H.
1894	Chapman, G. D. E., Capt. Intell. Corps, m. France	R.C.R.
1895	Chapman, H., Pte. Canadian Infantry, late Capt. (t. Maj.) Yorkshire Regt., w. France, Gallipoli (k. 15.8.17) E.H.	A.A.S
1896	Chapman, J., Lt. Grenadier Gds., att. Gds. T.M.B. France	A.C.J.
1914	Chapman, K. A. S., Lt. (t. Capt.) R.F.A. Balkans, Egypt, Gallipoli	K.S.
1896	Chapman, M., M.C., Lt. Grenadier Gds. France (k. 10.4.18)	W D
1894	Chapman, P., D.S.O., Capt. E. African Mounted Rifles, Nairobi F. F., and Staff, m. E. Africa	W.D.
1908	Chapman, T. M. G., Lt. R.A.S.C., M.T., late Tpr. R. 1st Devon Yeomanry. France	E.L.C.
1892	Chapman, W. C. 2nd Lt. Intell. Corps. France	R.C.R.

1898 Chapman, W. H., Capt. Yorkshire Regt. Gallipoli
(k. 6.8.15) E.H., A.A.S

1910 Charlesworth, A. K., M.C., Lt. 6th Dragoon Gds., w. France R.C.R., C.H.K.M.

1894 Charlesworth, C. B., Lt.-Col. K.O.Y.L.I., late 2nd Lt. R.A.S.C., w., m. France, Egypt H.W.M.

1912 Charlesworth, E. F., Lt. M.G.C., late The Queen's. Afghanistan P.W., F.E.R.

1910 Charlesworth, F. R., Capt. Montgomeryshire Yeomanry, att. R. Welch Fusiliers. France, Egypt, Palestine (d.w. 19.9.18) F.H.R., H. de H

1917 Charlesworth, J. B., P.O., Armoured Cars, att. R.N.A.S. Mesopotamia L.S.R.B.

1891 Charlesworth, J. S., the late, Maj. K.O.Y.L.I. France, Egypt (d. 10.11.18) A.C.J.

1895 Charlesworth, W. G., Capt. Yorkshire Hussars, att. K.O.Y.L.I. France H.W.M.

1889 Charlton, G. N., Capt. R. Defence Corps E.L.V.

1908 Charlton, St. J. A., Lt. Bedfordshire Regt. France (k. 26.10.14) H Br

1900 Charrington, A. C., Capt. 1st R. Dragoons. France (d.w. 20.10.14) A.C.A.

1904 Charrington, C. E. W., M.C., Capt. S. Staffordshire Regt., w. France C.L., R.S.K.

1877 Charrington, H. S., Maj., Sp. List E.H.

1903 Charrington, H. V. S., M.C. and Bar (F) Bt. Maj. 12th Lancers, m. 2. France C.H.A.

1907 Charrington, N. A., Lt. (t. Capt.) The Queen's Own (R. W. Kent Regt.). France K.S.

1915 Charrington, P. R. L., M.C., Lt. (t. Capt.) Rifle Bde., w. France R.P.L.B.

1897 Charrington, S. H., C.M.G., D.S.O. (F) Brig.-Gen. Tank Corps (15th Hussars), m. 3. France, E. Africa, Egypt, Gallipoli J.P.C.

1881 Charteris, Hon. E. E., Capt. R.A.F., and Staff. France E.W.

1903	Charteris, Hon. G. L., Lt. Scots Gds., att. Gds. M.G. Regt. France	E.I.
1915	Charteris, Hon. I. A., 2nd Lt. Grenadier Gds. France (k. 17.10.15)	K.S.
1911	Chattaway, P. S., 2nd Lt. Cheshire Regt. France (k. 14.10.16)	K.S.
1916	Cheney, J. N., Lt. K.R.R.C., w. France	H.M.
1915	Cherry, B. V., M.C., Lt. K.R.R.C., w. France	A.A.S.
1902	Cherry, L. A., Sub-Lt. R.N.V.R., att. R.N.D. Egypt, Gallipoli (k. 9.5.15)	S.R.J., H.F.W.T.
1911	Chesham, Lord, M.C., Lt. 10th R. Hussars, att. Cav. Corps Signals, w. France	C.M.W.
1913	Chester, H. K., Capt. Essex Regt. Egypt, Gallipoli, Palestine (d.w. 27.3.17)	K.S.
1914	Chester, R. C., 2nd Lt. Gds. M.G. Regt., late Pte. London Regt. France	A.B.R.
1887	Chetwode, Sir P. W., Bart., K.C.B., K.C.M.G., D.S.O. (F) Lt.-Gen. (19th Hussars), w., m. 9. France, Egypt, Palestine	G.E.M.
1905	Chetwynd-Stapylton, H. M., Capt. R.F.A. France (d.w. 14.11.15)	R.W.W.-T.
1866	Cheylesmore, Lord, K.C.M.G., K.C.V.O. (Eaton at Eton), Maj.-Gen. (Grenadier Gds.), Comdt. Musketry Camp, and Staff	E.B., E.W.
1889	Chichester, Earl of, O.B.E. (Pelham at Eton), Bt. Lt.-Col. R. Sussex Regt., and Staff	A.C.J.
1889	Chichester, C. H., Maj. Devonshire Regt., att. Labour Corps	J.C.
1894	Child, Sir S. H., Bart., C.B., C.M.G., D.S.O., M.V.O., Brig.-Gen. (R.A.), m. 4. France	R.A.H.M.
1869	Childers, E. S. E., the late, C.B., Col. R.E., and Staff. (d. 18.3.19)	W.E.
1905	Chinnery, E. F., Capt. Coldstream Gds., att. R.A.F., m. France (k. 18.1.15)	J.M.E.
1892	Chinnery, E. H., Lt. Oxfordshire Yeomanry, w. France	J.M.E.

1895	Chinnery, H. B., Lt. K.R.R.C. France (k. 28.5.16)	H B
1901	Chisenhale-Marsh, A. H., Capt. 9th Lancers, and Staff. France (k. 28.9.18)	F.C A L.
1884	Chisenhale-Marsh, T. E., Capt. Middlesex Regt., and Staff. France	C.L.L.-C., F.H.R.
1916	Chitty, F. J. P., Lt. Coldstream Gds. France	R.S. de H.
1915	Chitty, J. M., 2nd Lt. Grenadier Gds. France (k. 1.12.17)	R.S de H.
1913	Chitty, J. W., Capt. Essex Regt. Egypt, Gallipoli, Palestine	K.S.
1908	Cholmeley, G. H., Capt. London Rifle Bde., w. France	A.A.S.
1912	Cholmeley, H. L., Lt. Border Regt., w. France (k. 1.7.16)	A.A.S
1907	Cholmeley, H. V., 2nd Lt. Grenadier Gds., att. Gds. M.G. Regt. France (k. 7.4.16)	A.A.S.
1893	Cholmeley, Sir M. A. R., Bart., Capt. Grenadier Gds. France (k. 24.12.14)	F.C A L.
1904	Cholmondeley, Lord G. H., O.B.E., M.C., Capt. (t. Maj.) R.F.A., and Staff, m. 3. Egypt, Palestine	A.C.A., R.S. de H.
1917	Cholmondeley, H., M.C., 2nd Lt. Coldstream Gds., w. France	E.W.S.
1907	Cholmondeley, R., Capt. Rifle Bde., att. R.F.C., m. France (k. 12.3.15)	R.W.W.-T., C.M.W.
1906	Christian, J. O., Cpl. Southern Rifles, Cape Colony. S. Africa	P.W.
1900	Christie, J., M.C., Capt. K.R.R.C., w., m. France	R.W.W.-T.
1915	Christie, P. N. J., 2nd Lt. Bedfordshire Regt. France (k. 9.10.17)	H. de H.
1898	Christie-Miller, E. G., Maj. Coldstream Gds., w., p. France	J.P.C.
1900	Christie-Miller, G., D.S.O., M.C., Capt. Oxfordshire and Bucks L.I., att. Gloucestershire Regt., m. 2. France	J.P.C., F.H.R.
1915	Christy, B. R. F., 2nd Lt. Coldstream Gds. France (d.w. 3.10.16)	A C.G.H
1914	Christy, S. E. F., Lt. Irish Gds. France (k. 12.7.16)	A.C.G.H
1889	Church, J. F., Maj. 13th Hussars, att. Indian Cav. Corps. France	A.C.J.

1879	Churchill, Visc., G.C.V.O. (Spencer at Eton), Col. Oxfordshire Yeomanry. France, Italy	J.M.E.
1902	Churchill, A., 2nd Lt. W. Kent Yeomanry, Lt. att: Armoured Cars, R.N.V.R. S. Russia	R.W.W.-T.
1878	Churchill, A. G., C.B., C.B.E., Col. Imp. Gen. Staff	E.C.A.L.
1881	Churchill, H. F., O.B.E., Maj. (t. Lt.-Col.) Cameronians (Scottish Rifles)	E.C.A.L.
1904	Churchill, H. P., 2nd Lt. R.E., att. N. Z. Engineers. Gallipoli (d. 20.10.15)	R.P.L.B.
1916	Churchill, Lord I. S., 2nd Lt. R.A.S.C.	E.I., T.F.C.
1904	Churchill, J. A., M.C., Bt. Maj. Durham L.I., and Staff, m. 3. France	R.P.L.B.
1901	Churchill, W. M. (F) Maj. Cav. I.E.F., att. Middlesex Hussars, w., m. Egypt, Gallipoli (d. 4.11.18)	S.R.J., R.W.W.-T.
1898	Chute, C. L., M.C., Maj. Middlesex Regt., and Staff. France	K.S.
1897	Clanmorris, Lord (Mr. Bingham at Eton), Capt. (t. Maj.) Sp. List. France	P.W.
1889	Clanwilliam, Earl of, M.C. (F) (Mr. Meade at Eton), Capt. R.H.G., and Staff, m. France, Italy	R.C.R.
1916	Clapham, G., Lt. Shropshire L.I., att. Cheshire Regt., w. France	M.D.H.
1915	Clark, A. E. J., M.C., Lt. R.F.A. France	H.Br.
1898	Clark-Kennedy, A. R. W. S., Lt. R.A.F., late Lt. R.N.V.R. Gallipoli, Mediterranean	T.C.P.
1903	Clarke, A. C., Capt. Duke of Cornwall's L.I., att. R.A.F., w. France	J.M.E.
1895	Clarke, A. E. S., D.S.O., M.V.O. (F) Bt. Lt.-Col. Scots Gds., and Staff, m. 4. France	S.R.J.
1905	Clarke, C. F. (F) Capt. 3rd Hussars, w., m. France	R.C.R.
1890	Clarke, C. H. G. Mansfield, the late, M.V.O., Maj. Rifle Bde. France (d. 27.7.19)	A.C.J.
1910	Clarke, C. L. C., Capt. (t. Maj.), late Pte., Buckinghamshire Yeomanry, and Staff, w., m. Egypt, Gallipoli, N. Russia	H.Br.
1916	Clarke, E. D., M.C., Capt. R.A.F., w. France	H.Br.

1884	Clarke, E. J. A., Maj. R. N. Devon Yeomanry, and Staff	J.M.E.
1890	Clarke, E. P., Lt. R.N.V.R.	P.H.C.
1912	Clarke, E. S., Lt. Scots Gds., late R. Sussex Regt., w., m. France	R.S.K.
1892	Clarke, J. A. T. (F) Capt. The King's Own (R. Lancaster Regt.), w. France	J.M.E.
1913	Clarke, J. P. S., Lt., late Pte., R. Sussex Regt.	R.S.K.
1895	Clarke, M. F., D.S.O., Maj. Cheshire Regt., w. 3., m. France, Italy	K.S.
1899	Clarke, O. B., Capt. R.F.A., and Staff, E.E.F., m. 2. France, Egypt, Palestine	K.S.
1910	Clarke, R. S., Capt. Sussex Yeomanry, att. R. Sussex Regt., w. Egypt, Gallipoli, Palestine	R.S.K.
1898	Clarke-Jervoise, A. F., Maj. Scots Gds., att. Gds. M.G. Regt. France	E.L.V.
1910	Clauson, G. L. M., O.B.E. (F) Capt. Somerset L.I., and Staff, m. 2. Egypt, Gallipoli, Mesopotamia, Palestine	K.S.
1912	Clay, H. C. H., Lt. R.E., late 2nd Lt. N. Staffordshire Regt., w. France	J.H.M.H.
1895	Clayton, E. R., C.M.G., D.S.O., Bt. Lt.-Col. Oxfordshire and Bucks L.I., and Staff, m. 6. France	S.A.D.
1892	Clayton, H. D., Lieut. R.N.V.R. Home Waters	W.D.
1894	Clayton, R. S., Lt. H.L.I. France (d. 26.1.16)	F.T.
1887	Clayton-East, G. F. L., O.B.E., Maj. R.G.A., m. France	H.B.
1905	Clegg, J. A., Capt. Shropshire L.I., late Pte. London Regt., att. Suffolk Regt, and Staff	J.M.E.
1887	Clement, S. R., Capt. Australian Imp. Forces. Gallipoli (k. 26.4.15)	J.P.C.
1915	Clements, H. T. W., 2nd Lt. R.F.A., w. France	E.I., T.F.C.
1915	Clerke, D. H. H., Lt. 15th Hussars. France	R.S.K.
1905	Clerke, F. W. T., Lt. Coldstream Gds. France (k. 26.9.16)	R.C.R.
1905	Clifton, Lord, Maj. R.A.F., late Lt. R.N.V.R, att. R.N.A.S.	H.T.B.
1891	Clifton, P. R., C.M.G., D.S.O. (Bruce at Eton), Maj. (t. Lt.-Col.) S. Nottinghamshire Hussars, and Staff, m. 3. Egypt, Gallipoli, Palestine	H.G.W., S.R.J.

1906 Clifton Brown, C., Lt. Grenadier Gds., late Lt. Sussex and Worcestershire Yeomanry. France, Egypt, Gallipoli, Palestine   J.M.E., M.D.H.
1897 Clifton Brown, D., Capt. 1st (King's) Dragoon Gds., att. Worcestershire Regt. and Cheshire Regt., and Staff. France   J.M.E.
1886 Clifton Brown, H., Brig.-Gen. (12th Lancers), m. Egypt, Gallipoli   J.M.E.
1881 Clinton, Lord (Mr. Trefusis at Eton), Lt.-Col. R. N. Devon Yeomanry   W.E., J.M.E.
1901 Clinton, W. L., Capt. K.R.R.C. p., m. 2. France, Egypt (d. 22.11.18)   C.H.A.
1911 Clive, Visc., Capt. Welsh Gds., late Lt. Scots Gds. France (d.w. 13.10.16)   A.M G.
1890 Clive, P. A., M.P. (F) Capt. Grenadier Gds., empld. Lt.-Col. E. Yorkshire Regt., and Staff, w. 2, m. France (k. 5.4.18)   F.T
1895 Clonmell, Earl of (Scott at Eton), Capt. R.F.A. France   C.H.A., T.D., E.C.A.L.
1916 Close, B. S., Lt. Irish Gds., w. France (k. 27.9.18)   L.S.R B.
1900 Close, P. J. H., Lt. Irish Gds. France   C.H.A.
1902 Close, R. C. A., Lt. Irish Gds. France   C.H.A.
1892 Close, T., Capt. R. Berkshire Regt., att. Duke of Cornwall's L.I., and Staff. France, Balkans   A.C.A.
1873 Clowes, C. E., Maj. Staff, late Maj. K.R.R.C.   J.M.E.
1909 Clowes, C. G. E., Lt. K.R.R.C., w. France (k. 5.2.15)   J.M.E., M.D.H
1886 Clowes, E. W., D.S.O., Maj. 1st Life Gds.   E.W., S.A.D.
1886 Clowes, H. A., Lt.-Col. Staffordshire Yeomanry. Egypt (d. 8.3.16)   E.W., S A.D
1903 Clowes, H. M., D.S.O., Capt. (t. Maj.), late Pte., London Regt., and Staff, m. 3. France   S.A.D.
1907 Clowes, J. L. (F) Capt. K.R.R.C., empld. Maj. M.G.C., m. France, Balkans   J.M.E., M.D.H.
1902 Clowes, M., M.C. (F) Lt.-Col. R.F.A., m. France, Palestine   F.H.R.
1869 Clowes, P. L., C.B., Lt.-Col. Sp. List   W.E.

1894 Clowes, W. St. G., Capt. 19th Hussars, att. 1st Life Gds., and Staff, m. France   H.W.M.

1904 Clutterbuck, E. L., Lt. Somerset L.I., w. Egypt, Mesopotamia, Palestine   H.Br.

1874 Clutterbuck, H. F., V.D., Lt.-Col. Somerset L.I. Palestine   A.C.J.

1910 Coats, J. A., A.F.C., Capt. R.A.F., w. France   J.M.D., V.Le N.F.

1907 Coats, T. H., Lt. Ayrshire Yeomanry, att. 2nd Life Gds., France   R.S.de H.

1900 Cobbold, C. J. F., Maj. (t. Lt.-Col.) Suffolk Regt., w., m. France   R.W.T.-T., C.L.

1903 Cobbold, G. F., M.C., Maj. York and Lancaster Regt., w., m. France, Italy   A.C.B.

1915 Cobbold, J. M., Lt. Scots Gds., and Staff, w. France   P.V.B.

1893 Cobbold, P. W., Capt. (t. Maj.) Suffolk Regt. France   H.E.L.

1885 Cobbold, R. P., D.S.O. (F)Brig.-Gen. (K.R.R.C.), m.3. France   J.C.

1905 Cochrane, Lord, Capt. Scots Gds., and Staff. France, Egypt   A.C.B., A.M.G.

1871 Cochrane of Cults, Lord (Mr. Cochrane at Eton), Lt.-Col. Black Watch   F.Sr.J.T.

1904 Cochrane, A. K. O., 2nd Lt. R.A.F., late Capt. Yorkshire Regt. Gallipoli   T.C.P.

1904 Cochrane, G. D., Lt. Yorkshire Regt., att. Nigeria Regt. W. Africa   T.C.P.

1902 Cochrane, T. G. F., D.S.O., Maj. Black Watch, w. 3, m. 3. France, Mesopotamia, Palestine   H.E.L.

1914 Cochrane-Baillie, Hon. V. A. W. B., M.C., Capt. Scots Gds., late Lanarkshire Yeomanry, w. 2. France   M.D.H.

1912 Cockayne, M. H. D., Lt. 1st Brahmans, I.A., Aden F.F., late Lt. E. Surrey Regt. Balkans, Gallipoli   E.W.S.

1906 Cockburn, A. W., 2nd Lt. R.G.A. France   H.Br.

1906 Cockburn, E. H., Maj. R.A.F., and Staff, late Capt. R. Fusiliers. France   H.Br.

1874 Cockburn, G., C.B.E., D.S.O., Brig.-Gen. (Rifle Bde.). France   F.W.C.

1885	Cockburn, N. C., Maj. Lincolnshire Yeomanry, w. m. Egypt, Palestine	A.C.A.
1907	Cockburn, R. S., M.C., Maj. K.R.R.C., att. R.N.D., and Staff. France	H.Br.
1915	Cockerell, A. P., 2nd Lt. K.R.R.C. France (k. 14.8.16)	F.W.S.
1895	Cockerell, S. P., 2nd Lt. R.F.C. Egypt (d. 20.3.15)	C L.
1899	Cockshott, A. M., Maj. R.A.S.C., M.T., m. 2. France	R.C.R.
1906	Cohen, L. L., Capt. London Regt., and Staff, w. France	J.M.D.
1896	Coke, Visc., Maj. Scots Gds., and Staff. France, Italy	S.R.J.
1895	Coke, Hon. E., D.S.O., M.C., Capt. (t. Lt.-Col.) Rifle Bde., w. 2, m. 2. France	A.C.J.
1897	Coke, Hon. J. S., Capt. Scots Gds., p. France	A.C.J.
1899	Coke, Hon. Reginald, D.S.O., Capt. Scots Gds., att. Canadian E.F., m. 2. France	A.C.J.
1894	Coke, Hon. Richard, Capt. Scots Gds., att. R.A.F., w. 2, m. France	A.C.J.
1897	Colby, L., R. V., Maj. Grenadier Gds., m. France (k. 24.10.14)	P.W.
1893	Cole, Visc., C.M.G., (F) Maj. (t. Lt.-Col.) N. Irish Horse, m. France	E.C.A.L.
1894	Cole, Rev. H. B., M.C., C.F. France	P.W.
1901	Cole, J. J. B., M.C., Capt. Rifle Bde., w. 3, m. France	A.C.A.
1895	Cole, L. A. C., M.B.E., Lt. R.A.S.C., M.T., and Staff. France	E.C.A.L.
1899	Cole, Hon. R. B., Capt. E. African Mounted Rifles, Nairobi F.F. E. Africa	E.C.A.L.
1896	Coleridge, Hon. G. D., Capt. Devonshire Regt.	S.A.D.
1911	Coleridge, L. F. R., 2nd Lt. Coldstream Gds. France (k. 22.12.14)	A.A S.
1908	Coleridge, W. D., Capt. London Regt. France	L.S.R.B.
1910	Coles, A. N., Lt. Rifle Bde. France (k. 24.8.16)	P.W.
1900	Coles, E. L., M.C., Lt. The Queen's, late Pte. London Regt., w. France	H.B.
1915	Coles, J. D., 2nd Lt. R.F.A., att. R.H.G., w. France	R.S.K.

1902	Coles, J. H., D.S.O., Capt. E. Yorkshire Regt., w., m. 2. France, Balkans (k. 25.4.18)	C.L., R S K
1916	Colfox, T. D., 2nd Lt. R.F.A., w. France (k. 14.6.18)	E.I C.
1906	Colfox, W. P., M.P., M.C., Maj. R.F.A., w. 2. France	T.C.P., E.L.C.
1910	Collett-Mason, W. W., Lt. 8th Hussars. France	J.M.D., V.Le N.F.
1900	Collier, Hon. E. C. F., Lt. London Regt.	R.W.W.-T.
1891	Collier, M.C., O.B.E., T.D., Maj. R.A.S.C. Gallipoli	F.T.
1897	Collins, E. A. D., T. D. (F) Maj. Yorkshire Hussars, w. France	S.R.J.
1908	Collins, R. L. H., Capt. Rifle Bde., and Staff, m. 3. France, Italy	J.M.E., M.D.H.
1897	Collyer-Bristow, J., Lt. Northamptonshire Yeomanry, att. Remount Service. France	S.R.J.
1911	Colman, G. R. R., Capt. M.G.C., late Lt. Rifle Bde., w., m. France	R.C.R., C.H.K.M.
1917	Colquhoun, W. R., 2nd Lt. Scots Gds., w. France	K.S.
1898	Colston, Hon. E. M., C.M.G., M.V.O. D.S.O. (F) Brig.-Gen. (Grenadier Gds.), m. 6. France, Egypt, Palestine	S.A.D.
1882	Coltman, W. H., Maj. Gordon Highlanders, and Staff, w. France	R.A.H.M.
1913	Colvin, J. F., M.C., Lt. 9th Lancers, w. France	C.M.W.
1874	Colvin, R. B., C.B., T.D., Brig.-Gen. (Essex Yeomanry). France	R.D., R.A.H.M.
1878	Combe, B., Maj. Remount Service	C.L.L.-C.
1906	Combe, G. H. R., Lt. Rifle Bde., late Fife and Forfar Yeomanry. France (k. 16.9.16)	J.M.E., M.D H.
1908	Combe, H. C. S., D.S.O., Capt. R.H.G., empld. Maj. Tank Corps, w., m. France	A.C.G.H.
1913	Combe, J. F. B., Lt. 11th Hussars, att. M.G. Cav., w. 2. France	A.C.G.H.
1915	Combe, R. H., Sub-Lt. R.N. Home Waters, Baltic	A.A.S.
1882	Compton, Lord D. J. C., C.B.E., Col. Staff, m. France	E.C.A.L.
1906	Compton, E. R. F. (F) Lt. (t. Capt.) R. Scots Greys, att. M.G. Cav., w., m. France	R.P.L.B.

1917	Compton, H. R., 2nd Lt. Coldstream Gds.	J.H.M.H.
1916	Compton, Lord S. D., Lt. R.H.G. France (k. 13.5.15)	R.P.L.B
1902	Compton-Bracebridge, C., Lt. R.A.F., late Pte. R.A.S.C., M.T. France	H.W.M., S.A.D.
1877	Compton-Bracebridge, J. E. (Compton at Eton), Capt. R. Defence Corps	A.C.J.
1884	Compton-Thornhill, Sir A. J., Bart., Maj. R.G.A.	J.C.
1910	Compton-Thornhill, R. A., Lt. Scots Gds. France (k. 14.9.14)	F.H.R., H.de H.
1916	Conant, R. J. E., Lt. Grenadier Gds., w. France	R.P.L.B.
1909	Congleton, Lord, Lt. Grenadier Gds., m. France (k. 10.11.14)	A.A.S.
1889	Congreve, J., Maj. Westmorland and Cumberland Yeomanry	A.C.J.
1907	V.C. Congreve, W. La T., D.S.O., M.C. (F) Bt. Maj. Rifle Bde., and Staff, m. 4. France (k. 20.7.16)	H.M.
1904	Connal-Rowan, G. F., Capt. A. and S. Highlanders, p. France	A.A.S.
1900	Connaught, H.R.H. Prince Arthur of, K.G., K.T., G.C.V.O., C.B. (F) Bt. Lt.-Col. R. Scots Greys, and Staff, att. Canadian E.F. Staff, m. 2. France	E.C.A.L.
1901	Constant, N., Lt. E. Yorkshire Regt. France, Egypt	H.M.
1889	Conybeare, C. B., Lt., late Trooper, E. African Mounted Rifles, Nairobi F.F. E. Africa	H.W.M.
1899	Conyngham, Marquess, Lt. S. Irish Horse, and Staff. (d. 9.11.18)	J.P.C.
1888	Conyngham, Lord C. A., Capt. R. Defence Corps	S.A.D.
1903	Coode, D. R., Capt. (t. Maj.) R.F.A.	K.S.
1900	Cook, A. L. F., Capt. R.F.A., m. France	A.C.
1916	Cook, A. R., Lt. 1st R. Dragoons. France	C.H.K.M.
1884	Cook, C. C., D.S.O. (F) Col. Harlana Lancers, I.A., and Staff, m. 3. Mesopotamia	K.S.
1885	Cook, E. B., M.V.O. (F) Lt.-Col. 1st Life Gds. France (d.w. 4.11.14)	T.D.
1892	Cooke, B. H. H., C.M.G., D.S.O. (F) Brig.-Gen. (Rifle Bde.), w., m. 5. France	E.I.

1893 Cooke, E. D. M. H., D.S.O., Maj. R.F.A., m. 2. France, Palestine — S.R.J.

1897 Cookson, C. E., Capt. (t. Maj.) Bedfordshire Regt., att. Gold Coast Regt. W. Africa — K.S.

1883 Cookson, F., Capt. R.A.F., Staff, late Capt. R.E., and Interpreter att. 8th Hussars, m. France — H.W.M.

1889 Cookson, P. B., C.M.G., O.B.E., Lt.-Col. Northumberland Hussars, m. 2. France — F.H.R.

1912 Cookson, R. R. F., Capt. R.A.F., late Lt. R.M.L.I. — A.C.G.H.

1907 Cooper, A. D., D.S.O., 2nd Lt. Grenadier Gds. France — E.L.C.

1895 Cooper, A. H., Capt. Essex Regt., w. France, Gallipoli — A.C.B.

1914 Cooper, A. R., Lt. R. Scots Greys, att. M.G. Cav., w. 2. France — J.H.M.H.

1901 Cooper, B. R., M.B.E., Maj. Connaught Rangers, and Staff, m. Balkans, Gallipoli — H.M.

1908 Cooper, G. J. R. (F) Lt. R. Scots Greys, w., m. France — J.H.M.H.

1890 Cooper, H. A., Sergt. Canadian Infantry. France (k. 19.8.16) — T.D.

1877 Cooper, R. J., C.B., C.V.O., Brig.-Gen. (Irish Gds.), w., m. Gallipoli — J.P.C.

1902 Cooper, S. C. P., Lt. London Regt., empld. R.E. France — R.C.R.

1904 Cooper, S. L. (Hervey-Bathurst at Eton), Capt. Bedfordshire Regt., late Sergt. Scots Gds. France, India — R.A.H.M., R.S. de H.

1898 Cooper, W. C., Maj. R.E. France — E.H., F.J.T., R.W.W.-T.

1894 Cooper, W. G. D., Capt. R.A.S.C. France, Palestine — C.H.A., A.C.B.

1897 Cooper, W. R. F., D.S.O., M.C., Capt. (t. Maj.) 1st (King's) Dragoon Gds., w. 2, m. France, Afghanistan — E.I.

1914 Coote, C. G. E., Lt. 11th Hussars, late Northamptonshire Yeomanry. France (k. 22.3.18) — E.I., T.F.C.

1869 Coote, C. H. Eyre, Lt.-Col. Northamptonshire Yeomanry — J.W.H.

1909 Coote, C. M. J., Lt. Gloucestershire Regt., late Huntingdonshire Cyclist Bn., p. France — C.H.A., A.B.R.

1913 Coote, M. H., Lt. R.F.A., att. Lt. R.A.F., w. France,
Egypt, Gallipoli   E.L.V., A.C.R.-W.

1901 Cope, T. G., D.S.O. and Bar (F) Brig.-Gen. (R. Fusiliers),
w. 2, m. 6. France   R.A.H.M.

1892 Corbet, H. D., Lt. Shropshire L.I. France   J.P.C.

1896 Corbet, Sir R. J., Bart., Lt. Coldstream Gds., m.
France (k. 15.4.15)   A.B.R.

Corbett, Hon. A. C., Flight Sub-Lt. R.N.A.S. France
(k. 4.12.16)   A.B.R.

1887 Corbett, E. F. (F) Lt.-Col. R.G.A., w., m. France   E.L.V.

1891 Corbett, E. R. T., M.B.E., Maj. Shropshire L.I., and
Staff   H.W.M.

1914 Corbett, Hon. T. G. P., M.C., Lt. Grenadier Gds., late
2nd Lt. Ayrshire Yeomanry, w. France, Egypt,
Gallipoli, Palestine   A.B.R.

1894 Corbett-Winder, W. J., Maj. R. Welch Fusiliers.
Egypt   C.H.E., C.L.

1891 Corkran, C. E., C.M.G., Brig.-Gen. (Grenadier Gds.),
w., m. 6. France, Balkans   E.C.A.L.

1908 Corkran, R. S., 2nd Lt. Grenadier Gds., late Sergt.
H.A.C. France (d.w. 11.6.15)   H.B.

1882 Cornwallis, F. S. W., T.D., Maj. W. Kent Yeomanry   H.E.L.

1909 Cornwallis, F. W. M., M.C. (F) Lt. 17th Lancers, empld.
Capt. M.G. Cav. France   A.C.B., A.M.G.

1910 Cornwallis, W. S., M.C., Capt. R. Scots Greys, and
Staff, w. France   A.M.G.

1891 Cornwallis-West, G. F. M., Capt. (t. Maj.) Scots Gds.
Comm. Anson Bn. R.N.D., and Staff. France   W.D.

1893 Corrie, L., Paymaster Sub-Lt R.N.R. Home Waters
(d. 23.10.18)   J.P.C.

1911 Corry, J. P. I. M., Sub-Lt. R.N.V.R., late A.B., R.N.R.
Home Waters, Murman Coast   P.W.

1912 Corry, W. M. F., M.C., Lt. R.F.A. France   P.W., F.E.R.

1895 Corsellis, A. H. N., Lt.-Col. Sp. List, late Maj. Res.
Regt. of Cav.   E.H., A.A.S.

1910	Cory-Wright, R., M.C., Lt. R. Warwickshire Regt., w., m. France	J.M.D., V.Le N.F.
1907	Coryton, J. T., Capt. Rifle Bde., w. France	R.C.R.
1913	Coryton, W. A., M.V.O., Lt. Rifle Bde., att. R.A.F., w. France	C.H.K.M.
1918	Cosby, E. A. S., 2nd Lt. Rifle Bde. France	V.Le N.F., L.T.
1903	Cosens, G. P. L., D.S.O., Bt. Maj. (t. Lt.-Col.) 1st R. Dragoons, and Staff, m. 2. France, Egypt, Gallipoli, Italy	E.C.A.L.
1895	Cosens, F. U. W., Capt. R. Fusiliers. France	H.D.
1915	Coster Edwards, J. F., Lt. R. Welch Fusiliers, att. Derbyshire Yeomanry, and Staff, w. France, Palestine (d. 10.11.18)	R.S.K
1908	Cotes, J. C. C., Lt. R.A.F. Home Waters	C.H.A., A.B.R.
1897	Cotesworth, C. H., Capt. 21st Lancers, att. The Queen's Own (R. W. Kent Regt.). France	F.H.R.
1885	Cotterill, H. E., Maj. att. The Queen's	K.S.
1887	Cotterill, L., Maj. R.A.M.C. India	K.S.
1880	Cottesloe, Lord, V.D. (Fremantle at Eton), Col. Oxfordshire and Bucks L.I., and Staff	W.E., J.M.E.
1916	Cotton, A. F. R., Sub-Lt. R.N.V.R. Home Waters	P.V.B.
1909	Cotton Minchin, J. H., Capt. (t. Maj.) Cameronians (Scottish Rifles), att. R.A.F., w. France	F.H.R., H.de H.
1909	Cottrell-Dormer, C., Lt. Scots Gds. France (k. 26.10.14)	J.H.M.H.
1910	Cottrell-Dormer, C. M., D.S.O., Lt. Coldstream Gds. m. France (d.w. 8.2.15)	J.H.M.H.
1899	Couper, J. R., Maj. A and S. Highlanders, and Staff, w. France	J.P.C.
1890	Courage, M. R. F., D.S.O., Lt.-Col. R.F.A., w., m. 3. France	C.H.E.
1913	Courage, R. E. F., Lt. Northamptonshire Yeomanry, att. N. Somerset Yeomanry. France	K.S.
1903	Court, W. H. R., Capt. 9th Lancers. France (k. 24.5.15)	H.F.W.T.
1896	Courthope, G. L., M.P., M.C., T.D., Maj. R. Sussex Regt., and Staff, w., m. France	R.A.H.M.

1888	Courthope, W. G., Capt. Bedfordshire Regt., att. R.A.F., and Staff. France (d. 21.10.18)	K.S.
1883	Coventry, Hon. C. J., Lt.-Col. Worcestershire Yeomanry, w., p., m. Egypt, Gallipoli	E.W.
1884	Coventry, St. J. H., the late, Capt. Grenadier Gds. (d. 9.6.20)	W.D.
1908	Cowper, G. T., M.C., Maj. Westmorland and Cumberland Yeomanry, att. Border Regt. and R.G.A. France	L.S.R.B.
1917	Cox, H. K., 2nd Lt. R.G.A., w. France	V.Le N.F., L.T.
1915	Cox-Cox, G. G. (F) Lt. 16th Lancers, w. France	E.L.V., A.C.R.-W.
1875	Crabbe, A. B., Maj. N. Irish Horse	E.P.R.
1910	Crabbe, J. G., M.C. (F) Capt. R. Scots Greys, att. Bedfordshire Yeomanry, and Staff, m. 3. France	E.L.C.
1892	Crackanthorpe, O. M., Capt. R. Scots, att. Border Regt., w., m. France	P.W.
1906	Cracroft-Amcotts, W., M.C., Capt. R.E., m. 2. Gallipoli, Mesopotamia	K.S.
1896	Cradock, H. F. C. A., Capt. 2nd Life Gds., empld. Maj. R. Fusiliers, and Lt.-Col. Training Res. France	H.D.
1914	Craig, C. R., Lt. Northamptonshire Yeomanry. France, Italy	L.S.R.B.
1909	Craigie, J. C., M.C. (F) Capt. Grenadier Gds., w. 4, m. France	A.C.B., A.M.G.
1893	Craik, G. L., M.C., Capt. Lovat's Scouts, att. Cameron Highlanders, w., m. France, Balkans, Egypt, Gallipoli	K.S.
1911	Cranborne, Visc. (F) Lt. Grenadier Gds., and Staff. France	H.T.B., S.G.L.
1903	Crankshaw, E. N. S., M.B.E., Capt. (t. Maj.) R. Fusiliers, and Staff, w., m. 2. France	R.A.H.M., L.S.R.B.
1896	Cranworth, Lord, M.C. (F) (Mr. Gurdon at Eton), Capt. Staff, late Lt. R.F.A., m. 2. France, E. Africa	E.C.A.L.
1890	Crawford and Balcarres, Rt. Hon. Earl of (F) (Lord Balniel and then Lord Balcarres at Eton), Cpl. R.A.M.C. France	J.M.E.
1898	Crawfurd, R. B. J., D.S.O. (Jervis Smith at Eton), Lt-Col. Coldstream Gds., w. 2, m. 4. France	H.B.

1872	Crawley, A. P., Col. Staff, m. France	F.E.D.
1899	Crawley, W. H. T. E., Capt. R. Warwickshire Regt., m. France	A.A.S.
1912	Crawshay, J. W. L., M.C., Lt. Welsh Gds., late Sergt. and 2nd Lt. Scottish Horse. France	A.B.R.
1894	Crawshay, O. T. R., Capt. W. Riding Regt., att. Labour Corps. France	H.D.
1912	Crawshay, W. S. C., Capt. 5th Lancers, w. France	H.B.
1898	Crawshay-Williams, E., Capt. (t. Lt.-Col.) R.F.A. France, Egypt	C.H.E., C.L.
1899	Crealock, M. E. F., Paymaster Lt. R.N.R.	H.D.
1911	Creasy, R. L., M.C., Lt. R.F.A., w., m. France (d.w. 22.10.18)	K.S.
1892	Cresswell, A. F. Baker, Maj. K.R.R.C., and Staff. France	E.C.A.L.
1894	Cresswell, H. Baker, Capt. Res. Regt. of Cav., empld. Cheshire Yeomanry	E.C.A.L.
1900	Creyke, R., Maj. Scots Gds.	H.M.
1898	Creyke, W. L., Lt., late Gunner, R.G.A.	A.A.S.
1891	Crichton, Visc., M.V.O., D.S.O. (F) Lt.-Col. R.H.G., m. 2. France (k. 1.11.14)	E.C.A.L.
1894	Crichton, Hon. A. O., Capt. R.A.F., and Staff, m. 2. France, Egypt	E.C.A.L.
1891	Crichton, C. H., Maj. Scottish Horse	A.C.J.
1892	Crichton, Hon. G. A. C., M.V.O., Col. Coldstream Gds.	E.C.A.L.
1892	Crichton, H. F., Maj. Irish Gds., m. France (k. 1.9.14)	E.C.A.L.
1894	Crichton, Hon. J. A., D.S.O. (F) Capt. Rifle Bde., att. Nigerian Regt., W. African F.F. and Staff, w., m. France, E. Africa	E.C.A.L.
1914	Crichton-Browne, C. H. V., M.C., Capt. K.O.S.B., w. 2. France (d. 13.12.18)	A.C.G.H.
1874	Critchley, E. A., Maj. Staff. France	F.E.D.
1904	Critchley-Salmonson, R. E., M.C., Bt. Maj. (t. Lt.-Col.) R. Fusiliers, att. King's African Rifles, and Staff, m. 3. E. Africa	A.C.G.H.
1894	Crocker, F., Lt. Devonshire Regt., w. France	F.W.C., J.H.M.H.

1891	Crocker, J. A., Capt. Roughriders, att. Tank Corps. France, Egypt, Gallipoli	F.W.C.
1899	Croft, B. T. H., Capt. Grenadier Gds.	A.C.B.
1896	Croft, H. P., M.P., C.M.G., Brig.-Gen. (Hertfordshire Regt.), m. 2. France	E.H., T.C.P.
1889	Croft, R. P., Lt.-Col. Bedfordshire Regt. France	F.W.C.
1892	Croft, T. R., O.B.E., Capt. Sp. List.	J.M.E.
1903	Crofton, C. S. (Schneider at Eton) Capt. Sherwood Foresters, p. France	J.M.D.
1874	Crole-Wyndham, W. G., C.B., Col. Sp. List	O.B.
1895	Cromer, Earl of, C.V.O. (F) (Mr. Baring at Eton), Lt. Grenadier Gds.	W.D.
1882	Crompton-Roberts, C. M., Maj. R.E.	H.E.L.
1881	Crompton-Roberts, H. R., D.S.O., Lt.-Col. Grenadier Gds.	H.E.L.
1910	Cronk, W. G., 2nd Lt. The Buffs, att. K.R.R.C. France (k. 26.10.14)	E.L.C.
1908	Crookshank, A. C., Capt. R.F.A., w., m. France	H.B.
1912	Crookshank, H. F. C. (F) Lt. (t. Capt.) Grenadier Gds., late Hampshire Regt., and Staff, w. 2. France, Balkans	K.S.
1898	Cropper, J. W., Maj. Westmorland and Cumberland Yeomanry. France	C.H.E., S.A.D.
1906	Cross, J. K. C., Capt. Lancashire Fusiliers, w., m. France, Gallipoli	H.Br.
1892	Cross, J. L., Capt. (t. Maj.) R.G.A. France	H.W.M.
1906	Cross, R. C., Lt. Dorset Yeomanry, att. S. Lancashire Regt., late Pte. Strathcona's Horse, m. France (k. 7.6.18)	H.Br.
1913	Cross, R. H., Lt. Duke of Lancaster's Own Yeomanry, att. R.A.F., and Staff. France	R.P.L.B.
1916	Crosse, E. A. W., 2nd Lt. Coldstream Gds. France (k. 27.9.18)	R.S de H
1897	Crossley, A. A., Capt. 1st (King's) Dragoon Gds., empld. Maj. Essex Regt., and Staff. France, Palestine	C.L.
1904	Crossley, B., Lt. H.L.I., m. France (k. 18.5.15)	H.E.L., L S.R B.

1897	Crossley, E., O.B.E., Lt. 11th Hussars, empld. Maj. 3rd Hussars. France	H.F.L.
1907	Crossley, Hon. F. S., M.C., Capt. 9th Lancers, w., p., m. France	R.C.R., C.H.K.M.
1908	Crossley, Hon. J. de B., Capt. Suffolk Yeomanry, att: R.A.F., and Staff. France, Balkans, Egypt, Gallipoli, Palestine	R.C.R., C.H.K.M.
1914	Crossman, R. D., M.C., Lt. R. Scots, w. 2. France, Egypt (k. 27.9.18)	A.A.S
1908	Crowder, J. F. E., Lt. R.H.G., late Capt. Lincolnshire Yeomanry, and Staff	S.A.D., P.V.B.
1871	Crowder, J. St. V., Lt., late P.O., R.N.V.R.	E.P.R.
1884	Crum, A. S., Maj. Oxfordshire and Bucks L.I.	C.H.E.
1890	Crum, F. M., Maj. K.R.R.C., and Staff, m. 2. France	H.B., W.D.
1914	Crum-Ewing, A., 2nd Lt. Seaforth Highlanders, att. Cameron Highlanders, m. France (k. 22.12.14)	R.P.L.B
1911	Cubitt, Hon. A. G., Lt. 15th Hussars. France (k. 24.11.17)	A.M.G.
1909	Cubitt, H. A. (F) Capt. Coldstream Gds., m. France (k. 15.9.16)	A.M.G.
1916	Cubitt, Hon. R. C., Lt. Coldstream Gds.	A.M.G.
1914	Cubitt, Hon. W. H., Lt. 1st R. Dragoons. France (d.w 24.3.18)	A.M.G
1916	Cunard, V., Lt. Coldstream Gds. France	L.S.R.B.
1897	Cuningham, F. G. G., Lt.-Col. A. and S. Highlanders	C.H.A.
1906	Cuninghame, A. K. S., Capt. Grenadier Gds., w., m. France (k. 25.9.16)	I.H.M.H
1894	Cuninghame, Sir T. A. A. M., Bart., D.S.O., Bt. Lt.-Col. Rifle Bde., and Staff, m. 2. France, Balkans, Egypt, Gallipoli	J.P.C.
1907	Cuninghame, W. W. S., D.S.O., Capt. 2nd Life Gds., empld. Lt.-Col. Cameronians (Scottish Rifles), w. 2, m. France	J.H.M.H.
1885	Cunliffe, E. S., Lt.-Col. Shropshire L.I.	J.B.L., H.W.M.
1894	Cunliffe, Sir F. H. E., Bart., Maj. Rifle Bde. France (d.w. 10.7.16)	E.C.A.J

1910	Cunliffe, G., the late, Capt. Herts Yeomanry, and Staff. France, Egypt, Gallipoli, Palestine (d. 23.2.20)	E.L.C.
1-	Cunliffe, J. B., Maj. Northamptonshire Yeomanry. France (d. 20.4.17)	H.W.M.
1912	Cunliffe, Hon. R., Lt. R.A.F., m. Home Waters	H.M.
1913	Cunliffe, W. N., Capt. Remount Service	H.W.M.
1896	Curling, B. J., D.S.O. (F) Brig.-Gen. (K.R.R.C.), m. 3. France, Balkans, Egypt, Gallipoli	H.E.L.
1898	Curling, J. (F) Maj. R.F.A., w. France, Italy	H.E.L.
1902	Curling, R. R., D.S.O., Lt.-Col. R.A., m. 2. France	H.E.L.
1917	Currie, B. F. G., 2nd Lt. Scots Gds.	S.G.L.
1908	Curtis, A. R. W., M.C., Capt. 11th Hussars, att. R.A.F., w., m. France	E.I.
1894	Curtis, H. M. C., D.S.O. and two Bars, Capt. N. Staffordshire Regt., att. S. Staffordshire Regt. and The Buffs, m. France	R.C.R.
1907	Curtis, H. O., D.S.O., M.C., Bt. Maj. K.R.R.C., and Staff, w. 3, m. 3. France, Balkans, Palestine	E.I.
1916	Curtis, J. S., 2nd Lt. Rifle Bde. France (k. 21.3.18)	J.H.M.H.
1907	Curtis, T. L. C., Capt. Coldstream Gds., empld. Maj. M.G.C. France	J.H.M.H.
1876	Curtis, Sir W. M., Bart., Capt. R. Defence Corps (d. 19.12.16)	W.W.
1903	Curzon, Visc., Cr. R.N.V.R. France, Home Waters, Mediterranean	E.I.
1878	Curzon, Hon. A. N., Lt.-Col. Sherwood Foresters	C.W.D.
1916	Curzon, R. N., 2nd Lt. R. Scots Greys. France	C.H.K.M.
1876	Cusack-Smith, Sir T. B., Bart., K.C.M.G., Col. R.F.A. Mesopotamia	W.W., C.H.E.
1883	Cust, A. S. Cockayne-, Maj. Somerset L.I., and Staff. France	E.C.A.L.
1915	Cust, L. G. A., Lt. R.A., and Staff, p., m. France, Egypt	S.G.L.
1916	Cust, P. F. A., 2nd Lt. Grenadier Gds. France	A.M.G.
1894	Cuthbert, J. H., D.S.O., Capt. Scots Gds., w., m. France (k. 27.9.15)	F.D., C.H.A.

1896 Dalby, T. G., D.S.O. (F) Bt. Lt.-Col. K.R.R.C., and
    Staff, w. 2, m. France   R.C.R.
1908 Dale, E. C. B., M.C., Maj. R.F.A., w. 3, m. 5. France   J.M.E., M.D.H.
1908 Dale, R. C., 2nd Lt. R.F.A. France (k. 18.8.16)   T.C.P., I.L.C.
1914 Dale-Lace, L. E. C., M.C., Lt. R. Scots Greys, and
    Staff. France   R.S.K.
1883 Dalgety, F. J., Maj. Res. Regt. of Cav.   A.C.J.
1886 Dalgety, H. B., Lt.-Col. 7th Hussars. Mesopotamia   A.C.J.
1916 Dalgety, J. A. F., Lt. 15th Hussars. France   A.C.G.H.
1895 Dalhousie, Earl of, Capt. Scots Gds., w. France   R.A.H.M.
1913 Dalkeith, Earl of (Lord Whitchester at Eton), Lt.
    Grenadier Gds., and Staff. France   E.I.
1900 Dalmeny, Lord, D.S.O., M.C. (F) Lt. (t. Lt.-Col.)
    Grenadier Gds., and Staff, w., m. 2. France,
    Palestine   W.D., P.W.
1900 Dalrymple-Hamilton, N. V. C., M.V.O., Bt. Lt.-Col.
    Scots Gds., att. Maj. Howe Bn., R.N.D. France   A.C.B.
1906 Dalton, E. H. J. N. (F) Lt. R.G.A., late Lt. R.A.S.C.
    France, Italy   H.E.L., R.S.K.
1903 Dalton, H. F., 2nd Lt. R.A.S.C., M.T. France   HOME
1892 Dalton, T. E., M.M., Pte. Canadian A.M.C. France   T.D.
1904 Daly, V. A. H., M.C., Bt. Maj. W. Yorkshire Regt.,
    and Staff, m. 4. France   C.H.A.
1899 Daman, G. W., Capt. R. Fusiliers, and Staff, w. France,
    Italy   H.D.
1913 Dames-Longworth, T. R., Lt. Irish Gds., late 2nd Lt.
    Middlesex Regt. France   R.S.de H.
1914 Daniel, H. C., Lt. 17th Lancers. France   M.D.H.
1898 Daniell, H. A., O.B.E. (F) Capt. (t. Maj.) London Regt.,
    and Staff, w. 2. France, Italy   R.W.W.-T.
1882 Daniell, J. A. le N., Capt. 11th Hussars, empld. Maj.
    Res. Regt. of Cav.   C.I.I.-C., J.B.L.
1904 Daniell, N. A., Lt. Coldstream Gds., att. Capt. R.A.F.
    France   H.F.W.T.
1895 Daniell, R. H. A., Bt. Col. Hampshire Regt.   C.H.E., C.L.

1901	Daniell, W. A., Capt. R.A.F., late Lt. R.N.V.R. and Lt. R.N.A.S., w. Home Waters, Egypt, Gallipoli	H.F.W.T.
1878	Darbishire, R. N., Maj. Suffolk Regt., and Staff. France	F.E.D.
	Darby, M. A. A., Lt. Grenadier Gds., m. France (k. 11.3.15)	H.M.
1871	Darby, W. H., Bt. Col. Remount Service, m. Egypt	O.B.
1900	Darrell, G. M., M.C. (F) Maj. Coldstream Gds., and Staff, w. 2, m. 3. France	J.M.E.
1890	Darrell, H. F., D.S.O., Lt.-Col. Rifle Bde., m. France	F.T.
1893	Darrell, L. E. H. M., D.S.O., Maj. 1st Life Gds., and Staff, m. 2. Egypt, Gallipoli, Palestine	J.M.E.
1895	Darrell, W. H. V., C.M.G., D.S.O. (F) Bt. Col. Coldstream Gds., and Staff, m. 5. France	J.M.E.
1914	Darley, D. J., 2nd Lt. Suffolk Regt. France (k. 1.7.16)	K.S.
	Darley, J. E. C., Lt.-Col. 4th Hussars, m. France (k. 31.3.18)	F.T., J.H.M.H.
1904	Darling, J. C., D.S.O., Capt. 20th Hussars, w., m. 2. France	R.W.W.-T.
1910	Darnton, R. E., D.F.C., Capt. R.A.F., late Lt. R.N.V.R. France	H.F.W.T., A.E.C.
1898	Darroch, G. R. S. (F) Lt. Intell. Corps. France, Balkans	C.H.E., F.H.R.
1894	Darwin, B. R. M., Lt. R.A.O.C. Balkans	K.S.
1908	Daukes, A. H., Bt. Maj. K.R.R.C., and Staff, w. France	T.C.P., E.L.C.
1907	David, E. J. C., M.C., Capt. Glamorgan Yeomanry, att. Welch Regt., w. 2. France, Egypt, Palestine	J.M.E., M.D.H.
1903	Davidson, A. J., Capt. Gordon Highlanders	P.W.
1878	Davidson, D. F., Lt.-Col. Cameron Highlanders	F.E.D.
1897	Davidson, N. R., D.S.O. and Bar, Bt. Lt.-Col. R.F.A., and Staff, m. 3. France (d.w. 5.10.17)	K.S.
1900	Davies, C. M., D.S.O. (F) Bt. Lt.-Col. Rifle Bde., and Staff, w., m. 4. France, Egypt, Gallipoli	E.C.A.L.
1891	Davies, E. H., Lt. Middlesex Regt., att. E. Surrey Regt. France	P.H.C.

1881	Davies, Sir F. J., K.C.B., K.C.M.G., K.C.V.O. (F) Lieut.-Gen. (Grenadier Gds.), m. 6. France, Egypt, Gallipoli	R.A.H.M.
1912	Davies, G. L., M.C., 2nd Lt. K.R.R.C., att. Rifle Bde. France (k. 15.3.15)	H.M.
1882	Davies, H. R., C.B. (F) Maj.-Gen. (Oxfordshire and Bucks L.I.), w., m. 8. France	R.A.H.M.
1873	Davies, H. S. P., Lt.-Col. Staff	H.S.
1889	Davies, H. W., D.S.O., M.C., Capt. Worcestershire Regt., w., p., m. France	R.A.H.M.
1914	Davies, P. L., Lt. (t. Capt.) K.R.R.C., and Staff. France	K.S.
1908	Davies, R. G. R., M.C., Capt. 16th Lancers, empld. Capt. M.G. Cav., w., m. 4. France	P.W.
1912	Davies, R. H. S., Lt. R.F.A. France (d.w. 29.7.16)	C.M.W
1910	Davies, R. R., Capt. 16th Lancers, and Staff R.A., w., m. France	R.P.L.B.
1897	Davies, W. E., C.M.G., D.S.O. (F) Bt. Lt.-Col. Rifle Bde., and Staff, m. 4. France, Egypt, Palestine	E.C.A.L.
1914	Davies-Cooke, P. R., Lt. 1st R. Dragoons. France	E.L.C.
1896	Davis, H. A., Capt. Northumberland Fusiliers, att. S. Wales Borderers. Egypt, Gallipoli	H.D.
1910	Davis, L. F., Lt. R.N.V.R. Home Waters	P.W.
1911	Davis, R. G., 2nd Lt., late Pte., Buckinghamshire Yeomanry. France, Palestine	P.W.
1903	Davson, I. B., O.B.E. (F) Maj. City of London Yeomanry, empld. Lt.-Col. R.A.F., Staff.	T.C.P.
1906	Davson, T. G., Lt. R.H.G. France (k. 13.5.15)	T.C.P., E.L.C.
1909	Davy, M. B., Lt. R.G.A., late Pte., Rangoon Rifles. France	E.L.V.
1871·	Dawkins, H. S., C.B., Brig.-Gen. (R.A.)	F.W.C.
1904	Dawnay, A. G. C., C.B.E., D.S.O. (F) Bt. Maj. (t. Lt.-Col.) Coldstream Gds., and Staff, m. 8. France, Arabia, Egypt, Palestine	S.A.D.
1908	Dawnay, C. H., M.C., Capt. Yorkshire Regt., and Staff. France, Gallipoli, N. Russia	A.M.G.

1906	Dawnay, E. G., Lt. 20th Hussars, late Capt. Yorkshire Hussars, att. W. Yorkshire Regt., m. France	R.C.R.
1895	Dawnay, G. P., C.B., C.M.G., D.S.O., M.V.O. (F) Maj.-Gen. (Coldstream Gds.), m. 10. France, Egypt, Gallipoli, Palestine	S.R.J.
1893	Dawnay, Hon. H., D.S.O. (F) Maj. 2nd Life Gds., m. 2. France (k. 6.11.14)	R.A.H.M.
1890	Dawnay, Hon. J., C.M.G., D.S.O. (F) Lt.-Col. Staff. France	R.A.H.M.
1871	Dawson, Sir D. F. R., C.B., C.M.G., G.C.V.O. (F) Bt. Col. Staff	O.B.
1882	Dawson, E. A. F., Lt.-Col. Rifle Bde.	E.C.A.L.
1890	Dawson, J. M., Maj. W. Yorkshire Regt., att. Labour Corps	F.W.C.
1895	Dawson, R. L., Capt. Coldstream Gds., m. France (k 20.11.14)	J.M.E.
1870	Dawson, V. J., C.V.O., Maj.-Gen. (Coldstream Gds.)	O.B.
1916	Dawson-Greene, C. J., 2nd Lt. Grenadier Gds. France (d.w. 24.4.18)	H M
1899	Deane, G. H., Capt. (t. Maj.) Remount Service. France	E.L.V.
1880	Deane, J., C.M.G., Maj. Black Watch, and Staff	E.H.
1888	de Capell-Brooke, Sir A. R., Bart., Maj. Northamptonshire Regt.	E.C.A.L.
1915	de Caraman-Chimay, Count, Lt. Scots Gds.	J.H.M.H., M.D.H.
1884	Decies, Lord, P.C., D.S.O. (Mr. Beresford at Eton), Col. S. Irish Horse, and Staff. France	A.C.J.
1900	Deedes, W. H., C.M.G., D.S.O. (F) Brig.-Gen. (K.R.R.C.), m. 4. Egypt, Gallipoli, Palestine	R.A.H.M.
1884	Deerhurst, Visc., Lt.-Col. Staff, m. France	E.W.
1901	de Falbe, C. F. G. W., O.B.E., T.D., Lt.-Col., att. Yorkshire Hussars, and Staff, m. France, Egypt	A.C.A.
1893	de Forest, M. A., Lt.-Cr. R.N.V.R. France	W.D.
1890	de Freville, E. H., Maj. S. Nottinghamshire Hussars, att. 8th Hussars. France	J.P.C.
1901	de Grey, G., D.S.O., Bt. Maj. (t. Lt.-Col.) Norfolk Regt., w. 3, m. 5. France, Mesopotamia	W.D., H.Br.

1904	de Grey, N., O.B.E., Lt.-Cr., late C.P.O., R.N.V.R., late Flight Sub-Lt. R.N.A.S., m. Mediterranean	A.C B.-A.M.G.
1904	de Gunzburg, Baron, 2nd Lt. 11th Hussars, att. R.H.G. France (k. 6.11.14)	R P L B
1911	Deighton, G. W., M.C. (F) Capt. Suffolk Regt., m. France (k. 3.7.16)	K S.
1914	Deighton Simpson, H. R., Lt. 6th (Inniskilling) Dragoons, att. R.A.F., m. 2. France (k. accid. 19.12.16)	J.M.D., V L. N I
1915	Deighton Simpson, J., Ensign United States Naval Flying Corps	H.M.
1895	de Knoop, J. J. J., Capt. Cheshire Yeomanry, att. Imp. Camel Corps, late Interpreter Cav. Bde., and Staff, w., m. France, Egypt (k. 7.8.16)	P.W
1898	de la Rue, Sir E. A., Bart., Capt. R.A.F.; late E. Kent Yeomanry, and Staff, m. France	C.H.E., S.A.D.
1899	de la Rue, I. A., Lt., late Pte., R. Fusiliers, m. France	R.C.R.
1902	de la Rue, R. W., Capt. R.A.S.C. France	A.A.S.
1910	de Lavison, S., 2nd Lt. H.L.I. France	J.M.D., V.Le N.F.
1918	De La Warr, Earl, Deck Hand (Signaller) R.N.R. Home Waters	J.H.M.H.
1896	Delme-Radcliffe, R. H. J., Capt. London Regt., and Staff. France	H.W.M.
1899	Denison, E. B., D.S.O., M.C., Maj. K.R.R.C., empld. Lt.-Col. R. Fusiliers and R. Welch Fusiliers, w., m. 3. France	R.C.R.
1898	Denison, H., D.S.O., Maj. R.F.A., w., m. France, Gallipoli (d.w. 28.8.17)	R C.R
1897	Denison, W. F. E., 2nd Lt. Sherwood Foresters. France (d.w. 26.3.18)	R C R
1902	Denison-Pender, H., D.S.O., M.C., Bt. Maj. R. Scots Greys, and Staff, m. 3. France	H.W.M., H.M.
1899	Denison-Pender, J. C., M.P., Lt. Staff. France	H.W.M., H.M.
1914	Denman, R. C., Lt. Grenadier Gds., late Pte. H.A.C. France (k. 1.12. 17)	F W S

1913	Denman, R. P. G., Lt. Middlesex Regt., att. R.E. and R.A.F., m. France, Balkans, Egypt	E.L.V., A.C.R.-W.
1885	Dennistoun, A. H. O., Lt.-Col. Black Watch, m. France	J.P.C.
1895	Dennistoun, I. O., M.V.O. (F) Maj. Grenadier Gds., empld. Lt.-Col. Labour Corps, and Staff. France	J.P.C.
1887	Dennistoun, J. G., D.S.O., Lt.-Col. R.A., m. France	T.D.
1907	Denny, J. A., Lt. Grenadier Gds., att. Scots Gds., and Staff, w. France	R.S. de H.
1915	Dent, L. A., Lt. R.F.A., att. R.G.A., and Staff, w. France	E.L.V., A.C.R.-W.
1907	Dent, L. M. E., D.S.O. (F) Capt. (t. Maj.) Oxfordshire and Bucks L.I., late Capt. Carabiniers, and Staff, w. 2, m. 3. France	F.H.R.
1913	Dent, R. A. W., Lt. K.R.R.C., and Staff, w., m. France	E.L.V., A.C.R.-W.
1893	Denton, C. M., Capt. Loyal N. Lancashire Regt. France	E.I.
1915	de Paravicini, C. P. E., Lt. K.R.R.C., p. France	A.A.S.
1913	de Paravicini, J. M., Maj. K.R.R.C., w. 2, m. France (k. 30 11 17)	A.A.S.
1911	de Paravicini, P. G., Lt. K.R.R.C., w. France	A.A.S.
1915	de Pass, G. E., D.S.O., Lt. 4th Dragoon Gds., m. France	F.E.R.
1917	de Pass, J. A., 2nd Lt. Grenadier Gds. France	M.D.H.
1891	de Prée, C. G., Maj. Fife and Forfar Yeomanry, empld. Lt.-Col. Loyal N. Lancashire Regt., m. France, Egypt, Gallipoli	E.H.
1888	de Prée, H. D., C.B., C.M.G., D.S.O., Brig.-Gen. (R.A.), m. 4. France	E.H.
1914	de Quetteville, R. G., D.S.O., M.C., Capt. Yorkshire Regt., w., p., m. France	H.B., R.H. de M.
1882	Deramore, Lord, T.D. (Bateson de Yarburgh at Eton), Lt.-Col. Yorkshire Hussars	E.W.
1916	de Reuter, R. C. G., Lt. Grenadier Gds. France	A.A.S.
1904	Derham, J. A. T., Lt. London Regt., w. France	J.H.M.H.
1885	Dering, Sir H. E., Bart., Maj. E. Kent Yeomanry, and Staff. France	F.H.R.

1916	d'Erlanger, L. F. A., Lt. Grenadier Gds. France	H.Br.
1914	d'Erlanger, R. F. E. R., M.C., Lt. Rifle Bde., and Staff, m. France	M.D.H.
1904	de Roemer, C. W., Maj. R.F.A., att. R.A.F., and Staff, m. France	R.P.L.B.
1888	Derriman, G. L., Capt. Grenadier Gds., and Staff. France (d.w. 7.8.15)	C.H.T.
1894	de Rutzen, Baron, Lt. Pembroke Yeomanry, att. Imp. Camel Corps. m. Egypt, Palestine (k. 7.8.16)	T D.
1913	de Sales La Terrière, F. J. B., 2nd Lt. 21st Lancers, att. R.F.C. France	H.Br.
1882	de Sales La Terrière, F. L., Lt. R.A.F., late Capt. The Queen's	C.C.J.
1907	de Sales La Terrière, H. M. B., M.C., Maj. K.R.R.C., empld. Lt.-Col. Essex Regt., w., m. 2. France	L.S.R.B.
1916	De Salis, S. C. F., Lt. K.R.R.C., w. 2. France, N. Russia	E.W.S.
1890	de Satgé, H. V. B., C.M.G., D.S.O., Lt.-Col. R.F.A., m. 2. France	H.W.M.
1906	de Stein, E. A. S., Maj. K.R.R.C., att. M.G.C., and Staff. France	J.M.D.
1917	des Graz, E. P. A., 2nd Lt. Rifle Bde.	E.L.C.
1893	des Vœux, H. J., O.B.E., Lt.-Col. R. Fusiliers, late Maj. Northamptonshire Regt., empld. Lt.-Col. Labour Corps, m. France	W.D.
1909	de Teissier, A., 2nd Lt. R.A.F., late Pte. Canadian Inf. France (k. accid. 12.10.17)	M.D.H.
1904	de Teissier, G. F., Capt. Scots Gds., w. France	C.H.A.
1901	de Tuyll, Baron F. C. O., M.B.E.(F) Lt. 10th R. Hussars, and Staff, m. France, Balkans	A.C.J., L.F., R.S.K.
1905	Devas, G. C., M.C., Lt. Welsh Gds., late A.B., R.N.V.R., m. France	R.P.L.B.
1915	Deverell, J. L., Lt. R.F.A., w. 2. France	E.W.S.
1912	Devereux, R. G. de B., Lt. Welsh Gds., w. France	P.W., F.E.R.
1899	de Vesci, Visc. (Vesey at Eton), Maj. (t. Lt.-Col.) Irish Gds., and Staff. France	R.C.R.

1910	Dewhurst, G. C. L., Lt. Rifle Bde., w. France (k. 1.7.16)	E.L.V.
1917	Dewhurst, J. A., 2nd Lt. R. Scots Greys	A.C.R.-W.
1909	Dewhurst, R. C., M.C., Capt. Rifle Bde., and Staff, w. France	J.H.M.H.
1910	de Winton, W., 2nd Lt. Coldstream Gds. France (k. 6.9.14)	H.B.
1902	de Yerburgh Bateson, Hon. E., Lt. R.A.S.C., m. France	E.I.
1895	de Zoete, H. W., Lt. Essex Yeomanry	S.R.J.
1897	Dick-Cunyngham, G. A., Capt. (t. Maj.) Rifle Bde., w., m. France	A.C.A.
1907	Dickens, C. C., Maj. London Regt., w., m. France (k. 9.9.16)	H.Br.
1906	Dickens, P. C., Lt. Welsh Gds., w. 2. France	H.Br.
1888	Dickin, T., Lt.-Col. Shropshire L.I., att. Labour Corps, and Staff. France	A.C.
1890	Dickinson, A. H., M.C., Lt. Coldstream Gds., late Pte. R. Fusiliers, w., m. France	A.C.J.
1915	Dickinson, R. S. W., D.S.O. (F) 2nd Lt. Coldstream Gds., late Flight Sub-Lt. R.N.A.S. Mediterranean, Turkey	K.S.
1892	Dickson, G. F. H., Maj. (t. Lt.-Col.) R. Welch Fusiliers, w., m. 2. France	J.M.E.
1912	Digby, Lord, D.S.O., M.C. and Bar (F) (Mr. Digby at Eton), Capt. Coldstream Gds., w. 2, m. 2. France	R.P.L.B.
1906	Digby, A. E. H., 2nd Lt. R.M.L.I., R.N.D. Gallipoli	H.Br.
1883	Digby, G. H., the late, Maj. Dorset Yeomanry (k. accid. 20.10.14)	G.E.M.
1909	Diggle, L. W., M.C., Capt. 9th Lancers, att. Cav. Signals, m. 4. France	H.B.
1913	Dilbéroglue, A., Lt. 3rd Hussars. France (k. 1.4.18)	A.M.G.
1910	Dilbéroglue, P., Lt. Welsh Gds., w. France	A.M.G.
1914	Dilbéroglue, R. N., Lt. Coldstream Gds. France (k. 15.9.16)	A.M.G.
1908	Dill, J. M. Gordon, Capt. 5th Lancers, att. M.G. Cav., w. France	C.H.A., E.W.S.
1914	Dill, R. W. Gordon, M.C., Lt. 1st Life Gds., att. M.G. Cav., late Sussex Yeomanry, m. France	E.W.S.

1914	Dill, V. R. C., M.C., Lt. R.F.A., and Staff, w., m. 2. France	K.S.
1901	Dimsdale, E. C., Capt. Rifle Bde., att. Monmouthshire Regt. France (k. 8.5.15)	R.W.W.-T.
1911	Dingwall, C. F., Maj. E. Surrey Regt., att. M.G.C., w. France	H.Br.
1916	Dixon, M. V., 2nd Lt. R.F.A., w. France	K.S.
1893	Dodd, G. L. Ashley, Maj. Northumberland Fusiliers, and Staff. France	F.W.C.
1882	Dodington, R. Marriott-, O.B.E., T.D., Lt.-Col. W. Somerset Yeomanry, and Staff, m. France	G.E.M.
1874	Donaldson, Sir H. F., K.C.B., Brig.-Gen., Staff (drowned H.M.S. Hampshire 5.6.16)	G.R.D.
1905	Donaldson, S. H. M., Capt. King's African Rifles, w. E. Africa	S.A.D., P.V.B.
1892	Donaldson-Hudson, R. C., D.S.O. (F) Lt.-Col. R.A.F., and Staff, late Lt. 12th Lancers and Shropshire Yeomanry, m. 3. France	E.C.A.L.
1906	Donkin, A. W. F., Capt. R.G.A., att. R.E. France	H.B.
1893	Donoughmore, Rt. Hon. Earl of, K.P., M.V.O. (Visc. Suirdale at Eton), Col. Red Cross, m. 2. France	F.W.C.
1894	Dorrien-Smith, A. A., D.S.O., Maj. Rifle Bde., and Staff, m. France	J.M.E.
1914	Douglas, A. S. G., O.B.E., Capt. Rifle Bde., and Staff, w., m. France, Balkans, S. Russia	A.B.R.
1917	Douglas, D. S. W., 2nd Lt. Rifle Bde.	A.B.R.
1891	Douglas, H. A., Maj. (t. Lt.-Col.) I.A. Transport Corps, m. France, Mesopotamia	S.A.D.
1916	Douglas-Jones, S. V. D., 2nd Lt. Coldstream Gds., late 2nd Lt. R.F.C. France	M.D.H.
1898	Douglas-Pennant, A., Lt. (t. Capt.), late Sergt., Herts Yeomanry, and Staff. Egypt, Gallipoli	W.D.
1908	Douglas-Pennant, Hon. A. G. S., Lt. Grenadier Gds. France (k. 29.10.14)	H.T.B.
1895	Douglas-Pennant, Hon. C., Lt. Coldstream Gds. France (k. 29.10.14)	F C A.L.

1884	Douglas-Pennant, F., Lt.-Col. K.R.R.C. France	E.C.A.L.
1884	Douglas-Pennant, Hon. G. H., Capt. Grenadier Gds., m. France (k. 11.3.15)	E.C.A.L.
1913	Douglas-Pennant, Hon. H. N., Lt. R. Scots Greys, and Staff. France	H.T.B., S.G.L.
1910	Doune, Lord, M.C., Capt. Scottish Horse, att. R.A.F., and Staff, w. France	F.H.R., H.de H.
1910	Doyle, A. A. K. Conan, the late, Lt. Hampshire Regt., late Pte. City of London R.A.M.C., w. France (d. 28.10.18)	E.L.V.
1917	Doyne, R. H., 2nd Lt. Rifle Bde., w. France	E.W.S.
1887	Doyne, R. W., Capt. (t. Maj.) Westmorland and Cumberland Yeomanry, att. R.F.A. France	T.D.
1916	Drabble, G. A., Lt. 16th Lancers. France	P.W., F.E.R.
1879	Drage, G., Sub-Lt. R.N.V.R.	K.S.
1878	Drake, B. F., C.B., Brig.-Gen. (R.A.). France	E.H.
1913	Drake, F. C., M.C., Lt. 10th R. Hussars, w. France	J.H.M.H.
1904	Drake, F. V., M.C. (F) Capt. 11th Hussars, att. Cav. Signals, w., m. 3. France	J.H.M.H.
1902	Drake, J. H., O.B.E., M.C., Maj. Herts Yeomanry, and Staff, m. 3. France, Egypt, Gallipoli	J.H.M.H.
1910	Drake, R. F., Lt. 10th R. Hussars. France (k. 17.11.14)	J.H.M.H.
1916	Drake, R. H. M., 2nd Lt. R.F.A., and Staff. Palestine	H.Br.
1908	Draper, R. F., Capt. York and Lancaster Regt. Gallipoli (k. 21.8.15)	E.W.S.
	Drewe, A., 2nd Lt. R.G.A., m. France (k. 12.7.17)	R.C.R., C.H.K.M.
1913	Drewe, B., M.C. and Bar, Lt. R.G.A., late 2nd Lt. Devonshire Regt., w. France	C.H.K.M.
1914	Drewe, C., Lt. R.F.A., w. France	C.H.K.M.
1901	Drogheda, Earl of (Lord Moore at Eton), 2nd Lt. Irish Gds.	A.C.A.
1907	Drummond, F. B. H., M.C., Capt. Rifle Bde., and Staff, w. 2. France, N. Russia	E.W.S.
1910	Drummond, F. H. J., M.C., Lt. Grenadier Gds., late 2nd Lt. Warwickshire Yeomanry, w. 2. France	P.V.B.

1910 Drummond, F. J., Trooper Bowker's Horse. E. Africa
(k. 2.11.14) H.T.B., S.G.L.
1912 Drummond, F. W., Lt. R.E., late Pte. London Regt.
France H.T.B., S.G.L.
1900 V.C. Drummond, G. H. (F) Lt.-Cr. R.N.V.R., w. Home
Waters C.L.
1903 Drummond, J. H., D.S.C., Lt.-Cr. R.N. Home Waters H.T.B.
1909 Drummond, L., Lt, R. Scots Greys, att. M.G. Cav.
France J.M.E., M.D.H.
1877 Drummond, L. G., C.B., M.V.O., C.B.E., Maj.-Gen. (Scots
Gds.), and empld. under Admiralty. France, Mediterranean W.E.
1890 Drummond, M., Capt. K.R.R.C. F.H.R.
1896 Drummond, Hon. M. C. A., C.M.G., D.S.O. (F) Bt.
Lt.-Col. (t. Col.) Black Watch, and Staff, w., m. 4.
France P.W.
1914 Drummond, R. C., 2nd Lt. Coldstream Gds. France
(k. 28.11.17) C.M.W.
1902 Drummond, S. H., Capt. Rifle Bde. France (k. 30.7.15) C.L., H.T.B.
1906 Drury, D. D., Lt. R.A.F., p. France R.W.W.-T., C.M.W.
1910 Drury, V. D., Capt. R.E., w. France, Egypt, Palestine A.B.R.
1915 Drury, W. A., Lt. Sherwood Foresters, and Staff, w.
France K.S.
1909 Drury-Lavin, M. H., Lt. R.N.V.R., m. Home Waters,
Mediterranean R.C.R., M.D.H.
1902 Drury-Lowe, E. N., Capt. Sherwood Foresters, p. France E.L.V.
1896 Drury-Lowe, J. A. E., Capt. Scots Gds. France A.C.B.
1896 Drury-Lowe, W. D., D.S.O., Capt. Grenadier Gds.,
empld. Lt.-Col. R.F.A., m. 3. France (k. 25.9.16) A.C.B.
1892 Duberly, G. W., Maj. Grenadier Gds., m. France
(k. 13.3.15) H.F.L.
1908 Dubs, G. R., M.C. (F) Bt. Maj. K.R.R.C., and Staff,
w. 2, m. 3. France F.H.R., H. de H.
1892 Duckett, J. S., D.S.O. (F) Lt.-Col. 9th Lancers, and Staff.
m. 3. France E.H.

1888	Duckworth, A. C., Bt. Maj. R. Scots Greys, and Staff, m. 2. France	H.E.L.
1908	Duckworth-King, Sir G. H. J., Bart., Capt. Grenadier Gds., and Staff, w. France	E.W.S.
1884	Dudley, Rt. Hon. Earl of, G.C.B., G.C.M.G., G.C.V.O., T.D. (Visc. Ednam at Eton), Lt.-Col. Worcestershire Yeomanry, and Staff. Egypt, Gallipoli	J.M.E.
1887	Dudley, Lord (Lea-Smith at Eton), Lt.-Col. Worcestershire Regt.	H.G.W.
1910	Duff, B. P., 2nd Lt. Cameron Highlanders. France (k. 25.9.15)	P.W.
1913	Duff, D. F. G., Lt. (t. Capt.) 9th Lancers, empld. M.G. Cav. France	R.P.L.B.
1885	Duff, G. J. B., M.C. (F) Capt. Norfolk Regt., att. R.F.A., m. France	J.M.E.
1893	Duff, Sir R. G. V., Bart., Lt. 2nd Life Gds. France (k. 16.10.14)	A.C.J.
1889	Duff, R. W., Maj. R.F.A., and Staff. France	A.C.A.
1906	Dugdale, C. J. G., Lt. London Regt., w. France	H.F.W.T.
1895	Dugdale, E. T. S., Capt. Leicestershire Yeomanry, att. Intell. Corps. France	H.T.B.
1915	Dugdale, T. L., Lt. R. Scots Greys. France	A.E.C.
1882	Duleep Singh, H.H. Prince F. V., M.V.O., T.D., Maj. Norfolk Yeomanry, att. R.A. France	A.C.J.
1904	Duncan, H. H., Capt. Norfolk Yeomanry, att. R.E., and Staff. France, Italy	J.H.M.H.
1903	Duncan, Rev. J. M., C.F., w. 2. France, Gallipoli	K.S.
1889	Duncan, W. MacD., Capt. Leicestershire Yeomanry, and Staff. France	G.E.M., P.H.C.
1915	Dundas, H. L. N., M.C. and Bar, Lt. Scots Gds., w. France (k. 27.9.18)	C.H K.M.
1899	Dundas, J. C., D.S.O., Bt. Lt.-Col. R.F.A., and Staff, w., m. 2. France	H.E.L.
1903	Dundas, R. H., Capt. Black Watch, and Staff, w., m France, Mesopotamia	K.S.

1912	Dundas-Grant, J. H., Maj. R.A.F. France, Home Waters, Italy	J.H.M.H.
1905	Dunell, H. C. (F) Lt. R.G.A., m. France, Italy	E.I.
1895	Dunlop, A. H., 2nd Lt. Ayrshire Yeomanry, att. R. Scots Fusiliers. France, Egypt, Palestine (k. 6.11.17)	H.W.M.
1895	Dunlop, D. O., Lt. Lancashire Fusiliers	A.C.A.
1896	Dunlop, T. C. (F) Maj. Ayrshire Yeomanry, m. Egypt, Gallipoli, Palestine	H.W.M.
1888 V.C.	Dunmore, Earl of, D.S.O., M.V.O. (Lord Fincastle at Eton), Maj. 16th Lancers, and Staff, w. 2, m. 3. France	J.M.E.
1911	Dunn, J. H. M., 2nd Lt. R.F.A. France (k. 25.9.16)	E.I.
1873	Dunn, R. W. H., Brig.-Gen. (R. Welch Fusiliers), (d. from accid. 8.1.17)	F.St.J T.
1910	Dunne, A. S., Lt. 6th (Inniskilling) Dragoons. France (k. 2.7.17)	H.B.
1912	Dunne, L. R., M.C. (F) Bt. Maj. K.R.R.C., att. Rifle Bde., w., m. 2. France, Balkans, Black Sea	H.B.
1913	Dunning, G K., Lt. Hampshire Regt. Mesopotamia	R.P.L.B.
1901	Dunnington-Jefferson, J. A., D.S.O. (F) Bt. Maj. (t. Lt.-Col.) R. Fusiliers, and Staff, m. 6. France	H.Br.
1894	Dunsany, Lord (Mr. Plunkett at Eton), Capt. R. Inniskilling Fusiliers, and Staff. France	F.W.C., E.L.V.
1907	Dunsford, Visc., M.C. (F) (Mr. Brodrick at Eton), Capt. Surrey Yeomanry, and Staff, m. Gallipoli	S.A.D., P.V.B.
1883	Dunville, J. D., C.B.E., Lt.-Col. R.A.F.	W.D.
1914 V.C.	Dunville, J. S., 2nd Lt. Carabiniers, and 1st R. Dragoons. France (d.w. 26.6.17)	P W., F F.R
1911	Dunville, R. L., Capt. Grenadier Gds., att. 1st Life Gds., w. Gallipoli	P.W.
1882	Du Plat Taylor, G. P., O.B.E. (F) Maj. Grenadier Gds., and Staff	A.C.A.
1896	Du Pre, C. H., M.C., Lt. (t. Capt.) R.A.S.C., m. France	F.D., J.M.E.
1898	Du Pre, F. J., D.S.O., Maj. 3rd Hussars, w., m. 2. France	J.M.E.
1917	Dupuis, R. D. B., 2nd Lt. R.G.A. Aden, Egypt, Palestine	H.B., R.H.de M.

1893	Durand, H. M., D.S.O., Lt.-Col. 9th Lancers, and Staff, m. 3. France	A.C.J.
1907	Durant, N. H. C. F., Lt. Irish Gds. France (k. 30.11.17)	F.I.
1905	Durnford, H. G. E., M.C., Capt. R.F.A., p. France	K.S.
1914	Durnford, R. C., D.S.O., Capt. Hampshire Regt., m. Mesopotamia (k. 21.6.18)	K.S.
1904	Durnford, R. S., Capt. K.R.R.C. France (k. 30.6.15)	H.Br.
1910	Dyer, A. O., Capt. R.G.A., att. R.F.A., w. 2. France, Italy	H.Br.
1909	Dyer, Sir J. Swinnerton, Bart., M.C., Capt. Scots Gds., and Staff, w., m. France (k. 31.7.17)	A.A.S.
1898	Dyne, F. L. B., 2nd Lt. R. Fusiliers, late Pte. London Regt.	J.P.C.
1899	Eardley-Wilmot, Sir J., Bart., Maj. Rifle Bde., att. R.A.F., and Staff, w., m. France	C.H.A.
1907	Earl, A., C.B.E., Lt. (t. Maj.) R.G.A., and Staff, w. France	H.B.
1873	Earle, Sir H., Bart., D.S.O., Lt.-Col. Intell. Corps	G., E.C.A.L.
1908	Earle, J. V. (F) Lt. Sherwood Foresters, att. Cameroons E.F. W. Africa (k. 20.6.15)	K.S.
1896	Earle, J. W., Capt. Lancashire Hussars, m. France, Egypt	E.C.A.L.
1878	Earle, T. A., T.D., Lt.-Col. Lancashire Hussars. France, Egypt	E.C.A.L.
1911	Eastwood, C. S., M.C., Capt. London Regt. France	R.S.de H.
1910	Eastwood, F. M., Lt. The Queen's. France (k. 10.10.14)	R.P.L.B.
1915	Eastwood, G. A., Lt. R.F.A. France, Mesopotamia	R.S.de H.
1880	Eastwood, H. de C., D.S.O., Col. Comm. Army Cyclist Training Centre.	G.E.M.
1907	Eastwood, H. E., M.C. (F) Maj. R.A.O.C., and Staff. France	R.P.L.B.
1880	Eastwood, J. C. B., C.B., C.M.G., Col. Staff, m. 4. France	F.T.
1906	Eastwood, J. F., Lt. (t. Capt.) Grenadier Gds. France	R.P.L.B.
1908	Eastwood, J. P. B., Capt. R.F.A., m. France	R.S.de H.
1908	Eastwood, N. W., Lt. (t. Capt.) 3rd Hussars, w. France	R.P.L.B.

1908	Eastwood, T. R., D.S.O., M.C., Bt. Lt.-Col. (t. Lt.-Col.) Rifle Bde., att. N. Zealand E.F. Staff, m. 6. France, Egypt, Gallipoli, N. Russia, Samoa	H.M.
1912	Eaton, Hon. F. O. H., D.S.O., Capt. Grenadier Gds., m. France	A.A.S.
1913	Eaton, G. H., Lt. M.G.C. France (k. 25.3.18)	F.I
1905	Ebrington, Visc., M.C. (Mr. Fortescue at Eton), Bt. Maj. R. Scots Greys, and Staff, w. 2, m. 3. France	A.C.B., A.M.G.
1913	Eckstein, B. F., Capt. E. Surrey Regt., and Staff. France	J.H.M.H.
1905	Eckstein, H. F., Capt. 17th Lancers. France	J.M.D.
1911	Eckstein, L. A., Lt. King's African Rifles, Nairobi F.F. E. Africa (d.w. 24.11.16)	J.M.D., V.L.cN.F
1900	Eddis, L. A. (F) Maj. R.F.A., and Staff. France	J.M.E.
1915	Eddis, M. U., Lt. R.F.A. France	R.S.K.
1899	Ede, E. M. C., Capt. S. Staffordshire Regt., late Capt. R. Welch Fusiliers and 2nd Lt. S. Wales Borderers. Egypt	T.C.P.
1892	Eden, Hon. A. M., Lt. Sp. List, and Staff, late Pte. R.A.M.C. France	A.C.B.
1908	Eden, G. M., M.B.E., Lt. (t. Capt.) R.A.S.C., M.T., late Lt. E. Surrey Regt., m. 3. Aden	A.C.G.H.
1906	Eden, J., Lt. 12th Lancers. France (k. 17.10.14)	L.S.R.B
1915	Eden, R. A., M.C., Capt. K.R.R.C., and Staff. France	E.L.C.
1894	Eden, Hon. R. E., M.C., Maj. R.F.A., w. France	A.C.B.
1916	Eden, R. G. M., 2nd Lt. Scots Gds., w. France	M.D.H.
1910	Eden, T., M.C. and Bar, Capt. M.G.C., late Lt. The King's Own (R. Lancaster Regt.), m. France, Balkans, Egypt, Palestine	A.C.G.H.
1911	Eden, Sir T. C., Bart., 2nd Lt. K.O.Y.L.I., att. T.M.B. France	E.L.C.
1908	Eden, Hon. W. A. M., Lt. K.R.R.C., m. France (k. 3.3.15)	R.S de H
1908	Edge, J. V., Lt. Sherwood Foresters, w. 2. France	H.F.W.T.
1916	Edge, R. F., M.C., Lt. Coldstream Gds. France	J.H.M.H.
1907	Edge, R. T., M.C., Lt. (t. Capt.) R.E. France, Egypt	H.F.W.T.

1909 Edghill, V. J. C., 2nd Lt., late L/ce-Cpl., Somerset L.I. Mesopotamia — K.S.
1915 Edmonstone, W. G., Lt. Coldstream Gds., m. France (k. 15.9.16) — P.V.B.
1911 Edmunds, P. M. L., Capt. 12th Lancers, att. R.A.F., w., m. France, Balkans — R.S.K.
1912 Ednam, Visc., M.C., Lt. (t. Capt.) 10th R. Hussars, w. France — C.H.K.M.
1905 Edwardes, G. D'A., Capt. 1st R. Dragoons, empld. Maj. Welch Regt. France (k. 10.7.16) — F.L.C.
1890 Edwards, A. C., Capt. The Queen's Own (R. W. Kent Regt.). France (d.w., p., 27.9.15) — F.T.
1895 Edwards, A. H., Capt. R.F.A., and Staff, w. France — F.W.C., J.H.M.H.
1902 Edwards, A. N., Capt. 9th Lancers. France (d. gas poisoning 25.5.15) — C.L., R.P.L.B.
1909 Edwards, B. M. M., M.C. (F) Capt. (t. Maj.) Rifle Bde., and Staff, w., m. 2. France, Balkans, Egypt, Palestine — M.D.H.
1880 Edwards, F. A., Maj. R.F.A. — T.D.
1897 Edwards, F. W. L., the late, O.B.E. (F) Bt. Lt.-Col. K.R.R.C., att. Egyptian Army Staff, m. 3. Egypt, Gallipoli (d. 19.12.20) — J.H.M.H.
1900 Edwards, G. J., D.S.O., M.C., Lt.-Col. Coldstream Gds., w., m. 2. France — C.L.
1894 Edwards, G. O. C., 2nd Lt. W. Riding Regt. France (k. 7.7.16) — F.C.A.L.
1903 Edwards, H. L. G., Lt. R. Welch Fus. France (k. 16.5.15) — C.H.A.
1907 Edwards, R., Capt. Essex Yeomanry, att. Remount Service, w. France — R.P.L.B.
1911 Edwards, T. A. R., Capt. Sussex Yeomanry, and Staff, m. France, Egypt, Gallipoli, Palestine — P.W.
1892 Edwards-Heathcote, J. J., Lt. R.A.S.C., late 2nd Lt. Staffordshire Yeomanry. Balkans, Egypt — T.D.
1895 Edwards-Heathcote, J. S., Capt. Shropshire Yeomanry, att. R.F.A. France — H.E.L.

1901 Edwards-Moss, J., Lt. R.G.A.   C.L., T.C.P.

1897 Egerton, A. G. E., Lt.-Col. Coldstream Gds., w., m. France (k. 29.9.15)   A.C.B.

1906 Egerton, E. B., Capt. 17th Lancers. France (d.w. 1.9.16)   J H.M.H.

1913 Egerton, F., Capt. 17th Lancers, att. R.A.F., and Staff. France   P.W., F.E.R.

1893 Egerton, Hon. F. W. G., Maj. Duke of Lancaster's Own Yeomanry   W.D.

1889 Egerton, G. A., Maj. 9th Hussars. France (d.w. 13.5.15)   F.H.R.

1900 Egerton, J. S., Maj. Coldstream Gds., w., m. 2. France   A.C.B.

1899 Egerton, L. E. W., Capt. Buckinghamshire Yeomanry, att. R.A., and Staff. Egypt, France (k. 1.8.17)   A.C.B.

1912 Egerton, P. de M. W., Lt. 19th Hussars. France (k. 8.10.18)   H.F.W.T., A.E.C.

1897 Egerton, Hon. W. C. W., Lt.-Col. R.A.F.   W.D.

1914 Egerton-Green, C. S., Lt. K.R.R.C. France (k. 1.7.16)   H.M.

1910 Egerton-Green, J. W. E., Capt. Rifle Bde., and Staff. France (d.w. 9.10.17)   H.M.

1905 Egerton-Warburton, G., D.S.O., Capt. (t. Maj.) Cheshire Yeomanry, att. M.G.C. France, Egypt, Palestine   H.E.W.T.

1902 Egerton-Warburton, J., Capt. Scots Gds., att. R. Fusiliers. France (d.w. 30.8.15)   S.R.J., H.F.W.T.

1897 Eglinton and Winton, Earl of (Lord Montgomerie at Eton), Maj. Ayrshire Yeomanry, att. 2nd Life Gds., and Staff. France, Gallipoli   C.H.A.

1903 Elcho, Lord (Mr. Charteris at Eton), Capt. Gloucestershire Yeomanry, m. Egypt (k. 23.4.16)   F.I.

1916 Eley, W. A. D., 2nd Lt. K.R.R.C. France (k. 17.2.17)   E.I., T.F.C.

1900 Elgin and Kincardine, Earl of, C.M.G. (Lord Bruce at Eton), Lt.-Col. R.G.A., att. Labour Corps, and Staff, m. 2. France   H.E.L.

1892 Elkington, J. L. M., O.B.E., Capt. Censorship Dept., E. Africa, late Lt. Remount Service and Trooper E. African Mounted Rifles, m. E. Africa   T.D.

1891	Ellesmere, Earl of, M.V.O. (Lord Brackley at Eton), Bt. Col. R. Scots. France	W D.
1911	Ellicott, F. A. J., 2nd Lt. K.O.S.B. France (d.w. 9.7.16)	H.F.W.T., A.E.C.
1896	Elliot, F. B., O.B.E. (F) Capt. R. Berkshire Regt., w. France	K.S.
	Elliot, Hon. G. W. E., Lt. Scots Gds., late Lothians and Border Horse, and Staff. France (k. 6.8.17)	H.M.
1909	Elliot, H. W. A., Capt. Wiltshire Regt. Palestine	H.T.B.
1910	Elliot, R. B., Lt. A. and S. Highlanders	M.D.H.
1897	Elliott-Cooper, G. D'A., Maj. R. Fusiliers, w. France	J.P.C.
1900	Elliott-Cooper, M., Lt. R.E. France	J.P.C., R.P.L.B.
	V.C. Elliott-Cooper, N. B., D.S.O., M.C., Lt.-Col. R. Fusiliers, p., m. 4. France (d.w. 11.2.18)	H.M.
1911	Ellis, A. E. P., M.B.E., Capt. Rifle Bde., and Staff, w. France	L.S.R.B.
1900	Ellis, F. B., Capt. Northumberland Fusiliers. France (k. 25.9.16)	H.B.
1906	Ellison, C. T., O.B.E. (F) Maj. K.R.R.C., and Staff, w. France	A.C.B., A.M.G.
1873	Ellison, Sir G. F., K.C.M.G., C.B., Maj.-Gen. (R. Warwickshire Regt.), p., m. Egypt, Gallipoli	G.
1916	Ellison, P. J. M., Lt. Grenadier Gds., w. France	R.S. de H.
1884	Ellison, R. T., Maj. 2nd Life Gds.	C.H.E.
1874	Ellison, W. A., the late, M.V.O., V.D., Col. R. Berkshire Regt. (d. 1.11.17)	W.E., K.S.
	Elsmie, G. E. D. (F) Lt.-Col. Deccan Horse, I.A., m. France, India (k. 18.6.17)	K.S.
1914	Eltham, Earl of, Lt. 1st Life Gds., and Staff. France	A.A.S.
1893	Elveden, Visc., C.B., C.M.G. (Mr. Guinness at Eton), Capt. R.N.V.R.	P.H.C., C.H.A.
1892	Elwes, H. C., M.V.O., D.S.O., Maj. Scots Gds., empld. Lt.-Col. R. Irish Rifles, late Gloucestershire Yeomanry, m. 2. France, Egypt, Gallipoli	C.H.E.
1905	Elwes, R. H. A., Capt. R.A.S.C., M.T. France	H.M.

1884	Ennismore, Visc., Maj. R. Munster Fusiliers, and Staff. Egypt	G.E.M.
1913	Erle-Drax, J. C. W., Lt. Rifle Bde., w. France	A.A.S.
1883	Erskine, Lord (Mr. Erskine at Eton), Lt.-Cr. R.N.V.R.	H.E.L.
1913	Erskine, Lord J. F. A., Lt. Scots Gds., late A. and S. Highlanders, and Staff, m. France	C.M.W.
1916	Erskine, Hon. F. W., Lt. Scots Gds. France	C.M.W.
1877	Erskine, T. H., V.D., Lt.-Col. Fife and Forfar Yeomanry, and Staff. France	E.W.
1896	Erskine, Sir T. W. H. J., Bart., D.S.O., Maj. Cameron Highlanders, m. 3. France	F.T.
1911	Escombe, R. E. C., Lt. R.F.A., w. France	A.B.R.
1900	Essex, Earl of (Visc. Malden at Eton), Capt. Remount Service, m. France	A.C.B.
1896	Ethelston, H. W., Lt. Grenadier Gds. France (k. 13.3.15)	W.D.
1915	Eustace-Duckett, O. H., 2nd Lt. 16th Lancers	L.S.R.B.
1911	Evan-Thomas, H. A., Lt. Welsh Gds., w. France	A.M.G.
1891	Evans, E. F. H., Capt. Worcestershire Regt., w. France	H.B.
1899	Evans, G. C., Maj. R.A.S.C., M.T., and Staff, m. 2. Egypt, Mesopotamia	R.W.W.-T., H.B.
1889	Evans, G. P. E., Maj. Staff, m. France	H.D.
1903	Evans, J. J. P., M.C. and Bar, Capt. (t. Maj.) Welsh Gds., and Staff, m., w. 2. France	R.W.W.-T.
1898	V.C. Evans, L. P., C.M.G., D.S.O. and Bar (F) Brig.-Gen. (Black Watch), w., m. 3. France	H.W.M., R.W.W.-T.
1898	Evans, R. H., Capt. (t. Maj.) Shropshire Yeomanry, att. 12th Lancers. France	W.D.
1889	Evans-Freke, Hon. P. C., Lt.-Col. Leicestershire Yeomanry, m. France (k. 13.5.15)	J.L.V
1915	Evans-Freke, Hon. R., Lt. Rifle Bde., and Staff, w. 2, m. France	E.L.V., A.C.R.-W.
1883	Evans-Lombe, A. F., Maj. Staff	F.F.V., E.S.S.
1880	Evans-Lombe, E. H., Maj. Labour Corps	F.F.V.
1887	Evanson, E. F. C., Maj. Essex Regt.	F.W.C.

1892	Evelyn, J. H. C., Lt. A. and S. Highlanders, late Lt. Coldstream Gds., empld. Labour Corps, late Pte. R. Fusiliers. France	J.M.E.
1890	Everitt, A. F. G., Capt. R. Berkshire Regt. France	A.C.A.
1898	Ewing, I. A., Lt. Glasgow Yeomanry, empld. Maj. Remount Service. France	J.P.C.
1891	Exeter, Marquess of, C.M.G. (Mr. Cecil at Eton), Lt.-Col. R.F.A., and Staff, m. 2. France, Egypt, Palestine	W.D.
1909	Exmouth, Visc., Lt. R. Berkshire Regt., att. R.A.F. Egypt	H.B.
1901	Ezra, E., M.B.E., Lt. I.A. Staff, m. 4. Mesopotamia	H.F.W.T.
1914	Faber, C. V., 2nd Lt. K.R.R.C. France (k. 30.7.15)	J.H.M.H.
1913	Fairbairn, G. E., Lt. Durham L.I., late Pte. London Regt., w. France (k. 20.5.15)	H.Br.
1906	Fairbairn, S. G., M.C., Lt. Grenadier Gds., att. Buckinghamshire Yeomanry, w. France, Gallipoli	R.S.K.
1914	Fairbairn, S. I., Capt. R.H.G., w. France	K.S.
1910	Fairbank, C. A. H., M.C., Lt. R.F.A., w. 2, m. France, S. Russia	J.M.D., V.Le N.F.
1900	Fairbank, H. N., D.S.O., M.C., Maj. R.F.A., att. R.A.F., w. 2, m. 3. France	H.E.L.
1878	Fairtlough, C. E. G. M., the late, Maj. Oxfordshire and Bucks L.I. (d. 21.4.18)	R.A.H.M.
1895	Falconer, Lord (Mr. Keith-Falconer at Eton), Capt. Scots Gds.	A.C.A.
1898	Falkland, Master of (L. P. Cary), Bt. Maj. Grenadier Gds. France	E.C.A.L.
1905	Falmouth, Visc., D.S.O. (Mr. Boscawen at Eton), Capt. Coldstream Gds., att. R.A.F.	R.W.W.-T.
1900	Fane, H. N., Capt. Coldstream Gds., and Staff, w. France	C.L., H.T.B.
1886	Fane, W. V. R., Lt.-Col. Lincolnshire Regt.	A.C.J.
1886	Fane-Benett-Stanford, J. M. (Fane-Benett at Eton), Capt. 1st R. Dragoons, att. Wiltshire Regt. France	R.C.R.
1914	Fardell, H. G. H., Lt. E. Surrey Regt. France (k. 23.4.15)	R.S.de H.

1906	Farebrother, Rev. F. S., C.F. France	E.I.
1904	Farmer, C. G. E., Lt. K.R.R.C. France (k. 18.8.16)	A.A.S.
1912	Farmer, G. M. G., Lt. R.A.S.C., M.T., att. R.G.A., w., p. France	L.S.R.B.
1911	Farmer, H. C. M., 2nd Lt. K.R.R.C., late Trooper 3rd Dragoon Gds. France (k. 10.5.15)	A.B.R
1905	Farmer, H. G., Capt. Seaforth Highlanders. France (d.w., p., 12.11.15)	A.A.S
1913	Farquhar, E. H. G., L/ce-Cpl. Seaforth Highlanders, late 2nd Lt. Gordon Highlanders. France (k. 20.8.17)	A.A.S
1893	Farquhar, F. D., D.S.O., Lt.-Col. Coldstream Gds., Comm. Princess Patricia's Canadian L.I., m. 2. France (k. 20.3.15)	A.A.A
1875	Farquhar, F. J. W., O.B.E., Lt.-Col. Sp. List, m. 3. France, Italy	F.E.D.
1916	Farquhar, G. W. J., Lt. Coldstream Gds. France	A.A.S.
1912	Farquhar, H. L., M.C., Lt. (t. Capt.) Coldstream Gds., late Lt. 2nd Life Gds., att. Cav. Signals, w. France	H.M.
1889	Farquhar, J. E. M., Maj. Cameron Highlanders, late Pte. R. Fusiliers, w. France (k. 15.9.16)	J.M F.
1914	Farquhar, R., M.C., Lt. Grenadier Gds., m. France (d.w. 17.9.17)	H.M
1896	Farquhar, Sir W. R. F., Bart., Capt. R.F.A., late Capt. R.A.S.C., and Staff, m. France, Egypt, Gallipoli (k. 14.10.18)	A.A.A
1885	Farquharson, A. H., Lt.-Col. Gordon Highlanders, att. Labour Corps. France	G.E.M.
1901	Farrer, H. M., Capt. Staff, late Lt. R.N.V.R. and Drake Bn., R.N.D., m. France, Egypt, Gallipoli	S.R.J., R.W.W.-T.
1912	Farrer, J. O., M.C., Capt. Shropshire L.I., and Staff, w., m. France	E.I.
1906	Farrer, S. J., Lt. R. Sussex Regt., att. T.M.B., m. France	E.L.V.
1905	Farwell, A. W., Capt. S. Staffordshire Regt., att. R.F.C. and Manchester Regt. France	E.L.V.
1887	Faudel-Phillips, B. S., Lt. R.N.V.R. France	E.H.

1900	Faudel-Phillips, H. F. (F) Maj. 5th Lancers, and Staff. France, Balkans, Egypt	H.D., H.M.
1893	Faudel-Phillips, L. L. F., Lt. R. Defence Corps	P.H.C., A.C.B.
1886	Faunce-De Laune, A., Capt. R. E. Kent Yeomanry	E.L.V.
1891	Faunce-De Laune, E., Maj. R. E. Kent Yeomanry, att. R.F.A. France	E.L.V.
1889	Fawkes, F. H., Maj. Yorkshire Hussars	F.H.R.
1898	Fearon, P. J., D.S.O. (F) Lt.-Col. The Queen's, and Staff, w., m. 2. France, Egypt, Palestine	E.C.A.L.
1885	Feilden, J. H. G., Maj. K.R.R.C., att. Border Regt.	H.D.
1887	Feilden, P. H. G., Maj. K.R.R.C. France	J.H.M.
1900	Fellowes, Hon. C. C., Capt. 1st Life Gds. France (d. 22.10.15)	R.A. H.M.
1904	Fellowes, R. T., D.S.O., M.C., Bt. Maj. Rifle Bde., and Staff, w., m. 5. France	S.A.D.
1903	Fenn, A. A., D.S.O., Maj. (t. Lt.-Col.) R. Fusiliers, att. Intell. Corps, and Staff, m. 4. France	J.M.E.
1905	Fenwick, C. B., Capt. Northern Cyclist Bn., att. London Regt. and Cheshire Regt., w. France	H.M.
1888	Fenwick, G., Lt.-Col. R.F.A. France	E.H., R.C.R.
1882	Fenwick, H. T., C.M.G., M.V.O., D.S.O., Col. Middlesex Regt., w., m. France	E.C.A.L.
1894	Fenwick, L., Capt. Northumberland Yeomanry, m. France	E.H., R.W.W.-T.
1902	Fenwick-Owen, G., M.C. (Fenwick at Eton), Capt. Norfolk Yeomanry, w. 2. Egypt, Gallipoli	F.H.R.
1895	Ferguson, A. F. H. (F) Brig.-Gen. (2nd Life Gds.), w. 2. France	C.H.E.
1880	Ferguson, A. G., Lt.-Col. Rifle Bde., m. 2. France	R.A.H.M.
1867	Ferguson, H. S., Capt. London Regt.	J.W.H.
1916	Ferguson, V. J., Lt. 2nd Life Gds. France (k. 21.8.18)	A.B.R.
1882	Fergusson, Sir C., Bart., K.C.B., K.C.M.G., M.V.O., D.S.O. (F) Lieut.-Gen. (Grenadier Gds.), m. 7. France	J.M.E.
1911	Fergusson, D. H. L., Lt. Cameron Highlanders, w. France (d.w. 2.2.16)	F.H.R., H.de H.

1903	Fergusson, N. H., Capt. R. Defence Corps, late Sub-Lt. R.N.V.R.	F.H.R.
1901	Fergusson, N. M., Lt. Scots Gds. France	F.H.R.
1898	Fergusson, R. D., Lt. H.L.I., late Pte. R. Scots Fusiliers	H.W.M., H.F.W.T.
1899	Fermor-Hesketh, T., Capt. (t. Maj.) Lancashire Hussars	A.C.A.
1896	Feversham, Earl of (Visc. Helmsley at Eton), Lt.-Col. K.R.R.C., late Lt.-Col. Yorkshire Hussars, m. France (k. 15.9.16)	W.D
1898	ffrench Blake, A. O'B., T.D., Lt.-Col. R. E. Kent Yeomanry, att. Essex Regt. Egypt, Gallipoli, Palestine	S.A.D.
1911	Field, M., Capt. F.A., American Exp. Force. France	R.P.L.B.
1896	Field, N., Lt. E. Riding of Yorkshire Yeomanry, att. R.F.A. France	E.L.V.
1914	Field, R. G., Lt. 10th R. Hussars, late W. Kent Yeomanry. France (k. 5.4.18)	R.P.L.B.
1909	Fielden, A. N., Lt. R.N.V.R. Home Waters, Atlantic, Mediterranean	R.S.K.
1905	Fielden, C. M., Lt., late Cpl., E. African Mounted Rifles. E. Africa	E.C.A.L., E.W.S.
1904	Fielden, E. A., M.C., Capt. 10th R. Hussars, and Staff, w., m. France	R.S.K.
1910	Fielden, G., Lt. 7th Hussars, att. R.A.F. Mesopotamia	R.S.K.
1898	Fielden, J., Capt. Res. Regt. of Cav., att. R. Scots Greys. France	E.C.A.L.
1914	Fielden, L., Lt. R.G.A. Egypt, Gallipoli, Palestine	M.D.H.
1913	Fiennes, J. E., Capt. Gordon Highlanders, w. France (d.w. 18.6.17)	M.D.H.
1903	Fildes, G. P. A., Lt. Coldstream Gds., late Pte. and Lt. London Regt. France	E.C.A.L.
1896	Filmer, Sir R. M., Bart., M.C., Capt. Grenadier Gds. France (d.w. 27.1.16)	E.H., A.C.B
1906	Finch-Hatton, Hon. D. G., M.C., Lt. Loyal N. Lancashire Regt., late Somali Scouts, and Staff. E. Africa, Egypt, Mesopotamia	H.F.W.T.

1895	Findlay, S., Maj. (t. Lt.-Col.) Remount Service, m. France	A.C.B.
1915	Findlay, V. A. C., Lt. R.F.A., and Staff. Afghanistan, Egypt, Palestine	K.S.
1899	Findlay, W., Capt. R.A.O.C., and Staff	A.C.B.
1903	Finlay, D., D.S.O. (F) Maj. att. New Zealand E.F., and Egyptian Desert Column, Staff, late Capt. R.A.S.C. France, Egypt, Italy, Palestine	R.A.H.M., L.S.R.B.
1910	Finlay, E. L., 2nd Lt. Devonshire Regt., late London Regt. Mesopotamia (d.w. 20.3.16)	K.S.
1905	Finlay, E. N. A., 2nd Lt. Rifle Bde. France (k. 4.7.16)	K.S.
1894	Finlay, I. A., Capt. (t. Maj.) N. Irish Horse, att. R. Scots Greys, and Staff, w. France	S.A.D.
1897	Firth, R. C. D., Lt. S. Lancashire Regt. (d. 21.12.14)	F.T., T.C.P.
1898	Fisher-Rowe, C. V., M.C. (F) Capt. Grenadier Gds., and Staff, w. 3, m. 3. France	J.M.E.
1899	Fisher-Rowe, H. M., C.B.E., Lt.-Col. Surrey Yeomanry	G.E.M., P.H.C.
1900	Fisher-Rowe, L. G., M.C., Lt. (t. Capt.) Grenadier Gds. France	J.M.E.
1885	Fisher-Rowe, L. R., Lt.-Col. Grenadier Gds., m. France (d.w. 13.3.15)	G.E.M.
1909	Fison, W. G., M.C., Capt. R.F.A., and Staff, m. France, Balkans, Palestine	R.S. de H.
1883	Fitton, H. G., C.B., D.S.O., Brig.-Gen. (R. Warwickshire Regt.). France (d.w. 20.1.16)	K.S.
1879	V.C. FitzClarence, C., Brig.-Gen. (Irish Gds.), m. 2. France (k. 12.11.14)	J.C.
1915	FitzClarence, E. C., 2nd Lt. Irish Gds., late Pte. Oxfordshire and Bucks L.I.	C.M.W.
1907	FitzGerald, Lord D., M.C., Maj. Irish Gds., m. France (k. accid. 3.3.16)	H.T.B.
1910	FitzGerald, D., Capt. Remount Service. France	A.A.S.
1909	FitzGerald, Lord E., Lt. W. Riding Regt., w. France	H.T.B.
1874	FitzGerald, Lord F., Lt.-Col. K.R.R.C., and Staff	T.D.

1903 FitzGerald, G. H., Capt. 4th Dragoon Gds. France
(k. 13.9.14) I.C.A.L.
1902 FitzGerald, G. M., Capt. Sharpshooters, att. M.G.C., w.
France, Balkans, Egypt, Gallipoli, Palestine S.R.J., R.W.W.-T.
1881 FitzGerald, Lord H., Capt. Sp. List T.D.
1911 FitzGerald, J. S. N., M.B.E., M.C., Capt. Irish Gds., m.
France H.F.W.T., A.E.C.
1886 FitzRoy, Hon. E. A., M.P., Capt. 1st Life Gds., w. France A.C.J.
1889 Fitzwilliam, Earl, K.C.V.O., C.B.E., D.S.O. (Visc. Milton
at Eton), Lt.-Col. Oxfordshire and Bucks L.I., and
Staff, m. France W.D.
1902 FitzWygram, Sir F. L. F., Bart., the late, M.C., Capt.
Scots Gds., w. 2, p., m. France (d. 5.5.20) R.W.W.-T.
1890 Fleetwood-Hesketh, C. H. (Bibby at Eton), Maj. Duke
of Lancaster's Own Yeomanry, and Staff. France F.H.R.
1906 Fleming, G. B. Mac I., Lt. A. and S. Highlanders, att.
2nd Lt. Seaforth Highlanders. France R.C.R.
1908 Fleming, P., Maj. Oxfordshire Yeomanry. France R.S.K.
1900 Fleming, V., M.P., D.S.O., Maj. Oxfordshire Yeomanry, m. 2. France (k. 20.5.17) H.D., A.C.G.H.
1891 Fletcher, A. F., M.V.O., D.S.O. (F) Lt.-Col. 17th
Lancers, and Staff, m. 2. France W.D.
1896 Fletcher, A. M. T., Capt. R.A.S.C. P.W.
1903 Fletcher, B. L., Capt. Scots Gds., late Maj. Hawke Bn.,
R.N.D. France T.C.P.
1894 Fletcher, Sir E. L., Cr. R.N.R. France H.G.W., F.W.C., E.H.
1896 Fletcher, G. L., Lt.-Col. The King's (Liverpool Regt.) F.T., T.C.P.
1902 Fletcher, G. W.P., M.C., Lt. Coldstream Gds. France T.C.P.
1908 Fletcher, H. M., Capt. Lancashire Hussars, and Staff.
France E.C.A.L., E.W.S.
1908 Fletcher, H. W., Lt. R. Welch Fusiliers, late Pte.
Benbow Bn., R.N.D., and Staff. Egypt, Gallipoli,
Palestine (d.w. 26.3.17) K.S.
1910 Fletcher, R. W., 2nd Lt. R.F.A. France (k. 31.10.14) K.S.
1888 Fletcher, W. A. L., D.S.O. (F) Lt.-Col. The King's
(Liverpool Regt.), w. 2, m. 2. France (d. 14.2.19) E.W., H.G.W.

1906	Fletcher, W. G., 2nd Lt. Intell. Corps, att. R. Welch Fusiliers, m. 2. France (k. 20.3.15)	K.S.
1901	Flint, E. C. M., D.S.O., Capt. Suffolk Yeomanry, att. M.G. Cav., m. Egypt, Gallipoli, Palestine	R.A.H.M.
1868	Flint, E. M., Brig.-Gen. (R.A.). France	G.
1916	Floyd, Sir H. R. K., Bart., Lt. 15th Hussars. France	H.M.
1915	Foley, Lord (Foley at Eton), Lt. R.A.F.	F.E.R.
1887	Foley, C. P., Lt.-Col. E. Lancs. Regt., m. 2. France, Balkans	A.C.J.
1908	Foley, T. A. F., Lt. Norfolk Regt. France (k. 25.10.14)	F.H.R., H.de H.
1909	Foljambe, E. W. S., Capt. Rifle Bde., and Staff, w., p. France	A.C.B., A.M.G.
1875	Foljambe, G. S., C.B., V.D., Lt.-Col. Sherwood Foresters	E.W.
1896	Foljambe, Hon. G. W. F. S., D.S.O., Maj. (t. Lt.-Col.) Oxfordshire and Bucks L.I. France	S.A.D.
1891	Foljambe, H. F. F. B., Maj. K.R.R.C. France (k. 14.9.14)	S.A.D.
1900	Foljambe, Hon. J. C. W. S., Bt. Maj. Oxfordshire and Bucks L.I., m. 3. Mesopotamia (k. 6.4.16)	S.A.D.
1897	Follett, G. B. S., M.V.O., D.S.O. (F) Brig.-Gen. (Coldstream Gds.), w. 3, m. 4. France (k. 27.9.18)	R.C.R.
1899	Follett, R. S., D.S.O., Lt.-Col. Rifle Bde., and Staff, m. 3. France	E.L.V.
1896	Forbes, B. C., Lt. (t. Maj.) Coke's Rifles, I.A. N.W. Frontier, India	K.S.
1914	Forbes, J., Midshipman R.N.R.	J.H.M.H.
1890	Forbes, J. S., Capt. (t. Maj.) Res. Regt. of Cav.	W.D.
1882	Forbes, Hon. W. R. D., Capt. Staff	F.F.V.
1908	Forbes-Adam, C. G., Lt. I.A., and Staff. Mesopotamia, Palestine	K.S.
1902	Forbes-Adam, R., D.S.O., O.B.E., Maj. R.F.A., m. 3. France, Italy	R.A.H.M., L.S.R.B.
1891	Forbes-Gordon, A. D., Maj. Cameron Highlanders	J.P.C., S.R.J.
1876	Ford, R., Capt. Rifle Bde.	E.P.R.
1917	Forde, T. W., 2nd Lt. Coldstream Gds.	L.S.R.B.
1915	Fordham, R. G., 2nd Lt. R.F.C. France	E.I., T.F.C.
1917	Forrest, W. R. H., 2nd Lt. Scots Gds. France	H.M.

1899	Forster, A. P., Capt. (t. Maj.) K.R.R.C., att. M.G.C., w., m. 2. France (d. 25.9.18)	A.C.A.
1898	Forster, F. A., Capt. R. Fusiliers. France (k. 23.8.14)	A.C.A.
1895	Forster, H. C., Capt. R. Fusiliers, m. 2. France (k. 25.5.15)	F.T.
1908	Forster, J., 2nd Lt. K.R.R.C. France (k. 14.9.14)	A.A.S.
1895	Forster, L. A., Capt. Cheshire Regt. France (d.w. 4.11.14)	F.T.
1901	Forsyth-Forrest, T. R., Capt. K.R.R.C., empld. Lt.-Col. K.O.Y.L.I., m. France	A.C.A.
1885	Forte, H. A. N., D.S.O., Capt. E. Yorkshire Regt. France	H.W.M.
1891	Forte, P. L., Capt. R. Defence Corps	H.W.M.
1911	Fortescue, Hon. D. G., Capt. R. N. Devon Yeomanry, and Staff. France, Egypt, Gallipoli	A.M.G.
1909	Fortescue, G. G., Lt., late A.B., R.N.V.R.	A.B.R.
1876	Fortescue, H. (F) Bt. Col. Staff. France, Italy	E.W.
1915	Fortescue, J. G., Lt. Coldstream Gds., w. France	A.B.R.
1889	Foster, A., Lt.-Cr. R.N.R. Home Waters	H.B.
1909	Foster, A. C., 2nd Lt. Grenadier Gds., late Pte. R. Fusiliers. France (d.w. 12.3.15)	F.H.R., H.de H.
1902	Foster, A. W., M.C. (F) Maj. R.H.G., and Staff, w., m. France	A.C.J., H.Br.
1914	Foster, C. F., Lt. 9th Lancers. France (k. 27.3.18)	A.C.G.H.
1911	Foster, C. G., Lt. 13th Hussars, late Lt. (t. Capt.) Yorkshire Hussars, att. W. Yorkshire Regt., m. France	P.W.
1903	Foster, C. W., Capt. R.M.A., late R.M.L.I. France	F.H.R.
1897	Foster, E. B. G., Maj. Berks Yeomanry, att. Tank Corps and Cameronians (Scottish Rifles). France, Egypt, Gallipoli	S.A.D.
1904	Foster, G. R., Lt. 13th Hussars, late Lt. (t. Capt.) Yorkshire Hussars. India	R.S.K.
1900	Foster, J. B., Maj. Yorkshire Dragoons. France	H.W.M., H.F.W.T.
1909	Foster, P. W. W., Capt. 1st Life Gds. France	A.C.G.H.
1914	Foster, R. A. C., Lt. Rifle Bde., w. France	A.C.G.H.
1899	Foster, T. B. G., Capt. (t. Maj.) Cameronians (Scottish Rifles), att. Tank Corps, R. Scots Fusiliers, and Staff, m. France, Egypt	S.A.D.

1911	Foster, W. E., Capt. R.F.C., p. Mediterranean	P.W.
1884	Fothergill, S. R., T.D., Lt.-Col. Westmorland and Cumberland Yeomanry, and Staff. France	A.C.J.
1884	Foulkes, G. F. F., Maj. Labour Corps, late Maj. R. Scots, K.O.S.B., and London Regt. France	H.D.
1886	Foulkes, T. H., C.I.E., Lt.-Col. Indian Medical Service, and Staff, m. 2. Aden, India	H.D.
1916	Fowler, A. G. H., M.C., Lt. (t. Capt.) Coldstream Gds., w. France	E.L.C.
1914	Fowler, G. G., Lt. K.R.R.C. France (d.w. 26.9.15)	C.M.W.
1910	Fowler, J. D., Lt. 5th Lancers. France (k. 30.11.14)	R.S.K.
1910	Fowler, R. St. L., M.C., Capt. 17th Lancers. France	R.W.W.-T., C.M.W.
1896	Fox, J. St. V., Maj. Lincolnshire Regt. France	E.I.
1887	Foxcroft, C. T., M.P., Capt. Somerset L.I. India	E.C.A.L.
1891	France-Hayhurst, F. C., Lt.-Col. R. Welch Fusiliers. France (k. 9.5.15)	A.C.J.
1889	France-Hayhurst, W. H., Capt. Yorkshire Dragoons	A.C.J.
1913	Franchetti, Baron C., M.C. (F) Lt. Alpini, late Pte. Ciclisti, att. Aeroplani, Italian Army. Italy	A.C.G.H.
1910	Franchetti, Baron L., Lt. Italian Army. Italy	A.C.G.H.
1900	Francis, B. A., Lt.-Cr. R.N. Home Waters, Aden, E. Africa, Red Sea	E.I.
1901	Francis, H. D. P., M.C., Capt. E. Riding of Yorkshire Yeomanry, m. France, Egypt, Palestine	H.B.
1906	Francis, N. C. F., Lt. R.A.F., and Staff, late R.F.A. France	A.A.S.
1898	Frank, N. G., T.D., Maj. Manchester Regt., att. Norfolk Regt. France	A.C.J.
1901	Frankau, G. N., Capt. R.F.A., late Lt. E. Surrey Regt., and Staff. France, Italy	H.M.
1910	Frankau, R. H. W., 2nd Lt. Cyclist Corps, att. R.F.A., and Staff. France, Mesopotamia	J.M.D.
1915	Fraser, D. A. D., Lt. Gordon Highlanders, w. France, Italy	V.Le N.F.

1915	Fraser, H. A. H., Lt. 21st Lancers, late 2nd Lt. R. N. Devon Yeomanry. India	H. Br.
1884	Fraser, Sir K. A., Bart., Maj. Res. Regt. of Cav.	J. M. E.
1908	Fraser, M. H., the late, Capt. Seaforth Highlanders, att. King's African Rifles. E. Africa (d. 28.6.19)	H. Br.
1886	Fraser, W. A. C., Maj. Dorsetshire Regt., m. France, Mesopotamia (d. 14.6.15)	F. T.
1911	Fraser-Mackenzie, E. R. L., D.S.O., M.C., Capt. R.F.A., w., m. France, Egypt, Palestine	H. T. B., S. G. L.
1909	Fraser-Mackenzie, J. O. A., Lt., late Pte., E. African F.F., late 2nd Lt. Lovat's Scouts, m. E. Africa	H. T. B.
1916	Fraser-Mackenzie, R. A. L., 2nd Lt. Seaforth Highlanders, w., p. France	S. G. L.
1871	Fraser-Mackenzie, R. S. (Fraser at Eton), Capt. Cameron Highlanders	F. E. D.
1872	Fraser-Tytler, E. G., the late, Lt.-Col. Lovat's Scouts. (d. 12.3.18)	W. E.
1907	Fraser-Tytler, N., D.S.O. and Bar (F) Maj. R.F.A., and Staff, m. 3. France	H. T. B.
1877	Fraser-Tytler, W. T., Maj. Lovat's Scouts	W. E.
1894	Frederick, Sir C. E. St. J., Bart., O.B.E., Capt. Northamptonshire Yeomanry, and Staff, m. France	T. D.
1896	Frederick, E. B., Maj. R. Fusiliers, and Staff, w. France	T. D., J. H. M. H.
1895	Freeman, G. H. H., Capt. 1st Life Gds., empld. Maj. K.R.R.C., and Staff. France	T. D., A. A. S.
1910	Freeman, P. A. M., Lt. R.F.A.	R. P. L. B.
1912	Freeman-Thomas, Hon. G. F., 2nd Lt. Coldstream Gds. France (k. 14.9.14)	A. A. S.
1915	Freeman-Thomas, Hon. I. B., Lt. Skinner's Horse F.A.	A. A. S.
1905	Freer, G. H., 12th Lancers. France	A. C. G. H.
1907	Freer, R. C., M.C., Capt. R.F.A., w., m. France	A. C. G. H.
1899	Fremantle, A. E. A., Lt. R.N.V.R., and Staff. Balkans	K. S.
1896	Fremantle, A. F., Lt. (t. Capt.) 28th Light Cavalry, att. Khyber Rifles, I.A. N.W. Frontier, India	K. S.

1890	Fremantle, F. E., O.B.E., Lt.-Col. R.A.M.C., and Staff, m. 2. Egypt, Gallipoli, Mesopotamia	K.S.
1895	Fremantle, J. M., M.B.E., Maj. Sharpshooters, late att. Nigerian E.F. W. Africa	K.S.
1914	Fremantle, T. F. H., 2nd Lt. Oxfordshire and Bucks L.I. France (d.w. 17.10.15)	A.E.C.
1887	Fremantle, Hon. W., Capt. Oxfordshire and Bucks L.I., and Staff. France	J.M.E.
1899	French-Brewster, A. O., Capt. (t. Maj.) Tank Corps, late K.R.R.C., w. France	T.C.P.
1895	French-Brewster, R. A., Maj. Irish Gds. (d. 17.2.17)	F H.R.
1871	Frere, Sir B. C. A., Bart., D.S.O., Maj. Sp. List. France, Egypt	F.F.V.
1914	Frere, B. L. S., Lt. Bedfordshire Regt., m. France (k. 13.11.16)	R.S.K.
1900	Frere, E., 2nd Lt. London Regt., late Pte. R. Fusiliers. France (d.w. 22.5.16)	E.L.V.
1914	Frere, J. G., Capt. Norfolk Yeomanry, att. Norfolk Regt. Egypt, Gallipoli, Palestine	R.S.de H.
1902	Frewen, H. M., Lt. R.N.V.R., att. Benbow and Anson Bns., R.N.D., and Staff, w. France, Egypt, Gallipoli, Home Waters, Mediterranean	T.C.P.
1902	Frewen, O. M., Lt.-Cr. R.N. Home Waters, W. Africa	J.M.E.
1907	Fryer, E. R. M., M.C. and Bar, Lt. Grenadier Gds., late Pte. H.A.C., w. France	R.C.R.
1892	Fuller, Rev. A. R., C.F., m. Egypt, Gallipoli	J.C., F.D., E.I.
1905	Fuller, H. J. (F) Lt. Intell. Corps, and Staff, m. France	S.A.D., P.V.B.
1911	Fullerton, J. R. R., Lt. (t. Capt.) 19th Hussars. France	A.B.R.
1906	Furse, R. D., D.S.O. and Bar, Maj. King Edward's Horse, w., m. 2. France, Italy	H.E.L., H.T.B.
1880	Furse, Sir W. T., K.C.B., D.S.O. (F) Lieut.-Gen. (R.A.), Master-General of the Ordnance, m. 3. France	F.F.V.
1916	Fyers, F. R. H., Lt. Rifle Bde. France	E.L.C.

1878	Fyers, H. A. N., M.V.O., Maj. Rifle Bde., and Staff. France, Balkans, Egypt	R.A.H.M.
1907	Gaddum, W. F., Capt. Westmorland and Cumberland Yeomanry, att. Border Regt., w. France	H.B.
1914	Gage, Visc., Lt. Coldstream Gds., w. France	H.T.B., S.G.L.
1890	Gallup, H. C., Lt. R.F.A., p. Mesopotamia	F.W.C.
1877	Galsworthy, A. J., Maj. Somerset L.I. France	J.E.Y., C.C.J.
1907	Gambier-Parry, M. D., M.C., Bt. Maj. R. Welch Fusiliers, and Staff, m. 6. Egypt, Gallipoli, Mesopotamia	E.L.V.
1907	Gambier-Parry, R., Lt. R. Welch Fusiliers, att. Intell. Corps, R.A.F., and Staff, w. 2, m. France	E.L.V.
1901	Gambier-Parry, T. M., Pte., R.A.S.C.	J.M.E.
1916	Gamble, R. D., M.C., Lt. Coldstream Gds., and Staff. France (k. 22.8.18)	K.S
1902	Gardner, C. E., Capt. Gloucestershire Regt., empld. Maj. Lancashire Fusiliers, m. France, Balkans, Siberia	T.C.P., R.S.K.
1893	Gardner, H. C., Capt. (t. Maj.) Staffordshire Yeomanry	F.T.
1902	Garle, H. A., Lt. R.F.A. Mesopotamia	J.M.D.
1909	Garle, J. A. B., Capt. H.A.C., late Capt. W. Kent Yeomanry, att. The Buffs, w. Egypt, Gallipoli, Palestine	H.B.
1911	Garnett-Botfield, A. C. F., Lt. S. Wales Borderers, late 2nd Lt. Rifle Bde. France (k. 9.5.15)	J.L.C.
1900	Garnett-Botfield, W. McL., Lt. R.A.S.C., M.T.	A.A.S.
1886	Garnett-Orme, G. H., Capt. W. Riding Regt., and Staff	H.S.S.S., F.D.
1886	Garrard, C. F., Capt. 11th Hussars, att. R.N.A.S. France, Gallipoli	E.H.
1885	Garratt, L. C., O.B.E., Maj. (t. Lt.-Col.) Coldstream Gds.	R.A.H.M.
1911	Garstin, C. W. N., 2nd Lt. 9th Lancers. France (k. 24.8.14)	R S K
1898	Garth, H., L/ce-Cpl. R. Fusiliers, att. The Queen's Own (R. W. Kent Regt.). France (k. 27.9.16)	C L
1908	Garton, A. S., Lt. R.N.V.R. France, Balkans, Egypt, Mediterranean	E.L.V.

1904	Garton, C. L., Capt. Sp. List	E.L.V.
	Garton, E. C., 2nd Lt. Rifle Bde., w. France (d.w. 2.9.18)	H. Br.
	Garton, H. W., Capt. Rifle Bde., w. France (k. 15.9.16)	E.L.V.
1909	Garton, J. A., M.C., Capt. (t. Maj.) N. Somerset Yeomanry, w., m. France	A.B.R.
1911	Gartside-Tippinge, F., Lt. R.F.C. France (k. 6.11.17)	H.B.
1910	Gascoigne, A. D. F., Capt. Coldstream Gds., late 2nd Lt. 6th (Inniskilling) Dragoons, w., m. France	A.A.S.
1894	Gascoigne, C. C. H. O., D.S.O., Lt.-Col. Seaforth Highlanders, w., m. 3. France	A.C.J.
1886	Gascoigne, C. C. O., Capt. Seaforth Highlanders, w. France	A.C.J.
1889	Gascoigne, E. F. O., C.M.G., D.S.O. (F) Brig.-Gen. (Grenadier Gds.), m. 3. Egypt, Gallipoli, Palestine	A.C.J.
1912	Gaskell, F. R., Lt. 10th R. Hussars, w. France	H.T.B., S.G.L.
1904	Gatehouse, L. R. A., Capt. The King's (Liverpool Regt.), and Staff, w. France	J.H.M.H.
1898	Gathorne-Hardy, A. C., Capt. Cameronians (Scottish Rifles). France (k. 25.9.15)	W.D.
1896	Gathorne-Hardy, G. M., M.C. (F) Capt. R. Berkshire Regt., and Staff, w., m. France	W.D.
1891	Gathorne-Hardy, Hon. J. F., C.B., C.M.G., D.S.O. (F) Maj.-Gen. (Grenadier Gds.), m. 10. France, Italy	G.E.M., P.H.C.
1917	Gault, L. H., 2nd Lt. Grenadier Gds.	F.E.R.
1917	Gaussen, A. R. L., Midshipman R.N.V.R. Home Waters	E.L.C.
1875	Geary, Sir W. N. M., Bart., Maj. R. Warwickshire Regt., late Manchester Regt., and Staff. Mesopotamia	E.C.A.L.
1895	Gedge, C. B., 2nd Lt., late Pte., London Regt., w. (k. 25.9.15)	F.F.V., H.D.
1911	Gelderd-Somervell, R. C., Capt. K.R.R.C., att. R.A.F., w. France	K.S.
1904	Gelderd-Somervell, R. F. C., 2nd Lt. Grenadier Gds., att. Interpreter, I.A. France (k. 11.3.15)	K.S.
1916	Gell, P. V. W., Lt. R.F.A. France	H. Br.

1908	George, J. K., M.C. and Bar, Lt. Gloucestershire Regt., late Pte. R. Fusiliers, w. 2. France	R.S.K.
1914	George, R. A. K., Lt. Gloucestershire Regt., att. T.M.B., w. France, Balkans	R.S.K.
1903	George, S. C. K., Lt. Grenadier Gds., and Staff. France	H.E.L., R.S.K.
1898	George, W. K., Capt. Gloucestershire Regt. France (k. 25.1.15)	H.E.L.
1911	Gerard, C. R. T. M., D.S.O., Capt. Grenadier Gds., m. 2. France	A.A.S.
1884	Gerrard, T. G. (Collins at Eton), Maj. Res. Regt. of Cav.	H.E.L.
1898	Gibbon, E. L. L., Lt. R.F.A. France	A.C.A.
1897	Gibbon, J. H., D.S.O., Bt. Lt.-Col. R.F.A., and Staff, w., m. 4. France, Egypt, Gallipoli	A.C.A.
1911	Gibbons, G. S., 2nd Lt. R. Fusiliers, late Pte. Middlesex Regt., w. France	H. Br.
1913	Gibbs, A., M.C., Lt. Welsh Gds., w. France	E.W.S.
1892	Gibbs, A. H., Maj. N. Somerset Yeomanry. France	J.M.E.
1911	Gibbs, B. N., Lt. (t. Capt.) Welsh Gds., late Lt. 2nd Life Gds., w. France	E.W.S.
1903	Gibbs, E. L., Capt. N. Somerset Yeomanry, m. France (k. 11.2.15)	J.M.E.
1904	Gibbs, Rev. F. A. W., M.C. and Bar, C.F., w. 2. France, N. Russia	J.M.E.
1892	Gibbs, G. A., M.P., T.D., Lt.-Col. N. Somerset Yeomanry	J.M.E.
1908	Gibbs, G. M., Capt. N. Somerset Yeomanry, and Staff. France	J.M.E., M.D.H.
1897	Gibbs, J. E., M.C., Maj. Coldstream Gds., p. France	J.M.E.
1912	Gibbs, L. C., Lt. N. Somerset Yeomanry, and Staff, w., m. France	J.M.E., M.D.H.
1908	Gibbs, L. M., D.S.O., M.C. and Bar, Capt. Coldstream Gds., and Staff, w., m. 4. France	J.M.E., M.D.H.
1899	Gibbs, N. M., Trooper E. African Mounted Rifles, Nairobi F.F. E. Africa (k. 20.3.16)	J.M.E.

1909 Gibbs, R. C. B., Capt. N. Somerset Yeomanry, att. 7th
    Dragoon Gds., and Staff, w., m. France   J.M.E., M.D.H.
 ... Gibbs, R. C. M., 2nd Lt. Scots Gds. France (k. 28.10.14)   P.V.B.
1896 Gibbs, W. (F) Maj. 7th Hussars, and Staff, w., m. 2.
    France, Egypt, Gallipoli, Mesopotamia   J.M.E.
1907 Gibbs, W. D., Capt. Herts Yeomanry, m. 2. Egypt,
    Gallipoli, Mesopotamia, Palestine, S. Russia P.V.B.
1901 Gibbs, W. O., Maj. (t. Lt.-Col.) 10th R. Hussars, att.
    Tank Corps, w. 4, m. France   J.M.E.
1903 Giberne, H. B., Capt. R.A.S.C. France   H.E.L., L.S.R.B.
1899 Gibson, H. M., Capt. Westmorland and Cumberland
    Yeomanry, att. Lincolnshire Regt., and Staff.
    France   H.W.M., H.F.W.T.
1897 Gibson, Rev. J. A., Pte. R.A.M.C. France   H.W.M.
1907 Gibson, K. L., Lt. Carabiniers, and Staff, m. France   A.A.S.
1915 Gibson, M. H., Lt. R.F.A., w. France   M.D.H.
1892 Gibson-Watt, J. M., Maj. S. Wales Borderers. France   C.H.E.
1912 Gielgud, L. E., M.B.E. (F) Capt. Shropshire L.I., and
    Staff, w. France   K.S.
1904 Gilbey, A. R., Lt. 1st Life Gds., Capt. Oxfordshire and
    Bucks L.I. France   A.A.S.
1908 Gilbey, G. H., M.C., Capt. Rifle Bde., and Staff, w.,
    m. 2. France   A.A.S.
1904 Gilbey, W. H., Lt., late Trooper, Queensland L.H.,
    Australian Imp. Forces. France, Egypt, Gallipoli   A.A.S.
1910 Giles, G. C. T., Capt. W. Lancashire Divl. Cyclist Coy.,
    late att. The King's (Liverpool Regt.)   K.S.
1890 Gillett, F. W. H. A., Maj. Pembroke Yeomanry, and
    Staff   A.C.J.
1886 Gilliat, J. B., D.S.O., T.D., Lt.-Col. Herts Yeomanry   J.P.C.
1899 Gilliat, O. C. S., Capt. Rifle Bde. France (k. 30.10.14)   F.I.
1915 Gillies, H. G., 2nd Lt. R. Scots Fusiliers. France (k. 13.11.16)   K.S.
1896 Gillilan, E. G., D.S.O., Capt. Coldstream Gds., Maj.,
    att. Westminster Dragoons, w., m. France, Egypt,
    Gallipoli   J.P.C.

1906	Gillilan, H. P., Capt. King's African Rifles, late Trooper E. African Mounted Rifles, Nairobi F.F., m. E. Africa	H.M.
1911	Gilmour, C. D., M.C., Capt. Black Watch, and Staff, w. 2, m. France, Mesopotamia	E.W.S.
1905	Gladstone, A. C., M.B.E., Lt. I.A.R., empld. Capt. Gurkha Rifles, m. 3. Egypt, Gallipoli, Mesopotamia	H.M.
1907	Gladstone, C. A., Lt. Intell. Corps, att. R.F.C., p. France	H.M.
1896	Gladstone, H. S., Capt. K.O.S.B., and Staff	C.H.A., J.M.E.
1870	Gladstone, Sir J. R., Bart., Lt.-Col. Comdt. Prisoners of War Camp	J.L.J.
1911	Gladstone, K. S. M., M.C., Capt. Rifle Bde., and Staff, m. 3. France	R.S.de H.
1915	Gladstone, M. E., 2nd Lt. Rifle Bde. France	R.S.de H.
1913	Gladstone, N. W. H., Capt. Rifle Bde., w. France	R.S.de H.
1911	Gladstone, S. D., M.C., Lt. I.A.R., empld. Capt. Gurkha Rifles, m. Mesopotamia	H.M.
1906	Gladstone, T. H., Capt. 1st (King's) Dragoon Gds., and Staff. France	L.S.R.B.
1904	Gladstone, W. G. C., M.P., Lt. R. Welch Fusiliers. France (k. 13.4.15)	S.A.D.
1916	Gladstone, W. H., M.C., 2nd Lt. Coldstream Gds. France (k. 27.9.18)	H.M.
1895	Gladwin-Errington, G. L. (Errington at Eton), Capt. R.A.S.C. France	C.H.E., C.L.
1902	Glamis, Lord (Mr. Bowes-Lyon at Eton), Lt. Scots Gds., late Maj. Black Watch, w. France	R.W.W.-T.
1883	Glanusk, Lord, C.B., C.B.E., D.S.O. (Bailey at Eton), Col. S. Wales Borderers, m. Aden	W.D.
1908	Glasbrook, J. H. L., Lt. Welch Regt., att. R. Welch Fusiliers, m. France	E.L.C.
1899	Glazebrook, P. K., M.P., D.S.O., Maj. Cheshire Yeomanry, att. Shropshire L.I. Egypt, Palestine (k. 7.3.18)	T.D., R.W.W.-T.
1906	Gledstanes, S. A., Capt. Bedfordshire Regt., m. France (d.w. 9.5.15)	T.C.P., F.L.C.

1902	Glen-Coats, A. H. G., Maj. Glasgow Yeomanry, m. 2. Egypt, Gallipoli, Palestine	J.P.C., S.A.D.
1912	Glentanar, Lord (Mr. Coats at Eton), Lt. Black Watch, att. Worcestershire Regt., and Staff. France	R.S. de H.
1912	Glentworth, Visc., Capt. Warwickshire Yeomanry, att. R.A.F. France, Egypt (k. 18.5.18)	J.H.M.H
1888	Glyn, A. St. L. (F) Maj. Grenadier Gds., and Staff, m. 2. France	J.M.E.
1880	Glyn, G. C., C.M.G., D.S.O., M.V.O., T.D., Col. N. Somerset Yeomanry, and Staff, w., m. 4. France	R.A.H.M.
1914	Glyn, Hon. G. E. D. C., Lt. 10th R. Hussars, w. France	C.M.W.
1893	Glyn, R. F., D.S.O. (F) Capt. R.A.S.C., and Staff, w., m. 2. France	F.H.R.
1893	Goad, B. A., 2nd Lt. R.A.S.C., late Cpl. A.V.C.	F.W.C.
1912	Goad, C. E., 2nd Lt. R.A.S.C., late 2nd Lt. London Regt.	J.M.D., V. Le N.F.
1913	Goad, J. F. E., Capt. K.R.R.C., w., p. France	E.L.V., A.C.R.-W.
1916	Goad, R. F., Lt. Coldstream Gds. France	E.L.V., A.C.R.-W.
1906	Goddard, A. W., M.C. and Bar, Capt. R. Fusiliers, w. 2. France	P.V.B.
1915	Godfrey, J. T., Lt. R.E., w. France	K.S.
1901	Godman, J., Capt. (t. Lt.-Col.) 15th Hussars, p., m. 3. France, Egypt, Gallipoli	H.T.B.
1880	Godman, S. H., D.S.O., Lt.-Col. Scots Gds., and Staff, w., m. 2. France, Mesopotamia	H.D.
1913	Godman, W. W. W., 2nd Lt. K.R.R.C. France (k. 24.1.15)	E.W.S.
1898	Godsal, J., Lt. S. Wales Borderers. France	HOME
1898	Godsal, P., M.C., Capt. Oxfordshire and Bucks L.I., att. London Regt., w., p. (escaped). France, Palestine	HOME
1900	Godsal, W. H., D.S.O., M.C., Maj. Durham L.I., and Staff, w., m. 4. France, Egypt (d.w. 26.3.18)	HOME, A.A.S.
1893	Goff, L. T., Lt.-Col. R.F.A., m. France	H.D.
1886	Goff, T. C. E., Maj. R. Scots, and Staff. France, Egypt	E.C.A.L.
1916	Goff, T. R. C., Lt. Scots Gds., w. France	A.E.C.
1914	Gold, A. H., Lt. R. Berkshire Regt. France, Egypt	A.B.R.

1906	Gold, C. A., Lt. R. Berkshire Regt., m. France (k. 3.7.16)	
		E.C.A.L., E.W.S.
1895	Gold, H. G., O.B.E., Lt.-Col. R.A.F., and Staff	H.D.
1915	Gold, K. V. R., Lt. Bedfordshire Regt., w. France	H.B., R.H. de M.
1908	Gold, P. H., Lt. R. Berkshire Regt., w. France	E.C.A.L., E.W.S.
1896	Goldie, C. J. D., M.C., Capt. R.F.A., and Staff, m. France	
		H.G.W., S.R.J.
1909	Goldsmid, C. J. Hoffnung-, O.B.E. (F) Lt. (t. Capt.) 9th Lancers, and Staff, m. 2. France, Italy	J.M.E., A.B.R.
1910	Goldsmid, R. G. Hoffnung-, Lt. 12th Lancers, w. France	A.B.R.
1910	Goldsworthy, E. W., Capt. Roughriders, att. Lt. R.A.F., w. France, Balkans, Egypt, Gallipoli, Palestine	A.A.S.
1874	Golightly, R. E., C.B.E., D.S.O., Col. Staff	E.C.A.L.
1915	Gollan, S. A., Lt. R.H.G. France	H.M.
1902	Goodfellow, E. A. F., 2nd Lt. Connaught Rangers, att. T.M.B. France (k. 20.2.16)	C.H.A.
1914	Goodford, C. J. H., M.C., Lt. Hampshire Regt., m. France (k. 1.7.16)	H.M.
1897	Goodford, J. W., Maj. W. Somerset Yeomanry	R.C.R.
1900	Goodhart-Rendel, H. S. (Goodhart at Eton), Lt. Grenadier Gds., and Staff. France	E.I.
1917	Goodman, V. M. R., M.C., Lt. Coldstream Gds. France	A.E.C.
1911	Gordon, A. F. L., D.S.O., M.C., Capt. (t. Lt.-Col.) Irish Gds., w., m. 2. France	J.M.D., V. Le N.F.
1900	Gordon, C. L., Capt. Coldstream Gds. France	H.D.
1914	Gordon, C. S. G., Capt. Northumberland Fusiliers, late Lt. R.A.S.C., m. France	A.M.G.
1875	Gordon, C. T., Maj. R. Scots	F.F.V.
1899	Gordon, G. C. D., D.S.O. (F) Lt.-Col. Welsh Gds., m. 2. France	T.C.P.
1912	Gordon, G. S. Staveley, M.C., Capt. Northumberland Fusiliers, and Staff. France	A.B.R.
1900	Gordon, Rev. J. G. (F) C.F., and Staff, m. Italy	J.M.E.
1899	Gordon, J. L., Capt. A. and S. Highlanders. France	S.R.J., H.F.W.T.

1910 Gordon, K. E., Lt. R.F.A. France, Gallipoli   A.C.G.H.

1897 Gordon, R. G. S., M.C., Maj. Dorset Yeomanry. Egypt, Gallipoli, Palestine   F.J.T.

1906 Gordon-Canning, R. C., M.C., Capt. 10th R. Hussars. France   H.F.W.T.

1909 Gordon-Cumming, A. P., M.C., Capt. Cameron Highlanders, and Staff, w. 2, m. France   J.H.M.H.

1896 Gordon-Duff, L., Capt. Gordon Highlanders. France (k. 24.10.14)   J.M E.

1875 Gordon-Gilmour, R. G., C.V.O., C.B., D.S.O. (F) (Wolrige-Gordon at Eton), Brig.-Gen. (Grenadier Gds.), m. 2. France   E.H.

1896 Gordon-Lennox, Lord B. C., Maj. Grenadier Gds., m. France (k. 10.11.14)   E.I

1894 Gordon-Lennox, Lord E. C., C.M.G., D.S.O., M.V.O. (F) Brig.-Gen. (Scots Gds.), w. 2, m. 4. France, Italy   H.G.W., F.D., E.I.

1894 Gore, Sir R. St. G. C., Bart., Maj. Westminster Dragoons, empld. Lt.-Col. Berkshire Yeomanry. France, Egypt, Gallipoli, Palestine   E.L.V.

1890 Gore-Langton, Hon. C. G. T., Capt. 1st (King's) Dragoon Gds.   H.D.

1891 Goring, A., Maj. 20th Hussars, att. Remount Service, and Staff   F.H.R.

1902 Goring, F., Capt. R. Sussex Regt. France, Egypt, Gallipoli   P.W.

1898 Goring, H., Lt. 3rd Hussars, and Staff, m. France   P.W.

1880 Goring, W., Bt. Col. 3rd Hussars, m. France   G.E.M.

1883 Gorst, H. E., Lt. Yorkshire Regt., and Staff. France   J.M.E.

1897 Goschen, A. A., D.S.O. and two Bars (F) Lt.-Col. R.F.A., w., m. 6. France   A.C.B.

1899 Goschen, C. G., Capt. Grenadier Gds. France (k. 25.9.16)   A C.B.

1906 Goschen, G. G., Lt. Grenadier Gds., w., p. France   H.F.W.T.

1912 Goschen, Hon. G. J., 2nd Lt. The Buffs, m. Mesopotamia (d.w. 19.1.16)   H.T B., S G.L

1886	Gosling, C., C.M.G., Brig.-Gen. (K.R.R.C.), m. 3. France (k. 12.4.17)	J.C.
•1885	Gosling, F. R., Maj. K.R.R.C., att. Northamptonshire Regt., and Labour Corps	R.A.H.M.
1907	Gosling, G. E., M.C. (F) Capt. (t. Maj.) 10th R. Hussars, w., m. France	F.H.R.
1898	Gosling, H. M., Maj. K.R.R.C., w. 2, p., m. France	C.L.
1897	Gosling, H. W., Lt. R. Fusiliers, att. R.A.O.C. and Manchester Regt. France	R.A.H.M.
1889	Gosling, S. F., D.S.O., Lt.-Col. R.F.A., m. 5. France	R.C.R.
1896	Gosling, T. S., Lt. R.G.A.	R.C.R.
1906	Gosling, V. H., Sergt. Natal L.H. France, S.W. Africa, E. Africa	F.H.R.
1889	Gosling, Rev. W. C., C.F. France, Italy	H.G.W.
1888	Gosling, W. S., Maj. Scots Gds. France	W.D.
1890	Gott, W. W. M., Maj. Rifle Bde.	A.C.J.
1914	Gough, D. H., the late, M.C., Lt. 10th R. Hussars, w. France (d. 7.10.19)	A.E.C.
1905	Gough, E. J. F., Capt. Irish Gds., m. France (k. 30.12.14)	R.P.L.B
1905	Gough, G. P., Capt. Irish Gds., and Staff, w. France	S.A.D., P.V.B.
1904	Gough, G. V. H., Capt. K.R.R.C., p. France	S.A.D., P.V.B.
1886	Gough, Sir H. de la P., K.C.B., K.C.V.O., G.C.M.G. (F) Gen. (16th Lancers), w., m. 8. France	A.C.J.
1910	Gough, H. S., Lt. K.R.R.C. France (k. 16.6.16)	H.F.W.T., A.E.C.
1910	Gough, Hon. H. W., M.C., Bt. Maj. Irish Gds., and Staff, w., m. 2. France	F.W.S.
1887	V.C. Gough, Sir J. E., K.C.B., C.M.G., Brig.-Gen. (Rifle Bde.), m. 2. France (d.w. 22.2.15)	A.C.J.
1904	Gough, W. H. J., Capt. Welsh Gds., empld. Gds. M.G. Regt. France	S.A.D.
1901	Goulding, W. L. A., Capt. R. Irish Fusiliers, and Staff. France	R.A.H.M.
1895	Graham, Marquess of, C.V.O., C.B., Cr. R.N.V.R., and Staff. Home Waters	A.C.J.
1898	Graham, A. C., Capt. Grenadier Gds., late Lt.-Cr. Hood Bn., R.N.D. France (k. 12.9.16)	F.H., A.A.S.

1904 Graham, A. C. D., M.C., Bt. Maj. 9th Lancers, and Staff,
w., m. 2. France   E.C.A.L. E.W.S.

1901 Graham, A. K., Lt. Lothians and Border Horse, att.
M.G. Cav., and Staff. France, Balkans   A.A.S.

1898 Graham, C. P., C.B.E., D.S.O., Maj. Welch Regt., and
Staff, m. 6. France, Italy   R.W.W.-T.

1880 Graham, D. W., Maj. Monmouthshire Regt.   A.C.J.

1875 Graham, Sir E. R. C., K.C.B., K.C.M.G. (F) Maj.-Gen.
(Cheshire Regt.), m. 8. France   A.C.A.

1910 Graham, F. F., Capt. Irish Gds., and Staff, w. 2, m. 2.
France   C.M.W.

1902 Graham, G. M. A., C.B.E., Maj. Staff, late Capt. Middlesex Regt. and R.A.S.C., M.T.   J.M.E.

1892 Graham, H. J. C., Capt. Coldstream Gds., and Staff.
France   C.H.E.

1912 Graham, H. L., M.C., Lt. Scots Gds., late S. Staffordshire Regt., w. France   A.A.S.

1909 Graham, J. G. B. P., Capt. H.L.I., att. Nigerian Regt.,
W. African F.F., w. France, W. Africa   J.M.E., M.D.H.

1908 Graham, J. M., M.C., Lt. (t. Maj.) 6th (Inniskilling)
Dragoons, and Staff, m. France   J.H.M.H.

1917 Graham, J. M., 2nd Lt. R.G.A. Italy   H.M.

1911 V.C. Graham, J. R. N., Capt. (t. Maj.) A. and S. Highlanders, att. M.G.C., w. Mesopotamia, Palestine   H.Br.

1898 Graham, J. St. J., Maj. Staff, m. 3. France   J.M.E.

1900 Graham, M., D.S.O., Capt. (t. Lt.-Col.) 16th Lancers,
and Staff, m. 4. France   E.C.A.L.

1904 Graham, M. D., Lt. Coldstream Gds., late A. and S.
Highlanders. India   A.A.S.

1913 Graham, M. W. A. P., M.C., Capt. 2nd Life Gds., w. 2.
France   K.S.

1911 Graham, N. (F) Lt. Coldstream Gds., late Black Watch,
w. 3. France   J.H.M.H.

1894 Graham, Sir R. G., Bart., D.S.O., Maj. Yorkshire Regt.,
and Staff, m. 2. France, Italy   E.I.

1914 Graham, R. P., M.C., Lt. K.R.R.C., w. 2, p. France, Italy C.H.K.M.
1895 Graham, W. L. C., the Hon., Capt. I.A.R., and Staff India (k. accid. 14.7.15) J M I
1906 Graham-Campbell, J., Lt. A. and S. Highlanders, w. France S.A.D., P.V.B.
1911 Graham-Watson, A. F., Capt. R. Scots, p., m. France E.L.C.
1915 Graham-Wigan, A. J., M.B.E., Lt. The Queen's Own (R.W. Kent Regt.), att. R. Sussex Regt., and Staff R.S.de H.
1914 Grahame Stewart, J. C., 2nd Lt. K.R.R.C. France (k. 25.9.15) II M
1904 Granby, Marquess of (Lord Roos at Eton), Capt. Leicestershire Regt., and Staff. France A.C.A., R.S.de H.
1874 Granet, E. J., C.B. (F) Brig.-Gen. (R.A.), w. France, Gallipoli (d. 22.10.18) F.W.C.
1896 Grant, Sir A., Bart., C.B.E., D.S.O., Lt.-Col. Gordon Highlanders, and Staff. France H.B.
1917 Grant, A., 2nd Lt. Grenadier Gds. France (k. 27.9.18) H.de H.
1910 Grant, A. E. G., M.C., Capt. 9th Lancers, w., m. 2. France H.T.B., S.G.L.
1911 Grant, A. F. M., 2nd Lt. The Queen's. France (d. of gas poisoning 18.6.16) A A.S.
1893 Grant, A. S., D.S.O., Maj. Black Watch, and Staff, m. France H.W.M.
1896 Grant, C. J. P. McA., Capt. Deccan Infantry, I.A., and Staff. E. Africa, India, Mesopotamia P.W.
1879 Grant, H. G., Capt. Labour Corps, late Cheshire Regt. France, Balkans H.W.M.
1914 Grant, H. M., M.C. and Bar, Lt. (t. Capt.) Cameron Highlanders, w. France, N. Russia J.H.M.H.
1892 Grant, J. C. H. (F) Maj. (t. Lt.-Col.) R. Scots, w. France, E. Africa T.D.
1915 Grant, M. H., Lt. Durham L.I., w. 2. France, Italy V.Le N.F.
1913 Grant, P. F., Capt. R.F.A., w. 2. France J.H.M.H.
1872 Grant, Hon. R. A. O., Lt.-Col. R.A.S.C. France F.F.V.
1895 Grant, R. F. S., M.V.O., D.S.O., Maj. Rifle Bde., and Staff, w., m. 2. France T.D., A.A.S.

1897 Grant, W. D., Lt.-Col. Yorkshire Dragoons, att. Yorkshire Regt. France   C.H.A.

1907 Grant, W. G. S., M.C., Capt. R. Sussex Regt., late Capt. H.L.I., att. R. Scots and Bimbashi Egyptian Army, w., m. Egypt, Gallipoli   P.W.

1895 Grant-Suttie, G. D., Maj. Black Watch, att. M.G.C. France   H.B.

1889 Grant-Thorold, H., Maj. Northamptonshire Regt., att. Labour Corps. France   H.D.

1886 Grant-Thorold, R. S., D.S.O., Lt.-Col. Welch Regt., late Maj. R. Fusiliers, and Capt. Australian Imp. Forces, w., m. 2. France, New Guinea   H.D.

1890 Granville, B., D.S.O. and Bar, Lt.-Col. Warwickshire Yeomanry, w., m. 3. France, Balkans, Egypt, Gallipoli, Palestine   J.M.E.

1913 Gray, Master of, Hon. L. S. Campbell (Campbell at Eton), M.C., Lt. R.F.A., w. 3. France   P.W., F.E.R.

1888 Greathed, R. N., the late, Lt.-Col. R.A., and Staff. France (d. 26.3.20)   C.H.E.

1906 Greaves, G. M., Maj. R.H.G., late Duke of Lancaster's Own Yeomanry. France   J.M.E., A.B.R.

1898 Greaves, O. E. W., Capt. R.H.G. France   R.W.W.-T.

1909 Green, C. E. P., Lt. Coldstream Gds., and Staff, w. 2. France   H.F.W.T.

1905 Green, E. A. L. (F) Capt. Yorkshire Dragoons, late Lt. 2nd Life Gds., m. France   E.I.

1911 Green, G. H. W., M.C., Capt. (t. Maj.) Seaforth Highlanders, att. R.A.F., w. 2, m. 3. France   J.M.D., V.Le N.F.

1896 Green, H. B., Cpl. Canadian Scottish, Canadian E.F. France (k. 22.4.15)   T.D., F.J.T.

1907 Greenall, J. E., Capt. Duke of Lancaster's Own Yeomanry, att. R.F.C. France (k. 31.3.18)   R.S.K.

1906 Greene, B. S. C., Lt. R.N.V.R. Home Waters   H.T.B.

1897 Greene, E. A., M.C., Capt. Suffolk Yeomanry, and Staff, m. France, Gallipoli   C.L.

1887 Greene, Sir W. R., Bart., M.P., D.S.O., T.D., Lt.-Col. Sharpshooters, att. 9th Lancers, and Staff, w., m. France   F.H.R.

1909 Greenfield, H. R. H., Capt. A. and S. Highlanders, and Staff, w. France, Balkans   P.W.

1891 Greenfield, H. S. B., Lt. Staff   F.H.

1914 Greenfield, R. W., Lt. Rifle Bde. France (k. 23.10.16)   A.B.R.

1883 Greenfield, T. W. B., D.S.O., Maj. Irish Gds., and Staff, m. France   A.C.

1899 Greenhill, C. B., Capt. W. Somerset Yeomanry, att. Somerset L.I. France   J.H.M.H.

1892 Greenly, W. H., C.B., C.M.G., D.S.O. (F) Maj.-Gen. (12th Lancers), m. 7. France   J.M.E.

1904 Greenwell, E. E., the late, Lt. R.N.V.R. Home Waters (d. 23.2.19)   A.C.A., R.S.de H.

1913 Greenwell, G. E., Capt. R.E., late Pte. Hampshire Regt. France   E.L.C.

1906 Greenwood, V. J., M.C., Capt. 10th R. Hussars, w. France   E.I.

1910 Greer, E. B., M.C., Maj. (t. Lt.-Col.) Irish Gds., w., m. 3. France (k. 31.7.17)   E.I.

1912 Greer, F. St. L., M.C., Lt. Irish Gds., late 2nd Lt. 16th Lancers, m. France (k. accid. 1.2.17)   A.B.R.

1899 Gregge-Hopwood, E. B. G., D.S.O., Maj. Coldstream Gds., m. 2. France (k. 20.7.17)   A.A.S.

1901 Gregge-Hopwood, R. G., Capt. Rifle Bde., att. R.F.C. m. France (k. 24.8.16)   A.A.S.

1906 Gregory, G. F., Lt. R. Berkshire Regt. France (k. 25.9.15)   H.L.

1916 Gregson-Ellis, P. G. S., 2nd Lt. Grenadier Gds. France   R.P.L.B.

1902 Gregson-Ellis, R. G., Capt. Oxfordshire and Bucks L.I., att. Canadian Infantry, m. France (d.w. 17.4.17)   F.L.V.

1912 Greig, J. Y., Lt. Cameronians (Scottish Rifles), att. M.G.C., late Pte. R. Fusiliers, w. France   K.S.

1892 Grenfell, A. M., D.S.O., T.D., Maj. Buckinghamshire Yeomanry, att. 9th Lancers, and Lt.-Col. R.A.F., w. 2, m. 3. France   W.D.

1883	Grenfell, C. A., T. D., Brig.-Gen. (Buckinghamshire Yeomanry), m. France, Egypt, Gallipoli	J.M.E.
1899	V.C. Grenfell, F. O., Capt. 9th Lancers, w. 2, m. 2. France (k. 24.5.15)	W D
1908	Grenfell, Hon. G. W., 2nd Lt. Rifle Bde. France (k. 31.7.15)	A.C.B., A M.G
1887	Grenfell, H. M., C.M.G., M.V.O., Brig.-Gen. (1st Life Gds.). France	W.D.
1916	Grenfell, Hon. I. G. W., Lt. Grenadier Gds., and Staff. N. Russia	A.M.G.
1906	Grenfell, Hon. J. H. F., D.S.O., Capt. 1st R. Dragoons, m. 2 France (d.w. 26.5.15)	A.A.S.
1897	Grenfell, R. N., Capt. Buckinghamshire Yeomanry, att. 9th Lancers. France (k. 14.9.14)	W D.
1878	Grenville-Grey, G., O.B.E., Cr. R.N.V.R.	T.D.
1914	Greswolde-Williams, F. H. J., Lt. King's African Rifles, m. E. Africa (k. 3.8.17)	K S K.
1908	Greville, C. H., D.S.O., Capt. (t. Maj.) Grenadier Gds., w. 2, m. 3. France	H.M.
1908	Greville, G. G. F., Lt. 4th Hussars. France (k. 31.3.18)	H M.
1898	Grey, Earl (Visc. Howick at Eton), Maj. Northumberland Fusiliers, and Staff, m. 2. France	H.E.L.
1912	Grey, Sir J. F., Bart., Lt. 15th Hussars, w. France	H.T.B., A.A.S.
1881	Grey, T. R., Sub-Lt. R.N.V.R.	E.H.
1880	Grey-Egerton, Sir P. H. B., Bart., Maj. Cheshire Yeomanry	E.C.A.L.
1914	V.C. Gribble, J. R., Lt. (t. Capt.) R. Warwickshire Regt., w. France (p., d. 25.11.18)	A.C.G.H.
1885	Griffin, A. E. S., (F) Lt.-Col. R.F.A. France	A.C.A.
1910	Grimthorpe, Lord (Mr. Beckett at Eton), Capt. Yorkshire Hussars, att. R.A.F., and Staff, m. France	A.C.G.H.
1911	Grosvenor, Lord E. A. (F) Capt. R.A.F. France, Italy	A.B.R.
1897	Grosvenor, Hon. G., Maj. King Edward's Horse, att. Sherwood Rangers. France	R.C.R.
1893	Grosvenor, Lord G. R., Capt. Scots Gds., w., p. France	A.C.J.

1901	Grosvenor, Lord H. W., Capt. 1st Life Gds., m. France (k. 30.10.14)	A.C.B.
1910	Grove, E. T. N., Capt. Buckinghamshire Yeomanry, att. Egyptian Army. Egypt, Gallipoli	K.S.
1875	Grubbe, E. A., the late, Bt. Lt.-Col. Staff (d. 16.6.20)	T.H.S., J.E.Y.
1901	Guernsey, Lord, Capt. Irish Gds. France (k. 14.9.14)	A.C.A.
1889	Guest, Hon. C. H. C., M.P., Lt.-Col. 1st R. Dragoons, and Staff, m. France, Palestine	H.E.L.
1895	Guest, Hon. L. G. W., O.B.E., Capt. R.A.F., late Lt. R.N.D. France, Gallipoli	A.C.B.
1893	Guilford, Earl of, T.D., Lt.-Col. R. E. Kent Yeomanry. Egypt, Gallipoli	R.A.H.M.
1897	Guinness, Sir A. A. St. L., Bart., Lt.-Cr. R.N.V.R. and Staff. Home Waters	P.W.
1877	Guinness, C. D., Bt. Col. R.F.A.	O.B., E.S.S.
1917	Guinness, G. R. de C. B., 2nd Lt. Coldstream Gds. France	E.I., T.F.C.
1907	Guinness, R. S., Lt. R.N.V.R., att. Anson Bn., R.N.D., w. Home Waters, Gallipoli	A.A.S.
1899	Guinness, Hon. W. E., M.P., D.S.O. and Bar, Lt.-Col. Suffolk Yeomanry, and Staff, m. France, Egypt, Gallipoli	E.C.A.L.
1904	Guise, A. W. E., Capt. Gloucestershire Yeomanry. Egypt	C.H.A.
1911	Guise, H. G. C., 2nd Lt. Gloucestershire Regt. France (k. accid. 6.5.15)	H.E.W.T., A.F.C.
1908	Gull, F. W. L., Capt. Rifle Bde., and Staff, w., m. ?. France (k. 25.8.18)	H.M.
1913	Gull, R. C., Capt. Rifle Bde., and Staff, w., m. France	H.M.
1887	Gully, Hon. E. W. K., C.B., Lt. R.N.V.R.	T.D.
1913	Gunnis, G. G., M.C., Capt. Grenadier Gds., m. France (d.w. 13.10.16)	A.C.H.
1912	Gunter, F. J., Lt. 11th Hussars. France (k. 24.5.15)	M.D.H.
1916	Gunter, G. R., 2nd Lt. 11th Hussars. France	R.S.K.
1889	Gunter, Sir R. B. N., Bart., Lt.-Col. Yorkshire Regt. France (d. 16.8.17)	C.A.I.

1917	Gunther, G. R., M.C., 2nd Lt. Grenadier Gds. France (k. 4.11.18)	M.D.H.
1913	Gunther, N. O. F., M.C., 2nd Lt. R. E. Kent Yeomanry, att. The Buffs. France (k. 12.7.17)	M.D.H.
1912	Gunther, R. J. (F) Lt. 2nd Life Gds. France	M.D.H.
1916	Gurney, C. W., Lt. Coldstream Gds. France	H. de H.
1916	Gurney, D. W. T., M.C., Lt. K.R.R.C., w. 2. France, N. Russia	H. de H.
1904	Gurney, S., Capt. Norfolk Regt., att. Lancashire Fusiliers. France	E.L.V.
1897	Gurney, T. C., D.S.O., Maj. 2nd Life Gds., m. 2. France	A.C.J.
1883	Gush, F., Sergt., Welch Regt.	T.D.
1910	Guthrie, J. A., Capt. 15th Hussars, empld. Maj. M.G. Cav., and Staff. France, Afghanistan	E.W.S.
1911	Guthrie, P. S., Lt. 1st Life Gds., att. R. Inniskilling Fusiliers. France	R.P.L.B.
1912	Guy, C. G., Capt. Northamptonshire Regt., att. R.F.C. France, Gallipoli (d.w. 12.8.17)	K.S.
1897	Gwyer, A. G., Capt. Carabiniers. France (k. 22.10.14)	T C.P.
1917	Gwynne, D. R. H., 2nd Lt. Rifle Bde.	R.S.K.
1878	Gwynne, R. J., C.M.G., Brig.-Gen., Headquarters Staff, Canada	W.D.
1912	Gwynne, R. T. S., 2nd Lt. K.O.Y.L.I. France (d.w. 23.5.15)	R.S.K.
1912	Haddington, Earl of, M.C. (Mr. Baillie-Hamilton at Eton), Lt. R. Scots Greys, w. France	H.M.
1893	Haig, G. A. G., the late, Capt. R. E. Kent Yeomanry, (d. 9.4.19)	R.A.H.M.
1892	Haig, J., D.S.O., Maj. (t. Lt.-Col.) Westminster Dragoons, att. M.G.C., m. 3. France, Balkans, Egypt, Palestine	A.A.S.
1902	Haig, N. E., M.C., Capt. R.F.A., and Staff, w., m. France	J.H.M.H.
1885	Haig, N. W., C.B., C.M.G., Col. 6th (Inniskilling) Dragoons, m. 2. France	E.W., E.I.

1893	Haig, O., Lt.-Col. Westminster Dragoons, att. Remount Service. France	F.D., J.M.E.
1916	Hakim, R. B., Lt. R.G.A. France	K.S.
1911	Haldane, J. B. S., Capt. Black Watch, and Staff, w. 2. France, Mesopotamia	K.S.
1916	Haldeman, D. C., Lt. 19th Hussars. France	H. de H.
1879	Hales, Rev. J. T., O.B.E., Lt.-Col. C.F., p., m. France	W.D.
1878	Halford, C. H., Capt. Grenadier Gds.	C.W.D.
1912	Hall, A. A., Lt. R.E. France, E. Africa, Gallipoli	J.M.D., V. Le N.F.
1901	Hall, A. H., Capt. Essex Regt., att. M.G.C. France, Egypt	F.J.T., E.L.V.
1883	Hall, C. O., Maj. E. Riding of Yorkshire Yeomanry	C.C.J.
1910	Hall, D. M. B., D.S.O., Capt. Coldstream Gds., empld. Lt.-Col. N. Staffordshire Regt., w. 2, m. 3. France	P.W.
1909	Hall, F. G., Capt. Cheshire Regt. France (k. 7.7.16)	F.W.S.
1902	Hall, G. B., Capt. Gloucestershire Regt., att. S. Staffordshire Regt., w. 2, m. France	H.D.
1893	Hall, G. D., Capt. The Queen's Own (R. W. Kent Regt.), and Staff. France, Egypt	F.W.C.
1906	Hall, H. W., M.C. (F) Maj. 2nd Dragoon Gds. (Queen's Bays), and Staff, m. 5. France	J.M.D.
1897	Hall, J. E. K., 2nd Lt. S. Wales Borderers Gallipoli (d.w. 22.9.15)	K S
1881	Hall, Sir J. R., Bart., C.B.E., Maj. (t. Col.) Irish Gds.	G.E.M.
1893	Hall, L. K., Lt. R.G.A.	J.P.C.
1887	Hall, M. H., Capt. (t. Lt.-Col.) Sherwood Foresters, late Capt. Lincolnshire Regt. France	F.H.R.
1903	Hall, P. S. B., Capt. The Buffs, att. Hampshire Regt., and Staff. France (k. 9.8.16)	J.P.C., L.T., R.P.L.B.
1909	Hall, R. A., Pte. R.A.O.C.	H.B.
1898	Hall, R. H. E., Capt. Oxfordshire Yeomanry. France	C.H.A.
1910	Hall, W. D'A., M.C. and Bar, (F) Capt. 20th Hussars, att. R.A.F., m. France	J.M.D., V. Le N.F.
1916	Hall-Watt, R., 2nd Lt. Grenadier Gds. France (k. 13.10.17)	M.D.H.

1899	Halsey, Rev. G., Chaplain, R.N. Home Waters	W.D.
1890	Halsey, R., Maj. Herts Yeomanry., att. Westminster Dragoons. Egypt, Gallipoli, Mesopotamia, Palestine	W.D.
1916	Halsey, T. E., Sub-Lt. R.N. Home Waters, Black Sea, Mediterranean	C.M.W.
1887	Halsey, W. J., O.B.E., Capt. (t. Lt.-Col.) Bedfordshire Regt., and Staff, m. 3. Egypt, Palestine	W.D.
1891	Halswell, G., Capt. (t. Maj.) 1st Life Gds., att. M.G. Cav., late 13th Hussars. France	A.C.J.
1887	Hambleden, Visc. (Smith at Eton), Lt.-Col. R. 1st Devon Yeomanry, m. Egypt, Gallipoli	E.W., S.A.D.
1900	Hambro, A. V., M.P., 2nd Lt. Dorset Yeomanry, empld. Capt. Staff	A.C.A.
1898	Hambro, B. E., 2nd Lt. Interpreter, att. I.E.F. France (d. 25.4.15)	H.D.
1915	Hambro, C. J., M.C., Lt. Coldstream Gds., w. France	E.I., T.F.C.
1893	Hambro, H. E., C.B.E., Bt. Lt.-Col. R.A., att. Remount Service, and Staff. France	H.D.
1916	Hambro, P., 2nd Lt. K.R.R.C. France (d.w. 22.3.18)	E.I., T.F.C.
1889	Hambro, P. O., C.B., C.M.G. (F) Maj.-Gen. (15th Hussars), w., m. 7. France	H.D.
1903	Hambro, R. O. (F) Capt. Coldstream Gds., and Staff, m. 2. France	A.C.A., R.S.de H.
1910	Hamer, G. M., Lt. 14th Hussars, w. Mesopotamia	P.W.
1902	Hamilton, C. A. M. B., Lt. Sp. List	J.P.C., L.F., E.W.S.
1912	Hamilton, E. W., Capt. London Regt., w. France	K.S.
1893	Hamilton, F. A. C., M.C. (F) Maj. Cameronians (Scottish Rifles), empld. Lt.-Col. R. Fusiliers and Gloucestershire Regt., w., m. France	H.W.M.
1905	Hamilton, G. M., Capt. (t. Maj.) Sp. List, m. France	K.S.
1902	Hamilton, J., Capt. The Buffs, att. R.A.F., and Staff, w. France	A.C.J., A.C.G.H.
1891	Hamilton, Hon. L. d'H., M.V.O., Maj. Coldstream Gds., m. France (k. 29.10.14)	W.D.

1906	Hamilton, P. S., Lt. (t. Capt.) Border Regt, and Staff. Afghanistan	A.C.A., J.M.D.
1887	Hamilton, W. M. F., Maj. H.L.I.	E.C.A.L.
1890	Hamilton of Dalzell, Lord, K.T., C.V.O., M.C., Maj. Scots Gds., and Staff, m. 4. France, Italy	W.D.
1913	Hamilton-Fletcher, G., 2nd Lt. Grenadier Gds., att. Scots Gds. France (k. 25.1.15)	A.A.S.
1913	Hamilton-Fletcher, M. A., Lt. R.F.A., and Staff. France, Palestine	A.A.S.
1891	Hamilton-Russell, Hon. A., Maj. N. Irish Horse, m. France	A.C.J.
1899	Hamilton-Wedderburn, H. K., O.B.E. (Hamilton at Eton), Maj. Scots Gds., and Staff. France	A.A.S.
1874	Hammersley, F., C.B., Maj.-Gen. (Lancashire Fusiliers). Gallipoli	H.S.
1911	Hammersley, H. C., Capt. Scots Gds., m. France	E.L.V.
1898	Hammond, F. D., C.B.E., D.S.O. (F) Brig.-Gen. (R.E.) m. 6. France, Balkans, Mesopotamia, Palestine	K.S.
1893	Hammond, R. W., M.C., Capt. R. Fusiliers. France (d.w. 30.9.17)	C.H.A.
1904	Hammond-Chambers, H. B. B., Capt. The King's Own (R. Lancaster Regt.). France (k. 20.7.16)	J.M.E.
1902	Hammond-Chambers-Borgnis, J. A., Capt. R. Defence Corps	J.M.E.
1897	Hamond, P., D.S.O. and Bar, M.C., Maj. Norfolk Regt., att. M.G.C. and Tank Corps, w., m. France	A.A.S.
1887	Hampden, Visc., C.B., C.M.G. (F) (Brand at Eton), Brig.-Gen. (10th R. Hussars), m. 8. France, Egypt, Gallipoli	E.C.A.L.
1915	Hampson, D. F., 2nd Lt. Rifle Bde, late 2nd Lt. The Queen's Own (R. W. Kent Regt.) and L/ce-Cpl. Rifle Bde., w. France	H.Br.
1901	Hanbury, C., 2nd Lt. K.O.S.B., late Pte. R. Fusiliers, w. France	H.B.
1880	Hanbury, E. E., O.B.E., Maj. Scots Gds. France	J.P.C.

1900 Hanbury, E. R., Maj. Leicestershire Yeomanry, att.
M.G.C., w., m. France (k. 24.3.18)   A.A.S

1882 Hanbury, L. H., C.M.G., V.D., Lt.-Col. R. Berkshire
Regt., att. R. Warwickshire Regt., m. France   C.L.L.-C., H.W.M.

1896 Hanbury, N., M.B.E., Lt. (t. Capt.) Coldstream Gds.,
and Staff. France   J.M.E.

1902 Hanbury, R. F., Capt. Bedfordshire Regt., att. Border
Regt., w. France   S.A.D.

1911 Hanbury, R. H. O., M.C., Capt. 15th Hussars, m. 2. France   P.V.B.

1888 Hanbury-Tracy, E. T. H., O.B.E., Maj. Coldstream Gds.   J.M.E.

1909 Hankey, A. B., Lt. R.N.V.R., att. R.F.C., late A.B.,
R.N.A.S. France   R.S.K.

1889 Hankey, C. G. H. A., Lt.-Col. R. Sussex Regt. France   W.D.

1893 Hankey, E. B., D.S.O. (F) Brig.-Gen. (Worcestershire
Regt.), w., m. 3. France   R.A.H.M.

1904 Hankey, F. J. B., M.C., Capt. Tank Corps, late Capt.
K.R.R.C., w. 2. France   R.A.H.M., L.S.R.B.

1890 Hankey, G. F. B., O.B.E., Maj. K.R.R.C., w. France   R.A.H.M.

1891 Hankey, G. L., L/ce-Cpl. H.A.C.   A.C.A.

1885 Hankey, S. T., Lt.-Col. 2nd Life Gds., att. Lovat Scouts.
France   R.A.H.M.

1908 Hankey, T. B., M.C., Albert Medal (F) Capt. K.R.R.C.,
and Staff, m. 3. France   R.S.K.

1914 Hankey, T. S. D'A., Lt. 9th Lancers. France   A.A.S.

1884 Hanmer, Sir W. C. H., Bart., Maj. Remount Service.
France   H.E.L.

1907 Hannay, G. D., O.B.E., Lt.-Col. R.A.F., and Staff   T.C.P., E.L.C.

1908 V.C. Hansen, P. H., D.S.O., M.C. (F) Bt. Maj. (t. Maj.)
Lincolnshire Regt., att. Berkshire Regt. and Border
Regt., and Staff, m. 5. France, Egypt, Gallipoli   J.M.D.

1914 Harbord, Hon. V. A. C., Lt. Scots Gds, w. 2. France   H.M.

1895 Harcourt, R. V., Lt., late C.P.O., R.N.V.R., and Staff.
France, Balkans   A.C.A.

1917 Harcourt-Vernon, E. G. E., M.C., Lt. Grenadier Gds.
France   H.Br.

1909	Harcourt-Vernon, G. C. F., D.S.O., M.C., Capt. Grenadier Gds., w. 3, m. France	H.Br.
1903	Harding, C. E. H., Bt. Maj. R. Fusiliers, and Staff. France (d. 10.12.17)	R. A. H. M., L.S.R.B.
1873	Harding, G. M., Maj. Remount Service. France	J.W.H., F.F.V.
1909	Harding, R. A. C., M.B.E., Capt. R.F.A., and Staff, m. Mesopotamia	L.S.R.B.
1909	Hardman, F. McM., 2nd Lt. R. Fusiliers. France (k. 29.10.14)	J.M.E., A.B.R
1892	Hardwick, P. E., D.S.O., Lt.-Col. 1st R. Dragoons, att. 10th R. Hussars, w. 2, m. France (d. 9.6.19)	
1911	Hardy, A. E., Capt. Coldstream Gds. France	H.T.B., S.G.L.
1894	Hardy, B., Maj. Staffordshire Yeomanry	A.C.A.
1903	Hardy, E. J., D.S.O., Capt. R. Scots Greys, m. France	C.H.A.
1894	Hardy, F. H. (F) Lt.-Col. Coldstream Gds., and Staff, w. 2, m. France	W.D.
1870	Hardy, G. H., Maj. Staffordshire Yeomanry	J.L.J.
1896	Hardy, H. S., M.C., M.B.E., Maj. The Buffs, and Staff, w., m. 2. France	E.L.V.
1900	Hardy, L. H., M.C., Maj. (t. Lt.-Col.) 1st Life Gds., w., m. France	C.H.A.
1899	Hardy, R. M., Capt. Rifle Bde., late Pte. R. Sussex Regt. France (k. 23.7.15)	E.C.A L
1886	Hare, E. P. L., Capt. R.H.G., att. R.G.A., and Staff. France	A.C.A.
1883	Hare, Sir G. R. L., Bart., Lt. R. Defence Corps	G.E.M.
1912	Hare, H. K. C., Capt. Yorkshire Regt., att. W. Riding Regt., late Pte. The King's (Liverpool Regt.), w. 2., m. France	E.L.V., A.C.R.-W.
1886	Hare, P. R., T.D., Capt. Sharpshooters, and Staff. Balkans, Egypt, Gallipoli	F.H.R.
1885	Hare, S. W., C.B., K.C.M.G. (F) Maj.-Gen. (K.R.R.C.), w., m. 4. Balkans, Egypt, Gallipoli, Palestine	F.W.C.
1890	Harford, E. B., Capt. Somerset L.I., w., m. Palestine (d. 15.7.18)	F.H.R
1896	Harford, F. R., Capt. Scots Gds.	A.C.J.

1874	Harford, W. A., Maj. Remount Service	E.W.
1899	Hargreaves, A. K., D.S.O., Capt. Rifle Bde., w., m. France (k. 9.5.15)	A.C.A.
1905	Hargreaves, C. F., Maj. E. Lancashire Regt., att. R.E. Signal Service, w., p. France, S. Russia	C.H.A.
1905	Hargreaves, C. L., Capt. Scots Gds., and Staff, w., m. 3. France	A.C.A., R.S. de H.
1892	Hargreaves, F. (F) 2nd Lt. R.A.S.C. France	R.A.H.M.
1900	Hargreaves, G., Lt. (t. Capt.) Berks Yeomanry. France	R.A.H.M.
1900	Hargreaves, G. de la P. (F) Capt. Bedfordshire Yeomanry, m. France	H.D.
1917	Hargreaves, J., 2nd Lt. R.F.A. N. Russia	F.E.R.
1901	Hargreaves, L. R., M.C., Capt. Irish Gds. France (k. 15.9.16)	A.C.A.
1909	Hargreaves, R. C., M.C., Capt. Rifle Bde., att. Tank Corps, w., m. France	C.M.W.
1916	Hargreaves, S. J., 2nd Lt. Grenadier Gds. France (d.w. 19.5.18)	S.G.L.
1871	Harlech, Lord, T.D. (Ormsby-Gore at Eton), Col. Comm. Welsh Gds.	E.C.A.L.
1895	Harley, R. G. G., the late, Lt. R.N.V.R., late Capt. R. Fusiliers. France, E. Africa, Italy (d. 26.1.20)	E.C.A.L.
1914	Harley, T. W., M.C., Capt. The King's Own (R. Lancaster Regt.), m. France, Balkans	L.S.R.B.
1913	Harman, C. E., Lt. Middlesex Regt., w., p. France	K.S.
1917	Harmsworth, Hon. E. C., Lt. R.M.A.	H.Br.
1912	Harmsworth, Hon. H. A. V. St. G., M.C., Capt. Irish Gds., w. 3. France (d.w. 12.2.18)	H.Br.
1905	Harris, Hon. G. St. V., M.C., Capt. R. E. Kent Yeomanry, and Staff, w., m. France	E.I.
1892	Harris-St. John, C. E. St. J., D.S.O. (F) (Harris at Eton), Lt.-Col. 16th Lancers, and Staff, m. France	R.C.R.
1897	Harrison, B. C., Capt. Border Regt., w. 2, m. France (k. 11.8.18)	K.S.
1890	Harrison, C. E., Maj. Rifle Bde., w. France (k. 12.3.15)	C.H.E., C.L.

1897	Harrison, C. P., D.S.O., M.C., Maj. R.F.A., m. 2. France, Balkans, Egypt, Palestine	T.D., A.C.J.
1906	Harrison, J. F., Capt. (t. Maj.) R.H.G., w., m. France	J.H.M.H.
1881	Harrison, T. E., D.S.O., Lt.-Col. Hertfordshire Yeomanry, and Staff. France	W.E., J.M.E.
1892	Harrison, W. E., O.B.E., Lt.-Col. R.E.	P.H.C., C.H.A.
1909	Harrison, W. R. E., D.S.O., M.C., Capt. R.A., w. 2, m. France, Gallipoli, Mesopotamia	J.M.E., A.B.R.
1892	Hart-Davis, C. H., Capt. R. E. Kent Yeomanry, and Staff, m. Balkans, Gallipoli	K.S.
1892	Hart-Davis, R. V., Maj. R. Fusiliers, and Staff, m. 2. France	K.S.
1908	Harter, G. J., D.F.C., Capt. R.A.F. France, Palestine	E.I.
1907	Harter, J. C. F., 2nd Lt. Res. Regt. of Cav., att. Sherwood Rangers, late Trooper Westminster Dragoons. Balkans, Egypt, Palestine (k. 28.11.17)	H.T.D.
1913	Hartington, Marquis of, M.B.E. (F) Capt. Derbyshire Yeomanry, and Staff, m. France, Egypt, Gallipoli	E.I.
1909	Hartley, D'A. J. J., Lt. 7th Dragoon Gds., att. M.G. Cav., m. France (k. 14.7.16)	H.F.W.T
1915	Hartley, P. H. G. H. S., Lt. Coldstream Gds. France	E.L.V., A.C.R.-W.
1913	Hartmann, R. A. L., Lt. (t. Capt.) 11th Hussars, m. France	M.D.H.
1898	Harvey, C. G. S., D.S.O., Maj. (t. Lt.-Col.) R.F.A., m. France	A.C.J.
1911	Harvey, D. L., 2nd Lt. 9th Lancers. France (k. 2.11.14)	L.S.R.B.
1909	Harvey, F. L., Lt. 9th Lancers. France (k. 30.10.14)	L.S.R.B.
1890	Harvey, G. R. M., Pte. R. Fusiliers, att. Middlesex Regt. France, Siberia	A.C.A.
1909	Harvey, R. E. M. Coke, Lt. Durham L.I., empld. Lt. King's African Rifles, late Pte. R. Fusiliers, w. France, E. Africa, S. Russia	E.L.C.
1912	Harvey, R. G. C., Capt. Suffolk Regt., p. France	H.B.
1902	Harvey, S. E., Capt. 1st (King's) Dragoon Gds., and Staff, w. France	R.C.R.

1901	Harvey, W. J. St. J., Brig.-Gen. (Black Watch), m. 5. France, Mesopotamia (d.w. 2.2.16)	H.B.
..	Harvey-James, A. K. (James at Eton), Capt. Gen. List, att The Buffs, and Staff, late Pte. London Regt., m. 2. France (k. 15.4.17)	H W.M.
1902	Hasluck, N. R., Lt. E. Surrey Regt., att. R. Warwickshire Regt. and London Regt., w. France	C.L.
1900	Hastings, Lord (Mr. Astley at Eton), Lt. 7th Hussars, empld. Lt.-Col. Norfolk Yeomanry, m. 2. France	W.D.
1906	Hatfeild, C. E., M.C., Capt. R.E. Kent Yeomanry, att. The Buffs, m. France, Egypt, Gallipoli, Palestine (k. 21.9.18)	H T.B
1907	Hatfeild, H. S., Lt. 1st (King's) Dragoon Gds., I.E.F. France, Afghanistan	H.T.B.
1890	Havelock-Allan, Sir H. S. M., Bart., M.P. (Havelock at Eton), Maj. Lancashire Fusiliers, and Staff, late Maj. Durham L.I., w. France	H.E.L.
1884	Hawker, C. J., C.M.G., C.B.E. (F) Brig.-Gen. (Coldstream Gds.), m. 2. Egypt, Gallipoli, Mesopotamia, Palestine	E.C.A.L.
1906	Hawker, P. T. R., Lt. R.N.V.R. France, N. and S. Russia	E.L.C.
1916	Hawker, V. L., Lt. R.F.A. Palestine	C.H.K.M.
1878	Hawkins, H. P., C.B.E., Lt.-Col. R.A.M.C.	K.S.
1886	Hawkins, H. R. M., Capt. Dorsetshire Regt., att. S. Staffordshire Regt.	E.C.A.L.
1888	Hawkshaw, O., T.D., Lt.-Col. Engineer and Railway Staff Corps, R.E.	T.D.
1898	Hawley, Sir H. C. W., Bart., Capt. Labour Corps, late Capt. The Queen's Own (R. W. Kent Regt.), w. France	C.H.A.
1875	Haworth-Booth, B. B., Maj. E. Riding of Yorkshire Yeomanry	E.C.A.L.
1897	Hawtrey, G. V., Lt. Gloucestershire Yeomanry, late Lt. Lovat's Scouts. Egypt, Palestine	H.D.
1903	Hay, Lord A. V., Capt. Irish Gds. France (k. 14.9.14)	J.H.M.H.

1907	Hay, B. McE. A., Capt. 19th Hussars, att. R.F.C., w. 2. France	R.P.L.B.
1912	Hay, C. E. E., Lt. 17th Lancers. France (d.w. 9.8.18)	L.S.R B.
1899	Hay, Sir D. E., Bart., Sub-Lt. R.N.D., M.T., and Staff. France	R.A.H.M.
1906	Hay, Lord E. D. J., Lt. Grenadier Gds., att. Gds. M.G. Regt. France, Egypt, Gallipoli	E.W.S.
1878	Hay, H. C. F., T.D., Maj. Black Watch	F.S.S.
1901	Hay, Hon. I. J. L., Capt. 5th Lancers, p. France	A.A.S.
1908	Hay, R. A., Capt. Lothians and Border Horse. France	R.P.L.B.
1877	Hay-Drummond, A. W. H. (Drummond at Eton), Bt. Col. Black Watch, att. Devonshire Regt.	E.H.
1912	Hayes, W. W., Lt. 16th Lancers, w. 3. France	M.D.H.
1910	Hayes-Sadler, C. W. (F) Lt. R.E. France	J.M.D., V.Le N.F.
1897	Hazlerigg, Sir A. G., Bart., Capt. att. R.A.F., late Lt. R.N.V.R.	H E.L.
1898	Headlam, G. W., Lt. Coldstream Gds. France	K.S.
1912	Heath, L. C., Capt. Surrey Yeomanry, att. M.G.C. France, Egypt	H.T.B., S.G.L.
1904	Heath, R. A., M.C., Capt. (t. Maj.) Leicestershire Yeomanry, att. 5th Lancers	A.A.S.
1907	Heath, V. P., Lt. R.H.G. France (d.w. 5.9.14)	A.A.S.
1895	Heathcote, J. R. C., Maj. Cameron Highlanders, att. Lt.-Col. R.A.F. France	E.H., T.C.P.
1899	Heathcote, R. E. M., D.S.O., Capt. (t. Lt.-Col.) R. Scots, att. Shropshire L.I., w. 2, m. 4. France	R.A.H.M.
1889	Heathcote, W. J., 2nd Lt. Sp. List	G.E.M., A.C.J.
1912	Heaton, D. R., D.S.O., Capt. The Queen's, and Staff, w. 2, m. France	R.P.L.B.
1914	Heaton, J. B., Lt. K.R.R.C., w. 2. France	R.P.L.B.
1905	Heaton-Armstrong, J. D., Capt. 20th Deccan Horse, I.A., and Staff, w. France, Egypt, Palestine	R.A.H.M., R.S.de H.
1903	Heaton-Armstrong, W. D. F., Maj. Lancashire Fusiliers, and Staff, m. France	R.S.de H.
1898	Hebert, C., O.B.E., Maj. R.F.A.	T.C.P.

1901	Hebert, R., Lt. R.E. Egypt	T.C.P.
1914	Heffer, O. W., Capt. R. Berkshire Regt. France	J.M.D., V.LeN.F.
1911	Heinekey-Buxton, G. A. (F) Lt. 4th Hussars, att. Bimbashi Egyptian Army, w. 2. France, Egypt	J.H.M.H.
1913	Heinekey-Buxton, R. G., Capt. The Queen's, w., m. France	J.H.M.H.
1885	Heinemann, A. B., Lt. R.F.A., late Pte. R. Fusiliers. France	J.P.C.
1915	Helme, G. M., Lt. Coldstream Gds. France (d.w. .10.17)	E.I., T.P.C
1913	Helme, R. B., Lt. 1st R. Dragoons. France (k. 25.6.17)	E.I
1900	Helme, T. H., Capt. London Regt., w. 2. France, Balkans, Palestine (d.w. 3.11.18)	R.C R
1902	Hely-Hutchinson, C. D., M.C., Lt. R.F.A., late Lt. Transvaal H.A., and Staff, m. 3. France, S.W. Africa, Italy	E.L.V.
1904	Hely-Hutchinson, M. R., M.C., Lt. (t. Capt.) Irish Gds., and Staff, m. France	K.S.
1896	Helyar, M. H., Capt. Rifle Bde. France (k. 24.1.15)	E.L.V
1909	Hemsworth, A. H., 2nd Lt. K.O.Y.L.I. (k. accid. 6.6.15)	M.D.H.
1893	Henderson, Hon. A. P., Maj. Berks Yeomanry	E.I.
1905	Henderson, A. S., Capt. London Regt. France (d.w. 25.4.15)	A.C.G.H.
1907	Henderson, G. L. P., M.C., A.F.C., Maj. R.A.F., late Cpl. R.E., w. 2, m. 2. France	K.S.
1893	Henderson, Hon. H. G., C.V.O. (F) Lt.-Col. Berks Yeomanry, and Staff. Egypt, Gallipoli	E.I.
1914	Henderson, I. H. D., M.C., Capt. A. and S. Highlanders, att. R.A.F., m. France (k. 21.6.18)	A.C.G.H.
1902	Henderson, J. K., 2nd Lt. R.A.F.	P.W.
1900	Henderson, N. G. B., D.S.O., Maj. Black Watch, and Staff, w., m. France	E.I.
1899	Henderson, Hon. P., Maj. (t. Lt.-Col.) Westminster Dragoons, att. Tank Corps. France, Egypt	E.I.
1899	Henderson, R. E., Lt. R.H.G., late Lovat's Scouts, and Staff. France, Egypt, Gallipoli	C.L.

1912	Henderson, R. H. W., Lt. 1st R. Dragoons, w. France	E.I.
1898	Henderson, S. C., Capt. 17th Lancers	E.H., F.J.T.
1899	Heneage, A. P., D.S.O. (F) Maj. R.F.A., m. 3. France, Balkans, Egypt	E.L.V.
1886	Heneage, G. C. W., D.S.O., M.V.O., Maj. Grenadier Gds., and Staff, m. 5. France	J.P.C.
1883	Heneage, Hon. G. E., O.B.E., Lt.-Col. Lincolnshire Regt. France	C.L.L.-C., J.C.
1883	Heneage, Hon. H. G., D.S.O., Maj. 12th Lancers, empld. Lt.-Col. Lincolnshire Yeomanry. France	J.C.
1889	Heneage, I. D., Capt. Lothians and Border Horse. France	J.P.C.
1890	Henley, Hon. A. M., C.M.G., D.S.O., Brig.-Gen. (5th Lancers), m. 8. France	C.H.E.
1895	Henley, C. F., Maj. Oxfordshire and Bucks L.I., w. 2, p., m. Mesopotamia	H.D.
1893	Hennessy, G. R. J., M.P., O.B.E., Maj. K.R.R.C., w., m. France	P.H.C., C.H.A.
1890	Henniker, Lord, Lt.-Col. Rifle Bde. France	H.G.W., P.W.
1912	Henriques, P. B., 2nd Lt. K.R.R.C. France (k. 24.7.15)	H.F.W.T., A.E.C.
1895	Hensley, C. H. R., Air Mechanic R.A.F.	E.L.V.
1903	Henty, G. H., Maj. Suffolk Regt., w., m. 2. France (k. 30.11.17)	P.W.
1898	Herbert, Hon. A. N. H. M., M.P. (F) Capt. Irish Gds., empld. Lt.-Col. Staff, att. Australian and New Zealand E.F., w., m. France, Balkans, Gallipoli, Italy, Mesopotamia	A.C.B.
1889	Herbert, E. A. F. W., the late, T.D., Maj. Yorkshire Hussars (d. 25.7.20)	A.C., J.H.M.
1907	Herbert, E. R. H., Capt. (t. Maj.) K.R.R.C., and Staff, w. France	H.Br.
1905	Herbert, Hon. G. S., Capt. Wiltshire Regt.	H.T.B.
1910	Herbert, M. G., Lt. R.H.G., late 2nd Lt. R. Wiltshire Yeomanry, w. France	A.M.G.

1908	Herbert, S., Lt. R.H.G., late Lt. R. Wiltshire Yeomanry, w., m. France	A.M.G.
1899	Heriot, G. E., 2nd Lt. Sharpshooters. Egypt (d. 11.12.15)	C.H.A.
1904	Herman, G. L., Capt. The Queen's Own (R. W. Kent Regt.), and Staff. Mesopotamia	K.S.
1895	Hermon, E. W., D.S.O., Maj. King Edward's Horse, empld. Lt.-Col. Northumberland Fusiliers, m. 3. France (k. 9.4.17)	E.I.
1893	Hermon, J. V., D.S.O., Capt. Cheshire Yeomanry, att. 6th Dragoon Gds. (Carabiniers), w. 3., m. France	J.C., E.I.
1916	Hermon, R. O., Lt. Coldstream Gds.	E.I., T.F.C.
1899	Herringham, G. W., Capt. 6th (Inniskilling) Dragoons, att. 5th Dragoon Gds. France (k. 31.10.14)	K.S.
1896	Herschell, Lord, G.C.V.O. (F) (Mr. Herschell at Eton), Cr. R.N.V.R.	A.C.B.
1904	Hervey-Bathurst, A. R., D.C.M. (F) Sergt. R.F.C., late 2nd Lt. Rifle Bde., and Sergt. R.A.S.C., M.T., w. France	R.S. de H.
1899	Hervey-Bathurst, B. E., Maj. Northumberland Fusiliers, and Staff, w. 2. France	R.A.H.M.
1888	Hervey-Bathurst, Sir F. E. W., Bart., D.S.O (F) Maj. Grenadier Gds., and Staff, m. 3. France	R.A.H.M.
1885	Heseltine, C., O.B.E., Lt.-Col. R. Fusiliers, and Staff, m. 2. France, Balkans, Egypt, Italy	F.H.R.
1889	Heseltine, G., Capt. 6th Dragoon Gds. (Carabiniers), and Staff. France	F.H.R.
1898	Heseltine, J. E. N., D.S.O. (F) Bt. Lt.-Col. K.R.R.C., and Staff, w. 2, m. 2. France	F.H.R.
1904	Heseltine, N. E., Lt. Essex Regt.	F.H.R.
1905	Hewitt, G. S., Capt. King's African Rifles, late Trooper E. African Mounted Rifles, m. E. Africa	J.M.D.
1914	Hext, T. M., 2nd Lt. K.R.R.C. France (k. 28.4.17)	J.H.M.H.
1876	Heygate, R. H. G., D.S.O., Bt. Col. Staff	E.W.
1911	Heyman, W. A. C., Capt. 4th Hussars, att. R.A.F. France, Balkans, Egypt	J.M.D., V. Le N.F.

1903	Heywood, A. G. P., Maj. Manchester Regt., w. France, Egypt (d.w. 12.9.18)	C. H. A.
1898	Heywood, C. P., C.M.G., D.S.O. (F) Brig.-Gen. (Coldstream Gds.), m. 6. France, N. Russia	C.H.A.
1872	Heywood, H. de la P. B., Capt. R. Defence Corps	J.L.J.
1904	Heywood, M. B., M.V.O., D.S.O. (F) Capt. (t. Maj.) Northumberland Yeomanry, and Staff, m. 3. France, Italy	T.C.P.
1883	Heywood-Lonsdale, H. H., D.S.O., Lt.-Col. Shropshire Yeomanry, att. Shropshire L.I., m. 2. France, Egypt, Palestine	E.W.
1888	Heywood-Lonsdale, J. P. H., D.S.O., T.D., Maj. (t. Lt.-Col.) Shropshire Yeomanry, att. Shropshire L.I., and Staff, m. France, Egypt, Palestine	E.W., W.D.
1880	Heyworth, F. J., C.B., D.S.O., Brig.-Gen. (Scots Gds.), m. 3. France (k. 9.5.16)	C.W.D., H.D.
1914	Heyworth-Savage, R. F., Lt. 1st R. Dragoons, att. R.E. France	H.M.
1909	Hibbert, A. P. J. (F) Capt. (t. Maj.) R. Berkshire Regt., att. British W. Indies Regt., and Staff, w. France, Egypt	E.I.
1906	Hibbert, L. R., Capt. The King's Own (R. Lancaster Regt.), att. R.A.F. France	E.I.
1890	Hicks, R. S., Lt. (t. Capt.) Suffolk Yeomanry	J.C.
1910	Hicks-Beach, W. G., Lt., late Trooper, Roughriders	F.H.R., H.de H.
1908	Higgins, C. G., 2nd Lt., late Pte., W. Yorkshire Regt. France (d.w. 1.7.16)	A.A.S
1909	Higham, E. E., Lt., late Pte., London Regt., w. France	R.C.R., M.D.H.
1912	Higham, R. H., Capt. R. Welch Fusiliers, and Staff, w. 2. France	H.F.W.T., A.E.C.
1914	Hilder, T. M. M., Lt. 6th (Inniskilling) Dragoons. France	L.S.R.B.
1889	Hildyard, H. R., Maj. R. Defence Corps, att. W. Riding Regt., late Maj. Leicestershire Regt. France	A.C.A.
1913	Hill, Lord A. F. H., Lt. R. Scots Greys, att. R.E. France	C.H.K.M.

1904	Hill, Rev. A. P., C.F., w. France	K.S.
1916	Hill, C. I. H., 2nd Lt. R. Welch Fusiliers, att. Bedfordshire Regt. India	L.S.R.B.
1916	Hill, C. V., 2nd Lt. R.F.A., w. France	J.H.M.H.
1891	Hill, G. R., Capt. R. Defence Corps, att. R.A.F.	K.S.
1910	Hill, H. M., 2nd Lt. 5th Dragoon Gds., w. France	A.A.S.
1911	Hill, J. A., Capt. R.E., and Staff. France	E.L.V.
1915	Hill, R. A. G., Lt. R.A.F., late 2nd Lt. Somerset L.I. France (k. 12.8.18)	A.A.S.
1910	Hill, R. G., Lt. R.F.A. France	C.H.A., P.V.B.
1893	Hill, W. J. M., D.S.O. (F) Lt.-Col. Scots Gds., late att. Loyal N. Lancashire Regt., London Regt., and The Queen's, m. 2. France, Palestine	E.L.V.
1888	Hill-Wood, Sir S. H., Bart., M.P. (Wood at Eton), Capt. (t. Maj.) Cheshire Regt., and Staff	J.P.C.
1912	Hillier, F. J. H., Lt. R. Fusiliers, late Pte. S. African Infantry, Cpl. R.E., and Lt. King's African Rifles, m. E. Africa, S. Africa, S. W. Africa, Russia	H. de H.
1907	Hillingdon, Lord (Mr. Mills at Eton), Lt. W. Kent Yeomanry. Gallipoli	H.T.B.
1909	Hills, A. L. F., Capt. Cheshire Regt., w. France	R.S.K.
1912	Hills, C. H., 2nd Lt. Manchester Regt., att. R.A.F., late Trooper Botha's L.H. France, S. Africa (d.w. 5.9.16)	H M.
1885	Hills, J. W., M.P., Maj. Durham L.I., w., m. France	H.E.L.
1912	Hills, W. F. W., Lt. R.F.A., att. R.F.C. France, Balkans, Egypt (k. 6.3.17)	H.M.
1913	Hilton-Greene, C. C. H., 2nd Lt. 1st R. Dragoons, late R. Wiltshire Yeomanry, w. France	R.S.K.
1891	Hinckes, R. T. (Davenport at Eton), Capt. Herefordshire Regt.	H.E.L., A.C., H.W.M.
1895	Hindlip, Lord, O.B.E. (Mr. Allsopp at Eton), Capt. Sp. List, m. 2	F.T., R.A.H.M.
1903	Hippisley, H. H. S., Air Mechanic R.A.F., w. France, Balkans, Egypt, Mesopotamia	J.M.D.
1913	Hirsch, J. H., Lt. 13th Hussars. France, Mesopotamia	H. de H.

1896	Hoare, A. H., Lt. R.G.A., and Staff. France	S.A.D.
1890	Hoare, Rev. A. R., C.F., m. France	G.E.M., R.C.R.
1905	Hoare, A. S., Capt. 2nd Life Gds. France	H.T.B.
1894	Hoare, C. H., D.S.O. and Bar, Maj. W. Kent Yeomanry, empld. Lt.-Col. M.G.C., late att. W. Yorkshire Regt., w., m. 3. France, Egypt, Gallipoli	S.A.D.
1917	Hoare, E. B., 2nd Lt. Grenadier Gds.	A.C.G.H.
1912	Hoare, E. R., Lt. 21st Lancers, and Staff. France	R.S.K.
1912	Hoare, E. R. D., Lt. Grenadier Gds., att. Gds. T.M.B., w. France	E.I.
1890	Hoare, G. de M. G., Capt. London Regt.	S.A.D.
1897	Hoare, G. L., C.B.E. (F) Bt. Lt.-Col. R.A. France	E.I.
1898	Hoare, G. S., Maj. R.G.A., w. France, Balkans, Egypt	S.A.D.
1884	Hoare, Henry, Maj. Suffolk Yeomanry	E.W.
1878	Hoare, Herbert, O.B.E., Maj. 5th Dragoon Gds.	J.B.L.
1914	Hoare, J. E. A., D.S.C., Capt. R.A.F., late Sub-Lt. Armoured Cars, R.N.V.R., late L/ce Cpl. Middlesex Hussars. Home Waters, Gallipoli	E.W.S.
1898	Hoare, L. L., D.S.O., Maj. (t. Lt.-Col.) R.A.O.C., m. 2. France	E.I.
1902	Hoare, P. H. T., 2nd Lt. E. Lancashire Regt. France (d.w. 2.1.15)	H.M
1884	Hoare, R., C.M.G., D.S.O. (F) Brig.-Gen. (4th Hussars), w., m. 4. France, Egypt, Gallipoli, Palestine	F.T.
1901	Hoare, R. L., Capt. London Regt., late 2nd Lt. The Queen's Own (R. W. Kent Regt.), w. France (k. 1.7.16)	I.
1892	Hoare, V. R., Maj. London Regt. France (k. 15.2.15)	G.E.M., R.C.R.
1887	Hoare, W. R., Capt. Hampshire Regt., att. R.A.F.	G.E.M.
1888	Hobart, C. V. C., D.S.O., O.B.E., Maj. Grenadier Gds., empld. Lt.-Col. Staff, m. 3. France	E.C.A.L.
1902	Hobhouse, A. L., Lt. R.A.S.C., and Staff. France	H.E.L., H.T.B.
1879	Hobhouse, E., Lt.-Col. R.A.M.C.	W.E., J.M.E.
1911	Hobhouse, J. R., M.C., Capt. R.G.A., w. France	K.S.
1912	Hobhouse, P. E., Capt. Somerset L.I., w. 2, m. France (k. 21.3.18)	K.S.

1911	Hobson, A. C., Lt. 2nd Life Gds., w. France (k. 13.5.15)	I.L.C.
1900	Hodgkinson, G. W., M.C. and Bar (F) Capt. Westminster Dragoons, att. R.A.F., late E. African Mounted Rifles, Nairobi F.F. E. Africa	A.C.A.
1908	Hodgkinson, I. T., Lt. Somerset L.I. India	A.C.G.H.
1901	Hodgson, A. H. F., Maj. Remount Service	H.B.
1895	Hodgson, A. T., Lt. W. Yorkshire Regt., w. France	H.B.
1882	Hodgson, B. T., C.M.G., V.D., Lt.-Col. R. Sussex Regt.	E.C.A.L.
1904	Hodgson, C., M.C., Lt. The Queen's Own (R.W. Kent Regt.), late Sergt. R. Fusiliers. Egypt, Gallipoli, Palestine	A.C.A., R.S.de H.
1901	Hodgson, C. A. G., Capt. R. N. Devon Yeomanry, att. Devonshire Regt. Egypt, Gallipoli, Palestine (d. 20.3.18)	P.W.
1900	Hodgson, C. B. M. (F) Capt. The Queen's, att. London Regt., m. 2. France, Egypt, Gallipoli, Palestine (d.w. 1.4.18)	P.W.
1888	Hodgson, E. T., Capt. R. Sussex Regt.	E.C.A.L.
1895	Hodgson, G. C. S., M.C. (F) Maj. W. Somerset Yeomanry, and Staff, m. 3. France	W.D.
1899	Hodgson, H. E. A., Capt. The Queen's, empld. Capt. Norfolk Regt., and Staff. France, India	P.W.
1906	Hodgson, H. J., D.S.O., Capt. Cheshire Regt., empld. Lt.-Col. Wiltshire Regt., w., m. 2. France, Balkans	A.A.S.
1887	Hodgson, Sir H. W., K.C.M.G., C.V.O., C.B. (F) Maj.-Gen. (15th Hussars), m. 6. Egypt, Gallipoli, Palestine	E.C.A.L.
1896	Hodgson, M. R. K., Capt. R. Fusiliers, att. K.O.Y.L.I., m. France (k. 17.3.15)	W.D.
1898	Hodgson, W. T., D.S.O., M.C., Bt. Lt.-Col. 1st R. Dragoons, and Staff, m. 4. France, Palestine	E.C.A.L.
1892	Hogg, I. C., Lt.-Col. 4th Hussars. France (d.w. 2.9.14)	R.C.R.
1904	Hohler, A. P., D.S.O. and Bar (F) Lt.-Col. Middlesex Regt., m. Egypt, Gallipoli, Palestine (d. 7.3.19)	C.L., R.P.L.B.
1900	Holbech, W. H., Lt. Scots Gds. France (d.w. 1.11.14)	S.R.J., J.H.M.H.
1916	Holden, Hon. A W. E., 2nd Lt. Coldstream Gds.	A.M.G.

1880	Holden, E. C. S., the late, D.S.O., T.D., Maj Derbyshire Yeomanry (d. 17.5.16)	C.H.E.
1891	Holder, A. C., Capt. R.A.S.C., m. France	H.B.
1881	Holdsworth, G. L., C.B., C.M.G. (F) Brig.-Gen. (7th Hussars), m. 2. France, Egypt, Mesopotamia	C.C.J.
1880	Hole, S. H. F. (F) Maj. Sherwood Foresters, and Staff, m. France, Palestine	F.F.V.
1909	Hole, S. J. M., M.C. and Bar, Maj. R. Fusiliers, w. France	R.S. de H.
1877	Holford, Sir G. L., K.C.V.O., C.I.E., C.B.E., Bt. Lt.-Col. 1st Life Gds.	W.E.
1895	Holland, E., M.C., 2nd Lt. Scots Gds., late Lt. Worcestershire Yeomanry, m. France, Gallipoli (k. 13.9.16)	J.M.L.
1889	Holland, E. C. (F) Maj. Remount Service, m. Balkans, Egypt	A.C.J.
1885	Holland, M. J., M.C., Capt., late Trooper, King Edward's Horse. France, E. Africa	J.M.E.
1901	Holland, R. T., D.S.O., M.C. (F) Maj. R.F.A., and Staff, m. 2. France	E.L.V.
1885	Holland, W. F. C., Capt. Sp. List, att. Durham L.I., and Staff. (d. 8.11.17)	E.S S., A.C
1911	Holland, W. T. F., A.F.C., Capt. 21st Lancers, att. R.A.F., late att. 9th Lancers, w. 2. France	J.H.M.H.
1907	Holland-Hibbert, T., Capt. R. Scots Greys, late Lt. Herts Yeomanry. France, Egypt, Gallipoli	H.M.
1911	Holland-Hibbert, W., Capt. Herts Yeomanry. Egypt	H.M.
1916	Holland-Martin, E. G. R. (Martin-Holland at Eton), 2nd Lt. 16th Lancers. France (k. 26.3.18)	C. H K M
1910	Holley, E. J. H., M.C., Capt. R. 1st Devon Yeomanry, empld. Lt.-Col. Devonshire Regt., w., m. 2. France, Egypt, Gallipoli, Palestine	A.M.G.
1903	Hollings, J. H. B., Lt. 21st Lancers, att. 9th Lancers, w. France (k. 1.11.14)	H M
1895	Hollins, A. M., Capt. Loyal N. Lancashire Regt.	E.I.
1896	Hollins, F. H., Capt. Rifle Bde. France	E.I.
1897	Hollins, H. F., Maj. R.G.A. Mesopotamia (d. 19.8.17)	R C R

1909	Hollins, J. C. H., Lt. Loyal N. Lancashire Regt.	E.I.
1897	Hollins, P. L., Lt. R.A.S.C., M.T. France, Italy	E.I.
1911	Hollins, W. A., Lt. A. and S. Highlanders, late Pte. H.A.C., w., m. France	E.I.
1914	Hollond, G. E., Lt. Suffolk Regt.	A.B.R.
1910	Hollond, R. C., Capt. Rifle Bde., w., m. France	H.Br.
1913	Hollway, C. R., Lt. K.R.R.C., and Staff, w. France, Italy	K.S.
1873	Hollway, E. J., Bt. Col. Staff. France	F.F.V.
1887	Holmes-Tarn, H. (Tarn at Eton), Maj. K.R.R.C.	H.G.W.
1915	Holmes-Tarn, K. A., Lt. R.F.A., w. France	V.LeN.F.
1914	Holmesdale, Visc., M.C., Capt. Coldstream Gds., w. 2, m. France	V.LeN.F.
1904	Holmpatrick, Lord, D.S.O., M.C., Capt. 16th Lancers, w., m. 3. France	A.A.S.
1916	Holms-Kerr, R. K., Lt. Seaforth Highlanders. France	V.LeN.F., L.T.
1905	Holt, A. V., D.S.O. (F) Capt. Black Watch, att. R.A.F., w., m. France	A.C.B., A.M.G.
1903	Holt, F. V., C.M.G., D.S.O., Lt.-Col. Oxfordshire and Bucks L.I., and Brig.-Gen. (R.A.F.), m. 2. France	A.C.B.
1915	Holt, G. V., 2nd Lt. R.F.A. France (k. 2.9.17)	A.M.G
1881	Holt, H. E. S., C.B.E. (F) Maj. R.A.F., empld. Col. Instructor French Corps d'Aviation. France	A.C.J.
1897	Holt, R. V., D.S.O., Cr. R.N. Home Waters	A.C.B.
1906	Holt, V. H., M.C. (F) Capt. R.F.A., and Staff, m. France, E. Africa	E.L.V.
1892	Home, Earl of (Lord Dunglass at Eton), Lt.-Col. Lanarkshire Yeomanry, m. Egypt, Gallipoli	W.D.
1904	Homfray, H. C. R., Lt. Glamorgan Yeomanry	S.A.D., P.V.B.
1882	Homfray, H. R., V.D., Col. Welch Regt.	C.W.D., A.C.
1916	Honeywill, S. R., 2nd Lt. R. Fusiliers. France (k. 8.10.18)	H.B., R.H de M.
1884	Hood, Visc., O.B.E. (Mr. Hood at Eton), Maj. Grenadier Gds., empld. Lt.-Col. Staff	G.E.M.

1906	Hope, Lord C. M., Capt. Lothians and Border Horse. France, Balkans	E.L.C.
1905	Hope, G. E., M.C., Capt. Grenadier Gds., empld. Lt.-Col. Lancashire Fusiliers, and Staff, w., m. 3. France (k. 10.10.17)	A.C.B., A.M.G.
1900	Hope, G. M., Lt. R.N.V.R.	A.C.A.
1887	Hope, Sir J. A., Bart., M.P., O.B.E., Maj. K.R.R.C., empld. Lt.-Col. Staff, w. France	A.C.J.
1899	Hope, J. A. H., Maj. Manitoba Regt., Canadian E.F., w. 2, m. France	W.D., E.C.A.L.
1910	Hope, J. H., Lt. Field Survey Co., R.E. France	L.S.R.B.
1911	Hope, M. B., Lt. K.R.R.C., p. France	H.Br.
1896	Hope, S. J., C.P.O., R.N.A.S., late Lt. Seaforth Highlanders	A.C.A.
1903	Hope-Jones, W., Lieut. R.G.A., att. Field Survey Coy., R.E., m. France	K.S.
1906	Hope-Morley, Hon. C., Lt. Grenadier Gds., w., m. France	F.H.R.
1889	Hope-Wallace, J., Lt. Northumberland Fusiliers, m. France (d.w. 15.9.17)	H.B.
1912	Hopkins, H. P., Sergt. Tank Corps, American Army. France	L.S.R.B.
1893	Hopkins, R. B., O.B.E. (F) Capt. Manchester Regt., empld. Staff, m. E. Africa	E.I.
1899	Hopkins, R. S., D.S.O., M.C. (F) Maj. E. Yorkshire Regt., att. Welch Regt., w., m. 2. France, Balkans, Egypt	H.D.
1899	Hopkins, U. S., Capt. R. Berkshire Regt., w. 2. France, Palestine	H.D.
1897	Hopkinson, R. C., Capt. Northumberland Fusiliers, and Staff. France	C.L.
1907	Hopwood, R. H., Lt., late Pte., Middlesex Regt. France (k. 4.2.16)	C H.A., A.B.R
1913	Hordern, C. H., Capt. K.R.R.C., att. Seaforth Highlanders, w. 3. France	E.L.C.
1911	Hordern, H. M., M.C., Capt. R.G.A., m. France	E.L.C.

1907	Hore, C. W. C., Lt. R.N.A.S. France	H.F.W.T.
1905	Horlick, G. N., Maj. Gloucestershire Yeomanry, att. M.G.C., m. 2. Egypt, Gallipoli, Palestine (d. 5.7.18)	J.H.M.H
1904	Horlick, J. N., O.B.E., M.C. (F) Bt. Maj. (t. Lt.-Col.) Coldstream Gds., and Staff, m. 4. France, Balkans, S. Russia	J.H.M.H.
1907	Hornby, H. R., Lt. Duke of Lancaster's Own Yeomanry, and Staff. France	R.S.K.
1895	Hornby, R. P., M.C., Capt. Lancashire Fusiliers, and Staff, m. France, Egypt, Gallipoli, Palestine	J.M.E.
1912	Hornby, W. R., 2nd Lt. E. Lancashire Regt. Egypt, Gallipoli (k. 4.6.15)	R.S.K
1908	Horne, A. E., M.C. (F) Capt. Surrey Yeomanry, and Staff, m. 4. France, Balkans	P.W.
1916	Horne, D. E. A., Lt. Grenadier Gds., w. France	R.P.L.B.
1907	Horne, W. G., Lt. 19th Hussars, and Staff, p. France, S. Russia	P.W.
1906	Horner, E. W., Lt. 18th Hussars, late N. Somerset Yeomanry, and Staff, w. France, Egypt (k. 21.11.17)	E.I
1909	Hornsby, J. A., Capt. 5th Lancers, and Staff, w. 2. France	H.Br.
1910	Hornsby, R. L. W., 2nd Lt. Lincolnshire Regt. Gallipoli (k. 9.9.15)	H Br.
1914	Hornung, A. O., 2nd Lt. Essex Regt. France (k. 6.7.15)	H. de H
1911	Horsfall, E. D., M.C. (F) Maj. R.A.F., late 2nd Lt. Rifle Bde., m. France	P.W.
1885	Horsfall, H. L., Lt. Suffolk Regt.	J.M.E.
1906	Horsfall, R., Staff Sergt. R.A.S.C.	E.L.V.
1907	Horsfall, R. E., Capt. The King's (Liverpool Regt.). France (k. 20.11.17)	E.I
1907	Horsfall, T. H. S., 2nd Lt. R.G.A., w. 2. France	R.C.R.
1913	Horton, F. H. Le G., Capt. Rifle Bde., and Staff. France	H.Br.
1911	Horton, Le G. G. W., Capt. K.R.R.C., att. R.A.F. France	H.Br.
1914	Hoskins, H. M., Lt. R.A.F., late Lt. N. Staffordshire Regt., w. France	J.M.D., V.Le N.F.

1908	Hoskyns, E. C. L., Lt. R. Welch Fusiliers. France (k. 21.10.14)	H.T B
1889	Houghton, A. V., Lt. R.A.F., late R.N.V.R.	K.S.
1895	Houghton, R. J., O.B.E., Capt. Cheshire Yeomanry, att. Imp. Camel Corps, m. Egypt, Palestine	P.W.
1886	Houldsworth, Sir H. H., Bart., Maj. A. and S. Highlanders	H.D.
1914	Houldsworth, H. W., M.C., Lt. Seaforth Highlanders, w. 2., m. France	P.W., F.E.R.
1910	Houldsworth, J. F. H., Capt. Gordon Highlanders, p., m. France	P.W.
1885	Houldsworth, J. H., Capt. Staff	G.E.M.
1909	Houldsworth, W. G., Lt. Scots Gds. France (d.w. 23.9.14)	J.M.F., M.D.H
1893	Houldsworth, W. T. R., T.D. (F) Maj. (t. Lt.-Col.) Ayrshire Yeomanry, w. France, Egypt, Gallipoli, Palestine	H.D.
1908	Hoult, J. M., Capt. R.F.A. France, Egypt, Gallipoli	C.H.A., A.B.R.
1894	Houstoun-Boswall, Sir G. R., Bart., Lt. (t. Capt.) Grenadier Gds. France (k. 27.9.15)	C.H.E., C.L.
1900	Houstoun-Boswall, Sir T. R., Bart., Capt. R. Scots	R.W.W.-T.
1914	Howard, Hon. A. J. P. (F) Capt. Scots Gds., late Pte. London Regt., w. 4. France	H.Br.
1897	Howard, B. H., Maj. 47th Sikhs, I.A. Mesopotamia (k. 8.3.16)	F.L.V
1895	Howard, C. A., D.S.O. and Bar (F) Bt. Lt.-Col. K.R.R.C., and Staff, w., m. 2. France, Egypt	A.C.A.
1893	Howard, C. A. M., Maj. Staffordshire Regt., and Staff	F.W.C., J.H.M.H.
1910	Howard, Hon. D. S. P. (F) Capt. 3rd Hussars. France	H. Br.
1894	Howard, G. W., C.M.G., D.S.O. (F) Brig.-Gen. (Essex Regt.), and Staff, w., m. 7. France, Italy	H.E.L.
1899	Howard, H. C. L., C.M.G., D.S.O. and Bar (F) Bt. Lt.-Col. 16th Lancers, and Staff, w., m. 9. France, Italy	S.A.D.
1899	Howard, H. S., Lt. R. Warwickshire Regt.	F.L.V.

1914	Howard, J. B., Capt. R. Welch Fusiliers, w. France (d.w. 6.4.18)	F.V.B.
1911	Howard, Hon. R. H. P., 2nd Lt. E. Surrey Regt. France (k. .5.15)	H. Br.
1917	Howard, W. R. J., 2nd Lt. 1st R. Dragoons	H. de H.
1902	Howard-Bury, C. K., D.S.O., Lt.-Col. K.R.R.C., p., m. 4. France	P.W.
1897	Howard de Walden, Lord (Mr. Ellis at Eton), Maj. Westminster Dragoons, att. R. Welch Fusiliers, and Staff. France, Egypt, Gallipoli	E.C.A.L.
1914	Howard Vincent, V. N. E., Lt. (t. Capt.) K.R.R.C., and Staff, w. France	E.W.S.
1902	Howard-Vyse, R. G. H., C.M.G., D.S.O., Brig.-Gen. (R.H.G.), m. 5. France, Egypt, Palestine	R.W.W.-T.
1902	Howey, J. E. P., Capt. Bedfordshire Yeomanry, att. R.F.C. and 13th Hussars, p. France, Mesopotamia	R.W.W.-T.
1914	Hubbard, B. J., M.C., Lt. Grenadier Gds., late Pte. R. Fusiliers. France (k. 1.12.17)	E.L.V., K.S.
1904	Hubbard, E. W., 2nd Lt. Welsh Gds., att. Gds. M.G. Regt., w. France	A.A.S.
1906	Hubbard, Hon. F. S., Pte. R. Fusiliers. France	R.S.K.
1900	Hubbard, G. N., Capt. Irish Gds., w., m. France	A.A.S.
1901	Hubbard, Rev. H. E., D.S.O., M.C., C.F., w., m. 2. France	A.A.S.
1912	Hudson, A. J. B., M.C., Lt. Worcestershire Regt. France, Balkans (k. 7.6.17)	R.S.K.
1914	Hudson, A. U. M., Lt. R. Berkshire Regt., att. Gds. M.G. Regt., w. France	A.E.C.
1914	Hudson, B. M. M., Capt., late L/ce-Cpl., Middlesex Hussars. Balkans, Egypt, Gallipoli, Palestine	H.F.W.T., A.E.C.
1902	Hudson, J. H., Lt. R.F.A. France (d.w. 12.1.16)	H.B.
1894	Hudson-Kinahan, D. D., Lt. Irish Gds., late Scottish Horse. France (k. 9.4.16)	F.W.C., J.H.M.H.
1912	Hughes, A. W., Lt. R.F.A., w. 2. France	E.I.
1906	Hughes, G. R., Capt. Dorsetshire Regt., w. Gallipoli	E.I.

1903	Hughes, J. S., M.C., Capt. Grenadier Gds., w., m. France	R.C.R.
1902	Hughes, T. McK., Lt. K.R.R.C., att. R.F.C., and Staff, late Pte. London Regt., m. 2. France (k. 6.2.18)	F.F.
1915	Hughes-Hughes, E. P. A. de B., Lt. Welsh Gds., att. M.G.C. France	H.B., R.H. de M.
1880	Hughes-Onslow, A., Maj. 10th R. Hussars, att. Remount Service. France (d. 17.8.14)	C.C.J.
1912	Hughes-Onslow, O., Capt. Irish Gds. France	R.S. de H.
1907	Hulse, Sir E. H. W., Bart., Capt. Scots Gds., m. France (k. 12.3.15)	R.S.K.
1900	Hulton, H. H., D.S.O., Maj. R.F.A., att. Australian Staff, w. 2, m. 4. France	H.B.
1898	Hulton-Harrop, H. de L., Lt. 5th Lancers, att. 1st Life Gds., w. France (k. 12.5.15)	F.T., R.A.H.M.
1905	Hume-Williams, R. E., Capt. R.A.S.C. France	J.H.M.H.
1877	Hunt, R., M.P., Maj. Roughriders	O.B., H.W.M.
1893	Hunter, C. F., D.S.O. (F) Bt. Lt.-Col. 4th Dragoon Gds., and Staff, m. 5. France	P.W.
1875	Hunter, Sir C. R., Bart., M.P., Maj. Sp. List	G.E.M.
1911	Hunter, H. J. F., M.C., Maj. Rifle Bde., att. R.A.F., w., m. France	C.H.K.M.
1907	Hunter, K. S., Capt. 6th Dragoon Gds. (Carabiniers), w., m. France	A.C.G.H.
1914	Hunter, M., Lt. 9th Lancers. France (d.w. 11.4.18)	P.V.F.
1914	Hunter, T. V., Capt. Rifle Bde., att. R.F.C. France, Italy (k. 5.12.17)	C.H.K.M.
1888	Hunter, W. C., Lt.-Col. Oxfordshire and Bucks L.I., and Staff, m. France	A.C.J.
1916	Hunter Blair, C. E., Lt. Scots Gds., w. France	S.G.L.
1889	Huntington, A. W., D.S.O., Maj. Duke of Lancaster's Own Yeomanry, att. Loyal N. Lancashire Regt. France	J.P.C.
1906	Huntington, Sir C. P., Bart., Lt. R. Irish Regt., w. France	P.W.

1901 Huntington, G. W., 2nd Lt. K.R.R.C., late Pte. Ceylon
    Planters' Corps. France, Egypt, Gallipoli (k. 24.8.16)   H D., H T B

1902 Huntington, L. W., Lt. R.N.V.R., att. Armoured Cars,
    R.N.A.S. Home Waters, Egypt, Gallipoli   H. Br.

1914 Huntington-Whiteley, H. M. (Whiteley at Eton), Lt.
    R.N., w. Home Waters, Mediterranean   A.C.G.H.

1914 Huntsman, B. C., Capt. Sherwood Foresters. France
    (k. 7.4.17)   P.V.B.

1890 Hurst, G. H. J., Capt. (t. Maj.) R.G.A. France   K.S.

1880 Hussey, A. H., C.B., C.M.G. (F) Brig.-Gen. (R.A.),
    m. 7. France, Italy   E.W.

1895 Hussey, F. K. E., Lt., late Sapper, R.E. Balkans   S.R.J.

1917 Hustler, W. M. C., 2nd Lt. R. Irish Fusiliers, att.
    E. Lancashire Regt. Balkans   A.C.R.-W.

1890 Hutchison, C. G. G., Bt. Lt.-Col. empld. R.A.O.C.   A.C.A.

1896 Hutchison, C. K., Capt. R. Scots, late Capt. Coldstream
    Gds., p. France   R.A.H.M.

1898 Huth, A. H., Capt. E. Surrey Regt. France (k. 20.4.15)   C.L.

1897 Huth, G. E., Maj. E. Surrey Regt. France   C.H.E., C.L.

1888 Hutton, C. E., Maj. R.M., empld. Staff, R.N.D. France   G.E.M.

1896 Hutton-Riddell, G., M.V.O., Maj. 16th Lancers, and Staff,
    m. France, E. Africa   E.I.

1906 Huxley, J. S., 2nd Lt. Intell. Corps, late 2nd Lt. R.A.S.C.
    Italy   K.S.

1893 Hyslop, W., Lt. Oxfordshire and Bucks L.I., late Lt.
    E. Surrey Regt., w. 2. France, Balkans   E.L.V.

1892 Ilchester, Earl of, O.B.E. (Lord Stavordale at Eton),
    Capt. Coldstream Gds., and Staff, m. 2. France,
    Egypt, Gallipoli, Russia   G.E.M., T.D.

1900 Illingworth, D., Maj. R.A.F. Staff, late Lt. R.N.V.R.,
    att. Armoured Cars, R.N.A.S., w. Egypt, Gallipoli   E.L.V.

1914 Illingworth, H. C. H., M.C., Lt. K.R.R.C., w., p. France   M.D.H.

1879 Impey, E., Capt. Sp. List   K.S.

1914	Impey, J. E., Lt. Lincolnshire Regt., att. M.G.C. France (k. 27.3.16)	P.V.B.
1917	Impey, L. A. (F) 2nd Lt. Coldstream Gds., late French Red Cross	C.M.W.
1914	Impey, M. E., Sub-Lt. Hawke Bn., R.N.D. France	F.L., K.S.
1893	Ind, A. E. B., Maj. N. Staffordshire Regt., and Staff. France	R.A.H.M.
1902	Ind, R. J. W., Capt. W. Yorkshire Regt. France	E.I.
1889	Ingham, C. G. St. M., C.M.G., D.S.O. (F) Brig.-Gen. (R.A.), w., m. 4. France	K.S
1902	Ingleby, C. R., Maj. R.A.F., late Lt.-Cr. Benbow and Anson Bns., R.N.D., w. France, Egypt, Gallipoli	P.W.
1913	Ingleby, I. H. (F) Lt. (t. Capt.) Grenadier Gds., m. 3. France	A.B.R.
1899	Inglis, J. A. C., Lt. H.L.I., att. Seaforth Highlanders. France (k. 9.5.15)	C.H.A
1879	Inglis, W. R., Maj. Norfolk Regt., empld. Lt.-Col. The Queen's and R. Fusiliers. (d. 30.3.16)	R.A.H.M
1916	Inglis-Jones, J. A., Lt. Grenadier Gds., w. 2. France	A.M.G.
1909	Ingram, E. M. B., O.B.E., Capt. Staff	H.Br.
1897	Ingram, L. C., 2nd Lt. Sp. List, late Gunner R.G.A.	H.B.
1909	Inigo-Jones, H. R., Lt. Scots Gds. France (k. 14.9.14)	R.W.W.-T, C.M.W
1906	Innes, A. C. W., M.C. (Innes-Cross at Eton), Capt. R. Irish Fusiliers, late Lt. Irish Gds., w., m. France	A.A.S.
1911	Innes-Cross, S. M., 2nd Lt. R. Irish Rifles. France (k. 27.10.14)	A.A.S
1898	Innes-Ker, Lord A. R., D.S.O., Capt. R.H.G., att. Lt.-Col. R.A.F., w., m. 2. France	J.P.C.
1902	Innes-Ker, Lord R. E., Maj. Irish Gds., att. R.A.F., w., m. France	E.W.S.
1893	Ionides, A. A., Capt. Devonshire Regt., att. Oxfordshire and Bucks L.I. France	F.T.
1895	Ionides, A. C., Lt. K.R.R.C. France (k. 16.10.15)	I.T
1896	Ionides, G. A., Lt. The Queen's. France	H.P.

1915 Irby, C. E., M.C., Lt. Grenadier Gds., w. France — A.C.R.-W.
1908 Irby, G. N., Capt. Oxfordshire and Bucks L.I., att. Gloucestershire Regt. — E.C.A.L., E.W.S.
1890 Irby, L. P., O.B.E., Lt.-Col. K.R.R.C., late att. Rifle Bde. Italy — F.H.R.
1905 Ireland-Blackburne, G., Maj. S. Lancashire Regt. Mesopotamia — A.C.G.H.
1906 Ireland-Blackburne, J., Lt. S. Lancashire Regt., w. 2. France — A.C.G.H.
1877 Isham, Sir V., Bart., Maj. Yorkshire Regt., late Maj. Sherwood Foresters — C.W.D.
1909 Isherwood, L. C. R., Lt. (t. Capt.) 16th Lancers, and Staff, m. 2. France — H.Br.

1903 Jackson, B. R., Capt. Coldstream Gds. France (k. 15.9.16) — C.L., R.S K.
1905 Jackson, C. B. A., Capt. York and Lancaster Regt., empld. Maj. M.G.C., and Staff, w., m. France — J.M.E.
1914 Jackson, F. H., Lt. R. Sussex Regt., att. Duke of Cornwall's L.I., and R.F.C. France — S.G.L.
1900 Jackson, J. V. R., Maj. The Buffs, w., p., m. France — E.I.
1912 Jackson, P. A. D., 2nd Lt. R. Irish Rifles, w., m. France (k. 4.1.17) — M.D.H
1914 Jaffray, H. A., Lt. 11th Hussars, w. France — M.D.H.
1912 Jaffray, Sir J. H., Bart., Lt. Worcestershire Yeomanry, m. Egypt (k. 23.4.16) — M D H.
1913 Jaffray, Sir W. E., Bart., Lt. 1st (King's) Dragoon Gds., att. R.F.C. France — M.D.H.
1895 James, A. G., Lt. R.A.S.C., M.T., and Staff. Egypt — K.S.
1911 James, A. W. H., M.C., Lt. 3rd Hussars, empld. Lt.-Col. R.A.F., m. France — P.V.B.
1890 James, E. L. H., O.B.E., Lt.-Col. R.A.O.C. — F.H.R.
1901 James, G. C. B., Lt. S. Wales Borderers. France (d.w. 23.11.17) — H W.M., H M.
1892 James, R. E. H., C.M.G., D.S.O., Bt. Lt.-Col. Loyal N. Lancashire Regt., and Staff, m. 2. France — F.H.R.

1914	James, W. E. C., Lt. M.G.C., late Lt. Northumberland Fusiliers, m. Balkans, Palestine	R.S. de H.
1888	Jameson, H. B., Lt. (t. Capt.) 11th Hussars	F.T.
1907	Jameson, J. B., Lt. R.A.F. France (k. 24.8.18)	H P
1873	Jameson, S. B. (F) Brig.-Gen. (Seaforth Highlanders). France, Italy	F.W.C.
1893	Jameson, W. K. E., D.S.O., Lt.-Col. R.A., and Staff, m. 4. France, Egypt, Palestine	F.T.
1886	Jamieson, J. Fyfe-, Lt.-Col. R. Defence Corps	H.D.
1897	Janson, C. W., Capt. Coldstream Gds., late Hampshire Yeomanry, and Staff, w. France	F.H.R.
1898	Jardine, J. W., Maj. R.A.F., late A.B., R.N.V.R., w., m. France, Gallipoli	E.C.A.L.
1908	Jardine, R. J., 2nd Lt. R. Scots Greys, att. R.F.C. France (k. accid. 13.9.17)	H.B.
1901	Jardine-Paterson, J. J., 2nd Lt. Coldstream Gds.	T.C.P.
1896	Jardine-Paterson, R., Lt. Coldstream Gds. France	F.T., F.L.V.
1884	Jebb, H. S. F., Capt. R. Scots Fusiliers	A.C.J.
1909	Jeffcock, W. P., Lt. S. Nottinghamshire Hussars, att. Scots Gds., late 1st Life Gds.	R.C.R., C.H.K.M.
1911	Jefferson, L. H., Capt. 11th Hussars, att. R.A.F. France	H.T.B., S.G.L.
1908	Jeffrey, J. A., M.C., Capt. 13th Hussars, m. 2. France, Mesopotamia	J.H.M.H.
1914	Jeffreys, A. H., Lt. R.H.A., w., m. France	L.S.R.B.
1895	Jeffreys, G. D., C.B., C.M.G. (F) Maj.-Gen. (Grenadier Gds.), w., m. 8. France	H.E.L.
1901	Jelf, H. W., Sub-Lt. R.N.V.R. Home Waters	F.L.V.
1891	Jelf, R. G., C.M.G., D.S.O., Brig.-Gen. (K.R.R.C.), w., m. 5. France	H.E.L.
1898	Jelf, W. W., C.M.G., D.S.O., Bt. Lt.-Col. R.F.A., and Staff, m. 5. France	K.S.
1904	Jemmett, F. R., Capt. R.E.	H.E.L., F.W.S.
1894	Jenkins, W. R. H., Capt. 7th Dragoon Gds., Indian E.F. France	J.M.F.

1893 Jennings, E. C., C.B.E. (F) Lt.-Col. R. Fusiliers, att.
Rifle Bde., m. France F.W.C.
1892 Jervis, E. C. Scott, D.S.O., Bt. Maj. (t. Lt.-Col.) M.G.C.,
late Maj. 6th (Inniskilling) Dragoons, w. 2, m. 3.
France, Balkans, N. Russia F.D.
1877 Jervis, E. de R., Maj. S. Staffordshire Regt., m. France de R., H.E.L.
1909 Jessel, G., M.C., Lt. (t. Capt.) The Buffs, and Staff,
w., m. Mesopotamia R.P.L.B.
1914 Jessel, R. H., Lt. Hampshire Regt. Mesopotamia R.P.L.B.
1879 Jeudwine, Sir H. S., K.C.B. (F) Maj.-Gen. (R.A.), w.,
m. 8. France J.P.C.
1892 Jex-Blake, A. J., Capt. R.A.M.C. France K.S.
1911 Jobson, R. H., M.C., Lt. R.F.A. France P.V.B.
1914 Joel, G. J., M.C., Lt. The Queen's Own (R. W. Kent
Regt.), late Pte. R. Fusiliers, w. France H.B.
1907 Joel, W. S., Lt. Border Regt., att. R.A.F., and Staff, late
Pte. Natal L.H. France, S. W. Africa C.H.A., P.V.B.
1902 Johnson, Rev. A. D., M.C., C.F. Egypt, Palestine E.L.V.
1894 Johnson, B. C., 2nd Lt. Warwickshire Yeomanry, empld.
Lt. E. Lancashire Regt. and Capt. R.F.A. France H.G.W., H.E.L.
1895 Johnson, H. C., D.S.O., Bt. Maj. K.R.R.C., and Staff,
m. France (d.w. 1.1.15) H.W.M.
1903 Johnson, J. G. T., D.S.O., Maj. Derbyshire Yeomanry,
m. 2. Balkans, Egypt, Gallipoli E.C.A.L.
1909 Johnson, M. K., Lt. R.G.A., late 2nd Lt. London Regt.
France R.S.K.
1917 Johnson, M. M., 2nd Lt. Scots Gds. France L.S.R.B.
1897 Johnson, P. R., Bt. Maj. Devonshire Regt., w. Mesopotamia S.R.J., R.A.H.M.
1908 Johnson, R. L., Lt. R.F.A., and Staff, w. France (k. 28.5.17) E.L.V
1891 Johnson, W. L., Lt.-Col. Durham L.I. H.B.
1896 Johnston, C. E., D.S.O., M.C., Capt. (t. Lt.-Col.) London
Regt., m. France R.C.R.
1908 Johnston, G. S., Lt. Essex Yeomanry. France (k. 13.5.15)
R.C.R., C.H.K.M.

1901 Johnstone, B. C., Lt. Black Watch, m. France, E. Africa   F.J.T., T.C.P.

1914 Johnstone, F. J. L., M.C., Capt. K.R.R.C. France (d.w. 29.8.16)   H.B., R.H.de M.

1909 Johnstone, G. H., D.S.O. (F) Capt. R.F.A., m. 3. France, Mesopotamia   R.W.W.-T., C.M.W.

1913 Johnstone, H., Lt. Rifle Bde., and Staff, w. 2. France   F.I.

1911 Johnstone, J. A., 2nd Lt. R.F.A., att. R.F.C. France (k. 20.5.15)   H.M.

1900 Johnstone, M. C. J. S., Capt. R. Scots Greys, att. Maj. R.A.F., and Staff. France   J.M.E.

1902 Johnstone, R. F. L., Lt. Cameron Highlanders. France (k. 8.9.14)   J.M.F.

1914 Joicey-Cecil, J. F. J., Lt. Grenadier Gds. France (k. 25.9.16)   E.W.S.

1883 Joicey-Cecil, Lord J. P. (Cecil at Eton), Capt. Grenadier Gds., empld. Lt.-Col. R. Defence Corps   W.D.

1891 Jolliffe, C. H. H., Maj. A. Vet. Corps, and Staff. France   A.C.J.

1916 Jolliffe, Hon. W. G. H., Lt. Coldstream Gds. France   R.S.de H.

1875 Jones, B. N. H., the late, Capt. Cheshire Yeomanry, att. Res. Regt. of Cav. (d. 12.5.19)   F.F.D.

1898 Jones, J. W. B., Lt. Labour Corps, late Pte. Essex Regt. France   E.L.V.

1904 Jones, L. E., M.C., Capt. Bedfordshire Yeomanry, att. Maj. M.G.C., w., p., m. France   C.L., R.S.K.

1914 Jones, R. H. H., Lt. 6th Dragoon Gds. (Carabiniers). France   H.B.

1889 Jones, R. T., Capt. Shropshire Yeomanry, w. Egypt, Palestine   F.H.R.

1913 Judd, L. A., Capt. H.L.I., att. Middlesex Hussars, late att. K.O.S.B., w. France, Egypt, Palestine   M.D.H.

1886 Karslake, J. B. P., T.D., Lt.-Col. Berks Yeomanry, and Staff. France   J.P.C.

1905 Kavanagh, A. T. McMurrough, M.C., Capt. (t. Maj.) 7th Hussars, and Staff, m. 2. Egypt, Gallipoli, Palestine   F.I.

1904 Kavanagh, D. McMurrough, Capt. 11th Hussars, and
    Staff, m. France, Palestine   E.I.
1915 Kay, H. G. A., Lt. R.F.A., w. France   R.P.L.B.
1908 Kay-Shuttleworth, Hon. E. J., Capt. Rifle Bde., and
    Staff, m. France (k. accid. 10.7.17)   H.T.B.
1906 Kay-Shuttleworth, Hon. L. U., Capt. R.F.A., att.
    Canadian E.F., m. France (k. 30.3.17)   H.T.B.
1908 Kearley, Hon. G. C., Lt. Scots Gds., att. Remount Service, late R.N.D. France   R.P.L.B.
1891 Keate, R. D. M., Maj. R.G.A., and Staff. France   E.I.
1913 Keating, H. F. A., Lt. R.E., w. France (k. 28.6.18)   H.F.W.T., A.F.C.
1901 Keating, H. S., Lt. Grenadier Gds., att. Irish Gds.
    France (k. 20.1.15)   H.F.W.T.
1913 Keele, C. A., Capt. Rifle Bde. France (k. 12.7.16)   K.S.
1903 Keeling, E. A., Lt. att. Staff. Gallipoli   K.S.
1914 Keeling, J. H., Lt. Coldstream Gds., late Lt. The
    Queen's, m. Balkans, Gallipoli   A.M.G.
1903 Keene, R. L., 2nd Lt. R.A.S.C., M.T. Egypt, Italy, Palestine   P.W.
1907 Keiller, A., Capt. R.A.F., late Lt. R.N.V.R. France   J.H.M.H.
1900 Keith, G. T. E., D.S.O., O.B.E., Maj. (t. Lt.-Col.) The
    King's Own (R. Lancaster Regt.), and Staff, w., m. 4.
    France   T.C.P.
1906 Keith-Falconer, A. W., Capt. (t. Maj.) Oxfordshire
    Yeomanry, and Staff. France   F.H.R.
1901 Kekewich, A. St. J. M., Capt. Devonshire Regt., m.
    France (k. 25.9.15)   F.L.V.
1884 Kekewich, C. H., Lt.-Col. Staff   A.C.J.
1908 Kekewich, G., Capt. Roughriders, m. Balkans, Egypt,
    Gallipoli, Palestine (d.w. 28.10.17)   H.B.
1903 Kekewich, H. L., Maj. Sussex Yeomanry, att. Sussex
    Regt. Egypt, Gallipoli, Palestine (k. 6.11.17)   H.B.
1909 Kekewich, J., Capt. The Buffs. France (k. 26.9.15)   H.B.
1911 Kekewich, S., M.B.E., Capt. 21st Lancers, and Staff, w. India   H.B.
1899 Kelly, E. D. F., Capt. 7th Hussars, att. 1st Life Gds.
    France (k. 30.10.14)   J.P.C.

1899	Kelly, F. S., D.S.C., Lt.-Cr. R.N.V.R., att. Drake and Hood Bns., R.N.D., late Pte. R. Fusiliers, w., m. France, Gallipoli (k. 13.11.16)	H.D.
1914	Kelly, L. P. G., M.C., Lt. 9th Lancers. France	H. de H.
1897	Kemble, H. L., M.V.O., Capt. Scots Gds., w. France	T.C.P.
1872	Kemble, H. W., Maj. Cameron Highlanders	E.C.A.L.
1898	Kemmis, A. W. M., D.S.O., Maj. 10th Lancers, I.A., m. 3. Mesopotamia	E.I.
1885	Kemp, W. R., Capt. R.A.M.C.	F.W.C.
1897	Kemp-Welch, A., 2nd Lt. R.A.S.C., late Pte. London Regt. France	A.A.S.
1888	Kennard, A. C. H., Capt. Rifle Bde., empld. Lt.-Col. London Regt. and Labour Corps, m. 2. France, Egypt	R.A.H.M.
1883	Kennard, A. M., D.S.O., Lt.-Col. R.F.A., w. France (d. 2.1.17)	A.C.J.
1883	Kennard, C. W., Maj. Black Watch, and Staff. France	E.W.
1890	Kennard, E. C. H., Maj. W. Riding Regt., empld. Lt.-Col. W. Yorkshire Regt. France, Egypt	R.A.H.M.
1889	Kennard, H. G. H., C.B.E., Bt. Col. Irish Cavalry Depôt	E.W., C.H.E.
1892	Kennard, H. H. A., Lt. R.N.V.R., and Staff. Home Waters, Mediterranean	E.L.V.
1887	Kennard, L. E., the late, Maj. 15th Hussars. (d. 10.12.19)	R.A.H.M.
1895	Kennard, W. A., D.S.O., Capt. (t. Maj.) 13th Hussars, att. Northumberland Fusiliers, and Staff, w. 2, m. 2. France (d. 30.10.18)	J.H.M.H.
1900	Kennaway, A. L., Lt. Dorset Yeomanry. Egypt, Gallipoli (k. 21.8.15)	S.R.J., H.F.W.T.
1899	Kennedy, Lord A., Capt. R.A.F., late Lt. R.N.V.R. and Sub-Lt. R.N.R. Home Waters	C.H.A.
1893	Kennedy, A. E., Capt. A. and S. Highlanders. France (k. 26.8.14)	P.W.
1899	Kennedy, A. J. R., D.S.O., Maj. R.F.A., and Staff, m. 2. France	A.C.J., H.Br.
1892	Kennedy, Lord C., Capt. Ayrshire Yeomanry	H.G.W., C.H.A.

1907	Kennedy, E. N., Lt. R.F.A., and Staff, m. France	L.S.R.B.
1901	Kennedy, G. L., Lt. R.G.A., m. France	E.L.V.
1895	Kennedy, H. B. P. L., C.M.G., D.S.O. (F) Brig.-Gen. (K.R.R.C.), m. 7. France	A.A.S.
1910	Kennedy, J. D., Capt. The Queen's Own (R.W. Kent Regt.), w. France	L.S.R.B.
1907	Kennedy, J. F., M.C., Lt. R.F.A., w. France	L.S.R.B.
1917	Kennedy, P.G., M.C., 2nd Lt. Armoured Cars, R.N.V.R. Mesopotamia, Russia	E.L.C.
1905	Kennedy, S. V., M.C., Capt. (t. Maj.) 13th Hussars, and Staff, m. France	L.S.R.B.
1891	Kensington, Lord, C.M.G., D.S.O. (Mr. Edwardes at Eton), Lt.-Col. Welsh Horse, att. R. Welch Fusiliers, m. 3. France, Egypt, Gallipoli, Palestine	S.A.D.
1882	Kenyon, Lord, K.C.V.O., T.D., Col. Welsh Horse	C.L.L.-C., J.C.
1896	Kenyon, C., Capt. Hampshire Regt., att. London Regt: Egypt, Gallipoli, Palestine	E.H., C.L.
1896	Kenyon, J., the late, Maj. Lancashire Fusiliers, and Staff. Egypt, Gallipoli (d. 20.11.18)	E.H., C.L.
1905	Kenyon, M. N., Lt. Duke of Lancaster's Own Yeomanry, att. S. Lancashire Regt. Balkans	R.S.K.
1875	Kenyon-Slaney, F. G., C.B.E., Lt.-Col. Durham L.I., and Staff. France	W.E.
1909	Kenyon-Slaney, R. O. R., Capt. Grenadier Gds., empld. Maj. R. Defence Corps, w. France	R.W.W.-T., C.M.W.
1915	Keppel, Hon. A. E. G. A., Lt. Rifle Bde., m. France (k. 31.7.17)	E.L., T.F.C.
1901	Keppel, Hon. A. J. W., Lt. R.A.F. France	J.M.E.
1893	Keppel, B. W. A., Maj. Staffordshire Yeomanry, att. R.F.A. France	S.A.D.
1904	Keppel, Hon. R. O. D., Capt. Coldstream Gds., w., p. France	J.M.E.
1895	Ker, D. A. W., Maj. N. Irish Horse, and Staff, m. France	E.L.V.
1883	Ker-Seymer, E. C., the late, Maj. A. and S. Highlanders (d. 10.12.18)	R.A.H.M.

1913	Kerr, H. G., 2nd Lt. 9th Lancers. France (d.w. 1.7.17)	I I
1895	Kerr, M., Capt. Cameronians (Scottish Rifles)	A.C.J.
1881	Kerr, R. J., Lt.-Col. Gloucestershire Regt.	G F M.
1895	Kerr-Smiley, P. K., M.P. (Smiley at Eton), Maj. R. Irish Rifles, and Staff. Egypt	H.B.
1914	Kerrison, E. R., Lt. Norfolk Regt., att. R.A.F. France	L.S.R.B.
1904	Kerrison, R. F., Capt. Norfolk Regt., att. R. Berkshire Regt., and Staff. France	R.A.H.M., L.S.R.B.
1891	Kerrison, R. O., Lt.-Col. Res. Regt. of Cav., att. Australian R.A., and Staff. France (d. 18.9.17)	H G W , S R J
1889	Kerry, Earl of, M.V.O., D.S.O., Maj. (t. Lt.-Col.) Irish Gds., and Staff	S.A.D.
1909	Kersey, R. H., Capt. R.A.S.C.	E.W.S.
1906	Kesteven, Lord (Trollope at Eton), Capt. Lincolnshire Yeomanry, att. Jacob's Horse, Indian E.F. France (d.w. 5.11.15)	P W
1889	Keswick, H., M.P., Maj. K.O.S.B , late att. R. Scots	R.C.R.
1895	Kettlewell, H. W., Bt. Lt.-Col. Shropshire L.I., and Staff, m. 2. France	J.P.C.
1901	Keymer, S. L., Maj. R.F.A. France, Egypt, Gallipoli	C.H.A.
1903	Keyser, C. N., Lt. 20th Hussars	A.C.A., R.S. de H.
1899	Kilmorey, Earl of (Lord Newry at Eton), Maj. 1st Life Gds. France	E.I.
1911	Kincaid-Lennox, W. M. P. (Peareth at Eton), Capt. A. and S. Highlanders, and Staff. France	H.T.B., S.G.L.
1888	Kincaid-Smith, K. J., C.B., C.M.G., D.S.O. (F) Brig.-Gen. (R.A.), m. 6. France	J.P.C.
1892	Kincaid-Smith, T. M. H., Capt. 9th Lancers, empld. Lt.-Col. Wiltshire Regt., and Staff, m. France	J.P.C.
1917	Kindersley, H. K. M., M.C., Lt. Scots Gds. France	R.S.K.
1914	Kindersley, L. N., 2nd Lt. 15th Hussars. France (k. 24.11.17)	R S
1894	King, C. M., Capt. Coldstream Gds.	H.B.
1905	King, H. R., Capt. Durham L.I., att. R.A.F.	T.C.P., E.L.C.
1903	King, N. W. R., Lt. 16th Lancers. France (k 21.2.15)	I C P

1912 King, W. A. H., Lt. R. Sussex Regt., att. Intell. Corps A.M.G.
1898 King-King, E., Capt. N. Irish Horse. France J.M.E.
1916 Kingsborough, Visc., Lt. R. Scots Greys. France S.G.L.
1901 Kingscote, E. T., Maj. Gloucestershire Regt., att. Sherwood Foresters, and Staff. France A.C.B.
1903 Kingscote, J., Capt. Oxfordshire Yeomanry, w. France F.H.R.
1903 Kingscote, M. J., Capt. Berks Yeomanry. Egypt A.C.B.
1899 Kingsmill, A. de P., D.S.O., M.C., Lt.-Col. Grenadier Gds., att. The Buffs, w., m. France H.E.L.
1892 Kingston, Earl of (Visc. Kingsborough at Eton), Capt. Irish Gds., w. France T.D.
1874 Kinloch, Sir D. A., Bart., C.B., M.V.O., Brig.-Gen. (Grenadier Gds.), m. 2. France G.E.M.
1904 Kinloss, Master of (Hon. R. G. G. Morgan-Grenville), Capt. Rifle Bde., w. 2, m. 2. France (k. 19.12.14) H.B.
1904 Kinnaird, Hon. A. M., M.C., Lt. Scots Gds., and Staff, late L/ce-Cpl. R. Fusiliers. France (k. 27.11.17) H.E.L., H.T.B.
1898 Kinnaird, Master of (Hon. D. A. Kinnaird), Capt. Scots Gds. France (k. 23.10.14) H.E.L
1899 Kinnaird, Master of (Hon. K. F. Kinnaird), Capt. Scottish Horse, att. R.E., m. Egypt, Gallipoli H.E.L.
1916 Kinnaird, Hon. P. C., M.C., Lt. Scots Gds., w. France S.G.L.
1905 Kirby, A. G., Capt. London Regt., and Staff. France (d.w. 29.3.17) H.E.L., L S.R B
1901 Kirby, C. A., O.B.E., Lt.-Col. R.A.F., late Cr. R.N.A.S. and A.B., R.N.V.R. H.E.L.
1906 Kirk, G. L., Engineer, Submarine Service, R.N. Home Waters T.C.P., E.L.C.
1877 Knight, C. L. W. M., D.S.O., O.B.E., Lt.-Col. R.F.A., m. France E.S.S.
1910 Knott, H. B., Capt. Northumberland Fusiliers. France (d.w. 7.9.15) A.C.G II
1900 Knott, J. L., D.S.O., Maj. W. Yorkshire Regt., late Capt. Northumberland Fusiliers, m. France (k. 1.7.16) H.D., H.M.
1915 Knowles, A., Lt. R. Scots Greys. France E.I., T.F.C.

1891 Knowles, J., O.B.E. (F) Maj. 15th Hussars, and Staff, m. 3. France, Italy A.C.A.
1909 Knowles, J. B., Lt. R. Fusiliers, att. Dorsetshire Regt. Palestine J.H.M.H.
1914 Knowles, R. A. L., M.C., Lt. K.R.R.C., w., m. France, Balkans (k. 25.2.18) A.C.G.H.
1916 Knowles, R. K., Lt. R.A.F., late R.N.V.R. E.I., T.F.C.
1917 Koch de Gooreynd, A. L. W., 2nd Lt. Irish Gds. France C.M.W.
1893 Kynaston, W. R. O., Maj. Shropshire Yeomanry, att. Shropshire L.I., w. Egypt, Palestine J.C., F.D., E.I.

1906 Lacaita, F. C., M.C., Capt. 17th Lancers, att. M.G. Cav. France (k. 4.4.18) L.F., J.M.F., M.D.H
1903 Lacon, C. C. R., Lt. (t. Capt.) R. Warwickshire Regt., att. Nigerian Regt. France, Italy, W. Africa J.H.M.H.
1897 Lacon, Sir G. H. U., Bart., D.S.O., Lt.-Col. R. Warwickshire Regt., w. 2, m. 2. France J.H.M.H.
1904 Lacon, S. J. B., Capt. R. Warwickshire Regt., empld. Maj. R.A.S.C., M.T., m. France (k. 12.4.18) T.C.P., F.L.C.
1906 Laffan, Rev. R. G. D. (F) C.F. Balkans K.S.
1908 Lamb, A. J. R., D.S.O. (F) Capt. 2nd Dragoon Gds. (Queen's Bays), att. Egyptian Army, and Staff, m. France, Egypt J.H.M.H.
1903 Lambart, G. E. O. F., Capt. R. Scots Fusiliers, late 19th Hussars. France, W. Africa (d.w. 28.3.16) H Br.
1912 Lambart, J. H. L. (F) Lt. R.F.A., and Staff, w., m. 2. France K.S.
1913 Lambert, C. J., Capt. R. Scots, w., p. France E.W.S.
1874 Lambert, F. A. H., T.D., Col. Labour Corps, att. R.E., and Staff. France G.E.M.
1901 Lambert, J. B. W., Lt. R.A.S.C., M.T. France H.W.M., H.Br.
1903 Lambert, St. J. M. (F) Capt. R.F.A., late Trooper Sharpshooters, m. Egypt, Palestine E.I.
1896 Lambert, T. E., O.B.E., Capt. Sharpshooters, att. Maj. R.A.S.C. France E.I.

1906 Lambert, W. P., M.C., Capt. Connaught Rangers, and
    Staff. w., m. France   H.M.
1875 Lambton, Hon. C., D.S.O., Brig.-Gen. (Northumberland
    Fusiliers)   E.W.
1906 Lambton, C., D.S.O., Capt. Lanarkshire Yeomanry,
    att. R. Scots Fusiliers, and Staff, w., m. France,
    Gallipoli, Palestine   R.P.L.B.
1908 Lambton, Hon. F., 2nd Lt. R.H.G. France (k. 30.10.14)   S.A.D
1894 Lambton, G., Lt. Coldstream Gds. France (k. 1.9.14)   L.F.   R.P.L.B.
1902 Lambton, J. F., Capt. Northumberland Fusiliers, w.
    France   W.D., H.M.
1881 Lambton, Hon. Sir W., K.C.B., C.M.G., C.V.O., D.S.O.
    (F) Maj.-Gen. (Coldstream Gds.), m. 3. France   E.W.
1879 Laming, H. T., D.S.O., O.B.E., Maj. Res. Regt. of Cav.   A.C.A.
1917 Laming, R. C., 2nd Lt. 18th Hussars   M.D.H.
1877 Lamington, Lord, G.C.M.G., G.C.I.E., T.D. (Baillie-
    Cochrane at Eton), Lt.-Col. Lanarkshire Yeomanry   G.E.M.
1899 Lampson, A. C., Maj. Cameron Highlanders, w., m.
    France, Balkans   A.C.J.
1917 Lancaster, C. G., 2nd Lt. R.H.G.   R.P.L.B.
1900 Landale, D. B., Lt. Rifle Bde., m. France (k. 23.10.14)   H.F.W.T
1901 Landale, D. G., Lt. Rifle Bde., and Staff, w. France   H.F.W.T.
1893 Lane, G. A. O., Maj. Coldstream Gds., empld. Lt.-Col.
    Labour Corps, and Staff, m. France   H.G.W., S.R.J.
1899 Lane, G. E. W., Maj. Rifle Bde., w. France   S.R.J., H.F.W.T.
1911 Lane, G. R., Capt. Coldstream Gds., w. France (k. 16.9.16)   A.M.G.
1878 Lane, S. E. R., Capt. Black Watch   E.W.
1892 Lane-Fox, E., Capt. Yorkshire Hussars, and Staff. France   A.C.A.
1889 Lane-Fox, G. R., M.P., Maj. Yorkshire Hussars, w., m.
    France   A.C.A.
1884 Lanesborough, Earl of, M.V.O. (Lord Newton-Butler at
    Eton), Lt.-Col. London Regt. France   E.W.
1911 Langrishe, H. R., 2nd Lt. Montgomeryshire Yeomanry,
    att. R.A.F. (k. accid. 16.2.17)   A.C.B.
1912 Langrishe, T. H., Lt. Irish Gds., att. R.A.F. France, Italy P.V.B.

1917	Langton, J. C., 2nd Lt. Irish Gds.	A.B.R.
1889	Langton, S. J., Capt. London Regt.	T.D.
1898	Larcom, Sir T. P., Bart., D.S.O., Maj. R.F.A., Indian E.F., and Staff, m. 3. France	F.L.
1900	Lascelles, Visc., D.S.O. and Bar (F) Capt. Yorkshire Hussars, att. Lt.-Col. Grenadier Gds., w. 3, m. 2. France	S.R.J., R.W.W.-T.
1903	Lascelles, Hon. E. C., D.S.O., M.C., Bt. Maj. Rifle Bde., and Staff, m. 3. France	H.M.
1917	Lascelles, G. E., 2nd Lt. Rifle Bde. France (k. 28.3.18)	F.J.C.
1915	Lascelles, J. N. P., Lt. Coldstream Gds., w. France	C.H.K.M.
1874	Lassetter, H. B., C.B., C.M.G., Brig.-Gen. (N. S. Wales Mounted Rifles), m. France	H.S.
1889	Lassetter, W. H. B., Capt. R.A.S.C. France	F.W.C.
1889	Latham, S. G., D.S.O., M.C. and Bar, Capt. Northamptonshire Regt., m. 3. France (k. 25.4.18)	F.H.
1913	Lathom, Earl of, Capt. Lancashire Hussars. France	C.M.W.
1903	Lathom-Browne, H., M.C., Bt. Maj. R. Fusiliers. France	R.P.L.B.
1874	Laurie, Sir C. V. E., Bart., C.B., D.S.O. (Bayley at Eton), Lt.-Col. K.O.S.B.	J.L.J., T.D.
1910	Laurie, J. E., D.S.O. and Bar (F) Bt. Maj. (t. Lt.-Col.) Seaforth Highlanders, and Staff, w., m. 6. France	R.S. de H.
1887	Laurie, R. M., D.S.O., T.D. (F) Lt.-Col. R.F.A., m. France, Egypt, Palestine	F.T.
1914	Laurie, V. S., Lt. R.F.A., m. 2. France, Egypt, Palestine	C.H.K.M.
1914	Laurie, W. W., Lt. K.O.S.B. France (k. 19.5.17)	R.S. de H.
1913	Law, C. J., Lt. K.O.S.B. Egypt, Palestine (k. 19.4.17)	F.T.
1906	Law, Hon. H. A., M.C., Capt. K.O.Y.L.I., and Staff, m. France, Balkans	S.A.D., P.V.F.
1910	Lawford, A. B., 2nd Lt. Grenadier Gds. France	H.Br.
1907	Lawford, E. G., Lt., late Sergt., R.E., and Staff, m. France	E.W.S.
1914	Lawford, R. D., M.C., Lt. Grenadier Gds., w. France	H.Br.
1879	Lawley, Hon, Sir A., G.C.S.I., G.C.I.E., K.C.M.G., Col. Red Cross, m. 4. France, Mesopotamia	W.W., C.C.J.
1912	Lawrence, C. H., 2nd Lt. K.R.R.C. France (k. 13.10.14)	H.M.

1913	Lawrence, M. C., Lt. (t. Capt.) Coldstream Gds., late Lt. London Regt., w. France (k. 16.9.16)	H.M.
1905	Lawrence, M. E., Lt. K.R.R.C., late Pte. Canadian E.F. France (k. 10.1.15)	E.I
1911	Lawrence, O. J., 2nd Lt. London Regt., m. France (k. 26.5.15)	H.M
1902	Lawrence, P. R. B., M.C., Capt. Coldstream Gds., att. Gds. M.G. Regt., and Staff, w., m. 2. France	R.W.W.-T.
1881	Lawrie, C. E., C.B., D.S.O. (F) Brig.-Gen. (R.A.), m. 5. France	E.W.
1909	Lawson, E. F., D.S.O., M.C., Lt.-Col. Buckinghamshire Yeomanry, m. 4. Egypt, Gallipoli, Palestine	A.C.G.H.
1912	Lawson, R. L., Lt. R.A.S.C., M.T. France, Egypt, Mesopotamia	R.S.K.
1882	Lawson, Hon. W. A. W., D.S.O., Bt. Col. Buckinghamshire Yeomanry	E.H.
1911	Lawson, W. B. W., Lt. Scots Gds. France (k. 22.10.14)	I.I.
1904	Lawson-Johnston, A. McW., M.C., Lt. Grenadier Gds., late Lt. Buckinghamshire Yeomanry. France, Egypt (d.w. 22.2.17)	H.M.
1917	Lawson-Johnston, J. E., 2nd Lt. R.F.A.	H.M.
1887	Lawson-Tancred, Sir T. S., Bart. (Tancred at Eton), Maj. Central India Horse, I.A. France	R.C.R.
1904	Lawson-Walton, J. E. H., the late, Capt. King's African Rifles, late 2nd Lt. Rifle Bde. E. Africa (d. 1.1.20)	R.S.K.
1907	Lawson-Walton, J. H. H., Capt. K.R.R.C., att. R.F.C. and Tank Corps, w. France	R.S.K.
1884	Laycock, Sir J. F., K.C.M.G., D.S.O. (F) Brig.-Gen. (R.A.), m. 2. France, Egypt	E.C.A.L.
1915	Layland-Barratt, F. H. G., M.C., Lt. Grenadier Gds., w. France	A.C.G.H.
1914	Learmonth, D. J. Livingstone, 2nd Lt. R.F.A. France	R.P.L.B.
1891	Learmonth, F. L. C. Livingstone, C.M.G., Lt.-Col. R.A., and Staff, m. 3. France	E.L.V.
1894	Learmonth, J. E. C. Livingstone, C.M.G., D.S.O. (F) Brig.-Gen. (R.A.), w., m. 7. France	C.H.A.

1890	Learmonth, L. F. R. Livingstone, Capt. Dorset Yeomanry. Egypt, Gallipoli	F.L.V.
1887	Learmonth, N. C. Livingstone, Capt. R.F.A., and Staff. Balkans	F.L.V.
1895	Learmonth, N. J. C. Livingstone, Capt. 15th Hussars, att. Dorset Yeomanry, and Staff, m. Gallipoli (k. 21.8.15)	C.H.A.
1905	Learoyd, G. E. D., Capt. 21st Lancers, m. India (d. 30.10.18)	H.B.
1911	Learoyd, J. V., Lt. W. Yorkshire Regt.	H.B.
1905	Leatham, E. H., Lt. 12th Lancers, m. France (k. 31.10.14)	C.H.A.
1902	Leatham, R. E. K., D.S.O., Maj. (t. Lt.-Col.) Grenadier Gds., att. Gds. M.G. Regt., w., m. 2. France	H.M.
1911	Leather, R. T., A.F.C., Capt. Warwickshire Yeomanry, att. R.A.F. France, Egypt	P.V.B.
1909	Le Blanc-Smith, C. R., Lt. Rifle Bde., late P.O., R.N.V.R. France, North Sea (k. 27.11.15)	R.C.R., C.H.K.M.
1906	Leche, J. H., O.B.E., Lt. (t. Capt.) 12th Lancers, and Staff, m. 2. France	R.S. de H.
1906	Lee, A. K., Lt. (t. Capt.) Somerset L.I., and Staff. Mesopotamia	R.P.L.B.
1905	Lee, C. F., the late, C.M.G., A.F.C., Brig.-Gen. (R.A.F.), m. 3. France (k. accid. 2.9.19)	E.C.A.L., E.W.S.
1898	Lee, G., D.S.O., M.C. (F) Maj. (t. Lt.-Col.) The Buffs, m. 2. France, India	R.A.H.M.
1901	Lee, G. B., Capt. (t. Maj.) R. Irish Rifles, late Lt. Connaught Rangers, att. R. Munster Fusiliers, and Staff. France, Mesopotamia	K.S.
1892	Lee, H. R., C.M.G., D.S.O., Lt.-Col. 20th Hussars, and Staff, m. 3. France	R.A.H.M.
1911	Lee, M. P. E., M.C., Lt. 6th Dragoon Gds. (Carabiniers). France (k. 26.3.18)	R.C.R., C.H.K.M.
1886	Lee, N., V.D., Brig.-Gen. (Manchester Regt.), m. Gallipoli (d.w. 22.6.15)	H.L.L
1914	Lee, N. E., Capt. K.R.R.C., m. France (k. 24.8.17)	R.S.K.
1911	Lee Lee, L. C., 2nd Lt. Irish Gds. France (k. 1.2.15)	T.H.K.H.

1912	Lee-Steere, J. H. G., Lt. Grenadier Gds. France (k. 17.11.14)	F.L.C.
1908	Leech, J. C., Capt. 8th Hussars, att. R.A.F., p. France	E.L.V.
1880	Leeds, Duke of (Marquess of Carmarthen at Eton), Cr. R.N.V.R. Home Waters, Mediterranean	G.E.M.
1901	Leeke, R. H., Maj. Rifle Bde., att. King's African Rifles. E. Africa (d. 5.11.15)	H.C.A L.
1910	Lees, B. P. T., M.C., Capt. Dorset Yeomanry, w. Egypt, Palestine	R.W.W.-T., C.M.W.
1896	Lees, E. B., Maj. Westmorland and Cumberland Yeomanry, att. Sherwood Foresters. France (k. 31.7.18)	H B.
	Lees, J., 2nd Lt. H.L.I., att. Lt. Nigerian Regt. (drowned 24.3.15)	T.C.P., E.L.C.
1	Lees, J. M., Lt. N. Staffordshire Regt. France (k. 22.8.16)	M D H
1906	Lees, Sir J. V. E., Bart., D.S.O., M.C. (F) Maj. K.R.R.C., att. Australian Imp. Forces, Staff, w. 2., m. France	R.W.W.-T., C.M.W.
1883	Lees, R. L., D.S.O., O.B.E., V.D., Lt.-Col. Lancashire Fusiliers, att. Manchester Regt. and Suffolk Regt., m. 3. France, Egypt, Gallipoli	A.C.
1905	Lees, Sir T. E. K., Bart., Lt. 15th Hussars, att. Dorset Yeomanry, and Staff. Gallipoli (d.w. 24.8.15)	R.W.W.-T
1914	Leese, O. W. H., D.S.O., Lt. Coldstream Gds., w. 3, m. 2. France	P.V.B.
1897	Legard, A. D., C.B.E., Bt. Lt.-Col. K.R.R.C., and Staff. France	S.A.D.
1895	Legard, D. A. H., Capt. R.A.F., late Lt. R.N.V.R.	H.D.
1910	Legard, R. J., Lt. W. Yorkshire Regt. France (d.w. 9.5.15)	R.P L.P.
1913	Leggatt, L. C., 2nd Lt. Coldstream Gds., late Rifle Bde. France (k. 31.7.17)	K. S
1896	Legge, Hon. G., Capt. S. Staffordshire Regt. Gallipoli (k. 9.8.15)	W .
1907	Legge-Bourke, N. W. H. (Legge at Eton), Lt. Coldstream Gds. France (k 30.10.14)	H.T I

1908	Legh, Hon P. W., O.B.E. (F) Capt. (t. Maj.) Grenadier Gds., and Staff, m. 2. France, Italy	S.A.D., P.V.B.
1906	Legh, Hon. R. W. D., Capt. Lancashire Hussars, att. R.A., and Staff, m. France	P.V.B.
1907	Leigh, C. Egerton, Lt. (t. Capt.) The Buffs, and Staff, w. 2. France	E.C.A.L., J.M.D.
1910	Leigh, G. H., O.B.E., Capt. London Regt., empld. Maj. Worcestershire Regt. and Lt.-Col. S. Lancashire Regt., w. 2. France	R.S.K.
1906	Leigh, J. C. Gerard, Capt. 1st Life Gds., w. France	P.W.
1914	Leigh-Pemberton, R. D., M.C., Lt. Grenadier Gds. and Gds. M.G. Regt., att. R.A.F., w. France	A.M.G.
1911	Leigh-Smith, P., Lt. Intell. Corps, m. France	K.S.
1893	Leighton, B. E. P., Maj. 1st R. Dragoons, w. France	E.C.A.L.
1909	Leighton, J. B. T., M.C., Maj. Scots Gds., att. R.F.C., m. 2. France, Egypt (d.w. 7.5.17)	P.W.
1911	Leighton, Sir R. T., Bart., Capt. Westmorland and Cumberland Yeomanry, att. R.A.F., w., p. France	M.D.H.
1893	Leith, A. R., O.B.E. (F) Maj. K.R.R.C., and Staff, w. 2. France	P.H.C., A.C.B.
1895	Leitrim, Earl of, Maj. R. Inniskilling Fusiliers. France	J.M.F.
1885	Lely, H. M., Lt. Labour Corps. France	H.S.S.S., A.C.
1888	Le Marchant, E. T., C.B.E., Brig.-Gen. (R. Fusiliers), w. France	F.H.R.
1892	Le Marchant, W. G., Lt. K.R.R.C., late Pte. R. Fusiliers. France	P.W., H.B.
1896	Le Messurier, G. D. S., Maj. Wallajahbad L.I., I.A. India	C.H.A.
1877	Lennard, Sir H. A. H. F., Bart. (F) Lt.-Col. Border Regt., att. Cheshire Regt., and Staff. France	E.W.
1874	Lermitte, H. J., the late, Capt. Remount Service, late Lt.-Col. Essex Yeomanry. (d. 20.6.18)	G.R.D.
1879	Le Roy Lewis, H., C.B., C.M.G., D.S.O., T.D. (F) Col. Hampshire Yeomanry, and Staff, m. 2. France	F.W.C.
1913	Le Roy Lewis, S. H., Lt. 9th Lancers, empld. M.G. Cav. France	F.L.

1901 Leschallas, B. P., Capt. R.A.S.C., M.T., late Capt.
R. Berkshire Regt. France J.M.E.

1898 Leschallas, H. P., M.B.E., Capt. Gloucestershire Regt.,
w. France J.H.M.H.

1911 Leslie, H. W. E., M.C., Capt. Herts Yeomanry, m.
Egypt, Gallipoli, Mesopotamia E.I.

1874 Leslie, Sir J., Bart., C.B.E., Lt.-Col. R. Inniskilling
Fusiliers G., C.L.L.-C.

1913 Leslie, L. D. W., 2nd Lt. Irish Gds., late Pte. R. Inniskilling Fusiliers A.B.R.

1902 Leslie, N. J. B., Capt. Rifle Bde., m. France (k. 17.10.14) C.H.A.

1885 Leslie, W. N., Maj. Middlesex Hussars J.H.M.

1891 Leslie-Melville, A. B., Capt. Sherwood Foresters C.H.E.

1895 Leslie-Melville, C. Le D., Capt. R. Fusiliers. France C.H.E., S.A.D.

1910 Leslie-Melville, Hon. D. W., M.B.E. (F) Capt. Lovat's
Scouts, and Staff, m. Egypt, Gallipoli A.M.G.

1912 Leslie-Melville, Hon. I., Capt. Lovat's Scouts, att. Imp.
Camel Corps, and Staff. France, Egypt, Gallipoli A.M.G.

1879 Lethbridge, E. A. E., C.M.G., D.S.O., Lt.-Col. Oxfordshire and Bucks L.I., p., m. 3. Mesopotamia A.C.A.

1881 Lethbridge, Sir W. P. C., Bart., Capt. Grenadier Gds.,
att. R.A.F., and Staff. France, Egypt A.C.A.

1908 Letts, E. M., Lt. Oxfordshire and Bucks L.I., att. R.A.F.,
w. France J.M.D.

1914 Letts, F. C., Capt. R.F.A., w. France A.A.S.

1908 Leven and Melville, Earl of (Mr. Leslie-Melville at
Eton), Capt. R. Scots Greys, w., p. (escaped).
France A.C.B., A.M.G.

1909 Leverson, B. A. D., Capt. Loyal N. Lancashire Regt.,
w. 2. France H.F.W.T., A.E.C.

1904 Leverson, G. R. F., D.S.O. (F) Bt. Maj. (t. Lt.-Col.)
Northumberland Fusiliers, and Staff, w., m. 4.
France, Balkans, S. Russia E.L.V.

1907 Leveson Gower, Lord A. St. C. Sutherland-, M.C.,
Capt. R.H.G., w., m. France H.T.B., A.M.G.

1884	Leveson Gower, G. C. G., Maj. W. Kent Yeomanry, late Sussex Yeomanry	G.F.M.
1903	Leveson Gower, O. C. G., Lt.-Cr. R.N. Home Waters, Dardanelles, E. Africa	J.M.E.
1914	Leveson Gower, R. C. G. G., Lt. Coldstream Gds., late Lt. R. Sussex Regt., w. France (d.w. 1.8.17)	S.G.L.
1912	Leveson Gower, R. H. G., Lt. Grenadier Gds. France	H.T.B., S.G.L.
1901	Leveson Gower, W. G. G., Lt. (t. Capt.) Coldstream Gds., and Staff. France (k. 9.10.18)	K.S.
1880	Levett, B. J. T., Maj. Scots Gds., att. Capt. Northumberland Fusiliers, and Staff	C.L.L.-C.
1907	Levett, E. C., Capt. R.E.	F.H.R.
1915	Levett, R. W. B., 2nd Lt. K.R.R.C. France (k. 10.3.17)	F.W.S.
1896	Levinge, Sir R. W., Bart., Lt. 8th Hussars, att. 1st Life Gds. France (k. 24.10.14)	L.L.V.
1884	Levita, C. E., Capt. Staff, m. France	A.G.J.
1908	Levita, F. E., Lt. 4th Hussars. France (k. 12.10.14)	L.S.R.B.
1878	Levita, H. P., the late, (F) Lt.-Col. Staff. France (d. 17.4.19)	R.A.H.M.
1906	Lewis, E. J. P., Lt. R. Berkshire Regt., late Pte. R. Fusiliers	J.M.E.
1895	Lewis, H., Capt. R.F.A. France	T.D., F.J.T.
1895	Lewis, N. S., 2nd Lt. London Regt., att. Loyal N. Lancashire Regt., late Pte. R. Fusiliers. France	K.S.
1898	Lewis, R. W., M.C., Capt. Welsh Gds., late Capt. Glamorgan Yeomanry, w. 2, m. France	T.D., F.J.T.
1900	Lewis, W. H. P., O.B.E., Capt. Glamorgan Yeomanry, and Staff, m. 2. France	J.M.F.
1899	Lewisham, Visc. (F) Lt.-Col. Staffordshire Yeomanry. Egypt, Palestine	W.D.
1885	Leycester-Penrhyn, A., Maj. E. Surrey Regt., att. R.A.F.	C.H.E.
1911	Leyland, C. D., Capt. 1st Life Gds., att. M.G. Cav., w. France	H.F.W.T., A.E.C.
1907	Liddell, C. F. J., M.C. (F) Lt. K.R.R.C., att. T.M.B. France	J.M.E., M.D.H.

1902 Liddell, G. W., D.S.O., Bt. Maj. (t. Lt.-Col.) Rifle Bde., and Staff, w., m. 2. France — H. Br.

1903 Liebert, B. R., Maj. 7th Hussars, att. Leicestershire Yeomanry France (k. 13.5.15) — H.W.M.

1915 Lighton, C. R., Lt. K.R.R.C., and Staff, w. France — E.W.S.

1899 Lindop, K., Lt. Devonshire Regt., late Bombardier R.F.A. — T.C.P.

1910 Lindsay, D. C. M., Lt. Black Watch, late Pte. London Regt., w. France — H.B.

1904 Linlithgow, Marquess of (Earl of Hopetoun at Eton), Capt. Lothians and Border Horse, empld. Lt.-Col. R. Scots, and Staff, m. France — E.I.

1910 Lisburne, Earl of, Capt. Welsh Gds., w., m. France — E.I.

1907 Lister, Hon. C. A., Lt. R.M., late 2nd Lt. Middlesex Hussars, w. 2, m. Gallipoli (d.w. 28.8.15) — K.S.

1917 Lister, M. D. B., 2nd Lt. K.R.R.C., w. France — A.M.G.

1911 Lister-Kaye, K. A., Lt. W. Yorkshire Regt., att. R.A.F., w. France — P.V.B.

1871 Little, Archibald C., Bt. Maj. Remount Service — O.B.

1897 Little, Arthur C., D.S.O. and Bar, Bt. Lt.-Col. 20th Hussars, m. 5. France — H.W.M.

1887 Littledale, J. B., Capt., late Pte., R.A.S.C., M.T., m. France — F.W.C.

1914 Littledale, W. J., Lt. Oxfordshire and Bucks L.I., w. France (k. 23.3.18) — L.S.R.B.

1896 Littleton, Hon. W. H., Maj. N. Staffordshire Regt., att. Lincolnshire Regt., w. France — P.W.

1909 Livesey, T. R. M., Capt. Patiala Lancers, Indian E.F. Egypt, India, Mesopotamia — E.L.C.

1887 Llangattock, Lord (Rolls at Eton), Maj. R.F.A. France (d.w. 31.10.16) — F.H.R.

1912 Llewellin, J. J., M.C., Maj. R.G.A., w. France — A.B.R.

1908 Llewellin, W. W., Lt. Dorsetshire Regt., w. Mesopotamia — C.H.A., A.B.R.

1901 Llewellyn, W. H. C., Lt. S. Wales Borderers — C.L., H.T.B.

1882	Lloyd, A. H. O., C.B., C.M.G., M.V.O. (F) Brig.-Gen. (Shropshire Yeomanry), m. 4. Egypt, Palestine	C.W.D., J.H.M.
1910	Lloyd, C. E. H., Capt. R.F.A., and Staff. France	F.W.S.
1905	Lloyd, C. G., Capt. E. Riding of Yorkshire Yeomanry, att. Dorset Yeomanry, and Staff, m. Egypt, Palestine	P.W.
1903	Lloyd, E. A., Maj. R.E., late Lt. London Regt., and Staff, w., m. France	C.H.A.
1876	Lloyd, F., C.I.E., V.D., Lt.-Col. Sp. List	T.D.
1898	Lloyd, Sir G. A., G.C.I.E., D.S.O. (F) Capt. Warwickshire Yeomanry, att. Egyptian E.F. Staff and Australian and New Zealand Imp. Forces, m. 5. Arabia, Egypt, Gallipoli, Mesopotamia, Palestine, S. Russia	F.T., S.A.D.
1909	Lloyd, H. C., M.C., Capt. K.R.R.C., att. R.A.F., late Tank Corps, and Staff, w. 2, m. France	R.P.L.B.
1911	Lloyd, H. G., M.C., Lt. (t. Capt.) Duke of Cornwall's L.I., and Staff, w. France, Balkans	P.W.
1880	Lloyd, H. J. G., the late, Maj. Duke of Cornwall's L.I. (d. 13.4.19)	H.D.
1916	Lloyd, J. A., Lt. Grenadier Gds., m. France	R.P.L.B.
1897	Lloyd, J. C., M.C. (F) Capt. (t. Maj.) S. Wales Borderers, and Staff, m. 2. France	A.C.A.
1909	Lloyd, J. R., Lt. E. Riding of Yorkshire Yeomanry, att. M.G.C. France, Egypt, Palestine	P.W.
1908	Lloyd, L. S., Capt. R.F.A. France, Palestine	C.H.A., A.B.R.
1896	Lloyd, M. E., Capt. R. Welch Fusiliers. France (d.w. 23.11.14)	F.C.A.L.
1906	Lloyd, M. K. A., Capt. Grenadier Gds., w. France (k. 15.9.16)	F.L.
1884	Lloyd, T. O., C.M.G., Lt.-Col. Black Watch, m. 2. France	A.C.A.
1886	Lloyd, W. R., Lt.-Col. Loyal N. Lancashire Regt. France (k. 14.9.14)	H.F.
1902	Lloyd-Baker, A. B., D.S.O. (F) Maj. (t. Lt.-Col.) Oxfordshire and Bucks L.I., and Staff, m. 3. France, Italy	R.W.W.-T.
1891	Lloyd-Baker, M. G., Capt. Gloucestershire Yeomanry, w., m. Egypt, Gallipoli (k. 23.4.16)	J.M.F.

1887 Lloyd-Greame, Y., Lt. R.F.A., late Lt. Yorkshire Dragoons   E.H.
1900 Lloyd-Mostyn, Hon. E. L. R., Capt. R.H.G., late Capt.
       Denbighshire Yeomanry. France   E.C.A.L.
1901 Lloyd-Mostyn, I., 2nd Lt. R. Welch Fusiliers   W.D., H.Br.
1904 Lloyd-Mostyn, M. L., Capt. R. Welch Fusiliers, att.
       Dorsetshire Regt., and Staff, w. France   H.Br.
1902 Lock, C. F., Lt. Herts Yeomanry. Egypt, Gallipoli,
       Mesopotamia   A.C.J., H.F.W.T.
1894 Locker-Lampson, G. L. T., M.P., 2nd Lt., late Trooper,
       R. Wiltshire Yeomanry, and Staff. France   S.A.D.
1899 Locker-Lampson, O. S., M.P., C.M.G., D.S.O. (F) Lt.-
       Cr. Armoured Cars, R.N.V.R. France, Balkans,
       Gallipoli, Russia   S.A.D.
1909 Lockwood, R. W. M., 2nd Lt. Coldstream Gds. France
       (k. 15.9.14)   H.Br.
1904 Loder, B. C. R., Bt. Maj. Bedfordshire Regt., and Staff.
       France   J.P.C., F.H.R.
1902 Loder, E. R., Capt. Bedfordshire Regt., att. R.A.S.C.,
       M.T., m. 3. France, Italy   F.H.R.
1902 Loder, G. H., M.C., Capt. Scots Gds., and Staff, w., m.
       France   R.C.R.
1907 Loder, H. S., Lt. R. E. Kent Yeomanry, empld. Re-
       mount Service. Egypt, Gallipoli   R.C.R.
1914 Loder, J. de V., Lt. R. Sussex Regt., att. Intell. Corps,
       Egyptian E.F., and Staff, m. Egypt, Gallipoli, Pales-
       tine   R.P.L.B.
1904 Loder, N. W., Lt. The Buffs. France   R.C.R.
1906 Loder, R. E., Capt. R. Sussex Regt., and Staff, m. 2.
       Egypt, Gallipoli (d.w. 29.3.17)   L.F., E.W.S
1889 Loder-Symonds, J. F. L., Maj. S. Staffordshire Regt.
       France (k. 31.10.14)   P.H.C.
1884 Logan, C., Lt., late Pte., R.A.S.C., M.T.   J.M.E.
1887 Logan, E. P., Lt. Cheshire Regt. France, E. Africa   E.L.V.
1892 Logan, R. M., Maj. Oxfordshire and Bucks L.I.   F.W.C.
1916 Lomax, C. C., Lt. 9th Lancers, att. 5th Lancers. France   R.S.K.

1895	Londonderry, Marquess of, M.V.O. (Visc. Castlereagh at Eton), Bt. Lt.-Col. R.H.G., and Staff, m. 2. France	W.D.
1890	Long, W. E., O.B.E., Maj. (t. Lt.-Col.) 4th Hussars, att. Remount Service. France, Egypt, Palestine	A.C.A.
1916	Long, W. G., 2nd Lt. Tank Corps	S.G.L.
1896	Long-Innes, P. S., M.C. (Innes at Eton), Maj. Irish Gds., w. 2. France	E.I.
1900	Longman, H. K., D.S.O., M.C., Maj. Gordon Highlanders, and Staff, m. 3. France	R.C.R.
1901	Longman, R. G., Capt. Gordon Highlanders, att. R. Scots, w. France	R.C.R.
1893	Longstaff, C. L., Maj. N. Staffordshire Regt. France	F.H.R.
1892	Longstaff, F. V., Maj. E. Surrey Regt.	F.H.R.
1901	Longstaff, G. C., Lt. R.N.V.R. Home Waters, Italy	F.H.R.
1893	Longstaff, T. G., Capt. Hampshire Regt., att. Intell. Corps, I.A. India	F.H.R.
1911	Lonsdale, J. R. McC., Lt. 4th Hussars. France (d.w. 29.10.14)	C.H.K.M.
1915	Lord, A. A., Ensign U.S. Naval Res., late C.P.O., U.S. Naval Aviation, and Staff. France	V. Le N.F.
1917	Lord, F. M., 2nd Lt. R.E. France	S.G.L.
1915	Lord, J. A., Lt. 13th Hussars, late Worcestershire Yeomanry. Mesopotamia	E.W.S.
1884	Loring, W., D.S.M., Capt. Scottish Horse, m. Gallipoli (d.w. 24.10.15)	K S
1873	Lort-Phillips, J. F., Lt.-Col. Pembroke Yeomanry, and Staff, m. France	F.W.C.
1883	Lovelace, Earl of, D.S.O. (Mr. King-Noel at Eton), Maj. Northumberland Fusiliers, m. France	E.W.
1888	Low, F. S., Lt.-Col. Staff	C.H.E.
1892	Low, H. F., Maj. Durham L.I., att. Labour Corps	C.H.I.
1914	Lowe, W. J. M., Lt. 15th Hussars, and Staff. France, Egypt, Gallipoli	S.G.L.
1912	Lowinsky, R. E., Lt. York and Lancaster Regt., w. France	J.H.M.H.

1909	Lowinsky, T. E., Lt. Scots Gds., late Lt. The Queen's Own (R. W. Kent Regt.). France	J.M.E., J.H.M.H.
1916	Lowndes, W. G. L. F., 2nd Lt. 21st Lancers, and Staff. Afghanistan	A.B.R.
1908	Lowry-Corry, F. R. H., Lt. R.F.A. France (d.w. 30.10.15)	R.P.L.B.
1904	Lowry-Corry, H. C., M.C., Maj. R.F.A., w. France	L.F., R.P.L.B.
1916	Lowsley-Williams, J. S., 2nd Lt. R.F.A. France	E.L.C.
1907	Lowther, A. J. B., Capt., late Pte., Suffolk Regt., w. France	E.L.V.
1904	Lowther, C. W., Maj. Westmorland and Cumberland Yeomanry, and Staff, w., m. France	E.L.V.
1913	Loyd, A. T., Capt. The Buffs, att. R.F.C. France (k. 28.9.17)	C.H.K.M.
1898	Loyd, A. W. K., the late, Maj. R. Sussex Regt. France (d. 13.2.19)	F.H.R.
1908	Loyd, C. L., Lt. The Buffs, att. R.A.F. France	R.C.R., C.H.K.M.
1909	Loyd, E. E. F., Lt. R. Sussex Regt., att. R.A.F., p. France	R.C.R., C.H.K.M.
1899	Loyd, E. N. F., Capt. Warwickshire Yeomanry, late Cpl. R. Scots Greys. France	A.C.J.
1912	Loyd, E. W., Lt. Yorkshire Regt., att. M.G.C., w., m. France, Balkans	L.S.R.B.
1908	Loyd, G. A. (F) Lt. Scots Gds., m. France (k. 13.11.14)	F.H.R., H. de H.
1909	Loyd, H. C., D.S.O., M.C. (F) Capt. (t. Lt.-Col.) Coldstream Gds., and Staff, w. 4, m. 3. France	E.L.V.
1898	Loyd, L. F. I., Capt. Lovat's Scouts, empld. Maj. Worcestershire Yeomanry. Gallipoli (d. 21.9.18)	A.C.J.
1899	Loyd, L. R. W., Lt., late Air Mechanic, R.A.F. France, Egypt	W.D.
1904	Loyd, R. A., Capt. Remount Service. France	F.H.R.
1906	Loyd, R. L., M.C. (F) Lt. 16th Lancers, att. R.E. Signal Service, m. 3. France	F.H.R.
1914	Loyd, R. P., M.C., Lt. Coldstream Gds., late Hertfordshire Regt., and Staff, w. 2. France (k. 1.12.17)	E.L.V., A.C.R-W
1915	Lubbock, A., Lt. R.G.A., w. France	K.S.

1895	Lubbock, A. B., M.C., Lt. R.F.A. France	R.A.H.M
1912	Lubbock, Hon. E. F. P., M.C., Capt. R.F.C., late R.A.S.C., m. 2. France (k. 11.3.17)	A.M.G.
1892	Lubbock, Geoffrey, Maj. N. Somerset Yeomanry, and Staff, w., m. 2. France	R.A.H.M.
1887	Lubbock, Guy, C.M.G., D.S.O. (F) Brig.-Gen. (R.E.); m. 7. France, E. Africa, Egypt, Mesopotamia	R.A.H.M.
1906	Lubbock, Hon. H. F. P., Lt. Grenadier Gds., late Capt. W. Kent Yeomanry. France (k. 4.4.18)	A.C.B., A.M.C
1881	Lubbock, H. N., 2nd Lt. R. Defence Corps	R.A.H.M.
1902	Lubbock, M. G., M.C. (F) Lt. R.F.A., late Pte. R. Fusiliers, w. France, Balkans	R.A.H.M., L.S.R.B.
1910	Lubbock, R. H., M.C., Maj. R.F.A., late Trooper Roughriders. France	J.H.M.H.
1910	Lucas, A. R. F., M.C., Capt. R.F.A., m. France, Egypt, Palestine	E.W.S.
1904	Lucas, C. E., Capt. R. Fusiliers, and Staff. France	R.W.W.-T.
1893	Lucas, E. P., M.C., Capt. R. Berkshire Regt., and Staff, w. France	R.C.R.
1906	Lucas, G. M. E., Lt. (t. Capt.) R. Inniskilling Fusiliers, att. Cheshire Regt. and R.A.F., late Pte. R. Fusiliers, m. France, Balkans, Egypt, Palestine	R.W.W.-T., C.M.W.
1905	Lucas, J. M., M.C., Capt. R. Warwickshire Regt., att. R.A.F., w., p. France	R.C.R.
1916	Lucas, R. H. A., 2nd Lt. R.F.A., w. France	C.H.K.M.
1914	Lucas, R. S. C., Lt. R.F.A., late 2nd Lt. K.R.R.C. France	R.S.de H.
1900	Lucas, W. G., Lt.-Col. R.G.A., late Maj. R.M., att. R.N.A.S., late R. Fusiliers, m. 2. France	A.C.J., A.C.G.H.
1901	Lucas-Tooth, Sir A. L., Bart. (Tooth at Eton), Maj. H.A.C. France (d. 12.7.18)	W.D., H.T.P
1896	Lucas-Tooth, D. K. L., D.S.O. (Tooth at Eton), Capt. 9th Lancers, m. France (k. 13.9.14)	W.D.
1897	Lucas-Tooth, S. (Tooth at Eton), Capt. Lancashire Fusiliers. France (k. 20.10.14)	W.L.

1910 Luce, A. J., 2nd Lt. R.A.S.C., M.T. France — A.M.G.
1890 Luckock, E. H. M., Capt. S. Wales Borderers, and Staff — J.C., F.D.
1902 Luke, H. C. (F) (Lukach at Eton), Lt.-Cr. R.N.V.R., and Staff. Balkans, Gallipoli, Palestine — J.P.C., L.F., E.W.S.
1915 Lumley, L. R., Lt. 11th Hussars, w. France — C.M.W.
1880 Lumley, Hon. O. V. G. A., C.M.G., Brig.-Gen. (11th Hussars) — A.C.J.
1912 Lumley, R. J., 2nd Lt. 11th Hussars. France (k. 17.10.14) — C.M.W.
1898 Lumley-Smith, T. G. L., D.S.O., Maj. 21st Lancers, att. Herts Yeomanry and Staff, m. 2. France, Egypt, Gallipoli — W.D.
1902 Lumsden, B. N., Capt. Seaforth Highlanders. France (k. 25.4.15) — R.A.H.M., L.S.R.B.
1897 Lumsden, C. R., Capt. Gordon Highlanders. France (k. 25.8.14) — R.A.H.M.
1897 Lumsden, E. F., Capt. R.A.S.C., M.T., m. France, Egypt, Palestine — R.A.H.M.
1896 Lumsden, H. T., Capt. Cameron Highlanders, att. R.F.C. France (d. from accid. 21.6.15) — R.A.H.M.
1908 Lumsden, L. G., Capt. Seaforth Highlanders, w. France — E.L.V.
1903 Lumsden, W. V., D.S.O. and two Bars, M.C. (F) Bt. Maj. A. and S. Highlanders, empld. Lt.-Col. Cameronians (Scottish Rifles), w. 2, m. 4. France — R.A.H.M., L.S.R.B.
1916 Lund, J. E., Lt. Rifle Bde., w. 2. France, Balkans — L.S.R.B.
1892 Lupton, A. C., Capt. Remount Service. France, Mesopotamia — P.H.C., C.H.A.
1901 Luscombe, D. A., 2nd Lt. R.G.A., late Pte. London Regt. France — E.L.V.
1897 Luscombe, J. H., Capt. R. Guernsey L.I., att. R. Irish Regt., w. 2. France — E.L.V.
1910 Lushington, F., Capt. R.G.A., and Staff, w. France — J.M.D.
1879 Lushington, S., C.B., C.M.G. (F) Brig.-Gen. (R.A.), w., m. 4. France — F.T.
1914 Lushington, S. E. J. C., Lt. Hampshire Regt., and Staff. France (d.w. 22.9.16) — J.M.D., V.L., N.F.

1892 Lutley, J. T., Maj. (t. Lt.-Col.) Worcestershire Yeomanry F.H.R.
1886 Luttrell, A. C. Fownes, Maj. R.G.A., and Staff L.C.A.L.
1886 Luttrell, C. M. Fownes, Capt. N. Somerset Yeomanry W.D.
1906 Luttrell, R. P., Lt. (t. Capt.) Remount Service. Egypt
 A.C.B., A.M.G.
1906 Lutwyche, G. L., Capt. Montgomeryshire Yeomanry, att. M.G. Cav. France, India H.F.W.T.
1915 Luxmoore, C. M. G., Lt. R.M. Atlantic, White Sea R.S.K.
1912 Luxmoore, E. C. L., Capt. The Queen's, w. France E.W.S.
1915 Luxmoore, F. L., Capt. R.A.F., p. France E.W.S.
1890 Luxmoore, L. A., Maj. R.F.A. France H.E.L.
1890 Luxmoore, N., D.S.O. (F) Maj. (t. Lt.-Col.) Devonshire Regt., att. Manchester Regt., and Staff, w. 2, m. 2. France, Egypt H.E.L.
1894 Lyall, R. A., D.S.O., Maj. Staff, I.A., empld. Lt.-Col. Rajputs and Kashmir Rifles. E. Africa, Palestine A.C.J.
1910 Lycett-Green, F. D., Lt. Grenadier Gds., and Staff, w. France F.I.
1894 Lyell, Hon. C. H., Maj. R.G.A., and Staff. France (d. 18.10.18) J.M.E.
1901 Lygon, Hon. H. (F) Capt. Suffolk Yeomanry, att. R.A.F., and Staff. France, Balkans, Italy H E.L.
1895 Lygon, Hon. R., M.V.O., M.C., Lt.-Col. Grenadier Gds., att. Loyal N. Lancashire Regt., m. France R.C.R.
1898 Lynch, C. W. D., D.S.O., Capt. (t. Lt.-Col.) K.O.Y.L.I., m. 2. France (k. 1.7.16) F.H.R.
1912 Lyon, F. C., Lt. Grenadier Gds. France (k. 13.4.18) F.W.S.
1905 Lysaght, J. L. (F) Lt. Irish Gds., late 2nd Lt. 2nd Life Gds. France T.C.P., E.L.C.
1894 Lysley, W. L., Capt. R. Wiltshire Yeomanry T.D
1904 Lyttelton, Rev. the Hon. C. F., M.C., C.F. France A.C.B., A.M.G.
1900 Lyttelton, Hon. J. C. (F) Maj. Worcestershire Yeomanry, att. Australian Cav., and Staff, m. Egypt, Gallipoli, Palestine A.C.B.
1912 Lyttelton, O., D.S.O., M.C., Lt. (t. Capt.) Grenadier Gds., and Staff, w., m. 3. France H.T.B., S.G.L.

1913	Lyttelton, Hon. R. G. (F) Lt. R.F.A., w. France	A.B.R.
1896	Lytton, Hon. N. S., O.B.E. (F) Maj. R. Sussex Regt., and Staff, w., m. 3. France	S.A.D.
1874	Lyveden, Lord (Vernon at Eton), Lt. R.N.V.R.	O.B., H.W.M.
1885	Macalpine-Downie, J. R. (Macalpine-Leny at Eton), Lt.-Col. A. and S. Highlanders, att. Black Watch. France (d.w. 21.3.18)	H.B.
1886	Macalpine-Leny, R. L., D.S.O. (F) Bt. Lt.-Col. 16th Lancers, and Staff, m. 3. France, Egypt, Palestine	J.C.
1914	McBean, A. A., Lt. 12th Lancers, w. France	L.S.R.B.
1912	McBean, D. R., M.C., Lt. (t. Capt.) Rifle Bde., and Staff, m. 2. France	L.S.R.B.
1916	MacBrayne, D. C. H., 2nd Lt. R.F.C. France (k. 21.6.17)	L.S.R.B.
1903	MacBrayne, J. O., Maj. 16th Lancers, and Staff, w., m. France	H.B.
1904	McCalmont, D. H. B., M.C., Capt. 7th Hussars, and Staff, m. 3. France, E. Africa	A.A.S.
1899	McCalmont, R. C. A., D.S.O., Brig.-Gen. (Irish Gds.), m. 2. France	J.H.M.H.
1901	McCausland, E. T. W., Maj. 3rd Gurkha Rifles, I.A. India	H.B.
1906	Macclesfield, Earl of, Lt. R.A.S.C., M.T., late 2nd Lt. Oxfordshire Yeomanry. France, Egypt	P.W.
1904	McClure, I. H., D.S.O. (F) Capt. Intell. Corps, and Staff, late Sapper R.E., m. 4. France, Italy	P.W.
1907	McCormick, A. H., Flight Ensign U.S. Naval Res. Force. Home Waters	H.B.
1907	McCormick, E. H., Lt. U.S. Naval Res. Force	H.B.
1907	McCormick, L. J., Capt. Inf., U.S. Army. France	H.B.
1906	McCormick-Goodhart, F. H., Lt. R.N.V.R.	L.F., E.W.S.
1902	McCormick-Goodhart, L. McC., O.B.E., Lt.-Cr. R.N.V.R.	H.D., L.F., E.W.S.
1896	McCreagh-Thornhill, M.C., Capt. Derbyshire Yeomanry	A.C.B.
1916	McCreery, R. B., Lt. 17th Lancers	H.de H.
1915	McCreery, R. L., M.C., Lt. 12th Lancers, w. France	H.de H.

1913	McCulloch, S. H., Lt. Seaforth Highlanders, late 2nd Lt. H.L.I. France (d.w. 20.12.15)	S.R.E.
1878	Macdonald, G. G., Capt. Grenadier Gds.	G.F.M.
1891	Macdonell, E. N. N., C.M.G. (F) Col. Staff. E. Africa	F.T.
1889	Macdonell, H. E. E., the late, Capt. E. Surrey Regt., late Pte. H.L.I. France (d. 22.1.17)	G.F.M., F.T.
1897	McDonnell, Hon. A., C.B., C.M.G., Lt.-Col. Canadian E.F., m. 2. France	S.R.J.
1879	MacDonnell, C. R. A., Capt. R. Irish Regt.	A C.A.
1879	MacDonnell, L. G. A., Capt. (t. Lt.-Col.) Australian A.M.C. Egypt, Gallipoli, Mediterranean	A.C.A.
1877	McDonnell, Hon. Sir S. K., K.C.B., G.C.V.O., Maj. Cameron Highlanders, and Staff. France (d.w. 23.11.15)	L.F.D.
1904	MacDougall, I., Capt. Grenadier Gds. France (k. 1.9.14)	P.W.
1900	McEacharn, N. B. W., M.B.E., Capt. K.O.S.B., and Staff, m. 2. Balkans	H.D., H.F.W.T.
1912	McEwen, J. H. F., Capt. Cameron Highlanders, att. R.A.F., p. France	R.P.L.B.
1913	McEwen, J. R. D., Lt. R. Scots Fusiliers, and Staff. France (k. 12.10.16)	R.P.L.B.
1896	MacGregor, F. G., Capt. Gordon Highlanders, w. France	C.H.A.
1895	Macgregor, P. A., D.S.O., Bt. Lt.-Col. Coldstream Gds., m. 2. France	A.C.A.
1900	MacGregor, R., 2nd Lt., late Pte., R.A.S.C., M.T., late 2nd Lt. R.G.A. France (d.w. 23.7.17)	C.H.A
1895	MacGregor, W. W., D.S.O., Lt.-Col. Gordon Highlanders, att. Durham L.I. and Black Watch, m. 3. France	C.H.A.
1910	McGrigor, C. C., Capt. (t. Maj.) Rifle Bde., att. Tank Corps, and Staff, w. France	F.L.C.
1877	McGrigor, C. R. R., C.B., C.M.G., Maj.-Gen. (K.R.R.C.), m. France, Egypt, Gallipoli	J.P.C.
1896	McGrigor, F. J., Capt. Gordon Highlanders, w. France	C.H.A.
1913	McGrigor, J. N. G., 2nd Lt. Gordon Highlanders. France (d.w. 7.11.14)	F.L.C.

1878 McGrigor, W. C. G., Brig.-Gen. (Scots Gds.), m. France   J.P.C., E.S.S.

1897 Mackay, E. A., T.D., Maj. Wiltshire Regt., and Staff, w. Palestine   S.R.J.

1891 Mackay, G. E., T.D., Maj. R. Wiltshire Yeomanry, att. N. Irish Horse   H.G.W., S.R.J.

1905 Mackay, Hon. K., Lt. 12th Lancers, att. M.G. Cav. France   J.M.D.

1883 Mackenzie, A. C. O., the late, Sergt.-Maj. S. African Rifles. France. W. Africa (d. 23.4.20)   A.C.J.

1905 Mackenzie, A. K., Capt. Grenadier Gds., w. France (d.w. 16.9.16)   R.P.L.B.

1916 Mackenzie, C. H., Lt. Scots Gds., w. France   K.S.

1908 Mackenzie, D. W. A. D., D.S.O. (F) Bt. Maj. Seaforth Highlanders, and Staff, w., m. 2. France   P.W.

1910 Mackenzie, E. D., D.S.O., Capt. Scots Gds., and Staff, w. 3, m. 2. France   R.P.L.B.

1910 Mackenzie, H. W. Rawson, D.S.C. and Bar, Capt. R.A.F., late Lt. Grenadier Gds., m. 2. France, Balkans, Mediterranean, S. Russia   A.A.S.

1915 Mackenzie, R. K. (Martineau at Eton), Lt. Seaforth Highlanders, w. France   H.M.

1900 Mackenzie, Sir V. A. F., Bart., D.S.O., M.V.O. (F) Maj. (t. Lt.-Col.) Scots Gds., w. 2, m. 2. France   J.H.M.H.

1890 Mackenzie-Gillanders, E. B. (Mackenzie at Eton), Capt. Cameron Highlanders   T.D.

1880 McKerrell, A. de S., C.B. (F) Brig.-Gen. (Cameron Highlanders). (d. 24.4.16)   F.W

1911 Mackeson, G P., Paymaster-Sub-Lt. R.N.V.R., late 2nd Lt. London Regt. Home Waters, Mediterranean, Balkans, Egypt, Gallipoli   E.L.C.

1910 Mackinnon, A. H., Younger of, 2nd Lt. Cameron Highlanders. France (k. 14.9.14)   A.C.G.H.

1903 Mackintosh, A. A., Younger of, Capt. R.H.G., and Staff, w. France (d. 13.10.18)   L.H.R.

1897 Mackintosh, C. A. G. (F) Lt. (t. Maj.) R.A.F., and Staff, m. 2. Arabia, Egypt — K.S.
1897 Mackintosh, E. E. B., D.S.O. (F) Lt.-Col. R.E., att. Staff, Egyptian Army, m. 2. France, Egypt — K.S.
1902 Mackintosh, L. P. F., Lt. Wiltshire Regt., att. Devonshire Regt., late Pte. Somerset L.I. France, Egypt, Italy — T.C.P.
1901 Macklin, A. N. C., Lt. (t. Capt.) R.F.A. France, Egypt — H.B.
1910 Mackworth-Praed, C. W., Lt. Scots Gds. France, E. Africa — F.H.R., H.de H.
1894 Maclachlan, A. F. C., D.S.O. and Bar (F) Brig.-Gen. (K.R.R.C.), w., m. 3. France, Balkans (k. 22.3.18) — F.W.C., J.H.M.H.
1899 Maclachlan, K. D. M., Capt. Seaforth Highlanders, w. France (d.w. 27.4.15) — R.W.W.
1891 Maclachlan, R. C., D.S.O., Brig.-Gen. (Rifle Bde.), w., m. France (k. 11.8.17) — W.
1898 Maclagan, G. S., Lt. R. Warwickshire Regt. France (k. 25.4.15) — T.D.
1905 McLaren, Hon. F. W. S., M.P., 2nd Lt. R.F.C., late Lt. R.N.V.R. France, Egypt, Gallipoli (k. ac. 30.8.17) — H.L.
1916 McLaren, J. F. S., Lt. Black Watch, w. France — A.C.G.H.
1915 Maclean, D. C., Lt. A. and S. Highlanders, w. France — K.S.
1891 Maclean, H. F., Maj. Scots Gds. France — H.E.L.
1880 McLean, N., Maj. Dorset Yeomanry — J.P.C.
1873 Macleod, R. W., Capt. Sp. List — F.E.D.
1878 McMahon, Sir H. W., Bart., D.S.O., O.B.E. (F) Bt. Maj. (t. Lt.-Col.) R. Welch Fusiliers, m. 2. France — G.E.M.
1884 McMahon, N. R., Lt.-Col. R. Fusiliers, m. France (k. 11.11.14) — G.I.M.
1912 McMicking, N., D.S.O., M.C. (F) Capt. (t. Maj.) Black Watch, and Staff, w. 3, m. 5. France, S. Russia — A.C.G.H.
1904 Macmillan, D. de M., 2nd Lt. K.R.R.C. — K.S.
1895 Macmillan, Rev. J. V., O.B.E., C.F., m. France — K.S.
1909 Macmillan, M. H., Capt. Grenadier Gds., w. 3. France — K.S.
1899 Macmillan, W. E. F., Capt. Cameronians (Scottish Rifles), att. Intell. Corps, Staff. France — K.S.

1900	McMillan-Scott, T. A. F., Capt. K.O.S.B. France	F.L.V.
1905	McMinnies, W. G., A.F.C., Capt. (t. Maj.) R.A.F., late P.O., R.N.A.S., m. 2. France	H.M.
1900	Macnabb, R. J., Maj. Central India Horse, Indian E.F., m. France, Palestine	A.A.S.
1902	Macnaghten, A. C. R. S., Lt. Black Watch. France (k. 29.10.14)	E.C.A.L.
1893	Macnaghten, B., D.S.O., Lt.-Col. 12th Lancers, att. The King's Own (R. Lancaster Regt.), w. 2, m. France, Mesopotamia	P.W.
1898	Macnaghten, C. M., C.M.G., Lt.-Col., late Sergt., New South Wales Inf., Australian Imp. Forces, w. 4, m. 3. France, Egypt, Gallipoli	R.C.R.
1914	Macnaghten, Sir E. H., Bart., 2nd Lt. Black Watch, att. R. Irish Rifles. France (k. 1.7.16)	H M
1911	Macnaghten, G. E. M. (F) Capt. London Regt., and Staff. France	C.H.K.M.
1910	Macnaughtan, C. P. C., Capt. 2nd Dragoon Gds. (Queen's Bays). France, Palestine	E.I.
1915	Macneal, T. D. F., Lt. Gordon Highlanders, att. Black Watch. France	S.G.L.
1891	McNeile, H. D., Lt.-Col. 1st R. Dragoons, m. France (k. accid. 20.12.15)	F.W.C.
1891	McNeile, J., Lt.-Col. K.O.S.B. Gallipoli (k. 12.7.15)	F.W.C.
1910	McNeile, J. H., Lt. Coldstream Gds., w., p. France	L.S.R.B.
1899	Macneill, A. D., Capt. R.G.A. France (k. 29.7.17)	F.L.V.
1889	Macpherson-Grant, A., Lt. Seaforth Highlanders. France	F.T.
1886	Macpherson-Grant, G. B. (F) Capt. Cameron Highlanders, empld. under Admiralty	R.A.H.M.
1913	MacRae, J. D. G., Lt. Seaforth Highlanders, att. R.A.F., p. Mesopotamia	J H.M.H.
1907	MacRae, K. S., Capt. Black Watch, empld. Maj. R. Scots Fusiliers, w. France, Balkans, Egypt, Gallipoli	F.H.R.
1905	Madan, F. F., 2nd Lt. Behar and Orissa Regt., I.A. India	K.S.

1913	Madan, G. S., Lt. The King's Own (R. Lancaster Regt.), and Staff, late Pte. R. Fusiliers, w. France, Balkans, Egypt, Gallipoli, Italy, Mesopotamia	K.S.
1908	Madan, N. C., Lt. The King's Own (R. Lancaster Regt.). France (k. 2.3.16)	K.
1888	Madden, J. C. W., Lt.-Col. R. Irish Fusiliers. France	J.H.M.H.
1904	Maidstone, Visc., O.B.E., D.S.C. (F) Maj. (t. Lt.-Col.) R.N.V.R., att. R.A.F., and Staff. France	H.F.W.T.
1902	Maine, H. C. S., Lt. Grenadier Gds., and Staff, w. France	E.C.A.L.
1889	Mainwaring, C. F. K., Capt. Shropshire L.I., att. Tank Corps, and Staff. France	W.D.
1894	Mainwaring, W. R. K., C.B.E. (F) Lt.-Col. Denbighshire Yeomanry, and Staff, m. 4. Egypt, Gallipoli	S.R.J., H.B.
1910	Maitland, Hon. I. C., Capt. Cameron Highlanders, and Staff. Egypt, Palestine	A.C.G.H.
1907	Majolier, E., Lt. Yorkshire Regt., att. Norfolk Regt. France (d. 20.11.18)	H.W.
1917	Makgill, J. D. A. A., 2nd Lt. Coldstream Gds.	F.E.R.
1894	Makgill-Crichton-Maitland, F. L., D.S.O. (F) Maj. Gordon Highlanders, empld. Lt.-Col. R. Welch Fusiliers, and Staff, m. 3. France, Gallipoli, Italy	A.C.A.
1899	Makgill-Crichton-Maitland, M. E., D.S.O. (F) Maj. (t. Lt.-Col.) Grenadier Gds., att. The King's (Liverpool Regt.), w., m. 4. France	W.D., R.W.W.-T.
1899	Makins, H., Capt. London Regt. France (k. 4.11.15)	F.C.P.
1885	Makins, Sir P. A., Bart., Maj. Remount Service. France, Balkans, Egypt	J.P.C.
1882	Malcolm, C. E., Maj. Buckinghamshire Yeomanry	T.D.
1916	Malcolm, M. A. J., Lt. Scots Gds., w. France	H. de H.
1887	Malcolm, N., C.B., D.S.O. (F) Maj.-Gen. (A. and S. Highlanders), w., m. 8. France, Balkans, Egypt, Gallipoli	G.E.M.
1913	Malcolm, P., Lt. Grenadier Gds., w. 3. France (k. 25.8.18)	I.
1901	Malden, C. H., Maj. R.M.L.I., R.N., and R. Australian Navy, and Staff, m. Falkland Isles, N. America, W. Indies	K.S.

1898 Malden, Rev. R. H., Chaplain R.N. Home Waters, N. Atlantic — K.S.
1897 Malone, E. G. S. L'Estrange, Maj. R. Fusiliers, empld. Lt.-Col. W. Riding Regt. and M.G.C., and Staff, w., m. 2. France — K.S.
1894 Manchester, Duke of, Lt. R.N.V.R., att. Hawke Bn., R.N.D. — A.C.A.
1903 Mander, C. A., T.D., Maj. Staffordshire Yeomanry, w. Egypt, Palestine — H.Br.
1896 Manfield, A. H., Capt. R.A.M.C. France, Egypt, Palestine — A.A.S.
1910 Manley, R. S., Capt. Staffordshire Yeomanry, m. Egypt, Palestine — R.C.R., M.D.H.
1917 Manley, W. B. L., 2nd Lt. Grenadier Gds., w. France — L.S.R.B.
1895 Manley-Sims, R. F., C.M.G., D.S.O., Brig.-Gen. (K.R.R.C.), m. France — W.D.
1897 Mann-Thomson, J., Maj. Lothians and Border Horse, att. R.F.A. and R.G.A., late Lt.-Cr. R.N.R. France, Home Waters — A.A.S.
1914 Manners, Hon. F. H., M.C., Lt. Grenadier Gds., w. France — H.Br.
1910 Manners, Hon. J. N., Lt. Grenadier Gds. France (k. 1.9.14) — H.Br.
1893 Manningham-Buller, Sir M. E., Bart., Capt. (t. Lt.-Col.) Rifle Bde. France — S.A.D.
1908 Mansel, R. C., Maj. Rifle Bde., att. Tank Corps, w., m. France — J.M.E., M.D.H.
1915 Marchant, F. G. W., 2nd Lt. The Queen's Own (R. W. Kent Regt.), att. R.F.C. France (k. 22.10.16) — E.I., T.F.C.
1908 Marchant, H. S., Lt. The Buffs. Mesopotamia (k. 6.1.16) — R.P.L.B.
1884 Margesson, E. W., C.M.G., Bt. Lt.-Col. (t. Col.) Norfolk Regt., and Staff, m. 3. Egypt — F.W.C.
1884 Marindin, A. H., C.B., D.S.O. (F) Maj.-Gen. (Black Watch), m. 7. France — H.E.L.
1897 Marindin, C. C., C.B.E., D.S.O. (F) Lt.-Col. R.A.F., late Maj. R.G.A., and Staff, m. 2. France, Italy — H.E.L.
1891 Marker, E. R., Trooper R. 1st Devon Yeomanry. Gallipoli — S.A.D.

1885 Marker. R. J., D.S.O. (F) Lt.-Col. Staff, m. 2. France
(d.w. 13.11.14) F.W., S.A.D.
1912 Markham, C. H., Capt. Northumberland Fusiliers, att.
R.A.F., w., m. France A.B.R.
1902 Marks, C. H., Capt. R.F.C., late Lt. Middlesex Regt.
France (k. 23.10.15) H.B.
1906 Marriott, E. C., M.M., Pte. R. Fusiliers, late Lt. R.F.A.
France, N. Russia E.W.S.
1895 Marshall, A. P., Lt. Cameron Highlanders H.E.L.
1911 Marshall, F. G., Lt. Grenadier Gds. France (k. 22.3.15) A.A.S.
1882 Marshall, T. E., C.B., C.M.G., Brig.-Gen. (R.A.), m. 4.
France K.S.
1893 Marshall, W. S. D., Lt. (t. Maj.) R.F.A. France H.E.L.
1909 Marsham, Visc., Capt. Coldstream Gds., w. France H.F.W.T.
1891 Marsham, C. G. Bullock, Maj. W. Kent Yeomanry, att.
R.E. Egypt, Gallipoli, Palestine E.C.A.L.
1898 Marsham, C. H. Bullock, Capt. W. Kent Yeomanry, att.
The Buffs and R.A.F. Egypt, Gallipoli, Palestine R.A.H.M.
1901 Marsham, F. W. Bullock, D.S.O., M.C., Capt. (t. Lt.-
Col.) 19th Hussars, and Staff, m. 2. France R.A.H.M.
1897 Marsham, Hon. S. E., 2nd Lt. Grenadier Gds. France E.C.A.L.
1896 Marsham-Townshend, F., 2nd Lt. Scots Gds. France
(k. 16.5.15) J.M.E.
1895 Marsham-Townshend, H. S., Lt. Scots Gds., w. France J.M.E.
1908 Marson, A. A., M.C., Capt. R.F.A., m. France, Mesopotamia H.Br.
1900 Martin, C. H. G., Lt. Monmouthshire Regt. France
(k. 3.5.15) P.W.
1899 Martin, E. G., O.B.E., Lt.-Cr. R.N.V.R. Home Waters J.M.E.
1901 Martin, J. G. F. Napier, Capt. R. Dublin Fusiliers, and
Staff. France E.L.V.
1893 Martin, R. E., C.M.G., Lt.-Col. Leicestershire Regt.,
w. 2, m. France K.S.
1906 Martin, W. G., Lt. K.R.R.C. France (k. 14.1.17) H.M.
1908 Martineau, H. M., Lt. Welsh Gds., late Lt. R. Berkshire
Regt. R.W.W.-T., C.M.W.

1915	Maryon-Wilson, G. P. M., Lt. Grenadier Gds.	C.M.W.
1904	Mason, G. K. M., D.S.O. and Bar, Capt. 14th Hussars, att. Maj. Sherwood Rangers and Lt.-Col. Dorset Yeomanry, and Staff, w. 2, m. 2. France, Balkans, Palestine	E.C.A.L., J.M.D.
1912	Mason, P. R. F., Capt. The King's (Liverpool Regt.), w. France	H.F.W.T., A.E.C.
1917	Mason, R. B., Lt. Coldstream Gds. France	A.C.G.H.
1914	Massy-Beresford, T. H., M.C., Capt. Rifle Bde., w. France	R.S.de H.
1895	Master, C. E. H., Capt. The Queen's. India	J.M.E.
1912	Master, G. G. O., Lt. Gloucestershire Regt. France (k. 7.1.)	J.H.M.H.
1916	Mather-Jackson, E. A., Lt. Scots Gds. France	H.de H.
1911	Mather-Jackson, H., Capt. 9th Lancers, and Staff, m. France	F.H.R., H.de H.
1890	Matheson, T. G., C.B., C.M.G. (F) Maj.-Gen. (Coldstream Gds.), w., m. 10. France	E.H.
1904	Matthews, A. S., Lt. 8th Hussars, and Staff. France	E.L.V.
1895	Matthews, C. L., Bt. Lt.-Col. Durham L.I., empld. Lt.-Col. Hampshire Regt., and Staff, w., m. 3. India, Mesopotamia	F.T.
1894	Matthews, D. S., O.B.E., Maj. 17th Lancers, and Staff, m. 2. France	C.H.E., A.C.B.
1916	Matthews, E. J. W., 2nd Lt. Grenadier Gds., empld. Gds. M.G. Regt. France	A.B.R.
1877	Matthews, L. W., O.B.E., Maj. Remount Service	E.H.
1911	Matthews, M. L. W., Capt. The Queen's Own (R. W. Kent Regt.), m.. France (k. 3.7.16)	A.B.R.
1892	Matthews, R. L., Capt. The Queen's, empld. Maj. Labour Corps. France	J.P.C.
1903	Matthews, R. W., Lt. (t. Capt.) K.O.Y.L.I., and Staff. France	E.L.V.
1913	Matthey, J. T., A.B., R.N.V.R., att. R.N.D. France, Gallipoli (k. 13.11.16)	K.S.

1882	Maude, Sir F. S., K.C.B., C.M.G., D.S.O. (F) Lieut.-Gen. (Coldstream Gds.), w. 2, m. 7. France, Egypt, Gallipoli, Mesopotamia (d. 18.11.17)	F.W.C.
1911	Maude, G. H. F., 2nd Lt. R. Fusiliers, late 2nd Lt. The Buffs. France (d.w. 9.4.17)	F.W.
1903	Maude, J. W. A., 2nd Lt. K.R.R.C. France (k. 23.8.15)	A.C.L.
1892	Maudslay, C. C., Sub-Lt. R.N.V.R.	A.C.A.
1903	Maul, H. C., Maj. Oxfordshire and Bucks L.I. France	C.H.A.
1914	Mauleverer, A. A. M. G. (Gowan at Eton), Sub-Lt. R.N.V.R.	E.L.V., A.C.R.-W.
1913	Mauleverer, W. M. M. G. (Gowan at Eton), Lt. Dorsetshire Regt. India	E.L.V., A.C.R.-W.
1891	Mawson, W. W., O.B.E., Capt. (t. Maj.) Leicestershire Regt., w., m. 2. France	H.D.
1890	Maxted, H. R., M.C., Capt. (t. Maj.) King's African Rifles, and Staff, m. E. Africa	E.L.V.
1892	Maxwell, A. F., Capt. Lovat's Scouts, empld. Lt.-Col. Collingwood Bn., R.N.D. Belgium (k 9.10.14)	F.W.C., J.H.M.H.
1914	Maxwell, J. R. Perceval, Lt. K.R.R.C., w. 2. France	A.B.R.
1886	Maxwell, R. D. Perceval, D.S.O., Lt.-Col. R. Irish Rifles, att. R. Munster Fusiliers, w. 2, m. 2. France	A.C.J.
1895	Maxwell-Lyte, W., Lt. R.G.A., late C.P.O., R.N.V.R.	S.R.J.
1912	May, E. G. K. S. (F) Capt. Roughriders, and Staff, w., m. Balkans, Egypt, Palestine	H.B.
1908	Mayhew, A. J., Capt. Denbighshire Yeomanry, att. R. Welch Fusiliers. France, Egypt, Palestine	H.F.W.T.
1914	Mayhew, C. W., M.C. (F) Capt. Denbighshire Yeomanry, att. R. Welch Fusiliers, and Staff, w. France, Egypt, Palestine	H.F.W.T., A.E.C.
1905	Mayhew, G. D., Capt. (t. Maj.) Denbighshire Yeomanry	H.F.W.T.
1906	Maynard, A. L., M.C., Capt. Scots Gds., late Lt. 10th R. Hussars, w. 3. France	E.I.
1899	Meade, C. F., Lt. Surrey Yeomanry, and Staff. Balkans	A.C.B.
1896	Meade, Hon. E. B., Capt. 10th R. Hussars, att. 1st Life Gds., and Staff. France	P.W.

1901	Meade, H. E., O.B.E., Capt. R. Fusiliers, and Staff, w. France	E.L.V.
1913	Meade, J. W., Capt. Oxfordshire and Bucks L.I., w. 2. France, Mesopotamia, N. Russia	H. de H.
1912	Meade, R. P., 2nd Lt. Rifle Bde. France (k. 10.7.16)	H. de H.
1903	Meade-King, R. E. B., Lt. R.A.S.C., M.T., late Lt. Armoured Cars, R.N.V.R., m. France, Egypt	R.S.K.
1899	Meade-Waldo, E. R., D.S.O. (F) Maj. (t. Lt.-Col.) Rifle Bde., att. M.G.C., and Staff, m. 3. France	P.W.
1890	Meister, G. E. W., Lt. R. Defence Corps, late L/ce-Cpl. R. Fusiliers. France	K.S.
1901	Melles, G. F., Lt. R.F.A. Egypt (d.w. 6.11.15)	T.C.P.
1900	Melles, W. E., Capt. S. Nottinghamshire Hussars, att. Remount Service. France	T.C.P.
1898	Mellor, J. E. P., Capt. Hampshire Regt. Mesopotamia	P.W.
1898	Mellor, J. G. G., M.C. (F) Capt. (t. Maj.) Staff. France	J.M.E.
1901	Mellor, J. S., O.B.E., M.C. (F) Maj. (t. Lt.-Col.) K.R.R.C., and Staff, w., m. 2. France	J.M.E.
1912	Mellor, J. S. P., Lt. Somerset L.I., att. Oxfordshire and Bucks L.I., w. 2, p. Mesopotamia	F.H.R., H. de H.
1911	Mellor, V. C. S., Lt. K.R.R.C., att. Northamptonshire Regt., Suffolk Regt., and Cheshire Regt., and Staff. Egypt, Palestine (d. 21.3.19)	H. de H.
1878	Mellor, V. H., Lt.-Col. Labour Corps, late Lt.-Col. Sherwood Foresters, and Staff	W.E.
1913	Mellor, W. M., Capt. R.M. Staff, late Lt. R. Fusiliers, w. France	A.C.G.H.
1914	Melville, D. W. L., M.C., Capt. 21st Lancers, att. The Queen's Own (R.W. Kent Regt.), late 2nd Lt. Worcestershire Yeomanry, m. 3. France, Italy	A.C.G.H.
1915	Mendel, R. W. W., 2nd Lt. R.F.A. France (d. 19.9.17)	K.S
1914	Menzies, I. G., Lt. Coldstream Gds., w. France	E.I., T.F.C.
1906	Menzies, K. G., M.C. (F) Lt. Welsh Gds., and Staff. France	E.I.
1909	Menzies, S. G., D.S.O., M.C. (F) Bt. Maj. (t. Lt.-Col) 2nd Life Gds., and Staff, m. 3. France	E.I.

1907	Menzies-Jones, L. F., Lt. The Buffs, att. T.M.B. France	J.M.E., H.M.
1900	Meredith, H. C., O.B.E., T.D., Maj. Shropshire Yeomanry, att. Leicestershire Yeomanry, and Staff, m. 2. France	R.C.R.
1906	Meredith, L. A. de L., Lt. Gloucestershire Regt.	E.L.V.
1910	Meredith, W. M., Lt. (t. Capt.) The King's (Liverpool Regt.), att. Black Watch, and Staff, w. France (d. 7.12.18)	A.M.G
1905	Merivale, J. L., 2nd Lt., late Trooper, Australian L.H. Egypt, Gallipoli (k. 7.8.15)	J.M.E.
1894	Messel, H. G., Lt. R. Sussex Regt.	S.R.J.
1890	Messel, L. C. R., O.B.E., T.D., Lt.-Col. The Buffs	F.T.
1911	Messervy, E. D., Capt. London Regt., att. R.F.C. France (k. 20.7.17)	H. M
1911	Messervy, F. W. (F) Capt. Hodson's Horse, I.A. France, Palestine	H. Br.
1908	Messervy, G., M.C. (F) Capt. R.F.A., m. France (k. 9.10.18)	H.M.
1905	Methuen, Hon. P. A., Lt. Scots Gds., att. R. Wiltshire Yeomanry, and Staff. France	S.A.D., P.V.B.
1909	Meugens, G. E., Maj. (t. Lt.-Col.) Manchester Regt., att. Tank Corps, w. 2, m. France, Egypt, Gallipoli (d. 30.10.18)	K.S.
1902	Mewburn, S. W. R., Capt. 14th Hussars, att. 4th and 20th Hussars. France, Mesopotamia (k. 21.5.16)	E.L.V.
1883	Mexborough, Earl of (Mr. Savile at Eton), Capt. Remount Service. France	E.S.S.
1904	Meyer, F. C., Lt. Essex Yeomanry, att. R.E. Signal Service and R.A.F., w., m. France	R.S. de H.
1898	Meynell, F. H. L., D.S.O. (Wood at Eton), Maj. R.F.A., w., m. France	W.D.
1880	Meyrick, F. C., C.B., C.M.G., Brig.-Gen. (15th Hussars), m. France, Egypt	W.D.
1903	Meyrick, G. L. T. G., Capt. (t. Maj.) 7th Hussars, att. R.H.G., w., m. France	H.B.
1911	Meyrick, R. O., Lt. K.R.R.C. France	H.B.
1897	Meyrick, W. T. (F) Lt. R.A.S.C., M.T. France	A.A.S.

1904	Meysey-Thompson, A. de C. C., Lt. R.F.A. France	J.M.E.
1901	Meysey-Thompson, Hon. C. H. M., Capt. Rifle Bde. France (d.w. 17.6.15)	J.M.E.
1877	Meysey-Thompson, E. C., M.P., Lt.-Col. R.F.A. France	W.E.
1915	Meysey-Thompson, O. V. C., Lt. R.F.A., w. France, Italy	R.S.K.
1865	Meysey-Thompson, R. F., Col. W. Yorkshire Regt., and Staff	W.E.
1908	Michaelis, C. D. A., Capt. R.G.A., att. Field Survey Coy., R.E. France	J.H.M.H.
1905	Michelli, P. F. M. (F) Capt. R.E. France, Balkans, Egypt	J.M.D.
1911	Micholls, R. M. B., Lt. Bedfordshire Regt., late Lt. Nigerian Regt., W. African F.F., and The Queen's. W. Africa	R.P.L.B.
1905	Micholls, W. H. M. (F) Capt. 20th Hussars, empld. Lt.-Col. K.O.Y.L.I. and Cameron Highlanders, w. 2, m. 2. France	H.E.L., R.S.K.
1900	Micklem, R., C.M.G. (F) Maj. R.E., att. Egyptian Army, and Staff, w., m. Egypt, Gallipoli	K.S.
1914	Micklethwait, R. G., Lt. Yorkshire Dragoons	C.M.W.
	Middleton, E., 2nd Lt. Dorset Yeomanry. Egypt (k. 26.2.16)	H.M.
	Middleton, E., Capt. Dorsetshire Regt. Mesopotamia	H.W.M.
1893	Middleton, G., Pte. Mounted Infantry, S. African Defence Forces. S. Africa	A.C.J.
1894	Middleton, G. G., Maj. (t. Lt.-Col.) Northamptonshire Yeomanry, att. Scottish Horse, m. France	E.H.
1894	Middleton, N., Lt. H.L.I., and Staff	A.C.J.
	Middleton, W. A. A., Capt. Seaforth Highlanders. France (k. 15.4.15)	H.R.
1875	Middleton, W. C., C.B.E., Bt. Lt.-Col. Remount Service Staff	J.L.J.
1915	Miesegaes, C. G. V., Lt. R.F.A., att. R.E. Signal Service. France	A.M.G.
1897	Milbank, Sir F. R. P., Bart. (F) Capt. Yorkshire Regt., and Staff, m. 2. France	R.A.H.M.

1915	Milborne-Swinnerton-Pilkington, A. W., M.C., Lt. 16th Lancers. France	S.G.L.
1876	Milborne-Swinnerton-Pilkington, Sir T. E., Bart., Lt.-Col. K.R.R.C. France	E.C.A.L.
1913	Mildmay, A. S.-L. St. J., M.C., Lt. (t. Capt.) Grenadier Gds., w. 2. France	E.L.V., A.C.R.-W.
1879	Mildmay, F. B., P.C., M.P., T.D., Lt.-Col. W. Kent Yeomanry, and Staff, m. 4. France	G.E.M.
1874	Miles, A. E., Lt.-Col. Wiltshire Regt., att. Hampshire Regt.	E.W.
1901	Miles, E. W. T., M.C. (F) Capt. 1st R. Dragoons, w., m. France	S.A.D.
1900	Miles, T. G. A., Lt. Staff. France	A.A.S.
1915	Miles-Bailey, G. M., Lt. Hampshire Regt., att. Wiltshire Regt. Mesopotamia	A.E.C.
1880	Miller, A. D., C.B.E., D.S.O., Brig.-Gen. (R. Scots Greys). France	T.D.
1889	Miller, G. H. U., Maj. K.R.R.C., att. Essex Regt. and R. Defence Corps, w. France, Balkans, Egypt	E.H.
1895	Miller, J. W., Lt. R.N.V.R. Home Waters	F.H.R.
1898	Miller, R. B., Maj. R.F.A. France, Mesopotamia	T.C.P.
1903	Miller-Mundy, G. E., Maj. 1st Life Gds. France	R.C.R.
1908	Miller-Mundy, P. R., D.S.O., M.C. (F) Capt. (t. Maj.) S. Wales Borderers, w. 2, m. 2. France, Balkans, Gallipoli	J.H.M.H.
1911	Milligan, D. W., 2nd Lt. R.A.S.C., late Lt. Cameron Highlanders. France	H.Br.
1911	Milln, K. J., Capt. Somerset L.I., att. W. Riding Regt., and Staff, w. 2, m. France	R.S.de H.
1905	Mills, Hon. C. T., M.P., 2nd Lt. Scots Gds., late Lt. W. Kent Yeomanry. France (k. 6.10.15)	H.T.B.
1875	Mills, D. A., Bt. Col. Duke of Cornwall's L.I., late Lt.-Col. R.E. France	R.A.H.M.
1884	Mills, Hon. E. J., D.S.O., Maj. W. Kent Yeomanry	C.L.L.-C., F.H.R.
1892	Mills, Hon. G. E., the late, Cr. R.N.V.R., and Staff. (d. 14.8.17)	T.D.

1912	Mills, H. J. F., Capt. K.R.R.C., and Staff, w., p. France, Balkans	E.L.V., A.C.R.-W.
1917	Milne, I. R., 2nd Lt. Scots Gds.	L.S.R.B.
1875	Milner, E., Maj. K.R.R.C. France	H.W.M.
1880	Milner, G. F., C.M.G., D.S.O., Brig.-Gen. (1st Life Gds.)	W.E., J.M.E.
1896	Milnes-Gaskell, E., Maj. Yorkshire Dragoons, and Staff, m. 2. France	E.C.A.L.
1898	Milvain, H. R., Maj. 12th Lancers, att. R.F.A. France	R.C.R.
1905	Minto, Earl of (Viscount Melgund at Eton), Capt. Scots Gds. France	H.T.B.
1900	Mirrielees, F. D., Maj. Surrey Yeomanry. France, Balkans, Egypt, S. Russia	E.L.V.
1916	Misa, J. M., Lt. 17th Lancers. France	R.S. de H.
1914	Misa, L. E., Lt. 4th Dragoon Gds., w. France	R.S. de H.
1911	Misa, V. H., M.C., Capt. 2nd Dragoon Gds. (Queen's Bays), empld. M.G. Cav., w. 3, m. 2. France	R.S. de H.
1887	Mitchell, A. I., Capt. 3rd Dragoon Gds., att. Somaliland Camel Corps and M.G. Cav. France, E. Africa	F.T.
1900	Mitchell, C., D.S.O., O.B.E. (F) Capt. (t. Maj.) Grenadier Gds., and Staff, m. 4. France, Italy	A.A.S.
1902	Mitchell, C. R. G., Lt. 6th Dragoon Gds. (Carabiniers), w. France (k. 1.4.18)	R.A.H.M.
1893	Mitchell, R. H., 2nd Lt. R. Sussex Regt.	R.A.H.M.
1895	Mitchell, R. W., Lt. R. E. Kent Yeomanry, att. The Buffs. Egypt, Palestine (d.w. 19.11.17)	R.A.H.M.
1901	Mitchell, R. P. J., Capt. (t. Maj.) Baluchi Horse, I.A. Mesopotamia	J.M.E.
1912	Mitchell-Innes, G. R., Lt. 19th Hussars. France (d.w. 15.5.15)	A.B.R.
1909	Mitchison, G. R. (F) Capt. 2nd Dragoon Gds. (Queen's Bays), att. R.E. Signal Service, and Maj. Staff. France, Italy	S.A.D., P.V.B.
1911	Mitchison, W. A., Lt., late Cpl., R.E., w. 2. France (k. 20.9.17)	P.V.B.
1895	Mitford, Hon. C. B. O., D.S.O., Maj. 10th R. Hussars, w., m. France (k. 13.5.15)	J.M.E.

1899	Mitford, Hon. J. P. B. O., Lt. 1st Life Gds., att. Interpreter I.A., and Staff. France	J.M.E.
1874	Mitford, W. K., C.M.G., Col. Staff. France	W.W.
1916	Mitford, W. S., Lt. 17th Lancers. France	E.I., T.F.C.
1893	Moffat, J. A., Capt. Black Watch, att. Norfolk Regt., late Capt. Scottish Horse, w. France	J.C., F.D., A.C.B.
1917	Moir, J. W., 2nd Lt. Scots Gds. France	K.S.
1887	Molineux-Montgomerie, G. F., Maj. Grenadier Gds. France (k. 22.10.15)	A.C.J
1889	Molyneux, C. R., M.C., Maj. 10th R. Hussars, att. R.A.S.C., and Staff, w. France	W.D.
1901	Molyneux, R. C. A. F., Capt. S. Nottinghamshire Hussars, late Capt. London Regt.	E.L.V.
1893	Monck, Hon. C. H. S., Capt. Coldstream Gds., w. France (k. 21.10.14)	W.D.
1898	Monck, G. S. S., Capt. R.E. France, N. Russia	F.H.R.
1915	Monckton, C., 2nd Lt. R. Irish Fusiliers, att. R.F.C. France (d.w. 1.7.16)	H. de H.
1908	Monckton, F. A., Lt. Scots Gds. France (k. 8.11.14)	R.S. de H.
1912	Monckton, G. V. F., Lt. Scots Gds. France (k. 25.1.15)	R.S. de H.
1914	Monckton, L. R. S., Lt. (t. Capt.) R.E. Signal Service, late Lt. The Queen's Own (R. W. Kent Regt.). France	E.W.S.
1917	Monckton, M., Pte. E. Surrey Regt., w. France	H. de H.
1913	Monckton, R. F. P., Capt. Montgomeryshire Yeomanry, att. M.G.C., and Staff. Palestine	R.S. de H.
1899	Monckton-Arundell, Hon. G. V. A., D.S.O., O.B.E., Lt.-Col. 1st Life Gds., and Staff., m. 4. France	E.I.
1916	Money-Kyrle, R. E., Lt. R.A.F., w. France	S.G.L.
1909	Monins, J. E., Capt. (t. Maj.) The Buffs, and Staff. Aden, Afghanistan, Gallipoli	E.W.S.
1910	Monk, G. P. de B., Capt. Welch Regt. France (k. 3.10.15)	J.M.D.
1911	Monk, H. H. de B., M.C., A.F.C., Capt. K.R.R.C., att. R.A.F., w., m. France	J.M.D., V. Le N.F.
1887	Monk-Bretton, Lord, C.B. (Mr. Dodson at Eton), Maj. Sussex Yeomanry, att. Naval Intell. Staff. Mediterranean	C.H.E.

1894 Monkswell, Lord (Mr. Collier at Eton), 2nd Lt. R.F.A., Lt., att. Interpreter I.A. France   C.H.E., A.C.B.

1913 Monro, C. C. A., Lt. K.O.S.B., empld. Capt. M.G.C., w. France   K.S.

1899 Monson, Sir M. W. E. J., Bart., Lt. R.A.S.C., late Lt. Intell. Corps. France   R.W.W.-T.

1892 Monson, W. J., Col. Staff, m. E. Africa   K.S.

1905 Montagliari, Marchese F. di, Sergente Artiglieria Treno, Italian Army. Italy   J.M.D.

1894 Montagu, F. J. O., O.B.E., M.C., Capt. Coldstream Gds., and Staff, m. 4. France   H.D.

1906 Montagu, J. F., Lt. 15th Hussars, and Staff. France   H.B.

1910 Montagu, J. G. E. D., Capt. R.F.A., w. 2. France   A.A.S.

1885 Montagu of Beaulieu, Lord, K.C.I.E., C.S.I., V.D. (Mr. Montagu-Douglas-Scott at Eton), Brig.-Gen. (Hampshire Regt.), w. 2. France, Aden, Egypt, India, Italy, Palestine   G.E.M.

1905 Montagu-Douglas-Scott, D. J., O.B.E. (F) Capt. R. Scots, and Staff, w., m. France, Balkans   K.S.

1898 Montagu-Douglas-Scott, Lord F. G., D.S.O., Lt.-Col. Grenadier Gds., att. Irish Gds. and R. Fusiliers, w., m. France   R.A.H.M.

1885 Montagu-Douglas-Scott, Lord G. W., Lt.-Col. Lothians and Border Horse   E.W., S.A.D.

1888 Montagu-Douglas-Scott, Lord H. A., C.M.G., D.S.O. (F) Lt.-Col. London Regt., and Staff, m. 2. France, Gallipoli   W.D.

1886 Montagu-Douglas-Scott, Lord H. F., Col. Labour Corps, late empld. R. Fusiliers and Bedfordshire Regt., m. 5. France   E.W., S.A.D.

1886 Montagu-Douglas-Scott, W. G. L., Capt. Lovat's Scouts, att. Bimbashi Egyptian Army, and Staff. Egypt, Gallipoli, Palestine   J.H.M.

1914 Montagu-Douglas-Scott, Lord W. W., M.C., Lt. 10th R. Hussars, m. France   E.I., T.F.C.

1904	Montgomerie, Hon. F. C., Capt. 2nd Life Gds., att. Ayrshire Yeomanry, and Staff, m. Egypt, Gallipoli	A.C.B., A.M.G.
1888	Montgomery, H. M. de F., C.B., C.M.G. (F) Brig.-Gen. (R.A.), m. 5. France	F.T.
1897	Montgomery, R. H., M.C., Capt. E. Surrey Regt. France	F.W.C., J.P.C.
1869	Montrose, Duke of, K.T. (Lord R. Graham at Eton), Brig.-Gen. (Black Watch)	W.W.
1901	Moon, A., M.C., Capt. London Regt. France	S.A.D.
1902	Moon, B. O., 2nd Lt. London Regt., m. France (k. 24.5.15)	S.A.D.
1886	Moon, Rev. C. G., C.F. France	T.D.
1900	Moore, A. H., Surgeon-Lt. R.N. Home Waters, Atlantic, Black Sea, Mediterranean, Red Sea	H.E.L.
1894	Moore, G. H., Lt. R.N.V.R. Home Waters	R.A.H.M.
1902	Moore, L. G., D.S.O. and Bar, Bt. Maj. (t. Lt.-Col.) K.R.R.C., and Staff, w. 2, p., m. 4. France, N. Russia	E.I.
1908	Moore, N. A., M.C., 2nd Lt. Coldstream Gds., late Sergt. Rhodesian Regt. France, E. Africa, S.W. Africa	R.S. de H.
1902	Moore, W. A. M., T.D., Maj. R.F.A., and Staff, m. Egypt, Palestine	C.L., R.S.K.
1912	Moorsom, A. E., Lt. Suffolk Regt. France (d.w. 3.8.16)	H.B.
1910	Morgan, Hon. E. F., Lt. Welsh Gds.	M.D.H.
1872	Morgan, L. H. G., Lt. R. Defence Corps, late Remount Service and R.A.S.C.	J.E.Y.
1893	Morgan, P. V., Capt. R.A.O.C. France	H.W.M.
1908	Morgan-Grenville-Gavin, Hon. T. G. B., D.S.O., M.C. (F) (Mr. Morgan Grenville at Eton), Bt. Maj. (t. Lt.-Col.) Rifle Bde., and Staff, m. 4. France, N. Russia	H.B.
1909	Morignano, Duca di (F) Tenente Artiglieria and Liaison Officer, Italian Army. Italy	R.S. de H.
1871	Morland, H. C., Lt.-Col. The Queen's Own (R. W. Kent Regt.), late Lt.-Col. R. E. Kent Yeomanry	W.E.
1903	Morley, C., Lt. R.F.A. France	H.F.W.T.
1907	Morley, J., Lt. R. Wiltshire Yeomanry	H.F.W.T.
1902	Morrell, G. M., Capt. R.E., w. France	H.B.

1901	Morrell, J. H., Capt. Sp. List	H.B.
1880	Morrice, L. E., D.S.O., Bt. Lt.-Col. R. Warwickshire Regt., and Staff	C.C.J.
1900	Morris, T. H. P., M.C., Bt. Maj. (t. Lt.-Col.) Rifle Bde., m. 3. France (d.w. 18.9.16)	C.L., J.M.D.
1909	Morris-Eyton, C. R., M.C., Capt. R.F.A., w. France	R.S.K.
1892	Morrison, J. A., D.S.O., Maj. Grenadier Gds., empld. Lt.-Col. Middlesex Regt., w., m. 2. France	J.M.E.
1888	Morrison-Bell, A. C., M.P. (Bell at Eton), Maj. Scots Gds., p. France	F.T.
1885	Morrison-Bell, Sir C. W. H., Bart. (Bell at Eton), Capt. A. and S. Highlanders	F.T.
1887	Morrison-Bell, E. F., M.P., O.B.E. (Bell at Eton), Maj. 9th Lancers, empld. Lt.-Col. R. Wiltshire Yeomanry	F.T.
1892	Morrison-Bell, E. W. (Bell at Eton), Lt.-Col. Middlesex Hussars, late Capt. Rifle Bde., m. Egypt, Gallipoli, Palestine	F.T.
1898	Morritt, H. E., Maj. R. Warwickshire Regt., att. Tank Corps, m. 2. France	E.C.A.L.
1909	Morton, D. J. F., M.C. (F) Bt. Maj. R.F.A., and Staff, w., m. 4. France	H.F.W.T., A.E.C.
1912	Morton-Robertson, J. J. S., Lt. R. Scots, w. France	E.L.C.
1906	Moseley, H. G. J., 2nd Lt. R.E. Gallipoli (k. 10.8.15)	K.S.
1882	Mosley-Leigh, O., T.D., Lt.-Col. Cheshire Yeomanry, att. R. E. Kent and W. Kent Yeomanry. France, Egypt, Gallipoli	H.E.L.
1907	Mosley-Leigh, O. E. S., Capt. R.A.F., late Trooper King Edward's Horse and 2nd Lt. 11th Hussars, w. 2, m. France	P.W.
1906	Mostyn-Owen, R. A., D.S.O., Capt. (t. Lt.-Col.) Rifle Bde., att. The King's (Liverpool Regt.), and Staff, w., m. 3. France	E.I.
1913	Motion, A. K., Capt. Warwickshire Yeomanry, att. M.G.C. France, Egypt, Palestine	H.T.B., S.G.L.

1890	Mott, S. A., Maj. R. Scots Fusiliers, and Staff, w., m. 2. France	H.G.W., S.R.J.
1891	Mott, S. F., C.B. (F) Maj.-Gen. (K.R.R.C.), m. 6. Egypt, Gallipoli, Palestine	S.R.J.
1907	Mouchy, Duc de, D.S.O., M.C. (F) (de Noailles at Eton), Lt. de réserve 9me Cuirassiers. France, Balkans, Gallipoli	R.S.K.
1906	Moulton, C. E., Lt. Wiltshire Regt. France (k. 16.9.15)	T.C.P., E.L.C.
1895	Moulton, Hon. H. Fletcher, M.C., Maj. R.G.A., w. France	H.E.L.
1905	Moulton, J. C., O.B.E., T.D., Capt. (t. Maj.) Wiltshire Regt., and Staff, m. India	T.C.P., E.L.C.
1891	Mount, F., Capt. R. Berkshire Regt. France (k. 13.10.15)	F.H.R.
1912	Mozley, B. C., D.S.O., Capt. Dorsetshire Regt., w. 2, m. France	K.S.
1892	Mozley, E. N., D.S.O., Bt. Lt.-Col. R.E., and Staff, m. 3. France, Egypt, Gallipoli	H.W.M.
1906	Mozley, J. H., Lt. R.F.A., w. France	K.S.
1901	Muir, M. A., Capt. 15th Hussars, att. 1st King's African Rifles, m. E. Africa (d. 18.7.16)	R.A.H.M., T.C.P.
1909	Muirhead, A. J., M.C. and Bar, Bt. Maj. Oxfordshire Yeomanry, and Staff, w., m. 3. France, Italy	R.P.L.B.
1901	Mulholland, Hon. A. E. S., Capt. Irish Gds. France (k. 1.11.14)	S.A.D.
1904	Mulholland, Hon. C. H. G., D.S.O., O.B.E., Capt. 11th Hussars, and Staff, w., m. 2. France	S.A.D.
1911	Mulholland, Hon. G. J. A. M., M.C., Capt. R.A.S.C., m. France	P.V.B.
1907	Mulholland, Hon. H. G. H., Lt. R.A.F., late Lt. R.M. France	S.A.D., P.V.B.
1913	Mullens, C. J. A., Sub-Lt. R.N.V.R., att. R.N.A.S. Home Waters (drowned 5.5.16)	A.C.G.H.
1917	Mullens, G. J. de W., 2nd Lt. 4th Dragoon Gds.	A.B.R.
1889	Mullens, R. L., C.B. (F) Maj.-Gen. (4th Dragoon Gds.), w., m. 6. France	J.M.E.
1904	Mundey, H. R., Capt. R. Fusiliers, w., m. France	C.H.A.
1911	Mundey, L. C., Lt. R. Fusiliers. Gallipoli (k. 5.6.15)	J.H.M.H.

1906	Mundey, S. C. B., Capt. Oxfordshire and Bucks L.I., and Staff, p., m. Mesopotamia	J.H.M.H.
1914	Mundey, W. V., Lt. 19th Hussars. France	J.H.M.H.
1912	Mure, G. R. G. (F) Lt. R.F.A., m. France	K.S.
1916	Murphy, L. D., M.C., Lt. Irish Gds. France	M.D.H.
1901	Murray, A. J. L., D.S.O., O.B.E., Lt.-Cr. R.N., and Staff, w., m. Home Waters, Mediterranean, N. Russia	S.A.D.
1877	Murray, A. P., Maj. Gordon Highlanders. France	C.L.L.-C.
1868	Murray, C. J. (F) Maj. Sp. List. France	O.B.
1912	Murray, C. Wadsworth, Sub-Lt. R.N.V.R.	C.M.W.
1914	Murray, C. William, 2nd Lt. K.R.R.C. France (k. 25.9.15)	J.H.M.H.
1897	Murray, F. W. S., Capt. 12th Lancers. France (k. 30.10.14)	S.A D
1915	Murray, G., Lt. R.G.A., w. France	H.Br.
1883	Murray, G. R., Maj. (t. Col.) R.A.M.C. France, Italy	J.P.C.
1893	Murray, H. W., Capt. Scottish Horse	H.W.M.
1902	Murray, J., D.S.O. and Bar, T.D. (F) Lt.-Col. Scottish Horse, att. R. Scots, and Staff, m. 2. France, Egypt, Gallipoli	S.A.D.
1910	Murray, J. C., Lt. 1st Life Gds. France	J.H.M.H.
1904	Murray, K. R., Lt. (t. Capt.) Bedfordshire Regt., att. Oxfordshire and Bucks L.I., and Staff. Mesopotamia	J.M.E.
1899	Murray, R. A. C., Capt. Seaforth Highlanders. France (d.w. 11.3.15)	S.A.D.
1892	Murray, Hon. R. T. G., Maj. Black Watch, m. Mesopotamia	F.W.C.
1879	Murray, S. L., Maj. (t. Lt.-Col.) Gordon Highlanders	A.C.J.
1915	Murray, T. H., M.C., Lt. 7th Dragoon Gds., w. France	J.H.M.H.
1915	Murray, V. B., Lt. Cameron Highlanders. France	H.de H.
1885	Murray, W. G., D.S.O., Lt.-Col. 3rd Hussars, att. R.F.A. France	J.H.M.
1904	Murray, W. R. C., Capt. Grenadier Gds., empld. Maj. Nelson Bn., R.N.D., w. France (d.w. 25.2.17)	C.H.A.
1897	Murray-Graham, A. J. G., Capt. Black Watch, att. A. and S. Highlanders, and Staff. France	A.C.J.
1902	Murray-Johnson, F. K., Lt. (t. Capt.) 1st (King's) Dragoon Gds., w. France	J.H.M.H.

1916	Murray-Lawes, R. L., Lt. Grenadier Gds. France	A.A.S
1905	Murray-Smith, A. G., Lt. 2nd Life Gds. France (d.w. 2.11.14)	R.W.W.-T
1913	Murray-Smith, G., Lt. R. Fusiliers. France (k. 29.9.15)	H.T.B., S.G.L.
1907	Murray-Smith, J. E., Capt. (t. Maj.) R.H.G., w. France	H.T.B.
1908	Musgrave, T., Lt. Irish Gds., m. France (k. 6.2.15)	L.S.R.B.
1886	Mussenden, F. W., Lt.-Col. 8th Hussars, and Staff, m. 2. France	J.P.C.
1886	Myburgh, A. M., Maj. Res. Regt. of Cav., att. R.G.A., and Staff, late R.M. France, E. Africa, Egypt, Gallipoli	J.P.C.
1883	Myddelton, R. E. (Myddelton-Biddulph at Eton), Maj. R.F.A., m. France, Egypt	J.P.C.
1906	Myers, K., Sergt. Seaforth Highlanders, Canadian E.F., w. France (d.w. 22.7.18)	H.T.B.
1896	Mytton, A. R., Capt., att. Nigerian Regt., att. Belgian Forces, w. E. Africa, W. Africa	A.C.J.
1892	Mytton, G. H., Bt. Col. Montgomeryshire Yeomanry	A.C.J.
1890	Nairne, Lord C. M. (Lord Charles Fitzmaurice at Eton), Maj. 1st R. Dragoons, and Staff. France (k. 30.10.14)	R.A.H.M.
1897	Naper, W. L., M.C. (F) Capt. R.H.G., att. Remount Service, and Staff. France, Egypt, Palestine	J.P.C.
1900	Napier, Sir A. L. M., Bart., Capt. Grenadier Gds., and Staff, w. 2. France	A.C.B.
1910	Napier, H. A. M., Capt. R.E. Signal Service, late A. and S. Highlanders, w. France	K.S.
1914	Napier, I. P. R., M.C. (F) Capt. A. and S. Highlanders, att. R.A.F., and Staff. France	L.S.R.B.
1911	Napier, I. R., Lt. Cameron Highlanders, att. M.G.C., m. 2. France, Afghanistan, Balkans, Mesopotamia	F.H.R., H. de H.
1909	Napier, L. R. M., Capt. Cameron Highlanders, w., p. France (d.w. 28.7.16)	K.S
1905	Napier, R. A., Lt. R. E. Kent Yeomanry, att. The Buffs, late Pte. Roughriders, w. France, Egypt, Palestine	R.S.K.

1899 Napier, R. G. C., Lt. Grenadier Gds., late Capt. Warwickshire Yeomanry. France, Gallipoli (d.w. 2.8.17)   S.A.D.

1906 Narayan, Kumar H., Lt. Indian E.F., and Staff, m. France   T.C.P., E.L.C.

1905 Nash, E. R., Capt. 16th Lancers, m. 2. France (k. 21.2.15)   J.M.E.

1914 Nash, L. C., Capt. K.R.R.C., m. France (d.w. 28.9.15)   M D H

1890 Nathan, S. H., D.C.M., Capt. R.A.M.C. France, Italy   H.D.

1912 Naylor, H. M., Lt. 3rd Hussars. France   P.V.B.

1907 Naylor, J. M., Capt. London Rifle Bde., w. France   S.A.D., P.V.B.

1913 Naylor, R. E., Lt. R. Welch Fusiliers, w. France (k. 17.5.15)   P.V.B.

1909 Naylor, T. H., Capt. Montgomeryshire Yeomanry, att. M.G.C. and R. Welch Fusiliers, m. France, Egypt, Palestine   S.A.D., P.V.B.

1910 Naylor-Leyland, G. V., Lt. R.H.G., m. France (d.w. 21.9.14)   R.S. de H.

1915 Neale, A. F. H. (F) Lt. R.N.V.R., att. R.N.D., late 2nd Lt. The King's (Liverpool Regt.), and L/ce-Cpl. R.E., w. France   H.Br.

1910 Neame, E. M., Lt. The Queen's Own (R. W. Kent Regt.). Mesopotamia   E.L.C.

1915 Neame, L. G. C., Lt. Coldstream Gds., and Staff, w. France   E.L.C.

1899 Neame, L. V., T.D., Maj. The Queen's Own (R. W. Kent Regt.). Mesopotamia   J.H.M.H.

1901 Neame, P. L., Lt. R.A.S.C. France   J P.C., L.F., R.P.L.B.

1891 Neave, A. (F) Maj. 16th Lancers, m. France (d.w. 21.2.15)   F.D.

1898 Neave, R., Maj. Essex Regt., empld. Lt.-Col. New Zealand Forces, and Staff. Gallipoli   F.H.R.

1871 Neave, S. H. M., Maj. R.A.M.C.   H S

1891 Neave, Sir T. L. H., Bart., Maj. R. Welch Fusiliers and R. Defence Corps   E.C.A.L.

1905 Needham, E. J., Capt. Northamptonshire Regt., att. R.A.F., and Staff, w., in. France   L.S.R.B.

1903 Needham, Hon. F. E., Capt. (t. Maj.) Grenadier Gds., w. France   E.I.

1904	Nettlefold, E. J., Bt. Maj. 5th Dragoon Gds., empld. Lt.-Col. Dorset and Staffordshire Yeomanry, and Staff, w., m. 2. France, Egypt, Palestine	H.F.W.T.
1916	Nettlefold, H., Lt. R.F.A. France	A.M.G.
1908	Nettlefold, J. H., Lt. 5th Dragoon Gds., and Staff, w. 2. France	H.F.W.T.
1908	Neumann, Sir C. J. G., Bart., Capt. Norfolk Yeomanry, and Staff. Egypt, Gallipoli	R.P.L.B.
1901	Nevill, G. T. M., Capt. Scots Gds., late Capt. Sussex Yeomanry, and Staff. France	A.A.S.
1871	Nevill, Lord H. G. R., Lt.-Col. W. Kent Yeomanry	W.L.
1895	Nevill, P. L., Lt. R. Defence Corps	E.C.A.L.
1900	Nevill, R. W., the late, Capt. Rifle Bde., late Capt. Remount Service. (d. 3.11.18)	A.A.S.
1908	Neville, A. G., M.C., Capt. (t. Maj.) R.F.A., and Staff. France	F.H.R.
1915	Neville, J. E. H., M.C., Lt. Oxfordshire and Bucks L.I., w. 2. France, N. Russia	H.M.
1902	Neville, R. (F) Lt.-Cr. R.N. Home Waters, Mediterranean	F.H.R.
1910	Newall, L., 2nd Lt. London Regt. France (k. 2.9.15)	H.F.W.T., A E.C.
1914	Newall, N., Lt. Welsh Gds., late Pte. H.A.C., w. France (k. 12.10.17)	H.F.W.T., A.E.C.
1905	Newall, N. D., O.B.E., Capt. R.A.F. Staff, late R.N.V.R., att. R.N.A.S., m. France	J.H.M.H.
1906	Newman, W. P. M., Capt. R.A.F. Staff, late 2nd Lt R.F.A. and Bombardier H.A.C., w. France	R C.R.
1912	Newton, A. V., Capt. Somerset L.I., att. R.F.C., w. France (k. accid. 20.10.15)	H.F.W.T., A.E.C.
1907	Newton, C. H. F. A., Lt. K.R.R.C. France (k. 13.3.16)	L.S R.B
1901	Newton, C. N., M.C., Capt. Grenadier Gds., late Maj. Leicestershire Yeomanry, w. 2. France	H.Br.
1898	Newton, D. O. C., M.V.O. (F) Capt. Middlesex Regt., att Canadian E.F. France (d.w. 9.1.15)	A.A.S.

1879	Newton, H., Capt. R. Defence Corps	F.E.D., H.W.M.
1917	Newton, J. G., 2nd Lt. Rifle Bde.	S.G.L.
1906	Newton, R. G. Marsdin, Capt. 2nd Dragoon Gds. (Queen's Bays), att. Cyclist Corps and King's African Rifles. France, E. Africa	E.L.V.
1899	Nicholl, C. R. I., Lt.-Col. Oxfordshire Yeomanry, m. France	R.C.R.
1917	Nicholl, D. W. D., 2nd Lt. R.F.A.	C.H.K.M.
1888	Nicholl, H. I., D.S.O., Lt.-Col. Bedfordshire Regt., and Staff, m. 2. France	A.C.A.
1880	Nicholl, J. I. D., Lt.-Col. Glamorgan Yeomanry	C.L.L.-C.
1911	Nicholl, J. W. H., 2nd Lt. Welch Regt. France (k. 29.10.14)	H.B.
1903	Nicholl, K. I., Maj. R. Welch Fusiliers, m. France	R.C.R.
1915	Nichols, J. S., M.C., Capt. Lincolnshire Regt., w. 2. France	K.S.
1904	Nicholson, E. N., Capt. 12th Lancers, and Staff, m. France (d. 20.6.17)	R.C.R.
1901	Nicholson, G. C. N., Capt. R.F.C. (k. accid. 11.3.16)	C.L., J.M.D.
1886	Nickalls, G., Capt. R.E., att. Lancashire Fusiliers. France	A.C.J.
1917	Nickalls, G. O., 2nd Lt. Rifle Bde. Balkans	R.S.de H.
1913	Nickalls, H. Q., Lt. R. 1st Devon Yeomanry, att. R.F.C. and R.E. Signal Service, w. France (k. 22.7.17)	R.S.de H.
1883	Nickalls, N. T., Brig.-Gen. (17th Lancers), m. France (k. 26.9.15)	H.F.L.
1890	Nickalls, V. (F) Capt. R.F.A., w. France, Italy	T.D.
1910	Nickerson, G. A., Lt. Coldstream Gds., w. France	A.C.G.H.
1901	Nicol, R. J., O.B.E., Capt. (t. Maj.) A. and S. Highlanders, w., m. 3. France	J.P.C., R.P.L.B.
1917	Nisbet, F. C., Pte. The Buffs. France	K.S.
1891	Nix, C. G. A., Capt. R. Sussex Regt., and Staff	C.H.E.
1905	Noble, A. H., Lt. The King's (Liverpool Regt.), att. M.G.C., w. France	H.B.
1915	Noble, B. H. H., Pte. London Regt., att. R.N.D. France	H.B., R.H. de M.

1903	Noble, E. H., Capt. Grenadier Gds. France	E.I.
1916	Noble, G. P., Sub-Lt. R.N. Home Waters	E.W.S.
1911	Noble, H. B., M.C. (F) Capt. Northumberland Yeomanry, and Staff, m. 2. France	H.T.B., S.G.L.
1917	Noble, H. W., 2nd Lt. Scots Gds.	E.W.S.
1915	Noble, M. A. P., 2nd Lt. R.F.A. France (d.w. 1.7.17)	S.G.L.
1889	Noble, P. E., Lt. Northumberland Yeomanry	H.E.L.
1905	Noble, R. H., Pte. Canadian E.F., w. France	H.B.
1909	Noel, J. B., M.C., Capt. K.O.Y.L.I., w., p. France, N. Russia	R.S.K.
1912	Noel, T. C., M.C. and Bar, Lt. K.O.S.B., att. R.A.F. France (k. 22.8.18)	R S K
1917	Noel, W. H. M., 2nd Lt. (t. Lt.) Worcestershire Regt. India	R.S.K.
1915	Nolan, P. J., D.F.C., Lt. R.A.F., late Lt. R.F.A. France (k. 7.4.18)	L.S.R.B.
1911	Norbury, C. G., Capt. Rifle Bde., and Staff, w., m. France	J.H.M.H.
1914	Norbury, P. G., Lt. The Buffs, w. France (k. 1.7.16)	J.H.M.H.
1910	Norman, A. M. B. (F) Capt. (t. Maj.) Gordon Highlanders, w. 3. S. Russia	H.M.
1910	Norman, C. W., Capt. 9th Lancers, w., p., m. France	E.I.
1898	Norman, E. H., D.S.O., O.B.E., Maj. (t. Lt.-Col.) The Queen's Own (R.W. Kent Regt.), m. 5. France	E.I.
1886	Norman, H. H., Maj. Northamptonshire Regt., and Staff, w. France (k. 11.11.14)	A.C.J.
1888	Norman, R. L., Capt. R.A.M.C. Mediterranean (d. 23.12.19)	A.C.J.
1904	Norreys, Lord (Mr. Bertie at Eton), Lt. Grenadier Gds., late Lt. R.E. and Flight-Lt. R.N.A.S., w. 2. France	R.S.de H.
1911	Norrie, C. W. M., D.S.O., M.C. and Bar, Capt. 11th Hussars, and Staff, w. 4, m. 2. France	J H.M.H.
1914	Norrie, G. S. M., 2nd Lt. The Buffs. France (k. 7.10.16)	S.G.L.
1903	Norris, R. C., Capt. Rifle Bde., att. R.A.F. France	T.C.P.
1907	North, D. W. J., M.C., Lt. 19th Hussars, and Staff, w. 2. France	H.F.W.T.

1903	Northampton, Marquess of, D.S.O. (Earl Compton at Eton), Maj. R.H.G., att. R.E. Signal Service, w., m. 2. France, Palestine	A.C.B.
1885	Northey, Sir E., K.C.M.G., C.B. (F) Maj.-Gen. (K.R.R.C.), w. 2, m. 5. France, E. Africa	H.E.L.
1899	Northland, Visc., Capt. Coldstream Gds. France (k. 1.2.15)	W.D
1897	Northumberland, Duke of, C.B.E., M.V.O. (F) (Mr. Percy at Eton), Bt. Lt.-Col. Grenadier Gds., Staff, m. France	J.M.E.
1914	Norton, D. J. E., M.C., Lt. 13th Hussars. France, Mesopotamia	P.W., F.E.R.
1904	Noyes, T. R. A. H., Capt. Northumberland Fusiliers, late Pte. Grenadier Gds. France (k. 11.7.16)	K.S.
1876	Nugee, A. R., Lt.-Col. R.A.P.D.	G.E.M.
1881	Nugent, G. C., M.V.O., Brig.-Gen. (Grenadier Gds.). France (k. 31.5.15)	R.A.H.M.
1914	Nugent, T. E. G., M.C., Capt. Irish Gds., w. 2, m. France	R.S.de H.
1916	Nussey, T. M., Lt. 17th Lancers. France	A.E.C.
1905	Nutting, A. R. S., M.C., Capt. Irish Gds., w. France	T.C.P., E.L.C.
1901	Oates, B. W. G., Lt. R.N.V.R. Home Waters	E.W.S.
1915	O'Brien, Hon. D. E. F., Lt. Rifle Bde., w. 2. France	P.W., F.E.R.
1889	O'Brien, E. A. S., Maj. Northamptonshire Yeomanry	E.H.
1895	O'Brien, H. E., D.S.O., Col. R.E. Staff, m. 2. France, Italy, Palestine	E.L.V.
1901	O'Brien, H. H. S. (F) Maj. Northamptonshire Regt., and Staff, w., m. France	H.W.M., H.Br.
1911	Ochs, F. S., Lt. R.G.A., w. France	H.B.
1898	Ogilby, R. J. L., D.S.O. and Bar (F) Lt.-Col. 4th Dragoon Gds., att. London Regt. and Norfolk Regt., m. 4. France, Balkans, Palestine	H.D.
1910	Ogilvy, Sir G. N., Bart., Lt. Scots Gds. France (k. 29.10.14)	J.M.E., M D.H
1876	Ogilvy, Hon. L. G. S., D.S.O., Lt. Scottish Horse	E.W.
1913	Ogilvy, W. W., Lt. 20th Hussars, w. France (d.w. 23.3.18)	M.D.H.

1917	Oldfield, J. R. A., 2nd Lt. Coldstream Gds.	L.S.R.B.
1912	Oldham, E. A. S., Lt. Seaforth Highlanders, late Gunner H.A.C., w. France	H.de H.
1909	Oldham, R. A., Lt. R.F.A., and Staff, late Gunner H.A.C., w. France, Egypt, Mesopotamia	F.H.R., H.de H.
1914	Oldham, R. D'O., M.C., Capt. Hertfordshire Regt., att. S. Staffordshire Regt., w. 2. France	E.L.C.
1902	Olive, V. G., Capt. S. Staffordshire Regt., att. W. African Regt., and Staff. W. Africa	R.S.K.
1915	Oliver, M., Lt. R. Scots Greys, m. France	H.M.
1895	O'Neill, Hon. A.E.B., M.P., Capt. 2nd Life Gds. France (k. 6.11.14)	H.F.I.
1902	O'Neill, Hon. R. W. H., M.P. (F) Maj. R. Irish Rifles, and Staff. France, Egypt, Palestine	P.W.
1893	Onslow, Earl of, O.B.E. (F) (Visc. Cranley at Eton), Col. Intell. Corps, and Staff, m. 2. France	C.H.E.
1901	Oppenheim, A. C., D.S.O., Maj. K.R.R.C., att. London Rifle Bde., w. 2, m. 2. France	E.C.A.L.
1889	Oppenheim, A. H., Lt. (t. Capt.) R. Sussex Regt.	E.C.A.L.
1897	Oppenheim, R. W., O.B.E. (F) Bt. Maj. 4th Dragoon Gds., late att. Westminster Dragoons, empld. Lt.-Col. Staff, m. 2. France, Egypt, Gallipoli, Palestine	E.C.A.L.
1915	Oppenheimer, P. H. M., Lt. Dorsetshire Regt., att. R. Fusiliers. Egypt, Mesopotamia, Palestine	A.M.G.
1913	Ord, O. R., Lt. Rifle Bde. France (k. 18.9.16)	K.S.
1887	Orde-Powlett, Hon. W. G. A., M.P., Lt.-Col. Yorkshire Regt.	E.C.A.L.
1913	Orde-Powlett, W. P., Lt. Yorkshire Regt. France (k. 16.5.15)	A.M.G.
1879	Orlebar, R. R. B., Maj. (t. Lt.-Col.) Bedfordshire Regt.	F.F.V.
1906	Ormrod, L. M., M.C., Capt. R. Welch Fusiliers. France (d.w. 25.8.17)	R.P.L.B.
1910	Ormrod, M.S., D.S.O., Capt. (t. Maj.) K.R.R.C., m. France	J.H.M.H.
1904	Ormrod, O. H., Capt. R.F.A., att. R.F.C. France (k. accid. 12.9.16)	R.P.L.B.
1880	Ormsby-Gore, Hon. S. F., Capt. Staff. France	W.D.

1903	Ormsby-Gore, Hon. W. G. A., M.P., Capt. Shropshire Yeomanry, and Staff. Egypt, Palestine	E.C.A L.
1900	Orr-Ewing, E. P., Capt. Scots Gds. France (k. 15.9.16)	S A.D
1897	Orr-Ewing, N. A., D.S.O. (F) Brig.-Gen. (Scots Gds.), w. 2, m. 5. France	S.A.D.
1904	Orred, R. G., M.C. (F) Capt. R. Fusiliers, and Staff, w. France	E.I.
1914	Osborne, B. R., M.C., 2nd Lt. Grenadier Gds., late Trumpeter W. Kent Yeomanry, w. France, Gallipoli (k. 4.11.18)	H de H.
1889	Osmond-Williams, O. T. D., D.S.O., Lt. Welsh Gds., late Pte. R. Scots Greys, and Staff. m. 4. France (d.w. 30.9.15)	C H A
1901	Osmond-Williams, T. L. G., Capt. Sp. List, late Capt. R.A.S.C., and Staff. France	F.H.R.
1911	Ossulston, Lord, Capt. R.A.F., late Lt. R.N.A.S. Italy	P.W.
1875	Oswald, St. Clair, Bt. Col. Fife and Forfar Yeomanry	W.E.
1893	Otter, W. W., Capt. Sussex Yeomanry, and Staff	A.C.
1909	Ottley, R. B. H., M.B.E., Capt. R.A.S.C., and Staff. France, Egypt	K.S.
1900	Ovey, D., D.S.O. (F) Maj. (t. Lt.-Col.) Rifle Bde., and Staff, w., m. 2. France, Balkans, Egypt, Gallipoli, Palestine	A.C.J.. A.C.G.H.
1896	Ovey, R. L., D.S.O., Maj. (t. Lt.-Col.) Oxfordshire and Bucks L.I., m. France	A.C.J.
1910	Owen, A. R. B., Lt. E. Surrey Regt., w. France	E.L.C.
1882	Owen, W., Lt.-Col. Oxfordshire and Bucks L.I.	T.D.
1907	Oxley, G. S., M.C. (F) Capt. K.R.R.C., and Staff, m. 3. France, Balkans	E.W.S.
1916	Oxley, M. S., 2nd Lt. R.G.A. France	A.B.R.
1897	Paget, A. E. S. L., M.V.O., Maj. (t. Lt.-Col.) 11th Hussars, and Staff, w., m. 3 France (d. 2.8.17)	E.C.A L.
1899	Paget, G. M., Maj. Coldstream Gds., w. France	A.C.A.
1903	Paget, T. G. F., Lt. Scots Gds., empld. Maj. R.F.A., late att. Northamptonshire Regt., w. 2. France, Palestine	R.W.W.-T.

1877	Paget, V. F. W. A., Maj. (t. Lt.-Col.) R.F.A. France	E.W.
1907	Paget, Lord V. W., Capt. R.H.G., and Staff. France, Balkans, Egypt, Palestine	R.S.K.
1916	Paine, J. H., Lt. K.R.R.C., w., m. France, Italy	H.M.
1881	Pakenham, H. A., C.M.G. (F) Col. R. Irish Rifles, and Staff, m. 3. France	F.W.C.
1873	Pakenham, Sir W. C., K.C.B., K.C.M.G., K.C.V.O. (F) Vice-Admiral 3rd Cruiser Squadron, m. Home Waters	H.E.L.
1894	Paley, A. T., C.M.G., D.S.O. (F) Maj. (t. Col.) Rifle Bde., and Staff, m. 5. France	C.H.A.
1890	Paley, G., Maj. Rifle Bde., and Staff, m. France (k. 31.10.14)	R.A.H.M.
1902	Pallis, A. A., O.B.E. (F) 2nd Lt. Greek Army, Staff. Balkans	K.S.
1903	Palmer, A. E. G., D.S.O., M.C., Capt. (t. Maj.) Yorkshire Regt., and Staff, late att. R.E. Signal Service, m. 4. France	A.C.G.H.
1880	Palmer, Sir E. G. B., Bart., Maj. Leicestershire Regt.	H.E.L.
1910	Palmer, E. H. G., Lt. Derbyshire Yeomanry, att. Sherwood Foresters, late Pte. Hawke Bn., R.N.D. France	J.M.E., M.D.H.
1896	Palmer, G. M., M.P., Maj. Yorkshire Regt. France, Balkans	S.R.J.
1917	Palmer, J. A. B., 2nd Lt. 1st Life Gds.	H.Br.
1916	Palmer, R. H. R., M.C., Lt. Grenadier Gds. France	C.M.W.
1893	Palmer, R. S., Lt. (t. Capt.) R. Fusiliers. France, Italy	R.A.H.M.
1892	Palmer, W. H. E. H., Capt. Rifle Bde., late Lt. R.G.A. (d. 27.11.15)	J.C., H D.
1897	Palmer-Morewood, R. C. A., Capt. Sherwood Foresters	S.R.J.
1896	Pape, E. L., Lt. R.A.F. France	E.L.V.
1913	Pape, G. S. D. M., A.F.C., Capt. R.A.F., late Lt. Gordon Highlanders, w. France	P.W., F.E.R.
1899	Pape, H. R., M.C., Capt. (t. Lt.-Col.) Westminster Dragoons, att. Imp. Camel Corps and Tank Corps, m. France, Egypt, Gallipoli, Palestine	P.W.
1908	Pape, J. C. R. C., Capt. R.A.F., late Lt. Sp. List	P.W.

1903	Parbury, H. F., M.C., Capt. 17th Lancers, w. France	R.P.L.B.
1897	Pardoe, F. L., D.S.O., Maj. (t. Lt.-Col.) K.R.R.C., and Staff, w. 3, m. 5. France, Egypt, Palestine	R.A.H.M.
1873	Pares, E. H., T.D., Maj. Bedfordshire Yeomanry	E.H.
1877	Paris, Sir A., K.C.B. (F) Maj.-Gen. (R.M.A.), w., m. 5. France, Gallipoli	C.L.L.-C.
1909	Parish, C. D. W., Capt. Coldstream Gds., and Staff, w. France	A.M.G.
1904	Parish, J. B. A., Capt. R.F.A. France	C.H.A.
1899	Parker, A. E., Capt. Black Watch, att. Seaforth Highlanders. France (k. 7.11.14)	J.P.C.
1908	Parker, Charles E., M.C., Lt. Shropshire L.I., w. France	P.W.
1902	Parker, Cyril E., 2nd Lt. (t. Lt.) K.R.R.C., late 2nd Lt. Canadian E.F. France (k. 1.1.15)	H.F.W.T.
1884	Parker, E. D., Capt. Manchester Regt. France (k. 20.3.15)	C.C.J.
1913	Parker, F. A., Lt. Shropshire L.I., w. France E.L.V., A.C.R.-W.	
1889	Parker, F. M. S., Capt. The Queen's, att. R. Defence Corps and Intell. Corps	K.S.
1887	Parker, G. L., Lt. R.A.S.C.	W.D.
1896	Parker, H. A., Capt. Lincolnshire Yeomanry, att. Labour Corps, m. France	H.D.
1909	Parker, H. E., 2nd Lt. R.G.A., late Pte. Rhodesia Regt. S.W. Africa	H.F.W.T.
1882	Parker, H. R., Capt. Hampshire Regt.	J.P.C.
1917	Parker, I. M., Pte. Coldstream Gds.	R.S.de H.
1904	Parker, Hon. J. H., Lt. R.E. France	R.W.W.-T.
1904	Parker, J. O. (F) Maj. Essex Yeomanry, w., m. France	C.L., R.P.L.B.
1895	Parker, Hon. M. B. (F) Capt. Grenadier Gds., and Staff, m. 4. France, Egypt, Gallipoli	W.D.
1912	Parker, R. C. O., Lt. (t. Capt.) 6th Dragoon Gds. (Carabiniers), and Staff. France	H.B.
1899	Parker, R. F., Lt. (t. Capt.) R.F.A. France	A.C.B.
1908	Parker, R. H., M.C., Lt. 5th Dragoon Gds., w. France	H.F.W.T.
1899	Parker, T. F., 2nd Lt. Cheshire Regt.	W.D.

1894	Parker, V., Lt. R.F.A. France (d. 5.3.16)	F.H.
1879	Parker, W. F., Lt.-Col. Duke of Cornwall's L.I.	E.C.A.L.
1907	Parker, Sir W. L., Bart., O.B.E., Capt., late Pte., Hampshire Regt., m. Siberia	H.Br.
1913	Parker, W. L. O., Lt. 11th Hussars, att. R.F.C., w. France (k. 31.10.17)	C.M.W.
1914	Parker-Jervis, G., Lt. N. Staffordshire Regt., m. France	K.S.
1906	Parker-Jervis, T., Lt. Grenadier Gds., empld. Capt. R.A.F., and Staff, w. France	H.Br.
1909	Parkin, G. M., M.C., Capt. R.F.A. France	R.S. de H.
1913	Parnell, Hon. W. A. D., M.C., Lt. Grenadier Gds., m. France (k. 25.9.16)	A.A.S.
1895	Parratt, G. T., Capt. H.A.C., att. London Regt.	HOME
1909	Parry-Crooke, L. W., Pte. R. Fusiliers. France (k. 27.7.16)	L.S.R.B.
1904	Parsons, A. G., Capt. R.F.A. France (k. 26.4.18)	H.E.L., J.M.D.
1906	Part, A. O., Capt. Herts Yeomanry, m. Egypt, Gallipoli, Mesopotamia, Palestine	A.C.G.H.
1871	Partridge, W. C. St. I., Capt. Gloucestershire Regt., att. R. Berkshire Regt.	W.B.M.
1917	Paterson, J. S., 2nd Lt. Grenadier Gds.	J.H.M.H.
1899	Paton, G. A. L., Capt. Northumberland Fusiliers, and Staff. Gallipoli (k. 10.8.15)	H.B.
1916	Paton, J. A., Lt. Grenadier Gds., w. France	V. Le N.F., L.T.
1912	Patrick, C. M., Lt. 16th Lancers, att. R.A.F., w., m. France	P.V.B.
1903	Paul, H. M., Capt. Staff. France	H.B.
1890	Paulet, C. S., M.V.O. (F) Maj. Sp. List	A.C.J., P.H.C.
1903	Pauncefort-Duncombe, Sir E. P. D., Bart., D.S.O. (F) Maj. Buckinghamshire Yeomanry, and Staff, m. 3. France, Egypt, Gallipoli	A.C.B.
1916	Payne, A. F., 2nd Lt. Grenadier Gds., w. France	H.Br.
1900	Payne-Gallwey, W. T., M.V.O., Capt. Grenadier Gds. France (k. 14.9.14)	A.C.J., P.W
1897	Paynter, G. C. B., C.M.G., D.S.O. (F) Brig.-Gen. (Scots Gds.), w. 2, m. 5. France	T.D., J.H.M.H.

1905	Peacocke, W. J. R., D.S.O. and Bar (F) Lt.-Col. R. Inniskilling Fusiliers, att. The Buffs, m. 2. France	E.C.A.L., P.W.
1918	Peake, H., 2nd Lt. Coldstream Gds.	H.M.
1916	Peake, O., Lt. Coldstream Gds., w. France	H.M.
1914	Peake, R., Lt. Coldstream Gds. France (d.w. 30.9.16)	E.L.V., A.C.R.-W.
1893	Pearson, G. S. H., C.M.G. (F) Col. Staff	H.W.M.
1913	Pearson, H. C., M.C., Capt. 2nd Gurkhas, I.A., late Lt. K.R.R.C., att. M.G.C., w. 2, m. France	E.L.V., A.C.R.-W.
1916	Pearson, N. A., Lt. R.F.A., w. France	J.H.M.H.
1906	Pearson-Gregory, P. J. S., M.C., Maj. Grenadier Gds. France	E.I.
1909	Peart-Robinson, W. E., Lt. Westmorland and Cumberland Yeomanry	E.W.S.
1910	Pease, C., Capt. Irish Gds., w., m. France (d.w. 19.9.16)	L.S.R.B.
1878	Pease, Harold R., Lt.-Col. E. Yorkshire Regt. France, Egypt	C.C.J.
1878	Pease, Hugh R., Lt.-Col. Labour Corps, late Maj. E. Yorkshire Regt. France, Egypt	C.C.J.
1906	Pease, Hon. J., Lt. Lovat's Scouts, att. Cameron Highlanders, m. France, Balkans, Egypt, Gallipoli	A.A.S.
1909	Pease, R. A., Capt. Northumberland Yeomanry, w. 2. France	E.I.
1914	Pease, R. H. Pike, Lt. Coldstream Gds. France (k. 15.9.16)	A.A.S.
1911	Peat, J. H., Lt. 1st Life Gds., att. Middlesex Regt., w. France	H.M.
1894	Pechell, H. R. K., Lt., late, Pte. R. Fusiliers, w. France	F.H.R.
1906	Peek, R. G., Capt. 9th Lancers, and Staff, w., p. France	S.A.D., P.V.B.
1903	Peek, Sir W., Bart., D.S.O., Capt. (t. Maj.) R. 1st Devon Yeomanry, and Staff, m. 6. Mesopotamia	S.A.D.
1902	Peel, E. E., Lt. Grenadier Gds., att. Gds. M.G. Regt. France	A.A.S.
1887	Peel, E. J. R., C.M.G., D.S.O. and Bar, Brig.-Gen. (R.A.), w., m. 4. France, Gallipoli	K.S.
1911	Peel, E. O. E., M.C., Lt. 5th Dragoon Gds., m. France	M.D.H.

1888 Peel, H. E. E., Maj. Labour Corps, late Capt. Welsh
    Horse W.D.
1889 Peel, Hon. S. C., M.P., D.S.O., Lt.-Col. Bedfordshire
    Yeomanry, m. 2. France K.S.
1890 Pelham, Hon. D. R. H., D.S.O. (Mr. Anderson-Pelham
    at Eton), Capt. 10th R. Hussars, att. Australian
    L.H., and Staff, m. 2. France, Egypt J.C.
1884 Pelham, Hon. H. C. (Mr. Anderson-Pelham at Eton),
    Capt. Remount Service. France, Italy J.C.
1911 Pelham, Hon. M. H., Lt. 1st Life Gds. France P.V.B.
1904 Pelham, Rev. W. H., C.F. France, Italy R.C.R.
1910 Pelham-Burn, A. H., Capt. Rifle Bde., att. Egyptian
    Army, w. France, Egypt, Palestine E.W.S.
1912 Pelham-Clinton, G. E., M.C., Capt. R.E. France H.F.W.T., A.E.C.
1910 Pelham-Clinton, H. C. F., Capt. Sherwood Foresters,
    w. 2. Balkans, Egypt, Gallipoli, Palestine H.F.W.T., A.E.C.
1905 Pemberton, A. H., Capt. R.A.M.C. France H.F.W.T.
1914 Pemberton, F. S., O.B.E., M.C. (F) Lt. (t. Capt.)
    K.R.R.C., att. Intell. Corps, w. 3. France K.S.
1906 Pemberton, R. B., Capt. Oxfordshire and Bucks L.I.,
    and Staff. France, Balkans R.P.L.B.
1907 Pemberton, R. L. S., M.C. and Bar, Maj. Durham L.I.,
    m. France H.Br.
1904 Pemberton, R. O. W., Capt. Suffolk Yeomanry, w.
    France, Egypt, Gallipoli, Palestine R.A.H.M., R.S.de H.
1902 Pemberton, T. B., Lt. (t. Capt.) Canadian E.F. France
    J.P.C., R.P.L.B.
1898 Pembroke and Montgomery, Earl of, M.V.O. (F) (Lord
    Herbert at Eton), Maj. (t. Lt.-Col.) R.H.G., m. France A.C.A.
1905 Penn, A. H., M.C. (F) Capt. Grenadier Gds., w., m.
    France R.C.R.
1897 Penn, E. F., Capt. Grenadier Gds., late Norfolk Yeo-
    manry, m. France (k. 18.10.15) R.C.R
1905 Penn, G. M., 2nd Lt. Rifle Bde., att. Somerset L.I.
    France (k. 11.2.15) R.C.R.

1889	Pennell, V. H., Capt. R.A.S.C. France, Balkans	R.A.H.M.
1902	Pennyman, J. B. W., Capt. K.O.S.B., att. Worcestershire Regt., w. France	A.C.J., H.Br.
1883	Penrhyn, Lord (Douglas-Pennant at Eton), Maj. 1st Life Gds.	E.C.A.L.
1904	Penton, C. F., Capt. The Queen's Own (R. W. Kent Regt.), and Staff, w. France	E.C.A.L.
1910	Peploe, D. S., Capt. 20th Hussars, and Staff, m. France	E.I.
1906	Pepper, W., M.C., Capt. Oxfordshire Yeomanry, w. France	C.H.A.
1903	Perceval, A. A. C. P. S., Maj. Irish Gds., w. France	E.L.V.
1882	Perceval, P. D., Capt. R. Irish Regt. France	H.D.
1911	Perceval, R. R. M., M.C. and two Bars, Capt. R.F.A., w. 4, m. 2. France	C.H.K.M.
1899	Percy, Lord W. R., C.B.E., D.S.O. (F) Bt. Maj. (t. Col.) Grenadier Gds., and Staff, w., m. 2. France, Egypt, Gallipoli, Palestine	J.M.E.
1892	Perkins, C. A. C., Capt. (t. Maj.) R.A.S.C. France	R.A.H.M.
1914	Perkins, G. A. (F) Capt. Cheshire Yeomanry, att. R. Scots. N. Russia	M.D H.
1915	Perowne, V. J. T. W. T., Lt. Scots Gds., w. France	L.S.R.B.
1901	Perryman, C. R. E. W., D.S.C., Lt.-Cr. R.N. Home Waters	H.B.
1905	Perryman, H. A. F. W., Cpl. Canadian E.F., w. France	H.B.
1911	Perssé, R. A., 2nd Lt. Rifle Bde., att. K.R.R.C , m. France (k. 1.1.15)	A.M.G.
1907	Pery, Hon. E. C., D.S.O., Maj. Roughriders, att. Coldstream Gds., and Staff, w., m. France, Egypt, Gallipoli	R.P.L.B.
1904	Petersham, Visc., M.C. (Stanhope at Eton), Bt. Maj. 15th Hussars, and Staff, m. France	E.L.V.
1897	Peto, G. K., C.B.E., Capt., late Trooper, R. Wiltshire Yeomanry	K.S.
1904	Peto, H. F. M., Lt.-Cr. R.N., Submarine Service. Home Waters, Atlantic, Mediterranean	K.S.

1885	Petre, B. J., Lt.-Col. Remount Service. France	E.H
1906	Peyton, Sir A. T., Bart., Capt. 11th Hussars, and Staff, w., m. France	A.A.S.
1906	Peyton, H. S. C., M.C., Capt. Rifle Bde., m. France, Egypt, Gallipoli (k. 24.3.18)	A.A.S.
1906	Philipps, Hon. C. E. A., Capt. R.H.G., m. France (k. 13.5.15)	J.M.D
1889	Philips, F. C., Lt. R.A.S.C.	A.C.A.
1892	Philips, F. G. P., M.C., Maj. Shropshire L.I., att. Manchester Regt. France, Balkans	S.A.D.
1913	Philips, H. B., Capt. K.R.R.C. France	F.H.R., H.de H.
1897	Philips, J. L., D.S.O., Bt. Lt.-Col. R.F.A., w., m. 3. France, Mesopotamia, Palestine	S.A.D.
1904	Philips, M. H., 2nd Lt. S. Staffordshire Regt. France (k. 4.10.17)	F.H.R.
1910	Philipson, H., Lt. Scots Gds., att. Gds. M.G. Regt. France	R.P.L.B.
1914	Philipson, R. T., Capt. Coldstream Gds. France	R.P.L.B.
1914	Philipson, T., M.C., Lt. 2nd Life Gds., att. M.G. Cav. France	R.P.L.B.
1905	Phillimore, J. (F) Pte. R.A.S.C., M.T. France	C.H.A.
1914	Phillipps, R. W., 2nd Lt. Grenadier Gds. France (k. 26.10.15)	M.D.H.
1901	Phillips, E. C. M., D.S.O., Maj. Hertfordshire Regt., w., p., m. 2. France	A.C.A.
1912	Phillips, E. E. L., 2nd Lt. R. Berkshire Regt., France (k. 30.10.15)	A.C.G.H.
1903	Phillips, E. G. M., M.C., Capt. Black Watch, m. France, Balkans	A.C.A., R.S.de H.
1907	Phillips, F. R., M.C., Capt. Surrey Yeomanry, m. France, Balkans, Gallipoli	E.C.A.L., P.W.
1904	Phillips, H. L., M.B.E., Lt. (t. Capt.) R.A., and Staff, late Witwatersrand Rifles, w., m. France, S.W. Africa	E.C.A.L., P.W.
1897	Phillips, I. M. M., Lt. R.A.S.C., late Lt. Worcestershire Regt.	A.C.A.

1886	Phillips, L. C. W., Capt. Surrey Yeomanry	A.C.A.
1897	Phillips, N. McG., Lt. London Regt., att. R.E. Signal Service. France, Gallipoli	W.D.
1879	Phillips Brocklehurst, R. W. D., T.D. (Phillips at Eton), Lt.-Col. Cheshire Yeomanry, empld. Cheshire Regt. France, Egypt	H.D.
1898	Phipps, P., Capt. Sherwood Foresters, empld. Maj. Staff. France	R.C.R.
1897	Phipps, W. D., M.V.O., Cr. R.N., and Staff. Home Waters	R.C.R.
1907	Phipps-Hornby, G. H. (F) Bt. Maj. 9th Lancers, w., m. 2. France	R.C.R., C.H.K.M.
1900	Pickering, F. A. U., D.S.O., Capt. Lanarkshire Yeomanry, empld. Lt.-Col. Rifle Bde., and Staff, m. 2. France, Egypt (k. 23.12.17)	R.C.R.
191_	Pickersgill-Cunliffe, J. R., 2nd Lt. Grenadier Gds. France (k. 14.9.14)	H.T.B., S.G L.
1886	Piercy, B. H., Maj. S. Nottinghamshire Hussars	H.G.W.
1910	Piercy, V. H., M.C., Lt. (t. Capt.) R. Welch Fusiliers, w 2, m. France	R.S.de H.
1889	Piers, Sir C. P., Bart., Maj. British Columbia Regt., Canadian E.F., and Staff. France	C.H.E.
1899	Pigot, R., D.S.O., M.C., Brig.-Gen. (Rifle Bde.), m.5. France	R.C.R.
1878	Pigott, W. G., O.B.E., Lt.-Col Rifle Bde., m. 2. France	A.C.J.
1898	Pilcher, A. S., Maj. 21st Lancers, empld. 4th Dragoon Gds. France, India	A.C.A.
1893	Pilcher, C. F., Capt. Berks Yeomanry, att. M.G.C. France, Palestine	E.L.V.
1904	Pilcher, W. S., D.S.O., Bt. Maj. (t. Lt.-Col.) Grenadier Gds., w., m. 3. France	R.S.de H.
1895	Pilkington, C. C., Lt. R.A.F.	E.H.
1890	Pilkington, F. C., D.S.O., Maj. 15th Hussars, empld. Lt.-Col. Canadian L.H., m. 4. France, Italy	E.H.
1902	Pilkington, G. L., Maj. Lancashire Hussars, att. R.A.F. France, Egypt	C.H.A.

1898 Pilkington, H. C., Lt. Gds. M.G. Regt., late att. R.H.G. and Capt. Herts Yeomanry. France   E.H., R.A.H.M.

1885 Pine-Coffin, J. E., the late, D.S.O., Maj. Loyal N. Lancashire Regt., empld. Sherwood Foresters. (d. 22.8.19)   E.C.A.L.

1909 Pinto, R. J., M.C., Lt. Coldstream Gds., att. T.M.B., w. 3. France   R.S. de H.

1879 Pipe-Wolferstan, E. S., Lt.-Col. S. Staffordshire Regt.   W.W., C.H.E.

1900 Pirie, H. V. C., Capt. Gordon Highlanders, empld. Maj. R. Fusiliers, and Staff. France   J.M.E.

1901 Pirie, W. B., D.S.O. (F) Lt.-Cr. R.N. Home Waters, Mediterranean   J.M.E.

1914 Pitman, A. F. E., Capt. Seaforth Highlanders, att. R.F.C. France (k. 3.1.18)   C.H.K M.

1911 Pitman, F. A. H., Capt. R. Scots. France   R.P.L.B.

1895 Pitman, R. O., Lt. 11th Hussars, and Staff. France   F.W.C., P.W.

1887 Pitman, T. T., C. B., C.M.G. (F) Brig.-Gen. (11th Hussars), w., m. 4. France   F.W.C.

1888 Pitt, T. M. S. (F) Brig.-Gen. (1st R. Dragoons), m. 3. Egypt, Gallipoli, Palestine   R.C.R.

1909 Pitt-Rivers, G. H. L. F., Capt. 1st R. Dragoons, w. France   A.C.B., A.M.G.

1895 Pitt-Taylor, W. W., C.B., C.M.G., D.S.O. (F) Brig.-Gen. (Rifle Bde.), m. 9. France, Italy   W.D.

1916 Pittar, C. A., M.C., Lt. Coldstream Gds. France   K.S.

1874 Pixley, A. D., Maj. Sp. List, and Staff. France   J.P.C.

1915 Pixley, B. R. F., 2nd Lt. R.A.S.C., M.T. France   L.S.R.B.

1909 Pixley, E. G., 2nd Lt. Roughriders   L.S.R.B.

1914 Pixley, G. J., Lt., late L/ce-Cpl., Hampshire Regt.   F.W.S.

1904 Pixley, J. N. F., Capt. Grenadier Gds. France, E. Africa (k. 12.10.17)   R.P.L.B

1912 Pixley, R. G. H., M.C., Capt. R.F.A., att. R.F.C. France (k. 4.6.17)   L.S R.B

1873 Pixley, S. A., O.B.E., V.D., Bt. Maj. Staff. France   H.S.

1908 Pixley, S. E., Capt. R.F.A., w. 2. France   L.S.R.B.

1890	Platt, E. J. W., Capt. Remount Service	F.W.C.
1901	Platt, H. E. A., Capt. Coldstream Gds., late Capt. 19th Hussars. w. 2, m. France (k. 15.5.16)	H.M.
1896	Platt, J. E. H., Lt. Coldstream Gds. France	H.W.M.
1909	Platt, J. R., Lt. R.F.A. France (d.w. 27.3.16)	H.F.W.T.
1904	Platt, L. S., Capt. 17th Lancers, empld. Denbighshire Yeomanry, att. R.F.C. France, Egypt (k. 13.4.17)	J.H.M.H.
1905	Playfair, Hon. L. G. H. Lyon, Capt. R.F.A. France (k. 21.4.15)	H.Br.
1904	Pleydell-Bouverie, J. E., Lt. K.R.R.C. France (d.w. 1.11.14)	R.W.W.-T.
1915	Plowden, P. S. E., 2nd Lt. 17th Lancers. France	V.LeN.F.
1879	Plucknett, R., Sergt. R. Fusiliers	F.F.V.
1876	Plumer, Lord, G.C.B., G.C.M.G., G.C.V.O. (F) Field-Marshal (York and Lancaster Regt.), m. 8. France, Italy	R.A.H.M.
1907	Plumer, Hon. T. H. R., M.C. (F) Capt. Canadian E.F., and Staff, m. 2. France	A.A.S.
1865	Pole-Carew, Sir R., K.C.B., C.V.O., M.P. (F) Lieut.-Gen. (Coldstream Gds.)	J.L.J.
1917	Polhill-Drabble, C. R. P., M.C., Lt. Coldstream Gds. France	V.LeN.F., L.T.
1902	Pollak, H. L., Lt. Rifle Bde., late Lt. R.M. France, Gallipoli (k. 23.10.16)	H.D., H.M.
1912	Pollard, G. R., Capt. The King's (Liverpool Regt.), att. R.A.F., w. France	M.D.H.
1897	Pollen, J. L. H., Lt. R.F.A. France	A.C.
1902	Pollock, F. R., Lt. Coldstream Gds., m. France (k. 23.10.14)	H.M.
1893	Pollock, G. C., Capt. R.G.A., late Sub-Lt. R.N.V.R.	K.S.
1906	Pollock, M. V., Lt. S. Wales Borderers. France (k. 9.5.15)	H.M.
1897	Pollock, V. A., Capt. Durham L.I. France	A.C.A.
1897	Pollok, R. V., C.B.E., D.S.O. (F) Lt.-Col. Irish Gds., late 15th Hussars, and Staff, w. 4, m. 2. France, Egypt, Gallipoli	H.W.M.

1901	Poltimore, Lord (Bampfylde at Eton), Capt. R.N. Devon Yeomanry, att. Lincolnshire Yeomanry, and Staff, m. 2. Egypt, Gallipoli, Palestine	E.C.A.L.
1882	Polwarth, Lord, C.B.E., V.D. (Mr. Hepburn-Scott at Eton), Col. R. Scots	C.L.L.C., T.D.
1899	Ponsonby, A. W N., Capt. Oxfordshire and Bucks L.I., w. France (k. 8.9.15)	C.H.A.
1897	Ponsonby, C. E. (F) Capt. W. Kent Yeomanry, att. The Buffs, w. France, Egypt, Gallipoli, Palestine	C.H.A.
1886	Ponsonby, Sir F. E. G., P.C., G.C.V.O., K.C.B. (F) Lt.-Col. Grenadier Gds., and Staff, m. France	F.W.C.
1900	Ponsonby, H. C., D.S.O., M.C. (F) Maj. K.R.R.C., empld. Lt.-Col. Devonshire Regt., and Staff, m. 3. France, Balkans	A.A.S.
1885	Ponsonby, J., C.B., C.M.G., D.S.O. (F) Maj.-Gen. (Coldstream Gds.), w., m. 6. France	F.W.C.
1898	Ponsonby, Rev. M. G. J., M.C., C.F., w. France	C.H.A.
1905	Ponsonby, V. C., M.C., Capt. Herts Yeomanry, m. 2. Egypt, Gallipoli, Palestine	C.H.A.
1894	Pope, A. W. W., Capt. The King's (Liverpool Regt.), att. R.A.F. Balkans, Egypt	R.A.H.M.
1901	Pope, J. A., Lt. (t. Capt.) I.A.R., att. 31st Lancers and 130th Baluchis. India	K.S.
1913	Porchester, Lord, Lt. 7th Hussars. Mesopotamia	E.I.
1904	Portal, J. L., D.S.O., Capt. (t. Maj.) Oxfordshire and Bucks L.I., empld. Maj. King's African Rifles, m. 3. E. Africa	A.C.G.H.
1912	Portal, O. S., Lt. (t. Capt.) 17th Lancers, att. 1st Life Gds., w. France (k. 3.5.17)	P.V.B.
1903	Portal, W. R., M.V.O., D.S.O., Bt. Maj. 1st Life Gds., empld. Lt.-Col. Household Bn., m. 4. France	E.C.A.L.
1918	Porter, A. H., 2nd Lt. Grenadier Gds., att. R. Fusiliers. N. Russia	F.E.R.
1898	Porter, A. R. Z., Lt. R.E., late Pte. London Regt. France	F.H.R.

1893	Porter, A. S. M., Maj. R.A.S.C.	A.C., T.D.
1900	Porter, H. C. M., D.S.O., Lt.-Col. K.R.R.C., att. Army Cyclist Corps and M.G.C., w. 2, m. 3. France	J.M.E.
1916	Portman, E. C. B., Lt. 1st Life Gds. France	E.L.C., M.D.H.
1892	Portman, Hon. G. B., Capt. 10th R. Hussars	A.C.J.
1894	Potter, C. C. H., O.B.E. (F) Bt. Maj. 10th R. Hussars, and Staff, w. 2, m. 3. France	A.C.J.
1887	Powell, A. L., Bt. Lt.-Col. 19th Hussars, and Staff	A.C.A.
1895	Powell, E. B., D.S.O. (F) Maj. Rifle Bde., empld. Lt.-Col. Somerset L.I., and Staff, w., m. 2. France, Egypt, Gallipoli, Palestine	J.M.E.
1900	Powell, E. G. H. (F) Maj. Grenadier Gds., empld. Lt.-Col. London Regt., w., m. 2. France	P.W.
1910	Powell, E. I., Capt. R. Sussex Regt., att. Hampshire Regt. and Oxfordshire and Bucks L.I. France (d.w. 22.3.18)	K.S.
1905	Powell, E. W., O.B.E., Lt.-Col. R.A.F., m.3. France, Egypt	A.A.S.
1902	Powell, J., D.S.O., Lt.-Cr. R.N., m. Home Waters, N. Atlantic	P.W.
1897	Powell, J. H., Capt. Grenadier Gds., w. France	P.W.
1916	Powell, O. P., Sub-Lt. R.N. Baltic (k. 3.9.19)	E.I., T.F.C.
1898	Powell, R. H., 2nd Lt. R. Sussex Regt. France (k. 9.5.15)	K.S.
1897	Powell, R. M., D.S.O., Bt. Lt.-Col. R.G.A., att. R.E. Signal Service, m. 4. France	T.D., R.A.H.M.
1903	Powell, R. V., M.C., Lt. Scots Gds., w. 2. France	A.A.S.
1899	Powell, Rev. V. P., C.F., m. France, Italy	J.M.E.
1914	Powell, W. E. G. P. W., 2nd Lt. Welsh Gds. France (k. 6.11.18)	E.L.C.
1911	Power, J. W., Lt. Welsh Gds., late Lt. Somerset L.I. France (k. 10.9.16)	R.P.L.B
1914	Power, P. D., Lt. Somerset L.I., att. Labour Corps	R.P.L.B.
1880	Powney, C. Du P. P., Lt.-Col. Hampshire Regt.	A.C.J.
1885	Poynter, Sir A. M., Bart., Lt. R.N.V.R. Mediterranean	H.D.
1902	Poyser, A. H. R. W., Capt. (t. Maj.) M.G.C., late Pte. London Regt., m. Mesopotamia	R.A.H.M., J.M.D.

1899	Pratt, E. R., M.C., Bt. Lt.-Col. R.G.A., w., m. 2. France	S.A.D.
1911	Pratt, G. C. S., Lt. R.F.A., m. France (d.w. 27.11.15)	E.W.S
1912	Prentice, W. D. L., Pte. London Regt., late Pte. Border Regt., w. France	A.C.G.H., F.E.R.
1915	Prescott, J. A., Lt. Grenadier Gds., and Staff. France, Aden	L.S.R.B.
1917	Prescott, R. A., 2nd Lt. Worcestershire Regt., att. Somerset L.I., w. France	L.S.R.B.
1904	Preston, T., M.C., Capt. Yorkshire Hussars, att. Essex Yeomanry, empld. Maj. M.G. Cav., m. France	A.C.A., R.S.de H.
1883	Pretor-Pinney, C. F., D.S.O. (Pinney at Eton), Lt.-Col. Rifle Bde., w., m. 2. France (d.w. 28.4.17)	G.F.M.
1914	Pretyman, G. M. T., Capt. R.F.A. France, Egypt, Palestine	E.W.S.
1889	Prevost, W., Maj. Res. Regt. of Cav., att. 20th Hussars and Army Cyclist Corps. France	J.P.C.
1888	Price, R. K., Capt. Staff	R.A.H.M.
1910	Price, V. M. (F) Capt. A. and S. Highlanders, and Staff, m. France	E.I.
1910	Price-Davies, C. S., M.C., Capt. K.R.R.C., and Staff, m. 2. France, Balkans	J.M.D., V. Le N.F.
1908	Prideaux, G. A., M.C., Capt. Somerset L.I., and Staff, w. 2, m. France (k. 19.1.17)	R.S.K
1896	Prideaux, H. H., D.S.O., M.C. (F) Capt. (t. Maj.) Northumberland Fusiliers, and Staff, late L/ce-Cpl. Norfolk Regt., m. 3. France	C.H.E., C.L.
1909	Prideaux-Brune, D. E., D.S.O. and Bar, Bt. Maj. (t. Lt.-Col.) Rifle Bde., m. 6. France	R.W.W.-T., C.M.W.
1910	Pridgeon, R. C., Lt. Hampshire Regt., att. M.G.C. India	R.S.K.
1915	Priestley, C.H., 2nd Lt. Rifle Bde. France (k. 4.9.16)	E.L.V., A.C.R.-W.
1898	Priestley, J. G., M.C., Capt. R.A.M.C., w. France	C.L.
1899	Primrose, Hon. N. J. A., P.C., M.P., M.C., Capt. Buckinghamshire Yeomanry, and Staff, m. 2. France, Egypt, Gallipoli (k. 15.11.17)	W.D
1906	Prinsep, A. L., Lt. R.N.V.R.	A.C.G.H.

1913 Prinsep, N. J. A. L., Capt. R.A.F., late R. Scots Fusiliers, w. France — A.C.G.H.
1906 Prioleau, R. U. H., M.C., Capt. Rifle Bde., empld. Lt.-Col. Staff, w., m. France — J.M.D.
1907 Prior, E. F., Capt. Rifle Bde., w. France (k. 15.9.16) — K.S.
1903 Prior, G. E. R., D.S.O., M.C. and Bar, Bt. Maj. (t. Lt.-Col.) Devonshire Regt., and Staff, w. 3, m. 3. France — A.C.A., R.S.de H.
1908 Prior, H. C., Lt. (t. Capt.) I.A.R., att. 1st Gurkha Rifles and Assam Rifles, m. India — K.S.
1908 Probert, G. O. C., Capt. R.G.A., m. 2. France — M.D.H.
1913 Probert, Y. R. H. C., M.C., Lt. R.F.A., w. France — E.W.S.
1874 Proby, D. J. (Hamilton at Eton), Bt. Col. (t. Col.) Irish Gds., Comm. Regtl. District — W.W.
1902 Proby, G. (Hamilton at Eton), Capt. Bedfordshire Yeomanry, w. France — K.S.
1903 Proby, R. G., M.C. (Hamilton at Eton), Maj. Essex Yeomanry. France — K.S.
1912 Prothero, R. J., Lt. 7th Hussars. Mesopotamia (d.w. 11.11.18) — E.L.V., A.C.R.-W.
1879 Pryce, A. H., Maj. R. Welch Fusiliers, empld. Lt.-Col. Lincolnshire Regt. France — A.C.
1899 Pryce, H. B. Mostyn, Capt. Rifle Bde. France (d.w. 19.3.15) — E.C.A.L.
1882 Pryce, W. C., Maj. Shropshire L.I. — A.C.
1897 Pryce-Jones, H. M., M.V.O., D.S.O., M.C. (F) Bt. Lt.-Col. Coldstream Gds., and Staff, m. 6. France — E.L.V.
1902 Pryce-Jones, P. V., Capt. Welsh Horse, att. Central India Horse and Tank Corps. France — T.C.P.
1914 Pryor, N. S., Lt. R.F.A., m. Palestine — L.S.R.B.
1913 Pryor, R. S., Lt. The King's Own (R. Lancaster Regt.). France (k. 1.5.15) — C.H.K.M.
1915 Pryor, T. S., M.C., Lt. R.F.A. France — E.I., T.F.C.
1898 Pryor, W. M., D.S.O. and Bar (F) Bt. Maj. Hertfordshire Regt., empld. Lt.-Col. R. Warwickshire Regt., m. 3. France, Italy — H.E.L.

1894 Puller, F. C., Maj. Hertfordshire Regt., att. Bedfordshire Regt. S.A.D.
1877 Pulteney, Sir W. P., K.C.B., K.C.M.G., K.C.V.O., D.S.O. (F) Lieut.-Gen. (Scots Gds.), m. 5. France W.E.
1914 Purdey, T. D. S., Lt. A. and S. Highlanders, att. R.A.F. and Cameronians (Scottish Rifles). France A.M.G.
1897 Purves-Hume-Campbell, Sir J. H., Bart., Capt. 2nd Life Gds., late Lt.-Cr. R.N.D. and Lt. R.F.A., w. 2. Egypt, Gallipoli C.H.E., R.A.H.M.
1884 Puxley, F. L., Capt. Middlesex Regt. H.W.M.
1914 Pye-Smith, P. H. G., Lt. The King's (Liverpool Regt.), w. France (k. 15.5.17) A.A.S.
1897 Pym, C. E., O.B.E., Maj. Suffolk Yeomanry, and Staff, m. 2. France, Egypt, Gallipoli C.H.E., C.L.

1895 Quenington, Visc., M.P. (Hicks-Beach at Eton), Lt. Gloucestershire Yeomanry, m. Egypt, Gallipoli (d.w. 23.4.16) F.H.R
1898 Quilter, E. C., O.B.E., Capt. (t. Maj.) Suffolk Regt., and Staff, m. 2. France W.D.
1893 Quilter, J. A. C., Maj. Grenadier Gds., empld. Lt.-Col. S. Lancashire Regt. and Hood Bn., R.N.D., m. Antwerp, Gallipoli (k. 7.5.15) T.D
1901 Quirk, Rev. R., C.F. France K.S.

1913 Radcliffe, C. G., M.C. and Bar, Lt. R.F.A., m. France C.M.W.
1915 Radcliffe, E. C., Lt. 9th Lancers. France H.Br.
1917 Radcliffe, E. R. W., 2nd Lt. Coldstream Gds. R.P.L.B.
1904 Radcliffe, J. D. H., Capt. K.R.R.C. France (d.w. 30.7.15) P.W.
1881 Radclyffe, C. E., D.S.O.. Lt.-Col. Essex Regt., w. 2. France (k. 26.9.15) J.C., C.C.J
1914 Ralli, E. J., 2nd Lt. R.A.F., w. France (d. 13.10.19 of injuries received 8.5.18) M.D.H.
1895 Ralli, E. L., M.C., Capt. R.F.A. France H.D.
1908 Ralli, J. R., Capt. Irish Gds., w., m. France H.Br.

1902	Ralli, L. L., Capt. R.A.S.C. France (d. 20.4.17)	H.D., H.Br.
1916	Ralli, L. P., Lt. 20th Hussars. France (d.w. 14.11.18)	E.L.C.
1915	Ralli, S. A., Lt. 10th R. Hussars, w. France	E.L.V., A.C.R.-W.
1881	Ralli, S. S., Lt. Remount Service. Balkans, Egypt, Palestine	C.C.J.
1901	Ram, L. A. J. G., Capt. Herts Yeomanry, att. K.R.R.C. and S. Irish Horse, and Staff. France, Egypt, Gallipoli	C.L., J.M.D.
1911	Ramsay, A. H. M., Capt. Coldstream Gds., and Staff, w. France	E.W.S.
1894	Ramsay, I., Capt. A. and S. Highlanders. France	E.H.
1916	Ramsay-Fairfax-Lucy, B. F., Lt. Cameron Highlanders, w. France	A.B.R.
1887	Ramsay-Fairfax-Lucy, Sir H. W., Bart. (Ramsay-Fairfax at Eton), Lt. 2nd Life Gds., empld. Maj. Staff	J.C.
1883	Ramsden, C. J., Lt.-Col. R.M., m. France	E.H.
1908	Ramsden, E., M.C., Capt. 5th Lancers, and Staff, m. 3. France	C.H.A., A.B.R.
1896	Ramsden, G. T., M.P., Capt. R.F.A.	H.D.
1895	Ramsden, Sir J. F., Bart., Capt. Norfolk Yeomanry. Egypt, Gallipoli	S.A.D.
1895	Ramsden, J. V., C.M.G., D.S.O., Lt.-Col. R.F.A., and Staff, m. 2. France	S.A.D.
1891	Ramsden, R. E., D.S.O., Lt.-Col. R.F.A., m. 3. France, Balkans	J.M.E.
1888	Ramsden-Jodrell, H., C.M.G. (F) (Ramsden at Eton), Lt.-Col. R.F.A., and Staff. France	E.W., S.A.D.
1918	Randall, P. G., Midshipman R.N. Home Waters	A.C.G.H.
1914	Ranger, V. W. G., M.C. (F) Capt. Oxfordshire and Bucks L.I., att. R.A.F., Intell. Corps, and Staff, w. France, Italy	E.L.C.
1902	Ranken, L. D., Capt. Seaforth Highlanders, and Staff. France, Egypt, Mesopotamia, Palestine	R.A.H.M., L.S.R.B.
1894	Ranken, T., Maj. R. Scots, and Staff. France	R.A.H.M.
1889	Rankin, C. H., C.M.G., D.S.O., Brig.-Gen. (7th Hussars), m. 4. France	H.D.

1895	Rankin, E. C., 2nd Lt. Gloucestershire Yeomanry	A.A.S.
1890	Rankin, Sir J. R. L., Bart., Maj. W. Kent Yeomanry	H.D.
1901	Rankin, R., Capt. Irish Gds., att. Scots Gds., w. France	A.A.S.
1915	Raphael, C. E., Lt. Coldstream Gds., w. 2. France	A.E.C.
1898	Rasch, Sir F. C., Bart., Maj. 6th Dragoon Gds. (Carabiniers), and Staff, m. France, Egypt, Palestine	R.A.H.M.
1902	Rasch, G. E. C., D.S.O. (F) Bt. Maj. Grenadier Gds., and Staff, m. 3. France	R.A.H.M., R.S.de H.
1906	Rastrick, U., Lt. Northamptonshire Regt. France (k. 14.12.14)	H.F.W.T.
1899	Ratcliff, C. J., O.B.E., Capt. Gloucestershire Yeomanry, and Staff, m. 2. Palestine	H.W.M., H.F.W.T.
1910	Ratcliff, G. E., M.C., Capt. Gloucestershire Regt., att. R. Warwickshire Regt., m. France	H.F.W.T., A.E.C.
1901	Ratcliff, R. A., Maj. Staffordshire Yeomanry, m. Egypt, Palestine	H.W.M., H.F.W.T.
1910	Rathbone, R. R., M.C. and Bar, Capt. The King's (Liverpool Regt.), w. 2. France	E.L.V.
1898	Rathbone, W., Lt. (t. Capt.) R.E. France, W. Africa	C.L.
1887	Rathborne, L. St. G. P., Capt. Remount Service. France	H.W.M.
1913	Rawdon-Hastings, E. H. H., 2nd Lt. Black Watch. France (d. 15.9.15)	P.W., F.F.R.
1908	Rawdon-Hastings, P. C. J. R., Capt. Leicestershire Regt. France (k. 13.10.15)	C.H.A., H.Br.
1905	Rawle, J., Lt. 4th Dragoon Gds. France	H.Br.
1903	Rawle, T. F., M.C., Lt. S. Wales Borderers, w. France	H.Br.
1906	Rawle, W., Capt. S. Wales Borderers, att. Grenadier Gds., w. France, Gallipoli	H.Br.
1903	Rawlins, E. C. D., 2nd Lt. Intell. Corps, Staff. France, Balkans	H.E.L
1897	Rawlins, S. W. H., C.M.G., D.S.O. (F) Bt. Col. R.F.A., and Staff, w., m. 9. France	K.S.
1879	Rawlinson, Lord, G.C.B., G.C.V.O., K.C.M.G. (F) (Rawlinson at Eton) Gen. (Coldstream Gds.), m. 9. France	F.W.C.

1916	Rawlinson, J. C., Lt. Tank Corps. France	F.E.R.
1910	Rawnsley, J. R. C., M.C., Lt. 12th Lancers, m. France	K.S., R.P.L.B.
1876	Rawnsley, W. H., Maj. Cheshire Regt.	K.S.
1913	Rawson, P. C., 2nd Lt. R. Berkshire Regt. France (k. 28.9.15)	L.S.R.B
1913	Rawson, R. G. H., 2nd Lt. R.A.S.C., late 2nd Lt. Sussex Yeomanry	E.W.S.
1881	Rawson, R. H., the late, M.P., T.D., Col. Sussex Yeomanry. (d. 18.10.18)	F.W.C.
1908	Rawson-Shaw, K., Capt. R.F.A., att. R.F.C., p., m. France	R.P.L.B.
1914	Rawson-Shaw, T., Lt. 1st Life Gds., late Lt. Sussex Yeomanry. France	R.P.L.B.
1914	Rawstorne, G. S., M.C., Capt. Seaforth Highlanders, w., m. 2. France	E.W.S.
1912	Rawstorne, R. A., Capt. E. Yorkshire Regt., p. (Angora), Gallipoli	E.W.S.
1898	Rawstorne, T. G., Capt. Lancashire Hussars. France (d.w. 31.7.17)	E.H., A.A.S.
1897	Rayner, W. B. F., D.S.O., Maj. R. Fusiliers, att. London Regt., and Staff, m. 2. France	C.H.A.
1875	Reade, R. N. R., C.B., C.M.G. (F) Maj.-Gen. (Shropshire L.I.). Balkans	O.B.
1916	Reay, C. H. A., Lt. The Buffs. France	E.L.C.
1916	Reece, S. B., Lt. R.A.F., p. France	H.B., R.H.de M.
1871	Reeve, H. W., Maj. R. Irish Rifles, empld. Durham L.I. and Labour Corps. France, Egypt, Gallipoli	W.B.M.
1890	Reeve, J. S., Capt. Grenadier Gds.	F.T.
1909	Reeve, J. T. W., D.S.O., Capt. Rifle Bde., empld. Lt.-Col. M.G.C., and Staff, w. 2, m. 2. France	R.S.de H.
1901	Reid, P. L., O.B.E., Maj. (t. Lt.-Col.) Irish Gds., and Staff, w., m. 2. France	J.P.C., A.C.G.H.
1914	Reid, R. G. (F) Lt. R.A.F. Italy	H.M.
1905	Reid, S. K., M.C. (F) Capt. R. Sussex Regt. France, Egypt, Gallipoli, Palestine (d.w. 29.7.18)	A.C.G.H

1886	Reiss, E. L., Maj. 6th Dragoon Gds. (Carabiniers), empld. Lt.-Col. E. Lancashire Regt., late att. 2nd Dragoon Gds. (Queen's Bays), m. France, Egypt	A.C.A.
1916	Remnant, P. F., Lt. R.G.A. Balkans	H.Br.
1914	Remnant, R. J. F., Lt. R. Berkshire Regt., att. Wiltshire Regt., w. 2. France, Palestine	H.Br.
1903	Rennie, G., Capt. Grenadier Gds. France (d.w. 29.10.14)	W.D., A.C.G.H.
1917	Renshaw, T. A., 2nd Lt. Coldstream Gds.	T.F.C.
1912	Renton, A. J., Capt. Essex Regt., w. France, Palestine (k. 3.12.17)	R.S de H.
1915	Renton, J. M. L., Lt. Rifle Bde., w. France	M.D.H.
1916	Repton, G. J. S., Lt. Irish Gds., w. France	E.W.S.
1917	Repton, G. W., 2nd Lt. Irish Gds.	E.W.S.
1903	Reynolds, J. E., Lt. Winnipeg Rifles, Canadian E.F. France (k. 28.4.15)	C.H.A.
1871	Reynolds, J. H., Maj. att. Northumberland Fusiliers. Balkans, Egypt	F.E.D.
1916	Rhodes, F. W., Lt. 1st R. Dragoons. France	R.S.K.
1907	Rhodes, H. A., Lt. R.A.S.C., late 2nd Lt. Westmorland and Cumberland Yeomanry. France, Palestine	A.A.S.
1882	Rhodes, W., Capt. R.A.S.C.	C.H.E.
1892	Rhodes, W. W., Maj. K.R.R.C., and Staff	J.P.C.
1917	Rhys, Hon. C. A. U., M.C., 2nd Lt. Grenadier Gds., att. R. Fusiliers. N. Russia	R.P.L.B.
1916	Rhys-Davids, A. P. F., D.S.O., M.C. and Bar, Lt. R.F.C., m. France (k. 27.10.17)	K.S.
1906	Ricardo, F., Lt. (t. Capt.) Gloucestershire Regt., att. Oxfordshire and Bucks L.I. and M.G.C., w. France	H.B.
1884	Ricardo, W. F., D.S.O., Maj. R.H.G., late Maj. Leicestershire Yeomanry, w., m. 2. France	F.H.R.
1885	Riccardi-Cubitt, Count T., Lt. The Queen's Own (R.W. Kent Regt.), att. R. Defence Corps. Italy	E.H.
1918	Rice, E. D., L/ce-Cpl. The Buffs	C.M.W.

1907 Rice, H. Talbot, Capt. E. Riding of Yorkshire Yeomanry, att. Welsh Gds., w. 4. France — H.B.

1909 Rice, J. A. Talbot, M.C. (F) Capt. 5th Lancers, w. France (p., d.w. 14.4.18) — H.B.

1892 Richards, O. W., C.M.G., D.S.O., Col. R.A.M.C., m. 3. France — K.S.

1905 Richardson, A. K., Capt. R. Welch Fusiliers, and Staff. France, Egypt, Palestine — P.W.

1911 Richardson, A. T. L., Capt. W. Somerset Yeomanry. Egypt, Gallipoli, Palestine (k. 6.11.17) — H.B

1901 Richardson, D. C. H., M.C. and two Bars, Capt. 12th Lancers, w., m. 2. France — J.H.M.H.

1903 Richardson, E. St. J., Trooper R. Wiltshire Yeomanry — P.W.

1899 Richardson, F. J., O.B.E., Cr. R.N.V.R. Home Waters — A.C.A.

1900 Richardson, H. S. C., Capt. Rifle Bde., empld. Lt.-Col. York and Lancaster Regt. and Somerset L.I., w. 2, m. France — E.C.A.L.

1875 Richardson, J., D.S.O., Maj. (t. Lt.-Col.) H.L.I. — G.R.D., J.E.Y.

1903 Richardson, L., Capt. R.A.S.C., M.T. France — T.C.P.

1891 Richardson, R. E., Capt. London Regt., w. France — H.B.

1917 Richardson-Gardner, R. J. M., 2nd Lt. Coldstream Gds. — E.I., T.F.C.

1898 Richmond, H. C., Capt. Gloucestershire Regt., and Staff, m. France (k. 25.1.15) — J.H.M.H.

1900 Richmond, O. L. (F) Lt. (t. Capt.) Intell. Corps, and Staff, late Pte. London Regt. Italy — K.S.

1894 Rickards, A. W., Lt. R.G.A. France — E.L.V.

1904 Rickards, G. A., D.S.O., M.C. (F) Maj. R.F.A., and Staff, w., m. 2. France — K.S.

1888 Rickman, S. H., Maj. Rifle Bde., m. 2. France (d.w. 27.8.14) — F.W.C.

1893 Ridley, Visc., the late, Lt.-Col. Northumberland Yeomanry. (d. 14.2.16) — F.H.R.

1908 Ridley, A. H., Lt. (t. Capt.) Northumberland Yeomanry. France — F.H.R., H de H.

1905	Ridley, Hon. J. N., O.B.E. (F) Maj. Northumberland Yeomanry, att. Northumberland Fusiliers, and Staff, m. 3. France	F.H.R.
1904	Ridley, M. A. T., Lt. Grenadier Gds., and Staff, late Pte. E. African Mounted Rifles, w. France, E. Africa	J.M.D.
1916	Ridout, G. A. E., 2nd Lt. R.F.A. France (k. 21.3.18)	A.B.R.
1908	Rigden, C., Capt. R. E. Kent Yeomanry. France	A.A.S.
1901	Riley, A. C., Capt. London Regt. France (k. 25.9.15)	P.W.
1901	Riley, H. L., D.S.O. (F) Bt. Maj. Rifle Bde., empld. Lt.-Col. M.G.C., and Staff, w. 3, m. 5. France	E.C.A.L.
1903	Riley, L. A. M., 2nd Lt. R. Jersey L.I.	H.T.B.
1909	Riley-Smith, W., Lt. (t. Capt.) 13th Hussars, late Capt. Yorkshire Hussars. India	L.S.R.B.
1917	Rimington-Wilson, H. E., 2nd Lt. Grenadier Gds.	R.P.L.B.
1894	Ripley, Sir F. H., Bart., Capt. A. and S. Highlanders, late 2nd Life Gds., and Staff, m. France	E.I.
1901	Ripley, G. A., Lt. 1st R. Dragoons, att. R.A.F., and Staff. France	H.M.
1895	Ripley, Sir H. W. A., Bart., Capt. 1st R. Dragoons, att. R.A.F., and Staff. France	C.H.E., H.B.
1914	Ripley, J. M., M.C., Lt. R.F.A. France	H.M.
1917	Ritchie, H. D., 2nd Lt. Coldstream Gds. France (d.w. 27.9.18)	K.S.
1908	Rivière, G. G., Lt. Rifle Bde., empld. Capt. Staff, att. French Army, w., m. France	A.A.S.
1906	Rivière, H. G., Lt. R.N.V.R.	A.A.S.
1912	Rivière, P. G., Capt. 11th Hussars, w. France	A.A.S.
1897	Robarts, G., Capt. R.H.G., late Lt. Northamptonshire Yeomanry, and Staff, m. France	S.R.J.
1914	Robb, E. F., 2nd Lt. Coldstream Gds.	H.de H.
1915	Robb, H. A. B., M.C., A.F.C., Capt. R.A.F. France	A.B.R.
1846	V.C. Roberts, Earl, K.G., K.P., G.C.B., O.M., G.C.S.I., G.C.I.E., Field-Marshal (Bengal Art.). (d. at the Headquarters of the British Expeditionary Force on a visit to the Troops, 14.11.14)	R.

1894	Roberts, A. S. B., Maj. I.A., att. R. Scots Fusiliers. France, Egypt	H.D.
1916	Roberts, F. W. S., 2nd Lt. R. Scots, att. H.L.I.	J.H.M.H.
1914	Roberts, P. M., Capt. Staff, late Pte. R. Fusiliers. France	K.S.
1890	Roberts, W. L. H., Capt. 1st R. Dragoons, and Staff. France	F.H.R.
1908	Robertson, D. H., M.C., Lt. London Regt., att. Intell. Corps. Balkans, Egypt, Palestine	K.S.
1895	Robertson, F. M. B., D.S.O., Maj. Black Watch, and Staff, w., m. 3. France	J.M.E.
1915	Robertson, H., Lt. R. Welch Fusiliers, att. R.A.F. France	C.H.K.M.
1911	Robertson, H. A., Lt. (t. Capt.) Devonshire Regt., att. Army Cyclist Corps. France, Italy	K.S., C.M.W.
1900	Robertson, H. M., Capt. R. Welch Fusiliers. France (k. 26.1.16)	A.C., F.J.T.
1905	Robertson, J. A. St. G. Fitzwarrenne-Despencer-, O.B.E. (Robertson at Eton), Bt. Maj. R. Welch Fusiliers, and Staff	H.Br.
1908	Robertson, M. S., Lt. Cheshire Regt., att. Manchester Regt. and Durham L.I., late Pte. The Buffs. Balkans	F.H.R.
1908	Robertson, N.W., Capt. (t. Maj.) Cameronians (Scottish Rifles), and Staff, w. 2. France	F.H.R., H.de H.
1882	Robertson-Aikman, H. H., Maj. Remount Service, and Staff. France	A.C.
1910	Robertson-Aikman, T. F. D., Capt. R.A.F. France	R.S.K.
1879	Robertson-Aikman, T. S. G. H., Lt.-Col. Staff, late R. Defence Corps	W.W., A.C.
1900	Robertson-Luxford, J. O., Paymaster-Sub-Lt. R.N.R., late Stoker R.N. Home Waters	W.D., H.T.B.
1901	Robertson-Ross, P. M., Capt. The Queen's Own (R. W. Kent Regt.), late Pte. London Regt. France (k. 26.9.15)	R.P.L.B.
1880	Robinson, A. H., Lt. R. Defence Corps	H.D.
1910	Robinson, A. J., 2nd Lt. Gordon Highlanders	E.L.C.

1910	Robinson, C. R., Lt. R.N.V.R., late Lt. R. Sussex Regt. France	L.L.C.
1898	Robinson, H. C. (F) Maj. R.A.S.C., m. France	H.F.W.T.
1911	Robinson, Hon. H. E. J., 2nd Lt. The Buffs, late Pte. Alberta Dragoons, Canadian E.F. France (d.w. 25.10.15)	F.L.V
1896	Robinson, H. I., Maj. Lincolnshire Regt., w., m. France (k. 13.11.15)	J.H M.H.
1913	Robinson, I. P., Lt. (t. Capt.) The King's Own (R. Lancaster Regt.), w. France	H.M.
1898	Robinson, R. F., 2nd Lt. K.R.R.C. France (k. 30.7.15)	F.H.R.
1887	Robinson, S., Lt. (t. Maj.) Herefordshire Regt.	F.T.
1880	Robinson, W. A., C.B., C.M.G., Brig.-Gen. (R.A.), m. 5. France, Palestine	H.D.
1906	Robson, Hon. H. B. (F) Capt. Northumberland Yeomanry, m. France, Italy	E.L.V.
1874	Robson, H. D., Bt. Col. W. Yorkshire Regt.	W.W.
1906	Robson, R. G. G., Capt. R.E., m. France (k. 23.12.14)	K.S.
1898	Rocksavage, Earl of, Capt. 9th Lancers, att. Maj. Tank Corps, and R.A.F. France	R.C.R.
1911	Rodd, F. J. R. (F) Capt. R.F.A., and Staff, w., m. France, Egypt, Italy, Palestine	R.P.L.B.
1909	Rodney, Lord, Capt. R. Scots Greys, att. Tank Corps. France	L.S.R.B.
1910	Rodocanachi, H., Lt., late Driver, R.F.A. France, Balkans	A.C.G.H.
1912	Rodocanachi, J. E., Lt. R.F.A., w. France, Balkans	R.C.R., C.H.K.M.
1902	Rodwell, D. E. Hunter, Capt. Tank Corps, late Capt. N. Staffordshire Regt., and Staff, w. 2. France, Egypt	E.L.V.
1899	Rodwell, K. E. Hunter, Lt. Arab Rifles. E. Africa	E.L.V.
1917	Roe, W. N., M.C. and Bar, Lt. Coldstream Gds. France	K.S.
1909	Rogers, G. C., Capt. Shropshire Yeomanry, empld. Australian Imp. Forces. Egypt, Palestine	R.C.R., C.H.K.M.
1899	Rogers, J. L., Capt. R.E. France	H.B.
1908	Rogers, R. P., Capt. Wiltshire Regt., w., p. France	H.B.

1912	Rogerson, J. C., Lt. 15th Hussars, w., p., m. France, N. Russia	J.H.M.H.
1914	Rolleston, F. L., 2nd Lt London Regt. France (k. 26.4.15)	E.L.V., A.C.R.-W.
1905	Rollo, J. E. H., Capt. Black Watch, and Staff, w. France	J.M.D.
1908	Rollo, W. H. C., M.C., Lt. R. Scots Greys. France	J.M.D.
1912	Romanes, E. G. R., Lt. Worcestershire Regt., att. R. Fusiliers. Gallipoli (d.w. 8.6.15)	H.T.B., S.G.l
1903	Romanes, F. J., Capt. King Edward's Horse. France	H.T.B.
1911	Romanes, N. H., Lt., late L/ce-Cpl., Worcestershire Regt., and Staff. Mesopotamia, S. Russia	H.T.B., S.G.L.
1886	Romer, C. F., C.B., C.M.G. (F) Maj.-Gen. (R. Dublin Fusiliers), Chief of General Staff, m. 8 France	F.H.R.
1898	Romer, M., O.B.E., Lt.-Col. Scots Gds., m. France	S.R.J., H.F.W.T.
1916	Romilly, Lord, Lt. Coldstream Gds. France	A.E.C.
1904	Romilly, F. C., Lt. R.G.A. France	H.T.B.
1900	Rooke, D. G., Capt. Coldstream Gds., and Staff, m. France, Italy (d. 2.11.18)	P.W.
1917	Roper-Curzon, Hon. R. H., 2nd Lt. Coldstream Gds., late The Buffs, w. France	R.S.K.
1896	Rose, Sir F. S. D., Bart., Capt. 10th R. Hussars. France (k. 26.10.14)	R.A.H.M.
1901	Rose, H. G. St. C. (F) Capt. Hertfordshire Regt., and Staff. Gallipoli	J.H.M.H.
1898	Rose, I. St. C., Capt. Grenadier Gds., and Staff, w. France	J.H.M.H.
1898	Ross, H. C. E., D.S.O. (F) Capt. (t. Maj.) Scots Gds., w. 3, m. France, Italy	A.C.A.
1888	Ross, H. D., O.B.E., Lt.-Col. Rifle Bde., m. France	C.H.E.
1906	Ross, R. D., M.C. (F) Maj. N. Irish Horse, and Staff. France	E.L.V.
1910	Ross, W. M., Lt. Gordon Highlanders. France (k. 11.3.15)	J.H.M.H.
1891	Rosse, Earl of (Lord Oxmantown at Eton), Maj. Irish Gds., w. France (d.w. 10.6.18)	A.C.J.

1888	Rosslyn, Earl of (Lord Loughborough at Eton), Maj. K.R.R.C.	A.C.A.
1893	Rothes, Earl of (Lord Leslie at Eton), Lt.-Col. Highland Cyclist Bn., w. France	T.D.
1905	Rothschild, L. M. D., Maj. Tank Corps, late Capt. K.R.R.C., w. 2. France	R.S.K.
1901	Rouse, A.R., 2nd Lt. R.A.F., late Lt. R. Berkshire Regt., w. France	P.W.
1902	Rouse, G. N., Lt., late Sergt., London Regt., att. Manchester Regt. France	P.W.
1881	Rouse, H., C.B., D.S.O., Col. R.A., m. 2. France	C.H.E.
1888	Rouse, N. S., Capt. 2nd Life Gds., and Staff. France, Gallipoli	C.H.E.
1910	Rouse-Boughton, E. H., Lt. 15th Hussars, att. Herts Yeomanry, m. France	P.W.
1912	Rouse-Boughton-Knight, T. A. G. (Boughton-Knight at Eton), Lt. Rifle Bde. France (k. 18.10.16)	H.B.
1912	Rowlatt, A., Capt. Duke of Cornwall's L.I., and Staff. France, Balkans	E.I.
1913	Rowlatt, C. J., M.B.E., Lt. (t. Capt.) Rifle Bde., and Staff, w. France	K.S.
1917	Rowlatt, J., M.C., Lt. Coldstream Gds., w. France	K.S.
1908	Rowley, C. S., Capt. Grenadier Gds., w., p. France	R.S.de H.
1906	Rowley, G. R. F., Lt. R.H.G., late Lt. Coldstream Gds., w. France	H.B.
1894	Roxburghe, Duke of, K.T., M.V.O., Lt. R.H.G., w. France	J.P.C.
1894	Royds, A. H., O.B.E., Maj. Scots Gds., and Staff, m. 2. France	P.W.
1913	Royds, J. F., the late, Sub-Lt. R.N. Home Waters (k. accid. 9.11.17)	C.M.W.
1893	Royds, W. E., Maj. Duke of Lancaster's Own Yeomanry, and Staff, m. France	P.W.
1917	Rubin, H. de V., 2nd Lt. Coldstream Gds., empld. Lt. R. Fusiliers. Egypt, Palestine	M.D.H.

1901 Ruggles-Brise, E. A., M.C., Maj. Essex Yeomanry, att. 11th Hussars and 4th Dragoon Gds., w., m. France
S.R.J., H.F.W.T.
1905 Ruggles-Brise, E. C., Capt. Norfolk Yeomanry, att. Norfolk Regt. France, Egypt, Gallipoli, Palestine H.F.W.T.
1900 Rumbold, H. C. L. (F) Lt. Grenadier Gds., w. France
A.C.J., H.T.B.
1912 Ruspoli, Don E. M. B. G. (F) 9° Lancieri di Firenze, and Liaison Officer, Italian Army. Italy R.S.de H.
1908 Russell, A. D. C., Capt. Sp. List. France K.S.
1893 Russell, E. C., O.B.E. (F) Capt. Sp. List F.H.R.
1915 Russell, H. E., Lt. R.F.A., w. France, Palestine K.S.
1892 Russell, J. B. (F) Capt. I.A., late Cpl. R.E. France J.P.C.
1887 Ruthven, Lord, C.B., C.M.G., D.S.O. (F) (Master of Ruthven at Eton) Brig.-Gen. (Scots Gds.), m. 7. France F.T.
1888 V.C. Ruthven, Hon. A. G. A. Hore-, C.B., C.M.G., D.S.O. and Bar (F) Brig.-Gen. (1st [King's] Dragoon Gds.), w., m. 4. France, Gallipoli F.T.
1907 Rutter, E. M. (F) Bt. Maj. R.A.S.C., and Staff. France, Italy A.A.S.
1892 Rycroft, A. R. H., D.S.O., Maj. W. Kent Yeomanry, att. 3rd Dragoon Gds. and Tank Corps, w., m. France, Egypt, Gallipoli C.H.E.
1894 Rycroft, H. F., Capt. York and Lancaster Regt. France (k. 8.8.15) C.H.E., A.C.J.
1909 Rycroft, J. N. O., D.S.O., M.C. (F) Bt. Maj. Black Watch, empld. Lt.-Col. H.L.I., and Staff, w. 3, m. 4. France A.M.G.
1877 Rycroft, Sir R. N., Bart., Maj. London Regt., late Capt. Rifle Bde. A.C.J.
1877 Rycroft, Sir W. H., K.C.B., K.C.M.G. (F) Maj.-Gen. (11th Hussars), m. 7. France, Balkans A.C.J.
1910 Ryder, A. F. R. D., M.C. and Bar, Lt. R.F.A., w. 5. France E.W.S.
1906 Ryder, A. L. D., Capt. The Buffs, w., p. France R.W.W.-T., E.W.S.

1907	Rydon, H. E., Capt. R.A.F., late L/ce-Cpl. Australian Imp. Forces, w. 2. France, Egypt, Gallipoli	F.H.R.
1895	Sadler, H. K., D.S.O., M.C., Maj. R.F.A., and Staff, w. 2, m. 6. France	H.E.L.
1899	St. Aubyn, E. G., D.S.O. (F) Brig.-Gen. (K.R.R.C.), w. 2, m. 2. France	J.M.E.
1872	St. Aubyn, Hon. E. S., Maj. (t. Lt.-Col.) K.R.R.C., Sp. Service. France, Mediterranean (drowned 30.12.15)	E.W.
1913	St. Aubyn, F. C., Lt. Grenadier Gds., w. 2. France	P.V.B.
1888	St. Aubyn, G. S., Lt.-Col. K.R.R.C.	J.M.E.
1897	St. Aubyn, Hon. L. M., M.V.O., Capt. K.R.R.C., and Staff, m. France	H.E.L.
1910	St. Aubyn, M. J., M.C., Maj. K.R.R.C., w. 2, m. France (k. 23.3.18)	R.P.L.B.
1886	St. Aubyn, Hon. P. S., 2nd Lt. K.R.R.C. France (k. 31.10.14)	E.L.V.
1912	St. Audries, Lord (Mr. Acland-Hood at Eton), 2nd Lt. Grenadier Gds., late Lt. Somerset L.I.	H. Br.
1896	St. Clair, Hon. C. H. M., Capt. Seaforth Highlanders, m. France (k. 20.12.14)	J.P.C.
1908	St. Clair, W. F., Capt. A. and S. Highlanders, and Staff, w. France	C.H.A., A.B.R.
1913	St. George, H. A. B., 2nd Lt. 1st Life Gds. France (k. 15.11.14)	C.H.K.M.
1908	St. Germans, Earl of, M.C. (Mr. Eliot at Eton), Capt. R. Scots Greys, w., m. France	A.C.B., A.M.G.
1887	St. John, E. F. S., Maj. Remount Service	E.W., S.A.D.
1875	St. Levan, Lord, C.B., C.V.O. (St. Aubyn at Eton), Brig.-Gen. (Grenadier Gds.), m. France	E.W.
1911	St. Oswald, Lord (Mr. Winn at Eton), Capt. Coldstream Gds., att. R.A.F., w. France	R.C.R., C.H.K.M.
1878	Salisbury, Marquess of, P.C., K.G., G.C.V.O., C.B., T.D. (Visc. Cranborne at Eton), Brig.-Gen. (Bedfordshire Regt.)	G.E.M.

1915 Salisbury-Jones, A. G., M.C. and Bar, Lt. Coldstream
Gds., att. Gds. M.G. Regt., w. 2. France A.C.G.H.

1897 Salkeld, C., Maj. Westmorland and Cumberland Yeomanry, and Staff, m. 3. France, Gallipoli E.I.

1881 Salmon, H. R. P., Capt. Gloucestershire Regt. C.C.J.

1904 Salomons, D. R. H. P., Capt. R.E. Gallipoli (drowned 28.10.15) A.C.J., L.F., E.W.S.

1900 Salt, Sir J. W. T., Bart. (F) Lt.-Cr. R.N., m. Indian Ocean R.A.H.M.

1869 Saltmarshe, P., Col. R.F.A. France G.R.D.

1866 Saltoun, Lord, C.M.G. (Mr. Fraser at Eton), Brig.-Gen. (Grenadier Gds.) G.R.D.

1904 Saltoun, Master of (Hon. A. A. Fraser), M.C., Capt. Gordon Highlanders, p. France S.A.D.

1900 Saltren-Willett, G. A., Lt.-Cr. R.N., and Staff. Home Waters K.S.

1897 Sambourne, R. H., Capt. The Buffs A.C.A.

1869 Sampson, F. R. W., Lt.-Col. Staff W.B.M.

1900 Samson, A. L., M.C., Capt. R. Welch Fusiliers, m. France (k. 25.9.15) A.C.J., A.C.G.H.

1895 Samuda, C. M. A., Maj. Somerset L.I., att. R. Fusiliers and S. Wales Borderers, w. France (d.w. 2.7.17) E.L.V.

1903 Samuel, G. G., Lt. The Queen's Own (R. W. Kent Regt.), w. 2. France (k. 8.6.17) T.C.P.

1900 Samuel, W. H., M.C., Capt. W. Kent Yeomanry, att. R.G.A., and Staff, m. France, Egypt, Gallipoli T.C.P.

1906 Samuelson, B. G., Lt. (t. Capt.) Grenadier Gds., att. R. Fusiliers, w. France, Egypt, Palestine F.H.R.

1917 Samuelson, C. H. F., 2nd Lt. Grenadier Gds., att. Gds. M.G. Regt., w. France F.E.R.

1906 Samuelson, F. H. B., Capt. Yorkshire Hussars, att. Westminster Dragoons and Sherwood Rangers. France, Palestine H.B.

1914 Samuelson, G. B. F., M.C., Lt. Coldstream Gds., w. France (k. 27.11.17) R.S. de H

1917 Samuelson, R. E. H., 2nd Lt. Coldstream Gds. R.S. de H.

1894 Sandars, E. T., O.B.E., Maj. R.A.S.C., att. Intell. Corps, and Staff, m. France, Italy — A.C.J.

1877 Sandbach, A. E., C.B., D.S.O., Maj.-Gen. (R.E.), w., m. 3. France — F.E.D.

1910 Sandbach, G. R., Capt. Denbighshire Yeomanry, att. R. Welch Fusiliers. Egypt, Palestine (d.w. 3.7.17) — L.S.R.B.

1895 Sandbach, H. H., Capt. E. African Mounted Rifles, Nairobi F.F. E. Africa (k. 4.11.14) — C.H.E., C.L.

1883 Sandbach, W., Maj. The King's Own (R. Lancaster Regt.), m. Gallipoli (k. 10.8.15) — A.C.J.

1897 Sandeman, C. A. W., Capt. Intell. Corps, and Staff, late Pte. R.A.M.C., m. 2. France — A.C.A.

1902 Sandeman, G. A. C., Capt. Hampshire Regt. France (k. 24.4.15) — J.M.E.

1902 Sandeman, H. G. W., Lt. Grenadier Gds., late Pte. H.A.C., m. France — A.C.A., R.S.deH.

1914 Sandeman, P. W., M.C., Capt. R.G.A., m. France, Italy — R.S.deH.

1910 Sanderson, A. F., Lt. Seaforth Highlanders. France — R.S.deH.

1910 Sanderson, E. L., Capt. E. Riding of Yorkshire Yeomanry, and Staff. Egypt — J.M.D., V.LeN.F.

1916 Sanderson, J. F., Lt. 4th Dragoon Gds. France — V.LeN.F., L.T.

1906 Sanderson, O. B., Capt. 4th Dragoon Gds., w., p. France — J.M.D.

1910 Sandon, Visc., Capt. R.F.A., w. France — E.L.V.

1897 Sands, M. A., Lt. R.H.G., late Lt. Gloucestershire Yeomanry, empld. Capt. Staff, m. France, Egypt, Gallipoli — E.I.

1903 Sands, M. H., Lt. London Regt. — A.C.A., R.S.deH.

1911 Sartoris, C. F., Lt. Leicestershire Regt., att. R. Fusiliers. Gallipoli (k. 24.6.15) — E.L.V.

1911 Sartoris, G. U. L., Lt. R.N.V.R., late 2nd Lt. R.A.S.C. Mediterranean — E.L.V.

1897 Sartorius, E. F. F., Capt. Grenadier Gds. France (d.w. 5.4.15) — T.C.P.

1907 Sassoon, A. M., O.B.E., M.C., Capt. 13th Hussars, att. M.G. Cav., and Staff, m. 3. France, Mesopotamia — R.S.K.

1903 Sassoon, D., 2nd Lt., late Pte., Labour Corps. France — R.S.K.

1910	Sassoon, E., Lt. 5th Dragoon Gds., att. R.N.A.S. and Berks Yeomanry. France, Gallipoli, Palestine	R.S.K.
1910	Sassoon, F., Capt. R.F.A., att. Egyptian Army, w. France	R.S.K.
1907	Sassoon, Sir P. A. G. D., Bart., M.P., C.M.G. (F) Maj. R. E. Kent Yeomanry, and Staff, m. 4. France	H.F.W.T.
1910	Sassoon, R. E., M.C., Capt. Irish Gds., w. 2. France	M.D.H.
1914	Sassoon, R. E. D., Lt. K.R.R.C., late Pte. H.A.C., w. France	A.A.S.
1904	Sassoon, S. J., Capt. 6th (Inniskilling) Dragoons, att. 2nd Dragoon Gds. (Queen's Bays), and 15th Lancers I.A., and Staff. France	H.D., L.F., R.S.K.
1911	Satterthwaite, F. E. S., 2nd Lt. Loyal N. Lancashire Regt.	P.W.
1874	Saumarez, Hon. G. L. M., Lt. Sp. List. France	W.E.
1903	Saumarez, R. S., M.C., Capt. London Regt., and Staff. France (k. 23.3.18)	R.C.R.
1896	Saunderson, J. V., Capt. R.F.A., and Staff. France	A.A.S.
1893	Saurin, W. M., Maj. Yorkshire Regt., att. Lincolnshire Regt., and Staff, w. France	F.D., C.H.A.
1890	Savile, Hon. G., Capt. Remount Service, and Staff. France, Italy	E.L.V.
1874	Saye and Sele, Lord (Fiennes at Eton), Maj. Staff. France	G., F.T.
1874	Scarbrough, Earl of, K.C.B., T.D. (Visc. Lumley at Eton), Maj.-Gen. (Yorkshire Dragoons), Director-General of the Territorial and Volunteer Forces	A.C.A.
1905	Scarisbrick, C. E., Capt. R. Scots, p. France	H.F.W.T.
1907	Scarlett, C. H., Lt. R.G.A., late Lt. Cheshire Regt.	J.M.D.
1907	Schack-Sommer, G. (F) Lt., late Cpl., 12th Artirsky Hussars, Russian Army. Bukovina, Carpathians, Galicia.(d.w. 8.6.15)	R.C.R.
1914	Schilizzi, J. S., Capt. Northamptonshire Yeomanry, att. 6th Dragoon Gds. (Carabiniers). France	H.Br.
1917	Schofield, W. G. B., 2nd Lt. 2nd Life Gds., att. 3rd Hussars. France	M.D.H.
1895	Scholfield, E. P., Lt. R.G.A., late Capt. E. Riding of Yorkshire Yeomanry. France	F.H.R.

1909	Scholfield, W. S., Capt. W. Yorkshire Regt., and Staff, w., m. France	F.H.R., H.de H.
1905	Schweder, R. P., M.C., Lt. R.F.A. France	J.M.D.
1881	Scoones, F. T. F., Maj. Staff	F.W.C.
1903	Scott, F. J., M.C., Capt. 7th Dragoon Gds., and Staff, m. 3. France	C.L., H.T.B.
1916	Scott, F. P. D., 2nd Lt. R.A.F. Mesopotamia	K.S.
1890	Scott, F. W. A., D.S.O., Col. Dorsetshire Regt., m. France, Palestine	J.P.C.
1899	Scott, H. V., Capt. Rifle Bde., and Staff, m. 2. France (d. 1.9.15)	T.C.P.
1910	Scott, J. B., Capt. 7th Hussars, and Staff. Mesopotamia	A.A.S.
1899	Scott, J. M. C., Maj. R. Scots, att. Egyptian Army. Balkans, Egypt (d.w. 29.3.17)	T.C.P.
1911	Scott, O. A., D.S.O., Maj. Hampshire Regt., m. Balkans	A.A.S.
1899	Scott, R. C., Lt. R.A.S.C., M.T. France	T.D., A.C.A.
1890	Scott, Sir S. E., Bart., M.P. (F) Capt. R.H.G., late Maj. W. Kent Yeomanry, and Staff. Egypt, Gallipoli	E.C.A.L.
1915	Scott, S. M., Lt. Coldstream Gds. France (k. 15.9.16)	J.H.M.H.
1891	Scott-Elliot, W., D.S.O., Maj. (t. Lt.-Col.) R.A.S.C., m. 3. France	J.C.
1914	Scott-Elliot, W. T., Capt. Coldstream Gds., w. France	E.L.C.
1897	Scott-Hopkins, C., Capt. W. Yorkshire Regt., late Trooper Yorkshire Hussars. France	H.D.
1877	Scott-Kerr, R., C.M.G., C.B., M.V.O., D.S.O., Brig.-Gen. (Grenadier Gds.), w., m. France	G.E.M.
1877	Scott-Plummer, C. H., Maj. Lothians and Border Horse	T.D.
1909	Scott-Robson, H. N., Lt. R. Scots Greys, w., m. France	R.P.L.B.
1914	Scrase-Dickins, A. R. M., Lt. R.A.F., late Lt. K.R.R.C., w. France	E.I., T F.C.
1880	Scrase-Dickins, S. W., C.B., Maj.-Gen. (H.L.I.), m. 4. France	E.C.A.L.
1908	Scrimgeour, H., Lt. Suffolk Regt., w. France	A.A.S.
1902	Scrimgeour, H. C., Lt. Coldstream Gds., late Capt. N. Somerset Yeomanry and Pte. H.A.C. France	A.A.S.

1909	Scrimgeour, M., Lt. Rifle Bde. France (k. 30.7.15)	A.A.S.
1904	Scrimgeour, S., M.C. and Bar, Capt. Suffolk Regt. France	A.A.S.
1912	Scrutton, F. F. V., Capt. R.E., and Staff, late Lt. R.A.S.C. and Pte. R. Fusiliers. France	H.M.
1881	Scrymsoure-Steuart-Fothringham, W. T. J. (Fothringham at Eton), Lt.-Col. Scottish Horse, m. France, Gallipoli	A.C.A.
1914	Scudamore, J., 2nd Lt. K.R.R.C. France (k. 25.9.15)	E.W.S.
1910	Scudamore, J. V., Lt. R. Fusiliers. Egypt, Gallipoli (k. 25.4.15)	J.M.D., V.Le N.F.
1901	Seale, H. D. (F) Maj. M.G.C., late Lt. R.N.V.R. France, Mesopotamia, N. Russia	F.H.R.
1910	Sebag-Montefiore, G. E., M.B.E. (F) Lt. (t. Maj.) 21st Lancers, and Staff, w., m. France, Egypt, Palestine	J.M.D., V.Le N.F.
1896	Secker, J. St. J., Maj. Lovat's Scouts, att. Australian Artillery. France	H.E.L.
1897	Secker, Rev. W. H. N., M.C., C.F., w., m. France	H.E.L.
1885	Secker, W. O., Capt. R. Defence Corps, late Capt. Suffolk Regt. and Loyal N. Lancashire Regt.	R.C.R.
1912	Seely, C. G., Capt. Hampshire Regt., m. Egypt, Gallipoli, Palestine (k. 19.4.17)	V.Le N.F.
1916	Seely, H. M., 2nd Lt. Grenadier Gds.	V.Le N.F., L.T.
1914	Segrave, H. O'N. de H., Maj. R. Warwickshire Regt., att. R.A.F., and Staff, w. 3, m. 2. France	L.S.R.B.
1888	Selby-Lowndes, W., O.B.E., T.D. (F) Lt.-Col. Bedfordshire Yeomanry, and Staff, m. 2. France	F.T.
1914	Selby-Lowndes, W., Capt. 19th Hussars, w. France	C.M.W.
1886	Selwyn, H. J., the late, Maj. Worcestershire Yeomanry. (d. 21.4.19)	J.M.E.
1911	Selwyn, J., Capt. R.A. Staff, att. R.A.F., w., m. 2. France, Egypt	K.S.
1881	Sempill, Lord (Mr. Forbes at Eton), Col. Black Watch, w., m. France	J.P.C.

1907	Sempill, Master of (Hon. W. F. F. Sempill), A.F.C. (F) Col. R.A.F., and Staff. France	E.W.S.
1901	Senhouse, G. J. Pocklington, Maj. Westmorland and Cumberland Yeomanry, att. Border Regt. and R.F.A. France	W.D., H.M.
1905	Senhouse, O. W. Pocklington, 2nd Lt. Coldstream Gds., late Trooper Australian L.H. France, Egypt (k. 18.6.15)	H M.
1898	Sergison-Brooke, B. N., C.M.G., D.S.O. (F) (Brooke at Eton), Brig.-Gen. (Grenadier Gds.), w. 2, m. 7. France	R.C.R.
1894	Serocold, C. Pearce, O.B.E. (F) Cr. R.N.V.R., Intell. Dept. Staff	E.C.A.L.
1887	Serocold, E. Pearce, C.M.G. (F) Brig.-Gen. (K.R.R.C.), w., m. 4. France, Italy	E.C.A.L.
1883	Serocold, O. Pearce, C.M.G., V.D., Bt. Col. R. Berkshire Regt., m. 2. France	E.C.A.L.
1877	Seton-Karr, H. W., Capt. London Regt., late Lincolnshire Regt. and A. and S. Highlanders. Egypt, Palestine	H.W.M.
1908	Settle, R. H. N., D.S.O., M.C., Capt. 19th Hussars. empld. Lt.-Col. M.G.C., w. 4, m. 4. France (k. 24.3.18)	P.W.
1916	Settrington, Lord, Lt. Irish Gds., att. R. Fusiliers, p. France, N. Russia (d.w. 24.8.19)	E.I., T.F.C.
1904	Severne, E. C. W., Capt. Warwickshire Yeomanry, att. 9th Lancers, and Staff, w., m. France	P.W.
1909	Sewell, J. P. C., O.B.E. (F) Maj. R.A.F.; m. France	A.M.G.
1893	Seymour, A. G., D.S.O., Brig.-Gen. (R. Scots Greys), w., m. 3. France	P.W.
1896	Seymour, B., Maj. K.R.R.C., and Staff, w. France	H.E.L.
1891	Seymour, C. R., Lt. Remount Service. France	F.T.
1893	Seymour, E., D.S.O., M.V.O., O.B.E., Maj. Grenadier Gds., and Staff, m. 3. France	F.T.
1915	Seymour, E. W., Lt. Grenadier Gds., late 2nd Lt. R. 1st Devon Yeomanry, w. France	E.W.S.
1904	Seymour, F., Lt. K.R.R.C. France (k. 30.7.15)	R.W.W.-T.

1906	Seymour, L., O.B.E., Lt. Hertfordshire Regt., and Staff	A.C.B., A.M.G.
1893	Seymour, R. H., M.V.O., Maj. K.R.R.C., w. France	P.W.
1886	Shaftesbury, Earl of, C.B.E. (Mr. Ashley at Eton), Brig.-Gen. (10th R. Hussars)	A.C.A.
1906	Shafto, E. D., Capt. K.R.R.C., att. Cyclist Corps, m. France, Balkans	H.B.
1894	Shafto, S. D., Capt. Grenadier Gds.	H.B.
1885	Shand, S. G. F., Capt. Sp. List	E.S.S., H.D.
1905	Shaw, G. S., 2nd Lt. R.F.A.	A.C.B., H.M.
1914	Shaw, J. A. P., Surgeon-Sub-Lt. R.N.V.R. Home Waters	E.W.S.
1884	Shaw, J. R., the late, Lt.-Col. K.O.Y.L.I. (d. 5.11.16)	E.S.S., A.C.
1912	Shaw-Stewart, N., Lt. Rifle Bde., w. France (k. 21.8.16)	R.S. de H.
1906	Shaw-Stewart, P. H. (F) Lt.-Cr. Hood Bn., R.N.D., and Staff. France, Balkans, Gallipoli (k. 30.12.17)	K.S.
1911	Shaw-Stewart, W. G., M.C., Capt. (t. Maj.) Coldstream Gds., w. 2. France	R.S. de H.
1896	Shawe, C., C.B.E., Bt. Lt.-Col. Rifle Bde., and Staff. Egypt, Gallipoli	C.H.E., A.C.B.
1903	Sheepshanks, A. C., D.S.O., Lt.-Col. Rifle Bde., att. K.R.R.C., w. 2, m. 2. France	E.L.V.
1892	Sheffield, Sir B. D. G., Bart., Capt. Lincolnshire Yeomanry, and Staff. France	A.C.A.
1911	Shennan, D. F F., Lt. K.R.R.C. France (k. 8.5.15)	H Br
1867	Shephard, C. S., D.S.O., Lt.-Col. Labour Corps, late empld. Lt.-Col. Devonshire Regt., Loyal N. Lancashire Regt., and Wiltshire Regt. France	E.D.S.
'03	Shephard, G. S., D.S.O., M.C. (F) Brig.-Gen. (R. Fusiliers and R.A.F.), m. 5. France (k. accid. 19.1.18)	C.H.A
	Shepherd-Cross, C. H. S., Maj. Duke of Lancaster's Own Yeomanry, att. Hodson's Horse, I.A. and M.G.C. m. France (d.w. 15.10.17)	R.C.R.
1892	Shepherd-Cross, T. A. S., T.D., Maj. Duke of Lancaster's Own Yeomanry, and Staff	R.C.R.

1912	Shepley, R. G. S., Lt. 3rd Dragoon Gds., late Lt. Lanarkshire Yeomanry. France, Egypt, Gallipoli, Palestine	P.W., F.E.R.
1916	Sheppard, R. B., 2nd Lt. 19th Hussars. France	A.B.R.
1882	Sheppard, S. G., D.S.O., Lt.-Col. Herts Yeomanry. Egypt, Gallipoli (k. 21.8.15)	T.E.
1896	Sherbrooke, N. H. C., D.S.O. (F) Bt. Lt.-Col. R.F.A., and Staff, w., m. 3. France	K.S.
1890	Sherbrooke, P. C., the late, Capt. S. Nottinghamshire Hussars. (d. 7.9.15)	T.D.
1914	Sherlock, R. F., Capt. K.R.R.C., w. 2. France (k. 23.7.16)	A.A.S.
1914	Sherlock, W. N., Lt. Seaforth Highlanders, att. R.A.F., late 2nd Lt. R. Welch Fusiliers, w., m. 2. Mesopotamia	A.A.S.
1907	Shirley, E. C., Capt. (t. Maj.) Warwickshire Yeomanry, and Staff. Egypt, Gallipoli, N. Russia	R.P.L.B.
1911	Shirreff-Hilton, B. G., Capt. R. Fusiliers, att. Labour Corps. France	R.S.K.
1886	Shuldham, F. N. Q., Lt.-Col. W. Somerset Yeomanry, att. Somerset L.I., w., m. Egypt, Gallipoli, Palestine	J.C.
1889	Shuttleworth, A. U., Capt. Durham L.I. France	T.D.
1900	Sidmouth, Visc. (Addington at Eton), Capt. Devonshire Regt., and Staff. Aden, Balkans, Mesopotamia	S.A.D.
1916	Sillem, S. C., 2nd Lt. R.F.C. France (k. 12.8.17)	P.V.B.
1907	Sim, H. A. C., Lt. Cameronians (Scottish Rifles). France (k. 9.5.15)	J.M.D
1912	Sim, L. G. E., 2nd Lt. Grenadier Gds. France (k. 16.9.16)	H.B.
1904	Simeon, Sir J. W. B., Bart., Capt. Hampshire Regt., att. R.A.F. France	P.W.
1908	Simeon, L. S. B., M.C., Lt. R. Fusiliers, att. Intell. Corps, and Staff, late Pte. R. Fusiliers, w. France	R.S.K.
1896	Simonds, G. P., Lt. Gloucestershire Yeomanry. Egypt	A.C.J.
1901	Simpson, C. G., Pte. Calcutta Battery, Indian E.F. E. Africa	T.C.P.
1887	Simpson, C. H., T.D., Maj. (t. Lt.-Col.) Yorkshire Dragoons	F.T.
1895	Simpson, G. H., Lt. (t. Capt.) R.E., late Oxfordshire and Bucks L.I.	F.T.

1910	Simpson, G. P., M.C. (F) Capt. R.F.A., w., m. France, N. Russia	A.A.S.
1901	Simpson, Sir J. W. McK., Bart., Pte. R.A.F.	E.L.V.
1905	Simpson, O. L. D. M., Lt. Sherwood Foresters, late Pte. Canadian E.F., w. France (k. 13.7.18)	E.L.V.
	Simpson, R. V., Maj. Oxfordshire and Bucks L.I., m. Mesopotamia (k. 25.9.15)	F.T., T.C.P.
1915	Simson, J., Sub-Lt. R.N.V.R., late R.N.A.S. Home Waters, Mediterranean	P.W., F.E.R.
1901	Simson, R., O.B.E., Capt. Imp. Gen. Staff, late I.A.	C.L., H.T.B.
1908	Sinclair, Sir A. H. M., Bart. (F) Capt. (t. Maj.) 2nd Life Gds., and Staff. France	E.W.S.
1890	Sinclair, Master of (Hon. A. J. M. St. Clair), M.V.O. (F) Capt. R. Scots Greys, and Staff. France	R.C.R.
1897	Sinclair, R. C. H., Lt. R.G.A., late A.B., R.N.V.R.	T.D., A.C.B.
1909	Sitwell, F. O. S., Capt. Grenadier Gds. France	H.F.W.T.
1916	Sitwell, S., 2nd Lt. Grenadier Gds.	A.A.S.
1890	Skeffington-Smyth, G. H. J., D.S.O. (F) Bt. Lt.-Col. 9th Lancers, and Staff, m. 3. France	E.L.V.
1882	Skeffington-Smyth, R. C. E., D.S.O., Lt.-Col. Coldstream Gds., m. 2. France	J.C.
1887	Skelton, H. S., Lt. Armoured Cars, R.N.V.R. France	F.W.C.
1885	Skelton, S. S., Lt. R.A.O.C., att. Remount Service	R.C.R.
1899	Skene, P. G. M., O.B.E. (F) Lt.-Col. Black Watch, and Staff, w. 2, m. France, N. Russia	K.S.
1902	Skinner, E. L., Capt. Sp. List, late att. Leinster Regt. and The King's Own (R. Lancaster Regt.)	E.L.V.
1892	Skrine, H. L., Capt. Somerset L.I. France (k. 25.9.15)	A.C.J.
1912	Slade, Sir A. F., Bart., Lt. Scots Gds., att. W. Somerset Yeomanry and M.G.C. France	E.L.C.
1869	Slade, Sir E. J. W., K.C.I.E., K.C.V.O., Admiral Staff	J.W.H.
1897	Sladen, G. C., C.B., C.M.G., D.S.O. and Bar, M.C. (F) Brig.-Gen. (Rifle Bde.), w., m. 8. France, Italy	E.L.V.
1912	Slingsby, C., 2nd Lt. A. and S. Highlanders, late Pte. Seaforth Highlanders. (k. accid. 8.8.15)	L.S.R.B.

1904	Slingsby, H., M.C., Capt. (t. Maj.) Yorkshire Hussars, and Staff, m. 2. France, Italy	E.I.
1904	Slingsby, T., M.C., Capt. (t. Lt.-Col.) Lancashire Fusiliers, w. 2, m. France	E.I.
1893	Sloane-Stanley, R. C. H., Maj. Hampshire Regt., and Staff	H.D.
1883	Sloane-Stanley, R. F. A., Capt. 16th Lancers, empld. Lt.-Col. Hampshire Yeomanry	H.D.
1880	Smallwood, A. P., Pte. R.A.O.C. France (d.w. 25.5.15)	K.S.
1893	Smiley, Sir J. R., Bart., Capt. 6th Dragoon Gds. (Carabiniers), and Staff. France	F.T., H.B.
1909	Smith, A. F., D.S.O., M.C. (F) Capt. (t. Lt.-Col.) Coldstream Gds., and Staff, w. 3, m. 5. France	S.A.D., P.V.B.
1874	Smith, A. F. Eric, C.B., Lt.-Col. Remount Service, and Staff, m. E. Africa	R.D., R.A.H.M.
1881	Smith, Abel H., T.D., Lt.-Col. Herts Yeomanry	C.H.E.
1899	Smith, A. J. Hugh, M.C. (F) Capt. Coldstream Gds., and Staff, late Yorkshire Regt., w., m. France	A.C.B.
1910	Smith, A. L. Eric, M.C., Lt. 1st Life Gds., m. 2. France (k. 1.11.14)	P.W.
1896	Smith, B. Abel, D.S.O., M.C., Maj. (t. Lt.-Col.) S. Nottinghamshire Hussars, att. Middlesex Regt., m. 3. France, Balkans, Gallipoli	R.C.R.
1898	Smith, B. R. Winthrop, Lt. Scots Gds. France (d.w. 15.11.14)	J.M.F.
1898	Smith, C. H., Capt. Gloucestershire Regt., att. Army Cyclist Corps. France	E.I.
1914	Smith, C. J. Dudley, 2nd Lt. Grenadier Gds. France (k. 16.6.15)	A.A.S.
1911	Smith, D. Abel, M.C., Lt. Grenadier Gds., att. Gds. M.G. Regt., w. 2, m. France	H.T.B., S.G.L.
1915	Smith, D. Eric, Lt. Grenadier Gds., att. Gds. M.G. Regt., w. France	P.W., F.E.R.
1912	Smith, E. C. Eric, M.C., Capt. 9th Lancers, w., m. 2. France	P.W., F.E.R.
1916	Smith, E. F. H., Lt. Rifle Bde., w. 2, p. France	R.S.K.
1891	Smith, E. K., Lt. Armoured Cars, R.N.V.R.	T.D.

1885	Smith, E. P., Maj. R.F.A.	C.H.E.
1892	Smith, E. R. Martin, Capt. Welsh Gds. France	F.H.R.
1885	Smith, G. D., Capt. Remount Service	C.C.J.
	Smith, G. Howard, M.C., Lt. S. Staffordshire Regt., w. 3, m. France (d.w. 29.3.16)	S.A.D.
	Smith, Granville K. F., Lt. Coldstream Gds., w. France (k. 9.10.14)	S.A.D
	Smith, Granville L. I. Lt. Coldstream Gds. France (k. 26.9.15	
	Smith, Granville R. F. C.V.O., C.B., Col. Staff. France (d. 4.3.17)	C.H.F
1877	Smith, H. F., Maj. Norfolk Yeomanry	T.D.
1905	Smith, J. H. Martin, 2nd Lt. Intell. Corps. att. 9th Lancers. France (d.w. 8.9.14)	H.R
	Smith, J. H. Michael, 2nd Lt Manchester Regt. France (k 9.9.14)	
1888	Smith, L. G. Hugh, C.B.E., Lt. Westminster Dragoons	T.D.
1910	Smith, L. R. Abel, Lt. Grenadier Gds., w. 2. France	E.I.
1903	Smith, O. Martin, Capt. Grenadier Gds., late W. Kent Yeomanry, w. France, Egypt	F.H.R.
1916	Smith, O. W. Dudley, Lt. Grenadier Gds., and Staff, w. France	A.A.S.
1902	Smith, R., 2nd Lt. Welsh Gds., late Trooper W. Kent Yeomanry. France (k. 27.9.15)	R.A.H.M., L.S.R.B.
1908	Smith, R. H. M. Abel, M.C., Capt. Herts Yeomanry, m. Egypt, Gallipoli, Palestine	E.I.
1916	Smith, R. H. Vivian, Lt. 17th Lancers, w. France	C.M.W.
1872	Smith, W. A., C.B., C.M.G., Col. Staff	A.C.J.
1887	Smith, W. R. Abel, C.M.G., Lt.-Col. Grenadier Gds., m. 2. France (d.w. 19.5.15)	G.E.M.
1911	Smith, W. W., Lt. R.E., late Lt. R.A.S.C. France	E.L.V.
1903	Smith-Barry, R., A.F.C. (F) Brig.-Gen. (R.A.F.), w. France	E.C.A.L.
1883	Smith-Bosanquet, G. R. B., T.D., Maj. Res. Regt. of Cav.	C.H.E.
1916	Smith-Ryland, C. I. P., Lt. Coldstream Gds., w. France	R.S.K.

1895	Smyth-Osbourne, G. N. T., C.B., C.M.G., D.S.O. (F) Brig.-Gen. (Devonshire Regt.), m. 7. France, N. Russia	A.C.A.
1908	Snow, S. R. W., Capt. R. 1st Devon Yeomanry, att. Devonshire Regt., w., p. Egypt, Gallipoli, Palestine	P.W.
1874	Snow, Sir T. D'O., K.C.B., K.C.M.G. (F) Lieut.-Gen. (Somerset L.I.), m. 5. France	A.C.J
1899	Soames, A. A., D.S.O., Maj. K.R.R.C., empld. Lt.-Col. Wiltshire Regt. and R. Fusiliers, w., m. France, Balkans, N. Russia	S.R.J., H.F.W.T.
1904	Soames, A. G., O.B.E., Capt. Coldstream Gds., and Staff, w., m. France	A.C.G.H.
1902	Soames, A. H. L., M.C., Capt. 3rd Hussars, att. R.F.C., m. France (k. accid. 7.7.15)	J.M.F.
1896	Soames, A. L., Lt. R.A.S.C., M.T. France	S.R.J.
1901	Soames, H. M., Lt. 20th Hussars. France (k. 23.8.14)	H.F.W.T.
1911	Soames, J. A., Lt. R. Welch Fusiliers, late Sergt. 5th Dragoon Gds. and Capt. R.F.C., w. 2, p. France	A.A.S.
1902	Soames, J. B. (F) Lt.-Cr. Armoured Cars, R.N.V.R., late 2nd Lt. Res. Regt. of Cav. France, Balkans, Russia	H.F.W.T.
1901	Soames, M. G., Maj. R.F.A., m. France (d.w. 24.9.16)	H.B.
1897	Soames, M. H., Maj. London Regt., and Staff. France	S.R.J.
1901	Soames, R. M., Capt. R.A.M.C., p. France	H.B.
1895	Solly-Flood, R. E., C.M.G., D.S.O. (F) Brig.-Gen. (Rifle Bde.), m. 3. Balkans, Gallipoli	F.W.C., J.H.M.H.
1884	Soltau-Symons, G. A. J., Capt. K.R.R.C., empld. Lt.-Col. Staff	C.H.E.
1894	Soltau-Symons, L. C., D.S.O., Maj. Durham L.I., att. Northumberland Fusiliers, w., m. France	J.M.E.
1875	Somerleyton, Lord, P.C., K.C.V.O. (Sir S. B. Crossley, Bart., at Eton), Lt.-Col. Suffolk Yeomanry. France	F.E.D.
1913	Somers-Cocks, C. V., Capt. Black Watch, w. France, Mesopotamia	E.I.
1905	Somers-Cocks, J. C., Capt. Coldstream Gds. France	C.H.A., A.B.R.
1906	Somers-Smith, J. R., M.C., Capt. London Regt., att. Somerset L.I., m. France (k. 1.7.16)	H.B.

1902	Somers-Smith, R. W., 2nd Lt. K.R.R.C. France (k. 30.6.15)	R.C.R.
1874	Somerset, Hon. A. C. E., Capt. Rifle Bde.	J.E.Y.
1902	Somerset, Hon. F. R. (F) Capt. Grenadier Gds., att. Egyptian Army Staff. Egypt, Palestine	E.C.A.L.
1915	Somerset, H. R. S. F. de V., D.S.O., Lt. Coldstream Gds., att. 2nd Lt. R.A.F., w., m. France	R.S.de H.
1912	Somerset, N. A. H., 2nd Lt. Grenadier Gds. France (k. 23.10.14)	H.F.W.T., A.E.C.
1905	Somerset, Hon. W. F., Capt. Welch Regt., and Staff, w. France	E.C.A.L., E.W.S.
1905	Somerville, E. A., Capt. Sam Browne's Cav., I.A., w., m. France, Mesopotamia	K.S.
1917	Somerville, M. A., 2nd Lt. Rifle Bde., att. London Regt. Palestine (d.w. 21.9.18)	HOME
1904	Sopper, E., D.S.O., M.C., Capt. 17th Lancers, att. S. Nottinghamshire Hussars, Roughriders, Sharpshooters, and Leicestershire Regt., w., m. France, Balkans, Gallipoli, Palestine	H.D., L.F., E.W.S.
1913	Sotheby, L. F. S., 2nd Lt. A. and S. Highlanders, att. Black Watch, m. France (k. 25.9.15)	P.W., F.E.R.
1913	Sotheby, N. W. A., Lt. R.N. Home Waters	P.W., F.E.R.
1886	Southampton, Lord, O.B.E., Lt.-Col. Yorkshire Regt.	G.E.M.
1904	Southwell, E. H. L., Lt. Rifle Bde. France (k. 15.9.16)	K.S.
1893	Sowler, A., Maj. Remount Service. France	H.W.M.
1912	Speed, C. D. L., O.B.E., Capt. K.R.R.C., att. R.A.F. France	A.C.G.H.
1911	Speed, E. J. L., M.C., Capt. (t. Maj.) 2nd Life Gds. France	A.C.G.H.
1916	Speer, L. A. T., Lt. Shropshire L.I., w., p. France	M.D.H.
1893	Speir, G. T., Lt.-Col. S. Staffordshire Regt., att. Highland Cyclist Bn. and Northern Cyclist Bn., and Staff. France	H.E.L.
1899	Speirs, A. D., Capt. R.A.S.C. France, Egypt, Italy	J.H.M.H.
1902	Speirs, A. G., Capt. A. and S. Highlanders, att. Gordon Highlanders and R. Scots. France, Egypt, Gallipoli	C.H.A.

1896	Spencer, H. G., Maj. N. Somerset Yeomanry, w., m. France	E.L.V.
1900	Spencer, H. M., Capt. Seaforth Highlanders. France (k. 22.4.15)	E.L.V.
1905	Spencer, Hon. V. A., Bt. Maj. K.O.S.B., att. R. Scots Fusiliers, and Staff, m. France	J.M.E.
1894	Spencer-Churchill, E. G., M.C. (F) Capt. Grenadier Gds., w. 2, m. France	P.H.C., A.C.B.
1895	Spencer-Smith, D. C., Maj. R.F.A., m. France	K.S.
1900	Spencer-Smith, G. M., D.S.O., Maj. R.F.A., and Staff, w. 3, m. 3. France, Egypt	R.W.W.-T.
1900	Spencer-Smith, M. S., D.S.O., M.C., Capt. K.R.R.C., empld. Lt.-Col. Staff, m. 2. France, N. Russia	J.M.E.
1902	Spencer-Smith, R. O., Capt. (t. Maj.) Hampshire Regt., w., m. France, Egypt, Gallipoli, N. Russia	H.Br.
1892	Spender-Clay, H. H., M.P., C.M.G., M.C., Bt. Maj. 2nd Life Gds., empld. Lt.-Col. Staff, m. 3. France	R.A.H.M.
1895	Sperling, E. S. A., Lt. Gloucestershire Regt., att. London Regt. France	E.L.V.
1892	Sperling, R. H., Lt. (t. Capt.) R.E. France	E.L.V.
1885	Sperling, St. J. V. H., Lt. (t. Capt.) Essex Yeomanry, late 2nd Lt. Seaforth Highlanders	T.D.
1889	Speyer, A. W., D.S.O., Capt. Intell. Corps, Staff, m. 2. France, S.W. Africa	T.D.
1916	Spicer, R. H. S., Lt. Coldstream Gds., w. 2. France	K.S.
1916	Spottiswoode, R. A., 2nd Lt. R.A.S.C.	R.S. de H.
1901	Sprigg, H. A. G., Capt. Hampshire Regt., late Pte. Middlesex Regt., w. 2. France, Palestine (k. 9.4.18)	H.F.L.
1907	Sprot, H. M., Capt. (t. Maj.) Gordon Highlanders, w., m. France	H.M.
1907	Sprot, I. B., Lt. Cameron Highlanders. France (k. 22.10.14)	H.M.
1900	Squires, E. K., D.S.O., M.C., Maj. R.E., Indian E.F., and Staff, w. 2, m. 5. France, Mesopotamia	K.S.
1914	Squirl, M. E., Lt. A. and S. Highlanders, w. 2. France (d.w. 15.12.18)	P.W., F.F.R.

1883	Stacey, C., Maj. Res. Regt. of Cav., late Maj. Remount Service	H.W.M.
1891	Stacey, T., Capt. Remount Service	H.W.M.
1906	Stacpoole, G. E. G., Lt. R. Irish Regt. France (k. 27.1.15)	J.M.F.
1898	Stafford, H. G., Capt. R.A.S.C., m. France	H.W.M., H.M.
1910	Stafford-King-Harman, E. C., Capt. Irish Gds. France (k. 6.11.14)	E.L.V.
1915	Stainton, W. A., Lt. Grenadier Gds. France (k. 15.9.16)	H.Br.
1896	Stalbridge, Lord, M.C. (Mr. Grosvenor at Eton), Lt. Northamptonshire Yeomanry, att. M.G.C., m. 2. France, Italy	R.C.R.
1916	Stalkartt, C. M. B., 2nd Lt. R.G.A., w. France	J.H.M.H.
1913	Stamford, Earl of, 2nd Lt. Sp. List	R.S.K.
1914	Stancliffe, R. S., Lt. 2nd Life Gds., att. R.E. Signal Service, m. 3. France	A.B.R.
1876	Standish, W. P., O.B.E., Maj. E. Yorkshire Regt., att. Remount Service	C.W.D.
1903	Stanford, G. D., Lt. Devonshire Regt. France	H.E.L.
1899	Stanhope, Earl, D.S.O., M.C. (F) (Visc. Mahon at Eton), Capt. Grenadier Gds., empld. Maj. The Queen's Own (R. W. Kent Regt.) and Lt.-Col. Staff, m. 2. France	S.A.D.
1903	Stanhope, Hon. R. P., Capt. Grenadier Gds., late Lt. Lincolnshire Yeomanry. France (k. 15.9.16)	S.A.D
1916	Stanier, A. B. G., M.C., Lt. Welsh Gds. France	A.M.G.
1912	Staniland, E. A., Lt. 8th Hussars, att. R.E. Signal Service. France	A.A.S.
1912	Stanley, Lord, M.C. (F) Capt. Grenadier Gds., and Staff, w. France, Italy	H.F.W.T., A.E.C.
1880	Stanley, A. S. W., Lt.-Col. Suffolk Regt.	W.D.
1908	Stanley, A. W. W., M.C., Capt. R.H.G. France	A.C.G.H.
1913	Stanley, D. M., Lt. 14th Hussars. Mesopotamia	R.P.L.B.
1896	Stanley, E. A. V., Capt. 21st Lancers, late Lt. Berks Yeomanry and Pte. Rifle Bde., empld. The Queen's Own (R. W. Kent Regt.). France, Italy	T.D., J.M.E.

1910	Stanley, E. S., Lt. R.G.A., late Cpl. R.E., w. France	E.L.C.
1914	Stanley, Hon. O. F. G., M.C. (F) Lt. Lancashire Hussars, empld. Capt. R.F.A., m. France	A.E.C.
1899	Stanley, P. E., Maj., late Pte., R. Fusiliers. France	S.R.J., H.F.W.T.
1898	Stansfeld, J. A. H., Capt. Cameronians (Scottish Rifles), late Pte. R. Sussex Regt. France	J.H.M.H.
1890	Stanton, F. H. G., Brig.-Gen. (R.A.), m. France, Balkans	H.W.M.
1879	Stanyforth, E. W., T.D. (Greenwood at Eton), Lt.-Col. Yorkshire Hussars	H.S., A.C.A.
1911	Stanyforth, R. T., M.C., Capt. 17th Lancers, w., m. France	J.H.M.H.
1908	Stapleton, Sir M. T., Bart., Capt. R.E., I.W.T., att. Lt. R.A.F., and Staff. Italy	H.F.W.T.
1882	Starkey, A. H., Capt. Rifle Bde., m. Balkans, Egypt	E.S.S.
1876	Starkey, J. R., M.P., Capt. S. Nottinghamshire Hussars	H.E.L.
1878	Starkey, L. E., Lt.-Col. Sp. List	H.E.L.
1882	Starkey, T. R., Lt. R. Defence Corps. (d. 13.11.16)	E.S.S
1911	Steel, A. I., Lt. Coldstream Gds. France (k. 8.10.17)	F.I.
1904	Steel, J., Capt. Res. Regt. of Cav., late Lt. Staffordshire Yeomanry	F.H.R.
1899	Steel, S. S., T.D., Maj. Lothians and Border Horse. France, Balkans	A.C.J.
1906	Steel, W. L., Lt. Irish Gds., att. Gds. M.G. Regt. France	R.P.L.B.
1894	Steele, C. M., Lt. (t. Capt.) R.G.A. France, Italy	H.G.W., W.D.
1890	Steele, G. F., C.M.G., Lt.-Col. 1st R. Dragoons, m. France (d.w. 22.5.15)	G.E.M., H.G.W., W.D.
1889	Steele, J. M., C.B., C.M.G., D.S.O. and Bar (F) Brig.-Gen. (Coldstream Gds.), w., m. 7. France, Italy	G.E.M., H.G.W.
1917	Steer, W. R. H., 2nd Lt. R.F.A. France	J.H.M.H.
1896	Stephen, A. A. L., D.S.O., Capt. Scots Gds., m. 2. France (d.w. 31.10.14)	F.I.
1894	Stephen, D. C. L., Capt. Grenadier Gds., m. France (d.w. 11.9.14)	F.I.
1899	Stephenson, C. E. S., 2nd Lt. 9th Lancers, att. N. Somerset Yeomanry, late Trooper King Edward's Horse. France (d. 6.12.16)	F.H., H.D.

	Stephenson, D. C., D.S.O., M.C., Maj. R.F.A., w., m. 2. France (k. 13.3.18)	F. I.
1909	Stephenson, E. K., Capt. Coldstream Gds., and Staff, w. France	P.W.
	Stephenson, E. S., D.S.O., Capt. Gloucestershire Regt., att. Egyptian Army, and Staff. Gallipoli (d.w. 6.5.15)	F.H., H.D.
1912	Stephenson, H. F. B., Capt. Yorkshire Dragoons. France	H. de H.
1898	Stephenson, M. F. G., Capt. R.A.S.C., M.T., m. France	H. Br.
1897	Stern, A. G., K.B.E., C.M.G. (F) Lt.-Col. Tank Corps, late Maj. M.G.C., and Staff, late Lt. R.N.V.R., att. R.N.A.S., m. France	J.P.C.
1902	Stern, F. C., O.B.E., M.C., Capt. (t. Maj.) Westminster Dragoons, and Staff, w., m. 3. Egypt, Gallipoli, Palestine	J.P.C., R.P.L.B.
1892	Stern, H. J. J., Maj. S. Irish Horse. France	J.P.C.
1901	Steuart-Menzies, R., Capt. Scots Gds., p. France	R.C.R.
1914	Stevens, G. C., Capt. Oxfordshire and Bucks L.I., w. France	R.S. de H.
1899	Stevenson, F. H. L., Capt. H.L.I.	E.L.V.
1881	Stevenson, G. J. H., Maj. Sp. List	E.H.
1891	Stevenson, H. H. McD., Maj. H.L.I. France, N. Russia	H.D.
1909	Steward, C. W. D'A., Capt. Punjabis, I.A., w. Mesopotamia	R.P.L.B.
1911	Stewart, A. C., M.C. and Bar, Capt. Cameronians (Scottish Rifles), w. 2. France, Egypt	E.L.V.
1897	Stewart, Basil, 2nd Lt. R.E., late Pte. R.A.M.C., w. France	H.B.
1890	Stewart, Bertrand, Capt. W. Kent Yeomanry, att. Cav. H.Q. France (k. 12.9.14)	W.D.
1916	Stewart, C. D. A., 2nd Lt. 11th Lancers, att. 30th Lancers, I.A. Afghanistan	A.E.C.
1902	Stewart, E. O., Capt. Grenadier Gds. France	R.W.W.-T.
1896	Stewart, G., Capt. Coldstream Gds., late Maj. Leicestershire Yeomanry, and Staff, m. France (k. 22.12.14)	R.A.H.M.
1907	Stewart, J. C., Capt. H.L.I., and Staff. France	E.L.V.

1888	Stewart, J. S., Capt. R.F.A., late att. 3rd Dragoon Gds., w., m. France	H.E.L.
1892	Stewart, P. D., D.S.O., Capt. 3rd Dragoon Gds., empld. Lt.-Col. M.G.C. and London Rifle Bde., w. 2, m. 2. France	H.E.L.
1910	Stewart, W. A. L., M.C., Capt. Grenadier Gds., w. France (k. 25.9.16)	A.P.R.
1890	Stewart, W. N., D.S.O., Capt. Lothians and Border Horse, att. N. Somerset Yeomanry, empld. Lt.-Col. Leicestershire Regt. and Northumberland Fusiliers, m. 2. France (k. 23.3.18)	H.E.L.
1915	Stewart, W. S., Flight-Sub-Lt. R.N.A.S. (k. accid. 8.11.16)	F.J.C.
1891	Stewart-Murray, Lord G., Maj. Black Watch. France (k. 14.9.14)	J.M.E.
1897	Stewart-Murray, Lord J. T., M.C., Capt. Cameron Highlanders, w., p. France	J.M.E.
1892	Stewart-Richardson, J. L., 2nd Lt. Coldstream Gds., late Sergt. Wellington Mounted Rifles, N. Zealand E.F. France, Gallipoli (k. 17.5.16)	C.H.A.
1902	Stewart-Richardson, R. M., M.C. and two Bars, Bt. Maj. 11th Hussars, att. 2nd Dragoon Gds. (Queen's Bays), m. France	A.C.B., L.F., E.W.S.
1913	Stewart-Savile, D. N., M.C., Lt. 12th Lancers, att. R.A.F., and Staff, w. France	A.A.S.
1883	Stilwell, G. H., V.D., Lt.-Col. Hampshire Regt.	J.P.C.
1891	Stilwell, J. B. L., T.D., Lt.-Col. Hampshire Regt. France, Palestine	J.P.C.
1899	Stilwell, W. B., D.S.O., Lt.-Col. Hampshire Regt., att. Northumberland Fusiliers, m. Mesopotamia	J.P.C.
1885	Stirling, A. (Maxwell at Eton), Brig.-Gen. (Scots Gds.), m. Egypt, Gallipoli	G.E.M.
1886	Stirling, Sir G. M. H., Bart., C.B.E., D.S.O., Bt. Lt.-Col. Essex Regt., and Staff, w., m. 5. France	R.C.R.
1899	Stirling, J. A., D.S.O., M.C. (F) Maj. (t. Lt.-Col.) Scots Gds., m. 3. France	H.E.L.

1911	Stirling-Stuart, D. R., Lt. R. Scots Greys. France	R.W.W.-T., C.M.W.
1910	Stirling-Stuart, J., Lt. Scots Gds., w. France (d.w. 9.11.14)	R.W.W.-T., C.M.W.
1902	Stobart, H. M., C.B.E., D.S.O., Lt.-Col. Northumberland Yeomanry, and Staff, m. 2. France	J.M.E.
1910	Stobart, R. L., M.C., Capt. (t. Maj.) Northumberland Yeomanry, att. Northumberland Fusiliers, and Staff, w. France	J.M.E., H.M.
1910	Stock, A. B., the late, Capt. Ayrshire Yeomanry. (d. 12.12.15)	H.M.
1903	Stock, B. H., Lt. R. Defence Corps, late London Regt.	W.D., H.M.
1901	Stock, J. E. K., Capt. Remount Service. France, Egypt	W.D., H.M.
1916	Stocks, E. P., Lt. Coldstream Gds., w. France	E.W.S.
1910	Stocks, M. G., Lt. Grenadier Gds. France (k. 10.11.14)	E.W.S.
1900	Stokes, A. V. W., Bt. Maj. 4th Hussars, w. France	A.C.J., H.Br.
1908	Stokes, V. A. P., Capt. 10th R. Hussars, and Staff. France	R.C.R., C.H.K.M.
1901	Stone, C. R., D.S.O., M.C., Maj. R. Fusiliers, late Pte. Middlesex Regt., and Staff, m. 3. France	K.S.
1916	Stone, H. O., 2nd Lt. Baluchis, I.A.R., late Pte. Canadian R.E. Somaliland	R.H.de M.
1895	Stopford, Visc., O.B.E., Maj. Sp. List, m. France	E.I.
1871	Stopford, Hon. Sir F. W., K.C.M.G., K.C.V.O., C.B., Lieut.-Gen. (Grenadier Gds.). Gallipoli	J.M.E.
1909	Stopford-Sackville, L. C., D.S.O. (F) Bt. Maj. Rifle Bde., and Staff, m. 4. France, Balkans	A.A.S.
1909	Storey, A. T. T., O.B.E. (F) Capt. S. Lancashire Regt., att. Portuguese E.F., m. 2. France, E. Africa	J.M.E., M.D.H.
1907	Storey, R. A., Lt. R.A.S.C. France	J.M.E., M.D.H.
1912	Stovell, L. A. H., Lt. Devonshire Regt., att. Suffolk Regt. and Gloucestershire Regt., empld. Capt. Labour Corps, w. 2. France	H.B.
1909	Stracey, R. G., Capt. Scots Gds., m. France (k. 1.1.15)	H.B.
1872	Stracey Clitherow, C. E. (Stracey at Eton), Capt. Staff	G.
1869	Stracey Clitherow, J. B., C.B.E. (Stracey at Eton), Bt. Lt.-Col. Welsh Gds.	G.

1909 Strahan, W. R., Capt. London Regt., att. Middlesex
   Regt. France   E.L.V.
1908 Straker, I. A., Capt. 9th Lancers, empld. Maj. Worcestershire Yeomanry, w. France, Egypt, Palestine   H.Br.
1914 Straker, R., M.C., Lt. 12th Lancers, w. France   V.LeN.F.
1885 Strang-Watkins, W. J. Y., Lt. R. Defence Corps   E.S.S., A.C.
1874 Streatfeild, Sir H., K.C.V.O., C.B., C.M.G., Bt. Col.
   Grenadier Gds.   R.D., R.A.H.M.
1914 Streatfeild, H. G. C., Capt. Hampshire Regt. Aden   K.S.
1902 Streatfeild, H. S. J., D.S.O. (F) Lt.-Col. London Regt.,
   m. 6. France, Balkans, Egypt, Palestine   C.H.A.
1909 Strickland, A. W., Capt. Gloucestershire Yeomanry,
   p. Egypt, Gallipoli   H.T.B.
1877 Strickland-Constable, F. C., Lt.-Col. E. Yorkshire
   Regt., and Staff. France (d. 20.12.17)   C.W.D.
1913 Stronge, C. N. L., M.C. (F) Capt. R. Inniskilling Fusiliers, att. R. Irish Rifles, w., m. 2. France   A.C.G.H.
1910 Stronge, J. M., Lt. R. Fusiliers. France (k. 16.8.17)   A.C.G.H.
1911 Struben, L. F., 2nd Lt. 7th Dragoon Gds., att. R.F.C.,
   late Trooper Mounted Rifles, S. African Defence
   Force. France (k. 16.11.16)   A.C.G.H.
1914 Stuart, Hon. J. G., M.C. and Bar, Capt. R. Scots, and
   Staff. France   L.S.R.B.
1914 Stuart, W., D.S.O., Lt. Lothians and Border Horse,
   att. M.G. Cav., w., p. Palestine   H.B., R.H.de M.
1877 Stuart, W. D., Maj. K.R.R.C.   W.D.
1870 Stuart-Wortley, Hon. E. J. Montagu-, C.B., C.M.G., M.V.O.,
   D.S.O., Maj.-Gen. (K.R.R.C.), m. 2. France, Egypt   G.R.D.
1896 Stuart-Wortley, J. (F) Lt.-Col. S. Staffordshire Regt.,
   late R. Fusiliers and Cameronians (Scottish Rifles),
   w., m. France (k. 21.3.18)   E.L.V.
1909 Stuart-Wortley, R. N. Montagu-, M.C., Capt. Hampshire Yeomanry, att. R.A.F., m. 2. France, Egypt   E.W.S.
1905 Stubbs, K. S., Capt. Rifle Bde., and Staff, w., m. 2.
   France, Italy   J.H.M.H.

1894	Stucley, H. St. L., Maj. Grenadier Gds., m. France (k. 29.10.14)	E.C.A.L.
1889	Studd, H. W., C.B., C.M.G., D.S.O. (F) Brig.-Gen. (Coldstream Gds.), w., m. 5. France	W.D.
1917	Studholme, H. G., Lt. Scots Gds., w. France	R.S.K.
1916	Studholme, P. F. W., 2nd Lt. Devonshire Regt. France (k. 4.10.17)	H.Br.
1903	Sturgis, G. B., Lt. (t. Capt.) R.A.S.C., late The Queen's, and Staff. France	A.C.B.
1896	Sturgis, H. R., Maj. (t. Lt.-Col.) Rifle Bde., and Staff. France	A.C.B.
1899	Sturgis, J. B., Lt. Surrey Yeomanry, att. The Queen's. France	A.C.B.
1910	Sturt, Hon. G. P. M. N., Capt. Coldstream Gds., w. France (d.w. 11.11.18)	H.F.W.T., A.E.C.
1888	Style, G. M., Maj. W. Kent Yeomanry. Egypt, Gallipoli	F.T., R.A.H.M.
1914	Style, O. G., Lt. Coldstream Gds., w., p., m. France	A.C.G.H.
1897	Style, R. H., Capt. R. E. Kent Yeomanry. France	J.P.C.
1906	Styles, H. W., Capt. The Queen's Own (R. W. Kent Regt.), w. Afghanistan	T.C.P., E.L.C.
1902	Styles, W. R., M.C., Maj. 12th Lancers, att. M.G. Cav., m. 2. France	F.J.T., J.M.D.
1914	Summers, A. N. G., Lt. 9th Lancers, att. Lt. R.A.F. France, Egypt	P.V.B.
1905	Summers, A. S. M., Capt. 19th Hussars, att. R.F.C., m. France (k. 15.9.16)	R.C.R.
1911	Summers, W. A., M.C. 2nd Lt. (t. Capt.) 18th Hussars, att. R.F.C. France (k. 1.8.16)	P.V.B.
1889	Surtees, H. S. B., Capt. (t. Maj.) 2nd Life Gds., empld. R.G.A. France	A.C.J.
1894	Surtees, R. L., O.B.E., Capt. Shropshire L.I., m. France	A.C.J.
1905	Sutherland, Duke of (F) (Marquess of Stafford at Eton), Cr. R.N.R., and Staff. France, Egypt, Home Waters, Mediterranean, Red Sea	H.T.B.

1880 Sutherland, A. (Sutherland-Walker at Eton), Maj. (t. Lt.-Col.) A. and S. Highlanders. France J.P.C.
1909 Sutherland, A. H. C., O.B.E., M.C. (F) Capt. (t. Lt.-Col.) Black Watch, and Staff, w., m. France R.P.L.B.
1904 Sutherland, T. L. M., the late, 2nd Lt. Black Watch. (k. accid. 23.12.16) P.W.
1904 Sutton, B. E., D.S.O., O.B.E., M.C. (F) Capt. Westmorland and Cumberland Yeomanry, att. Maj. R.A.F., w., m. 3. France J.M.E.
1909 Sutton, C. L. M., Capt. R. Fusiliers, and Staff. France, Egypt E.L.V.
1917 Sutton, C. W. H., 2nd Lt. Coldstream Gds. France K.S.
1901 Sutton, F. A., M.C., Lt. R.E., and Staff, w. Gallipoli J.P.C., A.C.G.H.
1894 Sutton, F. H., M.C., Maj. 11th Hussars, w. France S.R.J., J.H.M.H.
1883 Sutton, H. C., C.B., C.M.G. (F) Maj.-Gen. (Coldstream Gds.), m. 4. France, Mesopotamia J.C.
1903 Sutton, H. J., Lt. Welsh Gds., late 2nd Lt. London Regt. France (k. 27.9.15) E.C.A.L.
1910 Sutton, L. T., the late, Lt. R.A.S.C., M.T. France (d. 27.4.20) J.M.D.
1914 Sutton, N. E. P. (F) Capt. Coldstream Gds., and Staff. France, Egypt P.V.B.
1909 Sutton, Sir R. V., Bart., M.C., Capt. 1st Life Gds., w. 2, m. France (d. 29.11.18) R.W.W-T., C.M.W.
1908 Sutton-Nelthorpe, C., M.C., Lt. Coldstream Gds., late 2nd Lt. Essex Regt., w. 3, m. France E.W.S.
1905 Sutton-Nelthorpe, O., D.S.O., M.C., Bt. Maj. Rifle Bde., empld. Lt.-Col. Staff, m. 4. France A.C.B., A.M.G.
1893 Swaine, F. L. V., Maj. Grenadier Gds., att. K.R.R.C., m. France J.M.E.
1902 Swan, P. C., Lt. Northumberland Fusiliers T.C.P.
1881 Swan, R. C., Lt.-Col. Lincolnshire Yeomanry C.C.J.
1896 Swann, H., Capt. R.F.A., att. R.G.A., and Staff. France A.A.S.
1909 Sweeting, G., Lt. R.H.G. France L.S.R.B.
1902 Sweeting, H. C., O.B.E., Capt. K.R.R.C., w., m. France T.C.P.

1893	Swetenham, F., Maj. R. Scots Greys. France (k. 28.8.14)	A.C.J.
1889	Swifte, L. C. (F) Maj. (t. Lt.-Col.) R. Dublin Fusiliers, and Staff. France, Balkans, Italy	K.S.
1914	Swire, A. G., 2nd Lt. Essex Yeomanry. France (k. 13.5.15)	R.P.L.B.
1908	Swire, C. G. W. (F) Capt. 1st R. Dragoons, att. R.A.F., and Staff, w., m. France	H.B.
1904	Swire, D. W., the late, Capt. Shropshire Yeomanry, att. Shropshire L.I., and Staff, m. Egypt, Palestine (d. 8.4.20)	H.B.
1901	Swire, G. W., Capt. (t. Maj.) Buckinghamshire Yeomanry. Egypt, Gallipoli	P.W.
1910	Swire, J. K., Lt. Essex Yeomanry, w. 2. France	R.P.L.B.
1903	Sydney, H., Capt. R.A.S.C., m. 2. France	H.F.W.T.
1893	Symonds, J. H., M.C., Lt. Imp. Light Horse, S. African F.F., m. 2. E. Africa, S.W. Africa (d. 15.11.18)	P.W.
1906	Symons, T. E. R., Bt. Maj. Grenadier Gds., and Staff. France	E.L.V.
1902	Symons-Jeune, B. H. B., Lt. R.A.S.C., and Staff. France, Mesopotamia	E.C.A.L.
1916	Synge, A. F., Lt. Irish Gds. France (k. 27.11.17)	A.C.R.-W.
1912	Synge, R. M., Capt. Coldstream Gds., w. 2. France	E.L.V., A.C.R.-W.
1911	Tabor, A. R., M.C., Capt. R.F.A., w. 2, m. France	E.L.V.
1915	Tabor, J., Lt. Grenadier Gds., w. France	E.L.V., A.C.R.-W.
1896	Tabor, J. C., T.D., Lt.-Col. Essex Regt., att. The Queen's Own (R. W. Kent Regt.), Welch Regt., W. Riding Regt., Durham L.I., and K.R.R.C., w. France	T.D., E.L.V.
1904	Tacon, D. G. T., Lt. R.F.A., late Lincolnshire Regt., m. France	T.C.P.
1872	Tagart, F. D., Maj. Westminster Dragoons	H.S.
1888	Tagart, Sir H. A. L., K.C.M.G., C.B., D.S.O. (F) Maj.-Gen. (15th Hussars), m. 4. France	E.H.
1910	Tailby, G. W. A., Capt. 11th Hussars, and Staff, w. France, Egypt, Palestine	H.M.

1903 Talbot, G. R. H., Flight-Lt. R.N.A.S. France (k. ac. 29.6.16) R.P.L.B.
1901 Talbot, H. J., Lt. R.A.S.C., M.T., att. R.G.A., late A.B., R.N.V.R. France H.E.L.
1903 Tallents, H., D.S.O., Maj. Sherwood Rangers, m. 2. Balkans, Egypt, Gallipoli, Palestine P.W.
1909 Tanner, W., Lt. R.A.S.C. France H.F.W.T.
1915 Tarratt, D. McN. F., 2nd Lt. Seaforth Highlanders. France (k. 4.10.17) E.L.C.
1897 Tarver, F. F., Capt. R.A.S.C., late Lt. Oxfordshire and Bucks L.I. F.T., C.L.
1889 Tarver, P. E., Pte. London Regt. France (k. 12.3.15) F.T.
1906 Tate, A. W., D.S.O. (F) Capt. Black Watch, empld. Lt.-Col. M.G.C., w., m. France A.A.S.
1902 Tate, H. B., Capt. Warwickshire Yeomanry, att. M.G.C., m. Egypt, Gallipoli A.A.S.
1913 Tatham, E. T., Lt. K.R.R.C., and Staff, m. France J.H.M.H.
1905 Tatham, M. (F) Lt. Sp. List. France R.P.L.B.
1917 Tatham, W. G., M.C., Lt. Coldstream Gds. France K.S.
1880 Tatham-Warter, H. de G. W. (Tatham at Eton), Lt. R. Defence Corps, late Pte. R. Fusiliers C.L.L.-C.
1914 Tatton, H., Lt. Duke of Lancaster's Own Yeomanry, att. R.A.F., w. France E.L.V., A.C.R.-W.
1901 Tatton, R. H. G., Capt. Oxfordshire and Bucks L.I., att. Duke of Cornwall's L.I., The Queen's Own (R. W. Kent Regt.), and Connaught Rangers, w. 2. France, Mesopotamia S.R.J., H.F.W.T.
1911 Tatton, T. A., M.C., Capt. Rifle Bde., att. Cameronians (Scottish Rifles), w. France E.L.V.
1892 Tayleur, H., Lt. R. Defence Corps J.C., F.D., E.I.
1891 Tayleur, J., Lt. R. Defence Corps J.C., F.D.
1890 Tayleur, W., O.B.E., T.D. (F) Lt.-Col. Labour Corps, late Maj. Manchester Regt. and Capt. Shropshire Yeomanry, m. 3. France J.C., F.D.
1909 Taylor, A. G. (F) Lt. R.F.A., att. I.A., and Staff, w. France J.M.E., A.B.R.

1899 Taylor, C. W. H., D.S.O. (F) Bt. Maj. The Queen's Own (R. W. Kent Regt.), and Staff, m. 3. France, Balkans, Egypt H.W.M., R.W.W.-T.

1903 Taylor, G. O., Capt. (t. Lt.-Col.) Norfolk Regt., att. Sherwood Foresters, w. France P.W.

1911 Taylor, G. R., Capt. Bedfordshire Regt., att. R.A.F., w. France, Egypt E.L.C.

1914 Taylor, G. R. M. S., Lt. R.F.A. France (d.w. 30.9.17) E.W.S.

1880 Taylor, G. W., Capt. Canadian E.F., and Staff C.L.L.-C.

1909 Taylor, G. W., Lt. R.F.A., w. France, Balkans, Egypt (d.w. 9.11.17) E.L.C.

1882 Taylor, J. F. W. B., Maj. R.A.S.C., late Capt. The Queen's. Egypt E.S.S.

1892 Taylor, L. H., Capt. R. Irish Rifles, att. Remount Service and R.F.A. France E.H.

1905 Taylor, L. W. M., 2nd Lt. R.F.A., late Driver H.A.C. France, Aden, Egypt, Gallipoli T.C.P., E.L.C.

1910 Taylor-Whitehead, G. E., 2nd Lt. 9th Lancers. France (k. 29.9.14) F.H.R., H.de H.

1909 Taylor-Whitehead, H. C., Capt. 9th Lancers, w. 2, m. France F.H.R., H.de H.

1889 Temple, Earl (Gore-Langton at Eton), Lt. Coldstream Gds., att. Irish Gds., and Staff H.D.

1907 Tennant, C. A. R., 2nd Lt. Dorsetshire Regt., att. Devonshire Regt., late Pte. London Regt. France (k. 9.5.15) F.H.R.

1905 Tennant, E. W. D., O.B.E., Lt. Intell. Corps, m. 2. France F.H.R.

1914 Tennant, H., 2nd Lt. R. Scots Greys, att. R.F.C. France (k. 27.5.17) V.Le N.F.

1909 Tennant, M., Lt. Scots Gds., late Capt. Seaforth Highlanders, att. Gds. M.G. Regt. France (k. 16.9.16) J.M.E., M.D.H.

1913 Tennant, M. F., D.S.O., Lt. Scots Gds., m. France S.G.L.

1913 Tennant, R. E., Capt. K.O.Y.L.I., m. France (k. 28.8.16) P.W., F.E.R.

1910 Tennyson, Hon. A. A., Capt. Rifle Bde., and Staff. France, Balkans (k. 21.3.18) A.M.G.

1897	Tennyson, A. B. S., Lt. Leicestershire Yeomanry, att. 5th Lancers. France	K.S.
1908	Tennyson, Hon. L. H., Capt. (t. Maj.) Rifle Bde., and Staff, w. 3, m. 2. France	A.M.G.
1917	Tennyson d'Eyncourt, A. E. C., 2nd Lt. Coldstream Gds.	A.E.C.
1917	Tennyson d'Eyncourt, W. L. F., 2nd Lt. Coldstream Gds.	A.E.C.
1895	Tew, T. P., Capt. (t. Maj.) Yorkshire Dragoons	F.T.
1885	Teynham, Lord (Roper-Curzon at Eton), Maj. The Buffs, and Staff. France	E.C.A.L.
1894	Thellusson, Hon. H. E., D.S.O. (F) Maj. (t. Lt.-Col.) R.F.A., m. 4. France	J.M.E.
1893	Thellusson, Hon. P. E., Capt. W. Kent Yeomanry, and Staff. France, Balkans, Egypt, Gallipoli	J.M.E.
1887	Thesiger, G. E. P., Maj. Surrey Yeomanry	J.C.
1885	Thesiger, G. H., C.B., C.M.G., Maj.-Gen. (Rifle Bde.), m. 2. France (k. 27.9.15)	J.C.
1901	Thomas, R. J. A., Maj. R.E. France	H.Br.
1917	Thomas, R. W., 2nd Lt. R.F.A. Palestine	H.de H.
1908	Thomas, W. H., M.C. and Bar, Lt. Berks Yeomanry, w. 3, m. Egypt, Palestine (d.w. 28.11.17)	E.L.V.
1897	Thompson, A. G., Capt. Bedfordshire Regt., att. Native Labour Corps. France, E. Africa	C.L.
1904	Thompson, H. C. St. J., D.S.O., Lt. Coldstream Gds., late att. Interpreters Corps, m. France (d.w. 1.12.17)	E.C.A.L., E.W.S.
1912	Thompson, J. F., O.B.E. (F) Lt. 3rd Dragoon Gds., empld. Capt. Tank Corps, m. France, S. Russia	K.S.
1914	Thomson, A. M. L., Capt. Gordon Highlanders, att. The Queen's Own (R. W. Kent Regt.) and R. Fusiliers, w. 2. France	H.de H.
1883	Thomson, Sir C., C.B., K.B.E. (F) Lt.-Col. Red Cross, and Staff, m. 4. France, Balkans, Egypt, Gallipoli, Italy, Palestine, S. Russia	H.E.L.
1902	Thorne, A. F. A. N., C.M.G., D.S.O. and two Bars (F) Brig.-Gen. (Grenadier Gds.), m. 7. France	H.D., H.M.

1908	Thorne, T. F. J. N., Capt. Grenadier Gds. France (k. 28.9.15)	H.M.
1870	Thornhill, Sir H. B., K.C.I.E., C.M.G., Lt.-Col. Staff	W.B.M.
1900	Thornhill, N., M.C., Lt. Grenadier Gds., late Bedfordshire Yeomanry, w. France	A.C.J., A.C.G.H.
1912	Thornton, E., Capt. R.A.F., late Lt. R. Fusiliers and R.E. Signal Service. France	A.M.G.
1904	Thornton, E. C., D.S.C., Lt. R.N., w. Home Waters, Mediterranean	L.S.R.B.
1912	Thornton, F., Lt. 16th Lancers, w., m. France, N. Russia	E.L.C.
1913	Thornton, R. W., M.C., Lt. R. Fusiliers, m. France (k. 16.6.15)	P.W., F.E.R.
1897	Thornycroft, C. M., C.B.E., D.S.O., Lt.-Col. Manchester Regt., m. 3. France	S.R.J.
1888	Thorold, J. G., Maj. Sp. List	H.W.M.
1895	Thorpe, G., C.M.G., D.S.O. and Bar, Brig.-Gen. (A. and S. Highlanders), m. 8. France	A.C.J.
1894	Thorpe, H., D.S.O., Lt.-Col. Sherwood Rangers, m. 3. Balkans, Egypt, Gallipoli	A.C.J.
1890	Thorpe, J. S., M.C., Maj. Scots Gds., w. 2, m. France (k. 16.9.16)	A.C.J.
1880	Thoyts, H. N. M., Bt. Col. King Edward's Horse, late Bt. Col. Res. Regt. of Cav.	C.C.J.
1894	Threlfall, C. M., Maj. 8th Hussars, Indian E.F. France	E.C.A.L.
1902	Thursby, A. D., Capt. K.R.R.C. France (k. 14.2.15)	H.Br.
1891	Thynne, Lord A. G., M.P., D.S.O. (F) Maj. R. Wiltshire Yeomanry, empld. Lt.-Col. Wiltshire Regt., w. 2, m. 2. France (k. 14.9.18)	A.C.J.
1905	Tichborne, Sir J. H. B. D., Bart., Lt. 4th Hussars, empld. Labour Corps, and Staff, m.	L.S.R.B.
1901	Tillard, T. A., Lt. Norfolk Yeomanry, att. R.F.C., w. France (k. 6.12.16)	A.C.J., H.Br.
1914	Tilney, L. A., M.C. (F) Maj. R.H.G., att. R.F.C., late 2nd Lt. Duke of Lancaster's Own Yeomanry, m. France (k. 9.3.18)	H.Br

1884	Tilney, R. H., D.S.O., T.D. (F) Col. Duke of Lancaster's Own Yeomanry, att. Labour Corps, and Staff, m. 2. France	R.A.H.M.
1884	Tilney, W. A. (F) Lt.-Col. 17th Lancers, and Staff, m. 2. France	R.A.H.M.
1914	Timmis, R. S., 2nd Lt. K.R.R.C. France (d.w. 10.5.15)	P.W., F.E.R.
1910	Tinline, G. C. M., 2nd Lt. Cameron Highlanders, w. France	L.S.R.B.
1910	Tinne, C. E., Lt. R.F.A., w., m. 2. France, Balkans, S. Russia	A.C.G.H.
1896	Tinne, J. A., Capt. R.F.A. France, Italy	C.H.E., C.L.
1911	Titchfield, Marquess of, Capt. R.H.G., and Staff. France, Egypt, Gallipoli	H.T.B., S.G.L.
1899	Tiverton, Visc., Maj. R.A.F. Staff, late A.B. and Lt. R.N.V.R. France, Home Waters	F.H.R.
1900	Tod, A. A., Maj. Rifle Bde., p. France	E.C.A.L.
1904	Tod, D., D.S.O., Lt. R. Berkshire Regt., att. M.G.C., m. France, Mesopotamia	H.F.W.T.
1905	Tod, W. N., O.B.E., Lt. (t. Maj.) London Regt., w. France	E.C.A.L., E.W.S.
1902	Todd, A. G. E., Lt. E. Surrey Regt., att. Hampshire Regt. France (k. 23.4.17)	H.M.
1874	Todd-Thornton, J. H. B., Capt. (t. Maj.) Northumberland Fusiliers, late Sherwood Foresters. (d. 12.1.18)	H.S.
1882	Toler, T. C., Maj. Sherwood Foresters	F.E.D., A.C.
1899	Tollemache, Lord (Tollemache at Eton), Capt. R.G.A., late Lt.-Cr. Armoured Cars, R.N.V.R., w. Mesopotamia	H.B.
1912	Tollemache, A. H. W., 2nd Lt. R.E., att. R.F.C. France (k. 19.7.16)	A.A.S.
1906	Tollemache, B. D., 2nd Lt. Coldstream Gds. France (k. 22.12.14)	A.A.S.
1902	Tollemache, E. D. H., D.S.O., M.C. (F) Bt. Maj. Coldstream Gds., and Staff, w., m. 3. France, Egypt, Gallipoli, Palestine	S.A.D.

1905 Tollemache, H. R. H., Capt. R.A.S.C., M.T., late Cameron Highlanders. France — S.A.D., P.V.B.
1889 Tollemache, Hon. M. G., Capt. Suffolk Regt. France — R.A.H.M.
1896 Tomkinson, C. W., Maj. Cheshire Yeomanry, att. Shropshire L.I., and Staff. France, Egypt, Palestine — H.B.
1901 Tomkinson, F. M., D.S.O. and Bar (F) Bt. Lt.-Col. Worcestershire Regt., m. 6. France, Italy — J.H.M.H.
1899 Tomkinson, H. A., D.S.O. and Bar, Maj. 1st R. Dragoons, att. 10th R. Hussars, and Staff, w. 2, m. 4. France — H.B.
1898 Tomkinson, J. E., Capt. Cheshire Yeomanry, att. Shropshire L.I., and Staff. Egypt, Palestine — H.B.
1899 Tomlin, G. A., M.C., Lt. Yorkshire Regt., att. Remount Service and R.A.S.C., m. France — J.M.E.
1881 Tomlin, M. J. B., O.B.E. (F) Lt.-Col. London Regt. France — F.T.
1894 Torkington, R. H., Maj. R. Fusiliers, w. France — T.D.
1903 Torrington, Visc., Capt. R.A.F., late Lt. R.N.V.R. and Trooper 18th Hussars, p. Balkans, Gallipoli, Mediterranean — A.C.B.
1876 Tottenham, R. G. Loftus, 2nd Lt. Labour Corps, late Col.-Sergt. Nigeria Regt. and Pte. R. Fusiliers, w. France, W. Africa — F.E.D.
1888 Toulmin, H. W., Lt. Suffolk Yeomanry — H.G.W.
1902 Toulmin, P. M., Lt. Leicestershire Yeomanry, late Trooper Northamptonshire Yeomanry. France (k. 22.6.17) — J.H.M.H.
1887 Tovey, D., the late, 2nd Lt. Sp. List, late Sergt. London Regt., w. France (d. 5.5.18) — HOME, F.D.
1902 Tower, C. C., Lt. Essex Yeomanry, and Staff. France (k. 2.10.15) — E.C.A.L.
1909 Tower, G. E., M.C., Lt. (t. Capt.) R.F.A. France, Egypt, Palestine — H.M.
1905 Townley, C. E., Lt. (t. Capt.) Suffolk Regt., and Staff, m. 2. France — J.M.E.
1881 Townley, M. G., Maj. Staff — J.M.E.
1900 Townshend, R. B., O.B.E., Lt. R.N.V.R. Home Waters — P.W.

1882	Tredegar, Lord, O.B.E. (Morgan at Eton), Cr. R.N.V.R. Home Waters	G.E.M.
1896	Treffry, D. K. de B., 2nd Lt. Coldstream Gds. France (k. 15.9.16)	F.T., J.P.C.
1885	Treffry, E., C.M.G., O.B.E., Lt.-Col. H.A.C., w., m. France	J.P.C.
1882	Trefusis, Hon. H. W. Hepburn-Stuart-Forbes-, Maj. Scots Gds., empld. Lt.-Col. Duke of Cornwall's L.I., and Staff	J.M.E., S.A.D.
1897	Trefusis, Hon. J. F. Hepburn-Stuart-Forbes-, D.S.O., Brig.-Gen. (Irish Gds.), m. 3. France (k. 24.10.15)	S.A.D.
1897	Trefusis, Hon. W. A. Hepburn-Stuart-Forbes-, Capt. (t. Maj.) Scots Gds., att. R.N.D., p. France	S.A.D.
1914	Treherne, E. H. A., Lt. R. Scots, and Staff. France, Balkans	A.B.R.
1915	Trelawny, H. W., Lt. Duke of Cornwall's L.I., w. France (k. 23.10.18)	A.A.S.
1888	Trelawny, J. E. Salusbury-, O.B.E., Bt. Lt.-Col. Duke of Cornwall's L.I., and Staff, w., m. France, E. Africa	C.H.E.
1902	Trelawny, L. D. St. A. Salusbury-, Capt. K.R.R.C., and Staff. France	E.L.V.
1910	Tremayne, C. H., M.C. and Bar, Capt. 19th Hussars, w., m. France	J.H.M.H.
1883	Tremayne, J. H. (F) Lt.-Col. 13th Hussars, empld. Derbyshire and Warwickshire Yeomanry. Balkans, Egypt	J.C.
1892	Trench, C. S. M., Capt. R. Fusiliers	T.D.
1913	Trench, Hon. F. S., Lt. K.R.R.C., att. R. Irish Fusiliers, w. France (d.w. 16.11.16)	R.S.K.
1913	Trench, Hon. R. P., Lt. The Queen's. France	R.S.K.
1904	Trevor, S. L., Capt. Bedfordshire Yeomanry, att. M.G. Cav. and Labour Corps. France	E.L.V.
1906	Tristram, G. H., Maj. R.F.A. France	R.W.W.-T., C.M.W.
1900	Tristram, L. B. C., Capt. Leicestershire Regt. France (k. 31.10.14)	K.S.
1876	Tristram, L. S. B., Maj. Welch Regt.	A.C.A.

1889	Tristram, M. H., Maj. 12th Lancers, empld. Lt.-Col. Eastern Cavalry Depôt	T.D.
1892	Tristram, U. H., Maj. S. Nottinghamshire Hussars, att. Remount Service	T.D.
1888	Tritton, H. L. M., Maj. Essex Yeomanry	C.H.E.
1909	Tritton, N. C., Lt. The Queen's, late E. Yorkshire Regt.	J.H.M.H.
1902	Trollope, R. J., Lt. R.F.A. France, Balkans, S. Russia	A.C.G.H.
1910	Trotter, A., Lt. Coldstream Gds., w. France (k. 31.12.14)	A.M.G.
1887	Trotter, A. R., M.V.O., D.S.O., Maj. 2nd Life Gds., empld. Col. Gds. M.G. Regt., w., m. France	H.G.W.
1908	Trotter, C. L., Lt. King's African Rifles. E. Africa (d. 22.1.18)	R.C.R., C.H.K.M.
1883	Trotter, C. W., C.B., T.D., Lt.-Col. S. Nottinghamshire Hussars, and Staff, m. 3. France	A.C.
1890	Trotter, E. H., D.S.O., Lt.-Col. Grenadier Gds., att. The King's (Liverpool Regt.), m. France (k. 8.7.16)	H.G.W., P.W.
1916	Trotter, F. L., Lt. K.R.R.C. France	P.V.B.
1911	Trotter, K. S., 2nd Lt. Rifle Bde. France (k. 27.4.15)	R.C.R., C.H.K.M.
1890	Trotter, R. B., Capt. Cameron Highlanders, m. France (k. 9.5.15)	H.G.W., P.W.
1905	Trotter, R. D., Capt. Rifle Bde. France	R.C.R.
1908	Trower, W. G., Capt. R.F.A., m. France, Egypt, Palestine	R.C.R., C.H.K.M.
1880	Troyte-Bullock, E. G., C.M.G., Lt.-Col. Dorset Yeomanry, m. 2. France, Egypt, Gallipoli	C.W.D., J.H.M.
1896	Truman, C. M., D.S.O., Bt. Lt.-Col. 12th Lancers, att. Black Watch, S. Irish Horse, R. Irish Regt., and Tank Corps, w., m. 3. France	A.C.A.
1889	Tryon, G. C., M.P., Bt. Maj. Grenadier Gds.	H.G.W., R.A.H.M.
1908	Tuck, G. L. J., C.M.G., D.S.O. and Bar (F) Lt.-Col. Suffolk Regt., w. 2, m. 4. France	E.L.V.
1911	Tuck, N. J., Lt. (t. Capt.) Norfolk Regt., att. Gds. M.G. Regt., w. 2. France	E.L.V.
1880	Tucker, C. Marwood, Lt.-Col. Devonshire Regt. Palestine	W.D.

1891	Tudor, H. O., Lt. Nigeria Regt., W. African F.F., late Pte. R. Fusiliers. W. Africa	E.H.
1917	Tudor-Craig, A. J. R., 2nd Lt. R. Scots, att. H.L.I. France	M.D.H.
1907	Tudway, H. R. C., Lt. Grenadier Gds. France (d.w. 18.11.14)	R.A.H.M., L.S.R.B.
1890	Tufnell, A. W., the late, C.M.G. (F) Brig.-Gen. (The Queen's), w., m. 3. France, Egypt, Gallipoli (d. 16.5.20)	H.G.W., S.R.J.
1912	Tufnell, C. E., Capt. Coldstream Gds., w. France (k. 15.9.16)	H.M.
1911	Tufnell, C. W., Lt. Grenadier Gds. France (k. 6.11.14)	P.W.
1916	Tufnell, G. J., the late, 2nd Lt. R.G.A. (d. 22.2.18)	S.G.L.
1909	Tufnell, L. H., 2nd Lt. R.F.A. France	P.W.
1906	Tufnell, N. C., Capt. Grenadier Gds., and Staff, w. 2. France	P.W.
1873	Tufton, G. R., Capt. Staff	R.D., R.A.H.M.
1913	Tufton, H. H. S. T., Lt. 15th Hussars, late R. Sussex Regt., att. Lincolnshire Regt., w. 2. France	E.I.
1892	Tufton, Hon. J. S. R., D.S.O. (F) Maj. R. Sussex Regt., and Staff, m. 2. France	H.G.W., R.A.H.M.
1912	Tupper-Carey, H. D., Capt. King's African Rifles, late Trooper E. African Mounted Rifles, w. E. Africa	H.T.B., S.G.L.
1914	Turing, R. A. H., Capt. Rifle Bde., att. M.G.C., w., m. France, Italy	A.E.C.
1902	Turner, H. B., Capt. Lancashire Hussars	R.C.R.
1888	Turner, R. F. L., Maj. R.F.A.	J.P.C.
1907	Turnor, A. C., M.C., Capt. R.H.G., att. Gds. M.G. Regt., m. France	J.M.E., J.H.M.H.
1905	Turnor, C. R., Lt. 10th R. Hussars. France (k. 26.10.14)	A.C.G.H.
1904	Turnor, H. B., M.C. and Bar, Capt. 17th Lancers, w., m. France	W.D., A.C.G.H.
1908	Turton, E. S., Lt. Yorkshire Hussars, att. Sherwood Foresters. France (k. 31.8.15)	H.B.
1878	Turton, R. B., Maj. Yorkshire Regt., and Staff. France	C.W.D.
1899	Tweeddale, Marquess of (Earl of Gifford at Eton), Capt. 1st Life Gds., att. R.F.A., w. France	J.H.M.H.

	Twining, C. F. H., Capt. Hampshire Regt., w. France	H.F.W.T.
1909	Twining, R. H., Bt. Maj. The Queen's, and Staff, w., m. France, Gallipoli	H.F.W.T.
1914	Twining, T. C., Lt. Grenadier Gds., and Staff. India	V.Le N.F.
1903	Twist, W. B., Capt. Durham L.I., w. France	L.F., R.P.L.B.
1917	Tyacke, A. J., 2nd Lt. R.F.A. France	R.S.K.
	Tylden-Pattenson, A. D., Lt. Oxfordshire and Bucks L.I., w. France (k. 5.1.15)	A.C.G.H.
1904	Tyler, G. E., M.C., Lt. R. Welch Fusiliers, att. R.F.C., late Pte. R. Fusiliers, w. France	T.C.P., E.L.C.
1897	Tyrer, O., 2nd Lt. R.F.A., w. France, Balkans	A.C.J.
1912	Tyringham, G. L., Capt. Scots Gds., and Staff, w. France	J.M.D., V.Le N.F.
1885	Tyringham, R. W. G., Lt. Sp. List	J.C.
1911	Tyrwhitt-Drake, T., M.C. and two Bars, Lt. Oxfordshire and Bucks L.I. France, N. Russia	H.Br.
1892	Tyser, H. E., 2nd Lt. Black Watch. France (k. 9.4.17)	H.E.L.
1913	Uffington, Visc., 2nd Lt. Hampshire Regt., att. Canadian E.F., w. France, Palestine	C.H.K.M.
1896	Unna, P. J. H., Lt. R.N.V.R. Home Waters, Mediterranean	H.B.
1894	Unthank, J. S., D.S.O., Lt.-Col. Durham L.I., att. Seaforth Highlanders, w. 2, m. 2. France	T.D.
1903	Upjohn, W. M., Lt. Welsh Gds. France (k. 24.8.18)	F.H.R.
1891	Upperton, C. B., the late, Capt. Somerset L.I. (d. 31.3.17)	T.D.
1903	Upton, Hon. E. E. M. J., Capt. K.R.R.C., m. 2. France (k. 9.5.15)	H.E.L.
1910	Upton, Hon. H. A. G. M. H., Lt. R. E. Kent Yeomanry	E.W.S.
1902	Vagliano, S. (F) 2nd Lt. Engineers, Greek Army. Balkans	T.C.P.
1901	Vallance, V. de V. M., M.C., Capt. 5th Lancers, att. Nigeria Regt., m. 2. France, W. Africa	A.C.A.
1900	Vandeleur, A. M., Capt. 2nd Life Gds. France (k. 30.10.14)	S.A.D.
1894	Van de Weyer, B. G., Maj. Scots Gds., w., p. France	E.C.A.L.

1899 Van de Weyer, J. B., Sergt. E. African Mounted Rifles, Nairobi F.F. E. Africa — E.C.A.L.

1890 Van de Weyer, W. J. B., M.V.O., Capt. R. Berkshire Regt., att. Hampshire Regt., m. France — E.C.A.L.

1900 Vane, Hon. H. C., Capt. R.F.A., late Maj. Yorkshire Hussars. France (d. 9.10.17) — A.C.B

1908 Vane, Hon. R. F., Capt. Durham L.I., att. Northumberland Fusiliers, K.O.Y.L.I. and Duke of Lancaster's Own Yeomanry, w. France — R.P.L.B.

1914 Vane-Tempest, C. S., Lt. Durham L.I., att. R.F.C. France (k. 25.3.17) — R.S.K.

1911 Vane-Tempest, E. C. W., D.S.C., Lt. R.N.V.R., w., m. 2. Mesopotamia — R.S.K.

1906 Van Neck, C., 2nd Lt. London Regt., late L/ce-Cpl. R.E., w. France — A.C.G.H.

1905 Van Neck, P., Lt. Grenadier Gds. France (k. 26.10.14) — A.C.G.H.

1904 Van Raalte, N. M., Lt. R.N.V.R. Home Waters — R.C.R.

1907 Vansittart, A. B., 2nd Lt. 11th Hussars. France (d.w. 12.5.15) — F.H.R.

1910 Vansittart, G. N., Capt. Central India Horse, I.A. Mesopotamia — F.H.R., H. de H.

1917 Vassall, L. S., 2nd Lt. K.O.Y.L.I. — A.C.R.-W.

1887 Vaughan, J., C.B., C.M.G., D.S.O. (F) Maj.-Gen. (7th Hussars), m. 3. France — E.L.V.

1917 Vaughan-Johnson, B. T., 2nd Lt. Coldstream Gds., w. France — H.M.

1916 Vaughan-Morgan, G. C., Lt. Irish Gds., w. France — J.H.M.H.

1889 Venables-Llewelyn, C. L. Dillwyn-, Lt.-Col. Glamorgan Yeomanry, att. R. Welch Fusiliers and Labour Corps. France — R.C.R.

1914 Venables-Llewelyn, J. L. Dillwyn-, Capt. Coldstream Gds., w. 2. France (k. 10.7.17) — R.P.L.B.

1907 Venn, E. N. L., Capt. 17th Lancers. France — H.B.

1908 Venn, H. W. S., O.B.E., Capt. W. Kent Yeomanry, and Staff, m. 3. France — H.B.

1907	Vereker, G.G.M., M.C., Lt. Grenadier Gds., m. 2. France	E.L.V.
1909	Verelst, H. W., M.C., Capt. Coldstream Gds., m. France (k. 26.9.16)	A.A.S.
1916	Verelst, R. W., Lt. 11th Hussars. France	A.A.S.
1896	Verey, H. E., D.S.O., Lt. (t. Lt.-Col.) Staff, late C.P.O., R.N.A.S., m. France, Italy	J.P.C.
1913	Verney, Hon. J. H. P., M.C., Lt. 17th Lancers, w. France	C.M.W.
1905	Vernon, Lord, Capt. Derbyshire Yeomanry. Gallipoli (d. 10.11.15)	H.Br.
1904	Vernon, Lord (Mr. Vernon at Eton), Lt.-Cr. R.N. Home Waters, Mediterranean	L.S.R.B.
1902	Vesey, Hon. O. E., C.B.E. (F) Maj. Westminster Dragoons, att. R.E. Kent Yeomanry, empld. Lt.-Col. Staff, m. 3. France, Egypt	R.C.R.
1903	Vesey, Hon. T. E. (F) Lt.-Col. Irish Gds., w. 3. France	R.C.R.
1916	Vickers, O. H. D., Lt. (t. Capt.) R.A.F. France	H.Br.
1914	Vickers, R. A., Midshipman R.N. Home Waters	A.C.G.H.
1911	Villiers, A. E., Lt. K.R.R.C., att. R.E. Signal Service. France	A.C.G.H.
1902	Villiers, Hon. A. G. Child, D.S.O. and Bar (F) Maj. Oxfordshire Yeomanry, w., m. 2. France	S.A.D.
1889	Villiers, C. W., C.B.E., D.S.O. (F) Lt. Coldstream Gds., empld. Lt.-Col. Staff, m. 7. Balkans, S. Russia	F.T.
1886	Villiers, G. F. M., Maj. K.O.S.B., late Maj. R. Scots Fusiliers	G.E.M.
1911	Vincent, A. F., Lt. Tank Corps. France	E.W.S.
1882	Vincent, S. A., Capt. Remount Service, late 2nd Lt. Scottish Horse. France, Egypt, Gallipoli	K.S.
1917	Vincentelli, C. A., Maréchal des Logis Cuirassiers, French Army. France	K.S., P.V.B.
1897	Vivian, Lord, D.S.O. (F) Maj. R. 1st Devon Yeomanry, att. Gloucestershire Regt., and Staff, m. 2. France, Egypt, Gallipoli	A.C.J.
1904	Vivian, G. N., O.B.E., Capt. Grenadier Gds., w., m. France	R.P.L.B.

1892 Vivian, Hon. O. R., M.V.O., D.S.O., T.D., Maj. Glamorgan
Yeomanry, empld. Lt.-Col. R. Irish Rifles and
Cameron Highlanders, m. France   W.D.
1915 Vivian, R. C. G., Lt. 2nd Life Gds. France   H M.
1898 Vivian, V., C.M.G., M.V.O., D.S.O. (F) Bt. Lt.-Col.
Grenadier Gds., and Staff, w., m. 7. France, N. Russia   E.H., J.P.C.
1906 Voules, H. St. G., Lt. R.A.O.C., late Coy.Q.M.S.,
R.A.S.C.   E.W.S.

1898 Wade-Palmer, A. N. (Wade at Eton), Capt. Sherwood
Rangers, and Staff. France, Egypt, Gallipoli   A.C., F.J.T.
1889 Wagg, H. J., O.B.E., Lt., late C.P.O., R.N.V.R.   J.M.E.
1869 Waithman, W. S., Capt. Sp. List   W.B.M.
1901 Waithman, W. W., Lt. R.A.S.C., M.T., m. France, Balkans   H.Br.
1896 Wake, G. R., Bt. Maj. K.R.R.C., and Staff, m. 4. France
    F.W.C., J.H.M.H.
1894 Wake, Sir H., Bart., C.M.G., D.S.O. (F) Bt. Lt.-Col.
K.R.R.C., and Staff, m. 4. France, Balkans, Italy
    F.W.C., S.R.J., J.H.M.H.
1906 Wakeman, E. O. R., 2nd Lt. Grenadier Gds., m.
France (k. 16.5.15)   H.B.
1905 Wakeman, O., Capt. Grenadier Gds., and Staff, w. France   H.B.
1907 Waley, E. G. S., O.B.E. (F) Capt. London Regt., and
Staff, m. France, Egypt, Palestine   H.B.
1893 Walker, C. C., Capt. A. and S. Highlanders. France
(k. 26.8.14)   T.D.
1902 Walker, C. F. A., M.C. (F) Capt. (t. Lt.-Col.) Grenadier
Gds., w. 2, m. 2. France   J.H.M.H.
1894 Walker, E. W., Capt. E. Yorkshire Regt. France
(k. 28.10.14)   P.H.C., C.H.A.
1901 Walker, F. G., Capt. R.A.S.C., M.T., m. 3. France, Italy   T.C.P.
1896 Walker, H. F. M., Lt. R.N.V.R., late Lt. Hampshire
Regt.   E.L.V.
1912 Walker, H. R., Capt. The King's Own (R. Lancaster
Regt.), w. France, Balkans, Gallipoli   K.S.

1909	Walker, J. P. E. (F) Lt. R. Scots Greys, att. M.G.Cav., w. 2, m. France	P.V.B.
1893	Walker, O. B., Capt. 15th Hussars. France (k. 23.8.14)	J.M.F.
1901	Walker, P. L. E., D.S.O., Capt. 7th Hussars, empld. Lt.-Col. E. Lancashire Regt., late att. R. Warwickshire Regt., W. Riding Regt. and R. Fusiliers, w. 2. France	J.H.M.H.
1914	Walker, R. H., Capt. Rifle Bde. France	A.C.G.H.
1906	Walker, Sir R. J. M., Bart., Capt. (t. Maj.) Coldstream Gds., late att. R. Fusiliers. France	S.A.D., P.V.B.
1893	Walker, W. B., Maj. Yorkshire Regt. France (k. 29.10.14)	J.M.F.
1896	Walker, W. E., Capt. Durham L.I. Balkans, S. Russia	T.D., T.C.P.
1898	Wallace, H. F., Sub-Lt., late P.O., R.N.V.R.	P.W.
1901	Wallace, J. T., D.S.O., M.C., Maj. R.F.A., and Staff, w., m. 4. France, Italy	C.H.A.
1899	Wallace, P. D., Capt. Scots Gds. France	P.W.
1895	Waller. A. J., Capt. Black Watch	W.D., T.C.P.
1915	Wallington, G. S., Lt. (t. Capt.) K.R.R.C., m. France (k. 9.9.17)	A.C.G.H.
1917	Wallis, T. H., 2nd Lt. K.R.R.C. France	P.V.B.
1877	Wallis-Wright, H. A. B. (Wallis at Eton), Maj. Remount Service	R.A.H.M.
1904	Walmesley, R., Lt. Yorkshire Regt. France (k. 21.10.14)	C.H.A.
1900	Walpole, H. S. (Vade-Walpole at Eton), Lt. Coldstream Gds., w. France (k. 9.4.18)	F.H.R.
	Walpole, J. R., Capt. The Queen's. France (k. 1.7.16)	C.H.A.
	Walrond, V., Capt. R.F.A., w., m. 2. France (k. 26.4.17)	R.W.W.-T., C.M.W.
1893	Walter, C. H., Maj. R.G.A.	H.G.W., S.R.J.
1894	Walter, F. E., D.S.O., Maj. (t. Lt.-Col.) Norfolk Regt., w., m. 3. France	S.R.J.
1908	Walter, G. L., M.C., Lt. Coldstream Gds., att. Gds. M.G. Regt., late Pte. Rhodesian Regt., w. France, S. W. Africa	C.H.A., P.V.B.
1878	Walter, R. L., Bt. Col. Hampshire Yeomanry. France	E.W.

1896	Walter, Stephen, Capt. R.A.F., late Lt. R.N.V.R., att. R.N.A.S.	S.R.J.
1911	Walter, Sydney, 2nd Lt. Grenadier Gds. France (k. 23.10.14)	R.S. de H.
1907	Walters, F. P., Capt. Oxfordshire and Bucks L.I., att. K.O.Y.L.I., w. France	K.S.
1899	Walton, H. C., Lt., late Sergt., R.A.S.C., and Driver Canadian F.A. France	H.D.
1895	Ward, A. S., M.P., Capt. Herts Yeomanry. Egypt, Gallipoli	K.S.
1912	Ward, C. S., Lt. R. Warwickshire Regt. France (k. 8.1.16)	H.P.
1899	Ward, E. S., Capt. Grenadier Gds., and Staff, w. France, Italy	J.M.E.
1905	Ward, F. W., Capt. Gloucestershire Regt. France (k. 9.10.17)	A.C.B., A.M.G
1896	Ward, Hon. G. E. F., M.V.O., Lt. 1st Life Gds. France (k. 30.10.14)	F.C.A.L.
1896	Ward, H. F., Capt. Irish Gds., late Capt. E. African Mounted Rifles, Nairobi F.F., m. France, E. Africa	R.A.H.M.
1913	Ward, H. S., Capt. R.A.F., w., p. (escaped). France	H.Br.
1889	Ward, Hon. Sir J. H., K.C.V.O. (F) Bt. Maj. Staff, m. 2. France, Egypt, Gallipoli, Italy	E.C.A.L.
1890	Ward, Hon. R. A., O.B.E. (F) Capt. Staff, m. 2. France, Egypt, Gallipoli, Italy	E.C.A.L.
1896	Ward, W. Dudley, M.P., Lt.-Cr. R.N.V.R., late Lt.-Cr. R.N.R., and Staff. Home Waters	A.C.A.
1883	Ward-Jackson, C. L. A., M.P. (F) Maj. Yorkshire Hussars, and Staff, m. France	A.C.
1916	Warde, J. R. O'B., Lt. R.F.A. France	R.S.K.
1911	Warde-Aldam, J. R. P., Capt. Yorkshire Dragoons, w. France	H.B.
1900	Warde-Aldam, W. St. A., D.S.O., Bt. Lt.-Col. Coldstream Gds., empld. Lt.-Col. London Regt., w., m. 4. France, Balkans, Egypt, Palestine	A.C.J., F.J.T.
1911	Wardell, J. M. S., M.B.E. (F) Lt. 10th R. Hussars, and Staff, w. France	H. de H.

1912	Wardell-Yerburgh, G. B., Flight-Sub-Lt. R.N.A.S. Home Waters	L.S.R.B.
1910	Wardley, G. C. N., Lt. R.G.A. France (d.w. 16.7.16)	K.S.
1904	Waring, C. H., Capt. 18th Hussars, att. R.A.F. Egypt	H.Br.
1900	Waring, H. A., D.S.O., Maj. The Queen's Own (R. W. Kent Regt.), empld. Lt.-Col. Lincolnshire Regt., m. 2. France	J.P.C., R.P.L.B.
1892	Waring, W., M.P. (F) Maj. Lothians and Border Horse, att. Naval Intell. Div. France, Balkans	C.H.E.
1897	Waring, W. A., Lt. The Queen's Own (R. W. Kent Regt.)	J.P.C.
1906	Warner, C. J., Lt. Oxfordshire and Bucks L.I. France (k. 16.5.15)	A C.G.H.
1903	Warner, E. C. T., D.S.O., M.C. (F) Bt. Maj. Scots Gds., and Staff, m. 7. France	A.C.G.H.
1896	Warre, E. L., Capt. K.R.R.C., att. R.A.F. France	E.C.A.L.
1915	Warre, F. R., Lt. K.O.Y.L.I., att. E. Yorkshire Regt. and Yorkshire Regt. India	E.L.C.
1897	Warre, F. W., O.B.E., M.C., Maj. K.R.R.C., and Staff, w., m. 2. France	E.C.A.L.
1894	Warre, G. F., C.B.E., Capt. R.A.S.C. France, Italy	T.D.
1883	Warre, H. C., D.S.O., Lt.-Col. K.R.R.C., and Staff, m. 4. France	E.W.
1894	Warre Cornish, G., Maj. Somerset L.I. France (k. 16.9.16)	F.W.C.
1891	Warre Cornish, W. H., 2nd Lt. (t. Capt.) N. Somerset Yeomanry, and Staff	K.S.
1897	Warren, R. D., Maj. Leicestershire Regt., empld. Lt.-Col. Leinster Regt. and Connaught Rangers. France, Balkans (k. 7.4.18)	K.S.
1885	Warrender, H. V., D.S.O., Lt.-Col. London Regt., m. 2. France, Italy	J.M.E.
1916	Warrender, Sir V. A. G. A., Bart., M.C. (F) 2nd Lt. Grenadier Gds., and Staff. France	R.P.L.B.
1910	Wasbrough, W. L., 2nd Lt. Loyal N. Lancashire Regt. France (k. 25.9.15)	L.S.R.B.

1911	Wasey, C. W. C., M.C. (F) Capt. R. Warwickshire Regt., att. R.F.C., w. 2, m. France (k. 28.10.17)	R.S.K.
1890	Waterhouse, A. T., Maj. R.A.M.C. France	S.A.D.
1907	Waterhouse, M. T., M.C., Maj. Sherwood Rangers, and Staff, m. 2. Balkans, Egypt, Gallipoli, Palestine	H.T.B.
1895	Waterhouse, P., Lt. R.E. France	E.I.
1905	Waterlow, C. B., Lt. R.A.S.C., M.T. Staff. France, Balkans, E. Africa, Mesopotamia	H.Br.
1897	Watkins, H. G., C.B.E. (F) Bt. Maj. (t. Lt.-Col.) Coldstream Gds., att. New Zealand E.F., and Staff, m. 3. France, Egypt	A.C.J.
1893	Watkins, H. T. G., Pte. R.A.M.C. Balkans	K.S.
1914	Watkins, W. L., Capt. R.G.A., w. France	E.L.V., A.C.R.-W.
1894	Watney, B. W. A., Lt. R.A.S.C., M.T. France, Egypt	A.C.A.
1887	Watney, C. N., C.I.E., T.D., Col. The Queen's Own (R. W. Kent Regt.). India	G.E.M.
1890	Watney, G. N., Capt. K.O.Y.L.I., att. Yorkshire Regt., The Queen's Own (R. W. Kent Regt.), and Labour Corps. France	G.E.M., P.H.C.
1906	Watney, M. H., Capt. R.A.M.C. France	A.A.S.
1898	Watney, W. H., Lt. Rifle Bde. France (k. 9.5.15)	A.A.S.
1895	Watson, B. B., O.B.E., Lt. (t. Capt.) Irish Gds. France	H.E.L.
1891	Watson, E. J. M., Capt. R.A.M.C., m. France	J.P.C.
1879	Watson, H. S., Lt. (t. Maj.) Glamorgan Yeomanry	H.D.
1916	Watson, Sir J., Bart., 2nd Lt. 16th Lancers. France (k. 23.3.18)	C.H.K.M.
1915	Watson, N. J., Lt. K.R.R.C., att. 2nd Lt. R.A.F. France	H.de H.
1911	Watson-Armstrong, Hon. W. J. M., Capt. Northumberland Fusiliers, w., m. France	H.T.B., S.G.L.
1910	Watson-Smyth, G. R., Lt. 13th Hussars, Indian E.F., att. R.F.C., w. France	R.C.R., M.D.H.
1894	Watts-Russell, A. E. (Birch at Eton), Capt. Coldstream Gds. France	S.R.J.
1886	Way, B. I., D.S.O., Lt.-Col. N. Staffordshire Regt., att. E. Yorkshire Regt., w. 2, m. 2. France	J.C.

1893	Webb, E. M., Capt. K.R.R.C., w. France (k. 23.7.16)	P.W., F.E.R.
1897	Webber, H. A. W., C.B.E., Maj. R.F.A., m. France	A.A.S.
1881	Webster, Sir A. F. W. E., Bart., O.B.E., Capt. (t. Maj.) Grenadier Gds.	E.H.
1916	Webster, G. V. G. A., 2nd Lt. Grenadier Gds. France (k. 4.8.17)	M.D.H.
1911	Wedderburn, A. H. M., Capt. Black Watch, and Staff, w., m. France	E.L.V.
1902	Weguelin, T. N., Capt. Hampshire Regt., att. R.A.F. France	A.C.A., R.S. de H.
1889	Welby, G. E. E., Maj. S. Wales Borderers. France (k. 27.9.14)	C.H.E.
1890	Welby, R. W. G., Lt. Grenadier Gds., m. France (k. 16.9.14)	H.M.
1901	Weldon, E. G., Maj. 8th Hussars, w., m. France	H.M.
1902	Weldon, G., Capt. R.F.A. France (d.w. 25.9.16)	H.M.
1896	Weller-Poley, E. H., M.V.O., Capt. Grenadier Gds. Egypt, Gallipoli	R.C.R.
1904	Wellesley, G. V., M.C., Capt. Oxfordshire Yeomanry, w. 2, m. France	J.M.E.
1894	Wellesley, Lord R., Capt Grenadier Gds., m. France (k. 30.10.14)	W.D.
1902	Wemyss, M. J., Capt. R.H.G., att. R.E. Signal Service, w., m. France	H.B.
1912	Wendover, Visc., Lt. R.H.G. France (d.w. 19.5.15)	H.M.
1913	Wentworth, G. W. (Withington at Eton), Lt. Norfolk Regt., att. R.F.C. and York and Lancaster Regt., w. France	A.A.S.
1905	Wentworth-Fitzwilliam, G. J. C., Lt. R.A.F., late Lt. Northamptonshire Yeomanry. France	J.M.D.
1910	Wentworth-Stanley, C. S. B., Lt. W. Kent Yeomanry. France, Egypt, Gallipoli, Palestine	A.C.G.H.
1913	Wernher, A. P., 2nd Lt. Welsh Gds., late Lt. Buckinghamshire Yeomanry. France, E. Africa (k. 10.9.16)	A.E.C.
1911	Wernher, H. A., Lt. 12th Lancers, empld. Maj. M.G.C., m. 3. France, Italy	H.F.W.T., A.E.C.

1905	West, A. H. P., Capt. Black Watch, and Staff. France	H.T.B.
1902	West, A. T., Maj. Berks Yeomanry, att. R. Berkshire Regt., and Staff. France	E.C.A.L.
1897	West, F. G., D.S.O., Maj. (t. Lt.-Col.) R.F.A., m. 2. France	E.L.V.
1906	West, L. R. E., Capt. London Regt. France (k. 23.4.15)	H.T.B.
1884	Westmacott, A., Lt. R.F.A., late 2nd Lt. R.G.A. India	J.H.M.
1883	Westmacott, C. B., C.B.E., Brig.-Gen. (Worcestershire Regt.), m. 2. France	J.H.M.
1896	Westmacott, G. P., D.S.O., Maj. Northumberland Fusiliers, w., m. France	H.W.M.
1910	Westmacott, G. R., D.S.O. (F) Capt. Grenadier Gds., and Staff, w., m. 3. France	L.S.R.B.
1885	Westmacott, R. G., O.B.E., Maj. Staff, m. France	H.W.M.
1897	Westminster, Duke of, G.C.V.O., D.S.O. (F) (Visc. Belgrave at Eton), Maj. Cheshire Yeomanry, att. Armoured Cars, M.G.C. and Tank Corps, m. 2. France, Egypt	S.A.D.
1876	Westmorland, Earl of, C.B.E. (Lord Burghersh at Eton), Col. Lancashire Fusiliers	R.A.H.M.
1878	Westropp, H. C. E., Brig.-Gen. (Manchester Regt.)	H.E.L.
1882	Wethered, F. O., C.M.G., V.D., Lt.-Col. R. Warwickshire Regt., m. 2. France	J.C.
1907	Wethered, H. E., Capt. (t. Maj.) Welsh Gds., late Lt. R.F.A., and Staff, w., m. France, Egypt, Palestine	A.A.S.
1875	Weyland, M. U., Maj. Staff. Italy	F.E.D.
1899	Whaley, H. E., Capt. Coldstream Gds., late Capt. R.F.A., w., m. France	R.C.R.
1897	Whaley, J. B., Lt., late Sergt., R.A.S.C., M.T. France	H.W.M.
1902	Wharton, H. E., Lt.-Cr. R.N. Home Waters, Mediterranean	F.H.R.
1900	Wharton, J. R., Capt. R. Warwickshire Regt., att. Northumberland Fusiliers, and Staff, w. France	F.H.R.
1876	Wharton, W. H. A., O.B.E., V.D., Lt.-Col. Yorkshire Regt.	C.L.L.-C.

1901	Whately, E. G., M.C. (F) Bt. Maj. Hertfordshire Regt., and Staff, late Pte. R. Fusiliers, m. 4. France, Italy	H.B.
1913	Whately, R. H., Lt. Rifle Bde., w. 2. France (k. 25.8.16)	R.P.L.B.
1892	Whatman, A. D., Maj. The Buffs, att. Suffolk Regt., w. France	S.A.D.
1907	Wheatley, C. J. H., Capt. Warwickshire Yeomanry, att. M.G.C., and Staff, m. France, Egypt, Palestine	A.A.S.
1877	Wheeler, E. V. V., O.B.E., T.D., Lt.-Col. Worcestershire Regt.	F.W.C.
1906	Wheeler, J. B., M.C., Bt. Maj. 15th Hussars, empld. Lt.-Col. Cav. Signals, m. 3. France	H.B.
1915	Wheeler, V. J., M.C. and Bar (F) Lt. Rifle Bde., att. R. Fusiliers, w. 3. France, N. Russia	R.S.de H.
1899	Wheler, C. W. G. H., Capt. R. E. Kent Yeomanry, att. The Buffs	C.H.A.
1892	Wheler, G. B. H., M.C., Maj. 21st Lancers, and Staff, att. R. E. Kent Yeomanry, m. 2. France, Gallipoli, Palestine	E.C.A.L.
1891	Wheler, G. C. H., M.P., C.B.E., Maj. Staff	E.C.A.L.
1899	Whitaker, G. C., Capt. (t. Maj.) Coldstream Gds., att. Gds. M.G. Regt. and Sussex Yeomanry. France	P.W.
1902	Whitaker, H., Capt. Rifle Bde. France (k. 1.12.14)	E.I.
1909	Whitaker, H. J. I., Sub-Lt. R.N.V.R., att. Nelson Bn., R.N.D. Gallipoli (k. 3.5.15)	E.L.V.
1902	Whitaker, H. S., Lt. R.N.V.R., att. R.N.A.S., and Staff. Italy	P.W.
1914	Whitaker, J. A. C., Lt. Coldstream Gds., w. 2, p. France	E.W.S.
1913	Whitaker, R., M.B.E. (F) Capt. Rifle Bde., and Staff, att. R.A.F., m. France	E.L.V., A.C.R.-W.
1896	Whitaker, W. H. B., Maj. Montgomeryshire Yeomanry, att. Middlesex Regt. and R.F.A. France	E.I.
1895	Whitbread, R. (F) Maj. Coldstream Gds., and Staff, w., m. France	H.G.W., C.H.A.
1886	Whitburn, C. W. S., T.D., Lt.-Col. W. Kent Yeomanry, m. Egypt, Gallipoli	F.F.V., H.D., E.S.S., A.C.

1910	Whitcombe, R. C. P., Surgeon-Lt. R.N. Home Waters, Mediterranean	K.S.
1904	White, A. B., Pte. R.A.S.C., M.T. France, Balkans, Egypt, Italy	T.C.P.
1876	White, Hon. C. J. (F) Maj. Norfolk Regt., and Staff, m. 2. France	H.S., J.P.C.
1914	White, C. M. F., Lt. R.F.A., and Staff, m. Balkans, Egypt, Palestine	R.P.L.B.
1902	White, F. S., Cpl. Engineers, Canadian E.F. France	A.A.S.
1887	White, G. H. A., C.B., C.M.G., D.S.O., Maj.-Gen. (R.A.), m. 6. France	R.C.R.
1912	White, H. J. F., Lt. Suffolk Regt., att. R.E. Signal Service, w. France	R.P.L.B.
1897	White, J. H. B., Capt. T.M.B., late Lt. R. Dublin Fusiliers, w. France	R.C.R.
1894	White, J. W. B., Capt. Middlesex Hussars, late Pte. Middlesex Regt. Balkans, Egypt, Palestine	R.C.R.
1877	White, Hon. R., C.B., C.M.G., D.S.O., Brig.-Gen. (R. Welch Fusiliers), w. 2, m. 5. France	J.P.C.
1883	White, R. E., V.D., Lt.-Col. Suffolk Regt.	W.D.
1908	White, R. J. S., Lt. Canadian E.F., att. R.F.C. France (d.w. 27.10.17)	J.M.D.
1914	White, R. P. F., M.C., Lt. The King's Own (R. Lancaster Regt.), att. Yorkshire Regt., w. 2. France	R.P.L.B.
1883	White-Thomson, Sir H. D., C.B., C.M.G., K.B.E., D.S.O. (F) Brig.-Gen. (R.A.), w., m. 6. France, Balkans	K.S.
1906	Whitehead, J. R. G., 2nd Lt. R.F.C. (k. accid. 3.8.16)	R.W.W.-T., C.M.W.
1905	Whitehouse, N. O., Lt. Engineer Corps, U.S.A. Army. France, N. Russia	H.E.L., R.S.K.
1908	Whiteley, Hon. R. G., O.B.E., Capt. R.G.A. France	C.H.A., A.B.R.
1902	Whiteley, Hon. W. T., Maj. R.A.F., late Lt.-Cr. R.N.V.R.	C.H.A.
1896	Whitfield, G. S. (F) Lt.-Col. Sussex Yeomanry, att. E. Yorkshire Regt., m. Egypt, Gallipoli, Palestine	R.C.R.
1907	Whitlark, J. H., Bt. Maj. R.A.S.C., m. France	E.C.A.L., J.M.D.

1890 Whitmore, F. H. D. C., C.M.G., D.S.O., T.D., Lt.-Col. Essex Yeomanry, att. 10th R. Hussars, w. 2, m. 4. France   A.C.A.

1874 Wickham, H., C.M.G., Lt.-Col. Northamptonshire Yeomanry, m. 2. France   E.H.

1903 Wickham, J. L., Capt. Welsh Gds., att. Scots Gds., w. France   H.F.W.T.

1885 Wickham-Boynton, T. L. (Wickham at Eton), Capt. Yorkshire Regt.   C.C.J., S.A.D.

1895 Wicklow, Earl of, Maj. (t. Lt.-Col.) S. Irish Horse, and Staff   S.R.J.

1899 Wienholt, E. A., Capt. 1st (King's) Dragoon Gds. France   T.C.P.

1909 Wigan, C. R., M.C., Capt. The Queen's. Mesopotamia   R.S.de H.

1912 Wigan, D. G., Capt. K.R.R.C. France   J.H.M.H.

1903 Wiggin, Sir C. R. H., Bart., Maj. Staffordshire Yeomanry, m. Egypt, Palestine   H.F.W.T.

1907 Wiggin, G. R., Capt. Worcestershire Yeomanry. Egypt (k. 23.4.16)   C.H.A., A.B.R.

1906 Wiggin, W. H., D.S.O. and Bar, Maj. (t. Lt.-Col.) Worcestershire Yeomanry, att. Sherwood Rangers, w. 2, m. 2. Egypt, Gallipoli, Palestine   C.H.A., A.B.R.

1910 Wiggins, A. F. R., Capt. Grenadier Gds., m. 2. France   A.C.G.H.

1914 Wiggins, H. G., M.C., Lt. Grenadier Gds., att. Hampshire Regt., w. 2. France   A.C.G.H.

1914 Wiggins, K., 2nd Lt. Hampshire Regt., att. S. Wales Borderers and R.A.F. Egypt, Mesopotamia   A.C.G.H.

1899 Wight-Boycott, T. A., D.S.O., Brig.-Gen. (Staffordshire Yeomanry), m. Egypt, Gallipoli (d. 30.3.16)   F.W.C.

1909 Wigram, R. F. (F) Capt. Sp. List   C.H.A., A.B.R.

1908 Wilberforce, E. V. S., A.F.C., Maj. R.A.F., late R.N.A.S. Home Waters   J.H.M.H.

1883 Wilberforce, H. W., C.B., C.M.G. (F) Brig.-Gen. (2nd Dragoon Gds. [Queen's Bays]), m. 5. France   E.W.

1914 Wilbraham, E. J., M.C., Capt. Rifle Bde., m. France   E.L.V., A.C.R.-W.

1875	Wilbraham, R. J., Bt. Lt.-Col. Staff	W.E.
1898	Wilder, F., 2nd Lt. R.F.A. France (k. 31.3.16)	T.C.P.
1893	Wilder, G., Capt. R.N.V.R. Home Waters	P.W.
1885	Wilkie-Dalyell, Sir J. B., Bart. (Wilkie at Eton), Maj. K.O.S.B., att. R. Scots, m. Balkans, Egypt, Gallipoli	A.C.A.
1906	Wilkinson, C. H., M.C. (F) Maj. Coldstream Gds., and Staff, w., m. France, Italy	J.H.M.H.
1917	Wilkinson, H. F., 2nd Lt. R.F.A.	H.Br.
1893	Wilkinson, R., D.S.O., Maj. (t. Lt.-Col.) Gloucestershire Regt., att. Hertfordshire Regt., w., m. France, Gallipoli	F.W.C., J.H.M.H.
1908	Wilkinson, W. A. C., M.C. and Bar, Capt. Coldstream Gds., late Lt. R.A.S.C. and Gunner H.A.C., w. 2. France	P.W.
1897	Willan, F. G., C.M.G., D.S.O. (F) Brig.-Gen. (K.R.R.C.), m. 5. France	E.C.A.L.
1900	Willan, R. H., D.S.O., M.C., Bt. Lt.-Col. K.R.R.C., att. R.E. Signal Service, w., m. 3. France	E.C.A.L.
1881	Willding-Jones, C. W., Capt. Northumberland Fusiliers	E.C.A.L.
1903	Willey, F. V., M.P., C.M.G., C.B.E., M.V.O., T.D., Lt.-Col. Sherwood Rangers, att. R.A.O.C., m. France, Egypt, Gallipoli	P.W.
1915	Williams, A. S. V., Lt. 18th Hussars, w. France	J.H.M.H.
1896	Williams, B. H., M.C., Capt. 11th Hussars, att. 13th Hussars, Leicestershire Yeomanry, and R.F.A., and Staff, m. France	A.C.A.
1877	Williams, C., C.B. (F) Brig.-Gen. (R. Scots Greys). France, Egypt	F.F.V.
1905	Williams, C., Lt.-Cr. R.N.V.R., att. R.N.D., and Staff. France, Egypt, Gallipoli	R.C.R.
1912	Williams, C. C. L., M.C., Lt. 12th Lancers. France	A.C.G.H.
1904	Williams, C. G., M.C., Lt. R.F.A., late Sergt.-Maj. H.A.C., w. France, Aden, Egypt, Gallipoli	T.C.P.
1904	Williams, C. Romer (F) Lt. (t. Capt.) Welsh Gds., late 4th Dragoon Gds., and Staff, w. 2. France	H.B.

1907	Williams, E. G., Lt. Grenadier Gds. France (k. 12.8.15)	C.H.A., A.B.R.
1913	Williams, H. A. C., M.C., Capt. K.R.R.C., w. 2, m. France, Balkans	C.M.W.
1905	Williams, H. de B., Lt. R.F.A., w. 2. France, Egypt, Palestine	J.H.M.H.
1911	Williams, H. E. E., 2nd Lt. Rifle Bde., late Pte. R. Fusiliers. France (k. 30.9.15)	K.S.
1897	Williams, J. N., Pte. New Zealand E.F. Gallipoli (k. 25.4.15)	S.A.D.
1880	Williams, L. O., Maj. 11th Hussars, att. King Edward's Horse	H.E.L.
1902	Williams, O. C., M.C. (F) Maj. Staff, m. 4. Egypt, Gallipoli, Palestine	K.S.
1882	Williams, Sir R., Bart., M.P., D.S.O. (F) Maj. Welsh Gds., late 2nd Lt. Grenadier Gds., att. Lt.-Col. Staff, w., m. 2. France, Italy, Mesopotamia	G.E.M.
1911	Williams, R. A. W., Lt. K.O.Y.L.I., w. France (k. 18.4.15)	A.B.R.
1917	Williams, R. C. O., 2nd Lt. Grenadier Gds.	F.E.R.
1904	Williams, T. L. O., M.C. (F) Capt. Canadian E.F., w. France (d. 21.10.18)	C.H.A.
1901	Williams-Bulkeley, R. G. W., M.C., Maj. Welsh Gds., late Lt. Grenadier Gds., w., m. France (d. 28.3.18)	J.M.D.
1906	Williams-Drummond, Sir J. H., Bart., 2nd Lt. Pembroke Yeomanry	J.M.E., H.F.W.T.
1907	Williams-Vaughan, J. C. A., 2nd Lt. S. Wales Borderers, att. M.G.C. France (k. 15.7.16)	C.H.A., A.B.R.
1914	Williams-Wynn, C. W., 2nd Lt. Coldstream Gds. France (k. 29.10.14)	R.S.de H.
1908	Williams-Wynn, W., Lt. 1st R. Dragoons, and Staff, w. France	R.S.de H.
1911	Williamson, G. H. G., Capt. London Regt., and Staff. France	H.B.
1911	Williamson, H. H. C., Lt. Coldstream Gds. France (k. 16.9.16)	L.S.R.B.

1902	Williamson, H. N. H., M.C. (F) Maj. R.F.A., and Staff, w., m. 2. France, Russia	J.M.D.
1906	Williamson, S. K. G., Capt. Westminster Dragoons, att. M.G.C., m. France, Egypt, Gallipoli, Palestine	A.A.S.
1910	Willink, F. A., Capt. R. Berkshire Regt. France	E.L.V.
1907	Willink, G. O. W., M.C., Capt. R. Berkshire Regt., m. France (k. 28.3.18)	E.L.V.
1912	Willink, H. U., M.C. (F) Capt. R.F.A., m. France	K.S.
1900	Willis, C. A., O.B.E. (F) Capt., att. Kaimakam, Egyptian Army, and Staff, m. Sudan	K.S.
1894	Willis, H. W. M., Capt. Sp. List, att. Manchester Regt. France	R.C.R.
1889	Willis, R. A. de A., Maj. Lancashire Hussars, att. Res. Regt. of Cav.	C.H.E.
1909	Willock, G. C. B., Capt. London Regt. France (k. 25.9.15)	A.B.R.
1916	Willock-Pollen, H. L. B., Lt. Coldstream Gds. France	E.L.C.
1879	Willoughby, Hon. C. H. C., Bt. Col. Sherwood Rangers, att. Remount Service	H.W.M.
1890	Willoughby, Hon. C. Heathcote-Drummond-, Maj. Coldstream Gds., empld. Lt.-Col. Tank Corps, late att. Cheshire Regt., m. 2. France, Gallipoli	R.A.H.M.
1888	Willoughby, Hon. C. S. Heathcote-Drummond-, C.B., C.M.G., Brig.-Gen. (Scots Gds.), m. 5. France	R.A.H.M.
1878	Willoughby, Sir J. C., Bart., the late, D.S.O., Maj. R.A.S.C., M.T., m. 2. E. Africa (d. 16.4.18)	E.W.
1878	Willoughby, Hon. T. L. F., Lt.-Col. Yorkshire Regt.	H.W.M.
1888	Willoughby de Broke, Lord, T.D. (Mr. Verney at Eton), Maj. (t. Lt.-Col.) Warwickshire Yeomanry	R.A.H.M.
1888	Willyams, A. H. V., Sergt.-Maj. Gordon Highlanders, Canadian E.F. France (k. 18.5.15)	E.H.
1905	Willyams, E. N., D.S.O., Capt. Duke of Cornwall's L.I., m. 2. France, Balkans	P.W.
1911	Wilmot-Sitwell, J. S., Lt. Coldstream Gds. France (d.w. 9.7.16)	P.V.B.
1907	Wilson, A. H. R., Lt. Black Watch, w. France	R.C.R., C.H.K.M.

1885	Wilson, A. S., M.P., Capt. E. Riding of Yorkshire Yeomanry, Sp. Service, p. (Austria). France, Mediterranean	C.H.E.
1911	Wilson, A. T. F., Lt. R.H.G. France	C.M.W.
1915	Wilson, B. A., M.C., Lt. 10th R. Hussars, late Lt. R. Wiltshire Yeomanry, m. 2. France	J.H.M.H.
1914	Wilson, C., Capt. Lincolnshire Yeomanry, att. M.G.C., m. France, Egypt, Palestine	A.M.G.
1901	Wilson, C. B., M.C., Capt. 10th R. Hussars, att. R.F.C., w., p., m. France	E.I.
1912	Wilson, C. F., Lt. 5th Dragoon Gds. France (k. 13.5.15)	H.B.
1892	Wilson, C. H. A., D.S.O., Maj. E. Riding of Yorkshire Yeomanry	C.H.E.
1899	Wilson, D. C., Lt. R.F.C. France (k. 10.5.15)	J.H.M.H.
1883	Wilson, E. Bryce, Capt. Res. Regt. of Cav., att. R.F.A. France	H.W.M.
1884	Wilson, G. C., M.V.O. (F) Lt.-Col. R.H.G., m. 2. France (k. 6.11.14)	F.W.C.
1894	Wilson, Hon. G. G., C.M.G., D.S.O., Lt.-Col. E. Riding of Yorkshire Yeomanry, m. 3. Egypt, Palestine	H.W.M.
1913	Wilson, G. H., Lt. E. Yorkshire Regt., and Staff. France	H.B.
1876	Wilson, Sir H. F. M., K.C.B., K.C.M.G. (F) Lieut.-Gen. (Rifle Bde.), m. 9. France, Balkans, Gallipoli	J.L.J., T.D.
1892	Wilson, H. H., D.S.O., Capt. R.H.G. France (k. 11.4.17)	F.W.C.
1898	Wilson, H. M., D.S.O., Bt. Lt.-Col. Rifle Bde., and Staff, m. 3. France	R.W.W.-T.
1903	Wilson, H. N. S., Maj. Worcestershire Yeomanry. Egypt, Gallipoli, Palestine	A.C.J., H.Br.
1900	Wilson, H. S. (F) Capt. Somerset L.I., att. K.O.Y.L.I., and Staff. France	C.H.A.
1909	Wilson, I. C., Capt. R.G.A. India	R.C.R., C.H.K.M.
1915	Wilson, L. G., Gunner R.F.A. France	A.M.G.
1902	Wilson, N. M., D.S.O., Maj. 7th Gurkha Rifles, I.A., and Staff, w., p., m. 3. Egypt, Mesopotamia	R.W.W.-T.

1894	Wilson, P. A., M.C., Maj. The Queen's Own (R. W. Kent Regt.), and Staff, m. France	P.H.C., C.H.A.
1915	Wilson, P. L., Lt. 1st R. Dragoons. France	E.I., T.F.C.
1911	Wilson, R. E., Lt. R. Scots, w. France (d.w. 28.9.15)	R.C.R., C.H.K.M.
1907	Wilson, R. M., O.B.E. (F) Capt. Cheshire Yeomanry, and Staff, m. 2. Balkans, Egypt	R.W.W.-T., C.M.W.
1905	Wilson-Fitzgerald, F. W., D.S.O., M.C., Capt. 1st R. Dragoons, and Staff, m. 2. France	R.A.H.M., R.S. de H.
1917	Wilson-Fox, G. H., 2nd Lt. 1st Life Gds. France	V. Le N.F., L.T.
1907	Wilson-Todd, J. H., the late, 2nd Lt. Scots Gds. (d. 3.3.19)	P.V.B.
1915	Windham, J. B. R., Lt. 18th Lancers, I.A., att. 30th Lancers, and Camel Corps, I.A. Afghanistan	A.C.R.-W.
1902	Windham-Wright, J., O.B.E., Lt.-Col. The Queen's. France (d. 14.2.19)	J.H.M.H.
1907	Windsor, Visc. (Mr. Windsor-Clive at Eton), Capt. Worcestershire Yeomanry, att. Intell. Corps, and Staff, m. France	S.A.D., P.V.B.
1909	Windsor-Clive, Hon. A., 2nd Lt. Coldstream Gds. France (k. 25.8.14)	S.A.D., P.V.B.
1895	Windsor-Clive, G., C.M.G., Bt. Lt.-Col. Coldstream Gds., and Staff, m. 4. France, Balkans, Egypt	S.A.D.
1909	Wingfield, A. E. F., Capt. Bedfordshire Regt., att. Essex Regt. and Suffolk Regt. France, Gallipoli	R.S.K.
1910	Wingfield, C. A. F., Lt. 13th Hussars. France, Mesopotamia	R.S.K.
1897	Wingfield, C. J. T. R., Capt. K.R.R.C. France (d.w. 29.4.15)	A.A.S.
1890	Wingfield, C. R. B., Maj. Shropshire L.I. France	F.W.C.
1891	Wingfield, M. E. G. R., Lt.-Col. Gloucestershire Regt., att. K.R.R.C. and Hampshire Regt. France	A.C.A.
1890	Wingfield, W. J. R., Maj. 19th Hussars, att. 7th Hussars, m. France, Mesopotamia	A.C.A.
1897	Wingfield-Stratford, E. C., Capt. The Queen's Own (R. W. Kent Regt.). India	J.P.C.
1905	Wingfield-Stratford, G. E., M.C. (F) Bt. Maj. The Queen's Own (R. W. Kent Regt.), and Staff, m. 2. France	L.S.R.B.

1914	Winkworth, H. S., Lt. 2nd Dragoon Gds. (Queen's Bays), att. R.A.F., late Pte. R.F.A. France	M.D.H.
1901	Winn, A., Capt. Suffolk Regt. France (k. 9.9.14)	A.C.A.
1914	Winn, Hon. C. J. F., Lt. 10th R. Hussars, and Staff, w. France	C.H.K.M.
1917	Winn, Hon. R. H., 2nd Lt. Grenadier Gds.	C.H.K.M.
1899	Winterbottom, A. D., D.S.O. (F) Capt. 5th Dragoon Gds., att. 18th Hussars, m. 2. France	H.D.
1909	Winterbottom, D. D., Capt. Manchester Regt. Gallipoli (k. 6.8.15)	R.C.R., C.H.K.M.
1907	Winterbottom, G. (F) Maj. Derbyshire Yeomanry, w., m. Balkans, Egypt, Gallipoli (k. 9.8.17)	J.M.D.
1908	Winterbottom, O. D., Capt. R.E., late 2nd Lt. Cameron Highlanders and Pte. London Regt., m. France	R.C.R., C.H.K.M.
1912	Winterbottom, W. R., Capt. Derbyshire Yeomanry, att. R.A.F., w. France	H. de H.
1901	Winterton, Earl, M.P. (F)(Lord Turnour at Eton), Maj. Sussex Yeomanry, att. Imp. Camel Corps, m. Arabia, Egypt, Gallipoli, Palestine	W.D., H.M.
1915	Winterton, W., 2nd Lt. R. Scots. France (k. 25.9.15)	A.C.G.H.
1886	Wisden, F., the late, Pte. R. Defence Corps, late Pte. Essex Regt. (d. 22.5.19)	C.C.J., F.D., S.A.D.
1883	Wisden, T. F. M., Maj. R. Sussex Regt. France	C.C.J.
1897	Witts, E. F. B., D.S.O., Maj. Gloucestershire Regt., m. 2. France, Balkans	F.J.T.
1902	Wodehouse, Lord, M.C. (F) Lt. 16th Lancers, and Staff, w., m. 2. France, Italy	T.C.P.
1916	Wodehouse, Hon. E., M.C., 2nd Lt. 16th Lancers. France (k. 30.3.18)	C.H.K.M.
1903	Wodehouse, Hon. P., Lt. Staff. France (d. 6.5.19)	T.C.P.
1899	Wollaston, F. H. A., D.S.O., Maj. Rifle Bde., empld. Lt.-Col. Suffolk Regt., m. 3. France, Balkans, Palestine (k. 7.3.18)	F.H.R.
1908	Wollaston, H. C., Capt. Sherwood Foresters, att. M.G.C. France	F.H.R.

1879	Wolley-Dod, A. H., Bt. Lt.-Col. R.A.	C.W.D., J.H.M.
1880	Wolley-Dod, O. C., C.B., D.S.O. Brig.-Gen. (Lancashire Fusiliers), w., m. 3. Gallipoli	C.W.D., J.H.M.
1879	Wolrige-Gordon, H. G., Maj. Cameron Highlanders, att. H.L.I. and Black Watch	E.H.
1876	Wolrige-Gordon, J. G., C.M.G., Lt.-Col. A. and S. Highlanders	E.H.
1906	Wolrige-Gordon, R., M.C., Capt. Grenadier Gds., w. 2, m. France	P.W.
1878	Wolrige-Gordon, W. G., Bt. Lt.-Col. R. Fusiliers, m. 4. France	E.H.
1899	Wolryche-Whitmore, G. C., Capt. Shropshire Yeomanry. Egypt	E.I.
1902	Wolryche-Whitmore, J. E. A., Lt. Shropshire L.I., and Staff, w. France	E.I.
1881	Wolverton, Lord (Glyn at Eton), Maj. N. Somerset Yeomanry	W.D.
1903	Wood, Rev. C. T. T., M.C., C.F., m. France	E.C.A.L.
1902	Wood, E. B., Capt. R.A.S.C., M.T., m. Mesopotamia	F.H.R.
1899	Wood, Hon. E. F. L., M.P., Maj. Yorkshire Dragoons, m. France	W.D.
1916	Wood, E. W. H., Lt. 2nd Life Gds. France	A.B.R.
1904	Wood, G. J., O.B.E., Lt. Intell. Corps, and Staff, m. 2. France	H.F.W.T.
1890	Wood, J. L., D.S.O., Capt. 18th Hussars. France (d.w. 11.6.15)	F.H.R.
1895	Wood, J. N. P., Lt.-Col. Bedfordshire Yeomanry, att. R. E. Kent Yeomanry and Lanarkshire Yeomanry	F.H.R.
1900	Wood, N. J., 2nd Lt. R.A.F.	H.F.W.T.
1896	Wood, R. B., Capt. 12th Lancers, empld. Lt.-Col. Tank Corps, and Staff, m. France, Egypt, Gallipoli (k. 21.8.18)	F.H.R.
1903	Wood, R. L., M.C., Capt. R.E., m. France	A.C.J., H.F.W.T.
1915	Woodcock, H. H. W. W., Lt. R.G.A. France	A.C.G.H.
1900	Woodhouse, H. M., Lt. Sherwood Rangers, att. Capt. R.A.F., and Staff. France, Balkans, Egypt	E.I.

1914	Woodhouse, L. M., M.C., D.F.C., Capt. Essex Yeomanry, att. R.A.F. France (k. 27.9.18)	R.S.de H.
1909	Woodhouse, R. C. H., Lt. Wallajabad L.I., att. Punjabi F.F., Indian E.F., m. Aden, Mesopotamia (d.w. 14.1.16)	J.H.M.H.
1904	Woodhouse, R. F., Lt. Northumberland Fusiliers, w. France	R.P.L.B.
1902	Woodhouse, R. P., Capt. Suffolk Yeomanry, empld. Maj. M.G.C. France, Egypt, Gallipoli, Palestine	E.I.
1911	Woodroffe, N. L., Lt. Irish Gds., m. France (k. 6.11.14)	H.Br.
1904	Woods, J. M., 2nd Lt. R.A.S.C., M.T.	H.B.
1904	Wormald, D. F. P., Capt. R.G.A., and Staff. Gallipoli, Mesopotamia (d. 4.11.18)	W.D., H.M.
1902	Wormald, G., Capt. Lancashire Fusiliers. France, Balkans (k. 14.9.16)	A.C.J., H.B.
1900	Wormald, J., M.C., Maj. K.R.R.C., and Staff, m. 2. France	A.C.J., H.B.
1909	Wormald, L. G., M.C., Capt. R.F.A. France	R.S.K.
1904	Worsley, Lord, Lt. R.H.G. France (k. 30.10.14)	S.A.D.
1905	Worsley, Lord, M.C. (Mr. Anderson-Pelham at Eton), Capt. 11th Hussars, w. France	S.A.D., P.V.B.
1910	Worsley, E. M., Capt. K.R.R.C., late Capt. Yorkshire Regt., w. 2. France, Gallipoli	A.A.S.
1908	Worsley, R. S. L., Lt. R.F.C., late 2nd Lt. R. Sussex Regt., p. France, Egypt, Gallipoli	C.H.A., P.V.B.
1909	Worsley, W. A., Capt. Yorkshire Regt., w., p. France	A.A.S.
1889	Worsley-Taylor, J., Lt.-Col. The King's Own (R. Lancaster Regt.). France	F.W.C.
1899	Wrench, J. E. L., C.M.G. (F) Maj. R.A.F., and Staff	C.H.A.
1917	Wright, A. H. N., 2nd Lt. Somerset L.I. France (k. 2.9.18)	K.S.
1911	Wright, E. G. E., M.C., 2nd Lt. Somerset L.I. France (k. 16.6.16)	F.H.R., H.de H.
1901	Wright, F. E. F., Capt. Bedfordshire Regt. France	S.R.J., H.F.W.T.
1889	Wright, H. F., Capt. R.F.A. France	J.M.E.
1914	Wright, M. T., Lt. Loyal N. Lancashire Regt., att R.F.C., p. France	V.Le N.F.

1901	Wright, R., Maj. Lincolnshire Yeomanry. w. Egypt, Palestine (k. 29.11.17)	I.J
1895	Wrottesley, Hon. W. B., Lt. S. Staffordshire Regt., late Pte. R. Fusiliers, w. France, Egypt	P.W.
1888	Wroughton, J. B., C.B., C.M.G. (F) Brig.-Gen. (R. Sussex Regt.), m. 8. France	H.G.W.
1906	Wroughton, P. M. N., Maj. Berks Yeomanry, w. Egypt, Gallipoli, Palestine (k. 19.4.17)	J.H.M.H
1900	Wyatt-Edgell, C. S. C., Maj. Devonshire Regt. France	J.M.E.
1890	Wyatt-Edgell, M. R. A., Maj. R. 1st Devon Yeomanry, att. Devonshire Regt., and Staff. France, Gallipoli, Italy	J.M.E.
1890	Wykeham-Musgrave, H. W., Lt. Gloucestershire Yeomanry, and Staff, m. Gallipoli	A.C.A.
1913	Wyld, J. W. F., M.C., Capt. Hampshire Regt., and Staff, w., m. 2. France	H.F.W.T., A.E.C.
1906	Wyndham, Hon. E. H., M.C., Capt. 1st Life Gds., m. France	A.C.B., A.M.G.
1901	Wyndham, Hon. E. S., D.S.O., Bt. Lt.-Col. 1st Life Gds., w., m. France	W.D., H.M.
1880	Wyndham, G. P., C.B., M.V.O., Col. Staff	R.A.H.M.
1895	Wyndham, Hon. H. A., Intell. Off., Staff. S.W. Africa	S.A.D.
1904	Wyndham, P. L., Lt. Coldstream Gds., and Staff. France (k. 14.9.14)	A.C.A., R.S. de H.
1893	Wyndham, Hon. W. R., Capt. Lincolnshire Yeomanry, att. 1st Life Gds. France (k. 6.11.14)	S.A.D.
1903	Wyndham-Quin, V. M., Lt. R.N. Home Waters, China Sea	J.M.E.
1872	Wyndham-Quin, W. H., C.B., D.S.O., Col. Staff. France, Balkans, Egypt	R.A.H.M.
1911	Wynne. E. H. J., Lt. Grenadier Gds. France (d.w. 16.9.16)	H.T.B., S.G.L.
1909	Wynne-Finch, J. C., M.C., Capt. (t. Maj.) Coldstream Gds., and Staff, w., m. 2. France	R.W.W.-T., C.M.W.
1911	Wynne-Finch, W. H., M.C., Capt. (t. Maj.) Scots Gds., and Staff, w. 2, m. 2. France	C.M.W.

1909	Wynne-Jones, C. L., Lt. 17th Lancers, and Staff. France	J.H.M.H
1909	Wynter, C. D., Lt. Irish Gds. France (d.w. 5.10.15)	H.E.L.
1899	Wynter, H. W., D.S.O., Bt. Lt.-Col. R.F.A., and Staff, m. 6. France	H.E.L.
1898	Wyvill, M. I., the late, Maj. Rifle Bde. (d. 6.3.16)	E.C.A.L.
1875	Yarde-Buller, Hon. W., Capt. Staff	R.A.H.M.
1903	Yeo, S. H., Capt. Devonshire Regt., w. France, Balkans	E.C.A.L.
1888	York, E., Maj. 1st R. Dragoons, att. Yorkshire Hussars, m. France	W.D.
1916	Yorke, H. C., Lt. R.G.A., w. France	H.B., R.H. de M.
1893	Yorke, R. M., C.M.G., D.S.O. (F) Brig.-Gen. (Gloucestershire Yeomanry), m. 4. Balkans, Egypt, Gallipoli	F.T.
1906	Young, B. W. M., Capt. Wiltshire Regt., and Staff. France, Balkans	A.A.S.
1896	Young, E. H., M.P., D.S.O., D.S.C. (F) Lt.-Cr. R.N.V.R., w., m. France, Balkans, N. Russia	H.E.L.
1889	Young, G., M.V.O., 2nd Lt. R.M., late Pte. H.A.C.	J.M.E.
1898	Young, H. T. L., Lt. R.A.S.C., M.T. Egypt, Palestine	T.D., F.J.T.
1902	Young, H. W., D.S.O. (F) Capt. (t. Maj.) 116th Mahrattas, I.A., and Staff, m. Arabia, India, Mesopotamia	K.S.
1905	Young, M. A., Lt. Rifle Bde., w., p. France	K.S.
1908	Young, N. E., M.C., Capt. R. Sussex Regt., late Pte. R. Fusiliers, w., p., m. France	K.S.
1911	Young-Herries, A. D. (Herries at Eton), Capt. K.O.S.B. France (k. 23.7.16)	H.F.W.T., A.E.C
1910	Younger, J. P., Capt. A. and S. Highlanders, w. France	H.T.B., S.G.L.
1877	Younger, Sir W., Bart., Maj. Lanarkshire Yeomanry	W.E.
1914	Younghusband, G. E., Lt. 11th Hussars, m. France	R.S.K.

ADDITIONAL NAMES

1911	Benson, T. G., M.B.E. (F) Capt., late Pte., R.A.S.C., M.T. France, Italy	M.D.H.
1886	Browne, A., Maj. R.A.S.C., M.T. E. Africa	C.H.
1898	Buckle, J. B., Lt. R.N.V.R.	E.L.V.
1899	Foy, K. C. S., Cpl. Rand Rifles. E. Africa	C.H.A.
1869	Heygate, W. H. B., Maj. R.F.A., att. R.G.A.	W.F.
1902	Hudson, R. S., 2nd Lt. Res. Regt. of Cav.	H.B.
1903	Knox, A. D., Lt. R.N.V.R.	K.S.
1903	Scholfield, A. F., Pte. Calcutta Port Defence, att. King George's Own Sappers and Miners, I.A. India	F.H.R.

CORRECTED ENTRIES

Brown, W. N. S., add 'the late (d. 1.8.19).'
Campbell, E. W., add 'the late (d. 4.10.20).'
Cochrane of Cults, Lord, and Egerton-Warburton, G. The Housemaster's initials should be 'F.St.J.T.' and 'H.F.W.T.' respectively.
Freeman-Thomas, Hon. I. B. For 'F.A.' read 'I.A.' and add 'India.'
Harrison, J. F. For '1906' read '1900.'
Wood, N. J. For '2nd Lt. R.A.F.' read 'Lt. R.A.F., late 2nd Lt. Res. Regt. of Cav., and Staff.'
To the entries of Bogle Smith, S., Gedge, C. B., Hindlip, Lord, Tichborne, Sir J. H. B. D., Bart., add 'France,' and in the case of Harrison, T. E., and Hindlip, Lord, 'Egypt.'

In the Libro d'Oro, any other corrections required will be made, and the names of battlefields, on which the fallen gave their lives, added.

APPENDIX
RED CROSS, Y.M.C.A., ETC.

1883	Askew, C. A. C., Hon. Maj. Serbian Army (drowned 5.10.17)	C.C.J.
1905	Atkinson, G. B., Ambulance Driver, French Red Cross. France	L.S.R.B.
1901	Barker, Rev. J. B., Motor Ambulance, Red Cross. France	J.P.C., R.P.L.B.
1888	Bevan, I., Ambulance. France, Italy, Russia	R.C.R.
1879	Bickley, B. F., Red Cross. France	H.W.M.
1915	Brooksbank, P. A., French Red Cross. France	A.E.C.
1907	Burkitt, M. C., Y.M.C.A. France	R.S. de H.
1875	Burrows, S. M., Y.M.C.A. Holland	K.S.
1876	Bury, L., French Red Cross. France	E.C.A.L.
1871	Buxton, B. H., American Red Cross. France	E.H.
1879	Cust, R. H. H., Y.M.C.A. Italy	T.H.S., E.P.R., A.C.
1881	Darbishire, H. B., Red Cross. France	E.C.A.L.
1910	Downshire, Marquess of (Earl of Hillsborough at Eton), Red Cross. France	C.H.K.M.
1878	Duncombe, Lt.-Col. C. W. E., C.B.E., Red Cross. France, Egypt	G.E.M.
1894	Fletcher, W., the late, Red Cross. France (d. 21.6.20)	T.D.
1869	Gascoigne, F. R. T. T., Red Cross and Y.M.C.A. France	T.H.S.
1880	Hill-Trevor, Hon. C. E., French Red Cross. France	F.T.
1906	Hoare, J. D. R., Red Cross. France	H.Br.
1895	Hunter, C. M., Water Expert, att. R.E. Balkans, Turkey	A.C.J.
1917	Knight, F. A., the late, French Red Cross. France (k. accid. 14.11.19)	A.A.S., F.W.D.
1885	Luard, G. M. C., French Red Cross. France	F.T., F.W.C.

1887	Malcolm, Sir I. Z., K.C.M.G., M.P., Red Cross. France, Italy, Russia	G.E.M.
1913	Murray, U. G., the late, Y.M.C.A. France (d. 17.2.19)	P.W., F.E.R.
1875	Noble, L., French Red Cross and Y.M.C.A. France	H.E.L.
1890	Noble, Rev. W. H., Y.M.C.A. France	J.M.E.
1893	Parr, R. C., Red Cross. France	E.C.A.L.
1883	Sotheby, W. E. S., Motor Ambulance, British and French Red Cross. France, Balkans	H.W.M.
1887	Spring-Rice, B. W. C., French Red Cross. France	H.E.L.
1897	Wicksteed, Rev. J. F. A., Church Army. France	K.S.
1917	Wilder, F. W., Red Cross, att. French Army. France	R.S.K.
1913	Wilder, H. A. J., Red Cross, att. French Army. France	S.G.L.

FROM THE STAFF OF ETON COLLEGE

Christie, J., Capt., M.C. (O.E.)
de Satgé, P. C. H., M.M., Maréchal-des-logis, Interprète, Mission Militaire Française, Guards Division. France
Duckworth, F. R. G., M.B.E., 2nd Lt. (t. Maj.) R.F.A., m. 2. France, Balkans
Durnford, R. S., Capt. (O.E.)
Fletcher, W. G., 2nd Lt. (O.E.)
Gladstone, C. A., Lt. (O.E.)
Headlam, G. W., Lt. (O.E.)
Hope-Jones, W., Lt. (O.E.)
Lee, H., Lt.-Col. R.A.F. France
Mason, E., 2nd Lt. Northamptonshire Regt., late Pte. R. Fusiliers. France (k. 9.5.15)
Morris, T. F., Capt. R.A.F., late Flight-Cr. R.N.A.S. Home Waters
Ovey, D., D.S.O. (F) Maj. (O.E.)
Powell, E. W., O.B.E., Lt.-Col. (O.E.)
Prior, E. F., Capt. (O.E.)
Robinson, F. L., D.S.O., M.C., Maj. R.A.F., late Lt. R.M.A., m. 2. France, Mesopotamia
Sheepshanks, A. C., D.S.O., Lt.-Col. (O.E.)
Slater, E. V., M.C., Capt. R.E., late Yorkshire Regt., w., m. France
Syson, A. E., O.B.E. (F) Maj. R.M., w., m. France, Gallipoli
Taylor, C. M. C., Lt. R. Sussex Regt., late Pte. Middlesex Regt. France
Wilkinson, C. H., M.C., Maj. (O.E.)
Wright, R. M., M.C. and Bar, Capt. Coldstream Gds., att. Gds. M.G. Regt., w. 3, m. France
Young, R. A., Capt. Yorkshire Regt., att. Northumberland Fusiliers. France

SOME STATISTICS

THE number of Etonians here recorded, according to information available up to date, is 5,650, of whom 31 are in the Appendix. Of this total, 798 did not serve overseas. The distribution is as follows:

ROYAL NAVY
R.N. (including 3 Surgeons and 2 Chaplains) 48
R.N.V.R. 105
R.M.A. 2
R.M.L.I. 8
—
163

HOME ARMY
Staff 317
Cavalry (including Household Cavalry, 140) 727
Yeomanry (including Irish Horse & King Edward's Horse, 17) 647
Remount Service 42
Royal Artillery 410
H.A.C. 7
Royal Engineers 76
Infantry (including Foot Guards 818, and Rifle Regiments, 410) 2,648
Tank Corps 9
Labour Corps 16
R. Defence Corps 34
R.A.S.C. 128
R.A.M.C. 27
R.A.O.C. 12
A.V.C. 2
Chaplains 27
R.A.P.D. 1
Sp. List 50
Red Cross (with Army rank) 3
—
5183

ROYAL AIR FORCES
136

COLONIAL, EGYPTIAN AND INDIAN CONTINGENTS
African 33
Australian 7
Canadian 25
Egyptian 1
Indian 49
New Zealand 1
—
116

ALLIED ARMIES
American 9
French 4
Greek 2
Italian 5
Russian 1
—
21

RED CROSS, Etc.
31

'Staff' in the above enumeration includes all generals of every grade, and those officers whose duties are shown as 'Staff' without mention of any regiment.

The unit mentioned first in the War List is that which is counted, and if anyone was in the R.F.C. or R.N.A.S. only, he is included in the R.A.F.

Of Lt.-Cols. and officers of higher rank, the numbers are as follows:

Admirals	2	Generals	3	Cols. and Bt. Cols.	90
		Lieut.-Gens.	12		
Field-Marshals	2	Maj.-Gens.	43	Lt.-Cols.	666
		Brig.-Gens.	151		

CASUALTIES

Died	1,157	Wounded	1,467	Prisoners	130

MENTIONED IN DISPATCHES

1,669

HONOURS AWARDED

V.C.	13	K.C.V.O.	7	M.C.	744 (including M.C. and Bar, 37; M.C. and two Bars, 4)
G.C.B.	3	C.V.O.	3		
K.C.B.	18	M.V.O.	21		
C.B.	76	K.B.E.	5		
C.S.I.	1	C.B.E.	69	D.S.C.	10 (including D.S.C. and Bar, 1)
G.C.M.G.	3	O.B.E.	187		
K.C.M.G.	21	M.B.E.	31	A.F.C.	16
C.M.G.	170	D.S.O.	548 (including D.S.O. and Bar, 44; D.S.O. and two Bars, 4)	D.F.C.	4
G.C.I.E.	1			D.C.M.	1
K.C.I.E.	1			M.M.	2
C.I.E.	4			Albert Medal	1
G.C.V.O.	4			T.D.	35
				Total	1999

Number of officers who have received Foreign Decorations   591

The following Etonians, who otherwise would probably have been fighting in the War, were interned as civilians at Ruhleben:

1912	Balfour, J.	C.H.K.M.
1914	Belmont, A. S.	P.W., F.E.R.
1913	Cottrell Dormer, T.	J.H.M.H.
1910	Kearley, Hon. M. H.	M.D.H.
1906	Kindersley, R. F.	K.S.
1910	Pemberton, C. G.	K.S.
1909	Phillip, W. T.	C.H.A., A.B.R.

FLOREAT ETONA

Compiler:	E. L. Vaughan
	of The Marches, Willowbrook, Eton
Publishers:	P. H. Lee Warner
	G. W. Howard
	N. de Grey (O.E.)
Production Assistant:	C. H. Busby
Proof Readers:	W. G. Lingley
	T. A. Till
Engravers:	H. G. Williams
	O. J. Fender
Compositors:	S. W. Hartley
	W. McFarlane
	A. G. Redman
Machine Manager:	T. C. Byford

PRINTED PRIVATELY FOR ETON COLLEGE
IN THE RICCARDI PRESS FOUNT BY PHILIP
LEE WARNER, PUBLISHER TO THE MEDICI
SOCIETY LIMITED, VII GRAFTON
STREET, LONDON, W
MDCCCC
XXI

LIST OF ETONIANS WHO
FOUGHT IN THE GREAT
WAR MCMXIV-MCMXIX

ETONIANS
WHO
FOUGHT IN
THE GREAT
WAR
MCMXIV
MCMXIX

THE LIBRARY
UNIVERSITY OF CALIFORNIA
Santa Barbara

THIS BOOK IS DUE ON THE LAST DATE
STAMPED BELOW.

Series 9482

There is given in the following pages information as to the places where the one thousand and thirty-one Etonians, whose deaths are attributable to enemy action, were killed or received a fatal wound.

> "IF OUR TIME BE COME,
> LET US DIE MANFULLY
> FOR OUR BRETHREN, AND
> LET US NOT STAIN OUR
> HONOUR."

FRANCE, 1914

Ainsworth, Lt. J. S.	Meteren	Burn, 2nd Lt. A. H. R.	Hollebeke
Alexander, Lt.-Col. R.	Armentières	Cadogan, Maj. Hon. W. G. S.	Ypres
Allgood, Capt. B.	Armentières	Cameron, Capt. A. G.	The Aisne
Anderson, 2nd Lt. G. R. L.	Hooge	Campbell, Lt. A. W. G.	The Aisne
Annesley, Sub-Lt. Earl	French Coast	Campbell, Lt. G. A.	Gheluvelt
Annesley, Capt. Hon. A.	Klein Zillebeke	Cathcart, Capt. A. E.	The Aisne
Anstruther, Lt. J. A. St. C.	Zandvoorde	Cavendish, Maj. Lord J. S.	
Antrobus, Lt. E.	Kruiseecke	Cecil, Capt. Hon. W. A.	Soupir
Baillie, 2nd Lt. Sir G. G. S., Bt.	The Marne	Chance, Lt. G. O. de P.	Menin
Baird, Capt. W. F. G.	Neuve Chapelle	Charlton, Lt. St. J. A.	Festubert
Balfour, Capt. R. F.	Gheluvelt	Charrington, Capt. A. C.	Ypres
Banbury, Capt. C. W.	Soupir	Cholmeley, Capt. Sir M. A. R., Bt.	
Barrett, Capt. C. J. C.	Hooge		Festubert
Beauchamp, Lt. E. A.	Givenchy	Colby, Maj. L. R. V.	Ypres
Benson, Lt.-Col. R. E.	The Aisne	Coleridge, 2nd Lt. L. F. R.	Givenchy
Berners, Capt. H. H.	The Aisne	Compton-Thornhill, Lt. R. A.	The Aisne
Bingham, Lt. D. C.	The Aisne	Congleton, Lt. Lord	Klein Zillebeke
Blacklock, 2nd Lt. A. H.	Le Maisnel	Cook, Lt.-Col. E. B.	Messines
Blake, Lt. M. F.	The Aisne	Cottrell-Dormer, Lt. C.	Ypres
Boden, Maj. A. D.	The Aisne	Crichton, Lt.-Col. Visc.	Wytschaete
Boscawen, 2nd Lt. Hon. V. D.	Gheluvelt	Crichton, Maj. H. F.	Villers-Cotterets
Bowes-Lyon, Lt. C. L. C.	Ypres	Cronk, 2nd Lt. W. G.	Zonnebeke
Bradford, Lt.-Col. Sir E. R., Bt.	Soissons	Crum-Ewing, 2nd Lt. A.	Givenchy
Brooke, Lt. G.	The Aisne	Dawnay, Maj. Hon. H.	Ypres
Brown, Capt. G. Hargreaves	Gheluvelt	Dawson, Capt. R. L.	Zillebeke
Browning, Capt. C. H.	Le Cateau	de Gunzburg, 2nd Lt. Baron	Ypres
Browning, Maj. J. A.	Messines	de Winton, 2nd Lt. W.	The Marne
Bulkeley, Capt. T. H. R.	Zonnebeke	Douglas-Pennant, Lt. Hon. A. G. S.	
Buller, Capt. L. M.	Frameries		Kruiseecke
Burleigh, Capt. Master of	Le Cateau	Douglas-Pennant, Lt. Hon. C.	Gheluvelt

Drake, Lt. R. F.	Zonnebeke
Duff, Lt. Sir R. G. V., Bt.	Oostnieuwkerke
Eastwood, Lt. F. M.	Gheluvelt
Eden, Lt. J.	Wervick
V.C. FitzClarence, Brig.-Gen. C.	Ypres
FitzGerald, Capt. G. H.	The Aisne
Fletcher, 2nd Lt. R. W.	Veldhoek
Foley, Lt. T. A. F.	Festubert
Foljambe, Maj. H. F. F. B.	Troyon
Forster, Capt. F. A.	Mons
Forster, 2nd Lt. J.	Noyon
Forster, Capt. L. A.	Violaines
Fowler, Lt. J. D.	Hollebeke
Freeman-Thomas, 2nd Lt. Hon. G. F.	Soissons
Garstin, 2nd Lt. C. W. N.	Audregnies
Gibbs, 2nd Lt. R. C. M.	Ypres
Gilliat, Capt. O. C. S.	Ypres
Gordon-Duff, Capt. L.	
Gordon-Lennox, Maj. Lord B. C.	Zillebeke
Gough, Capt. E. J. F.	Bethune
Grenfell, Capt. R. N.	Mons
Grosvenor, Capt. Lord H. W.	Zandvoorde
Guernsey, Capt. Lord	The Aisne
Gwyer, Capt. A. G.	Wytschaete
Hamilton, Maj. Hon. L. d'H.	Gheluvelt
Hardman, 2nd Lt. F. McM.	Neuve Chapelle
Harvey, 2nd Lt. D. L.	
Harvey, 2nd Lt. F. L.	Messines
Hay, Capt. Lord A. V.	The Aisne
Heath, Lt. V. P.	Néry
Herringham, Capt. G. W.	Messines
Hogg, Lt.-Col. I. G.	Haramont
Holbech, Lt. W. H.	Kruiseecke
Hollings, Lt. J. H. B.	Messines
Hoskyns, Lt. E. C. L.	Ypres
Houldsworth, Lt. W. G.	Vendresse
Inigo-Jones, Lt. H. R.	The Aisne
Innes-Cross, 2nd Lt. S. M.	
Johnstone, Lt. R. F. L.	The Marne
Kelly, Capt. E. D. F.	Zandvoorde
Kennedy, Capt. A. E.	Le Cateau
Kinloss, Capt. Master of	Ploegsteert
Kinnaird, Capt. Master of	Zonnebeke
Lambton, 2nd Lt. Hon. F.	Zandvoorde
Lambton, Lt. G.	Villers-Cotterets
Landale, Lt. D. B.	Armentières
Lawrence, 2nd Lt. C. H.	
Lawson, Lt. W. B. W.	Steenstraate
Leatham, Lt. E. H.	Hollebeke
Lee-Steere, Lt. J. H. G.	Ypres
Legge-Bourke, Lt. N. W. H.	Ypres
Leslie, Capt. N. J. B.	Armentières
Levinge, Lt. Sir R. W., Bt.	Ypres
Levita, Lt. F. E.	Mont-des-Cats
Lloyd, Capt. M. E.	
Lloyd, Lt.-Col. W. R.	Troyon
Lockwood, 2nd Lt. R. W. M.	Soupir
Loder-Symonds, Maj. J. F. L.	
Lonsdale, Lt. J. R. McC.	Godewaersvelde
Loyd, Lt. G. A.	Zonnebeke
Lucas-Tooth, Capt. D. K. L.	Vendresse
Lucas-Tooth, Capt. S.	Le Touquet
Lumley, 2nd Lt. R. J.	Ploegsteert
Lumsden, Capt. C. R.	Mons
MacDougall, Capt. I.	Villers-Cotterets
McGrigor, 2nd Lt. J. N. G.	Fauquissart
Mackinnon, 2nd Lt. A. H., Younger of	Vendresse
McMahon, Lt.-Col. N. R.	Ypres
Macnaghten, Lt. A. C. R. S.	Gheluvelt
Manners, Lt. Hon. J. N.	Villers-Cotterets
Marker, Lt.-Col. R. J.	Hooge
Maxwell, Lt.-Col. A. E.	Antwerp
Monck, Capt. Hon. C. H. S.	St. Julien
Monckton, Lt. F. A.	Hooge
Mulholland, Capt. Hon. A. E. S.	Ypres
Murray, Capt. F. W. S.	
Murray-Smith, Lt. A. G.	Warneton
Nairne, Maj. Lord C. M.	Klein Zillebeke
Naylor-Leyland, Lt. G. V.	Soissons
Nicholl, 2nd Lt. J. W. H.	Ypres
Norman, Maj. H. H.	Ypres
Ogilvy, Lt. Sir G. N., Bt.	Ypres
O'Neill, Capt. Hon. A. E. B.	Ypres
Paley, Maj. G.	Hooge
Parker, Capt. A. E.	Ploegsteert
Payne-Gallwey, Capt. W. T.	Troyon
Pickersgill-Cunliffe, 2nd Lt. J. R.	The Marne
Pleydell-Bouverie, Lt. J. E.	Gheluvelt
Pollock, Lt. F. R.	Langemarck
Rastrick, Lt. U.	La Bassée
Rennie, Capt. G.	Kruiseecke
Rickman, Maj. S. H.	Le Cateau
Robson, Capt. R. G. G.	Rue-du-Bois
Rose, Capt. Sir F. S. D., Bt.	
St. Aubyn, 2nd Lt. Hon. P. S.	Gheluvelt
St. Clair, Capt. Hon. C. H. M.	Festubert

St. George, 2nd Lt. H. A. B.	Zillebeke	Tudway, Lt. H. R. C.	Ypres
Smith, Lt. A. L. Eric	Wytschaete	Tufnell, Lt. C. W.	Ypres
Smith, Lt. B. R. Winthrop	Ypres	Turnor, Lt. C. R.	Zandvoorde
Smith, Lt. Granville K. F.	Gheluvelt	Vandeleur, Capt. A. M.	Zandvoorde
Smith, 2nd Lt. J. H. Martin	Naugis	Van Neck, Lt. P.	Kruiseecke
Smith, 2nd Lt. J. H. Michael	The Marne	Walker, Capt. C. C.	Le Cateau
Soames, Lt. H. M.	Mons	Walker, Capt. E. W.	Armentières
Somerset, 2nd Lt. N. A. H.	Ypres	Walker, Capt. O. B.	Mons
Sprot, Lt. I. B.		Walker, Maj. W. B.	Ypres
Stafford-King-Harman, Capt. E. C.	Klein Zillebeke	Walmesley, Lt. R.	Ypres
		Walter, 2nd Lt. Sydney	Kruiseecke
Stephen, Capt. A. A. L.	Gheluvelt	Ward, Lt. Hon. G. E. F.	Zandvoorde
Stephen, Capt. D. C. L.	The Marne	Welby, Maj. G. E. E.	Vendresse
Stewart, Capt. Bertrand	The Marne	Welby, Lt. R. W. G.	Cour-de-Soupir
Stewart, Capt. G.	Ginchy	Wellesley, Capt. Lord R.	Kruiseecke
Stewart-Murray, Maj. Lord G.	The Aisne	Whitaker, Capt. H.	Laventie
Stirling-Stuart, Lt. J.	Ypres	Williams-Wynn, 2nd Lt. C. W.	Ypres
Stocks, Lt. M. G.	Ypres	Wilson, Lt.-Col. G. C.	Zillebeke
Stucley, Maj. H. St. L.	Gheluvelt	Windsor-Clive, 2nd Lt. Hon. A.	Landrecies
Swetenham, Maj. F.	St. Quentin		
Taylor-Whitehead, 2nd Lt. G. E.	Longueval	Winn, Capt. A.	Soissons
		Woodroffe, Lt. N. L.	Klein Zillebeke
Tollemache, 2nd Lt. B. D.	Givenchy	Worsley, Lt. Lord	Zandvoorde
Tristram, Capt. L. B. C.	Bethune	Wyndham, Lt. P. L.	The Aisne
Trotter, Lt. A.	Festubert	Wyndham, Capt. Hon. W. R.	

FRANCE, 1915

Ackerley, Lt. R. H.	Festubert	Boles, 2nd Lt. H. F.	
Agar-Robartes, Capt. Hon. T. C. R.	Loos	Bonvalot, 2nd Lt. E. St. L.	
Anson, Lt. A.	Hohenzollern Redoubt	Bowes-Lyon, Capt. Hon. F.	Loos
Arbuthnot, Capt. A. H.	St. Julien	Bowlby, Capt. G. V. S.	Ypres
Armstrong, 2nd Lt. E. W	Poperinghe	Brabourne, Lt. Lord	Neuve Chapelle
Armstrong, 2nd Lt. G. C.	Cuinchy	Bromley, Lt. H. A.	Ypres
Atkinson, Capt. W. H. J. St. L.	Ypres	Brooksbank, Capt. S.	Loos
Bacon, 2nd Lt. D. F. C.	Hohenzollern Redoubt	Brooman-White, 2nd Lt. R. G.	Ypres
		Bryant, Capt. H. G.	St. Julien
Bailey, 2nd Lt. Hon. G. S.	Menin Road	Buckland, Lt. T. A.	Hohenzollern Redoubt
Barnett, 2nd Lt. C. F. R.	Ploegsteert		
Barrington-Kennett, Bt. Maj. B. H.	Festubert	Bulkeley, Capt. C. I. R.	Festubert
		Bull, Lt. R. E. B.	Festubert
Batchelor, L.'ce-Cpl. G. A.	St. Eloi	Burbury, 2nd Lt. J. F.	Ypres
Beech, Lt. R. A. J.	Ypres	Burness, Lt. A. R.	Ypres
Benson, Lt. H. C.	Hooge	Burrell, 2nd Lt. R. F. T.	Loos
Bentall, 2nd Lt. E. H.	Hulluch	Bury, Capt. E. W.	Fleurbaix
Bibby, Lt. J. Patrick	Neuve Chapelle	Bury, 2nd Lt. H. S. E.	La Bassée
Bigge, Capt. Hon. J. N.	Festubert	Campbell, 2nd Lt. H. B.	Ypres
Birchall, Capt. A. P.	Pilckem Ridge	Campbell, Capt. Hon. J. B.	Cuinchy
Blacker, 2nd Lt. J. R.	Vermelles	Campbell, Maj. W. R.	Hooge
Blane, Lt. M. G. S.	Loos	Chaplin, Lt.-Col. C. S.	Hooge
Blofeld, 2nd Lt. F. D'A.	Ypres	Chapman, Capt. A. H. D.	Loos

Charteris, 2nd Lt. Hon. I. A.	Loos
Chetwynd-Stapylton, Capt. H. M.	Ypres
Cholmondeley, Capt. R.	Chocques
Clowes, Lt. C. G. E.	St. Eloi
Compton, Lt. Lord S. D.	Verlorenhoek
Corbet, Lt. Sir R. J., Bt.	Givenchy
Corkran, 2nd Lt. R. S.	Festubert
Cottrell-Dormer, Lt. C. M.	La Bassée
Court, Capt. W. H. R.	Hooge
Crossley, Lt. B.	Richebourg-l'Avoué
Cuthbert, Capt. J. H.	Loos
Darby, Lt. M. A. A.	
Davies, 2nd Lt. G. L.	Voormezeele
Davson, Lt. T. G.	Ypres
Derriman, Capt. G. L.	Cambrin
Dimsdale, Capt. E. C.	
Douglas-Pennant, Capt. Hon. G. H.	Neuve Chapelle
Drummond, Capt. S. H.	Hooge
Duberly, Maj. G. W.	Neuve Chapelle
Duff, 2nd Lt. B. P.	Loos
Durnford, Capt. R. S.	Hooge
Earle, Lt. J. V.	
Eden, Lt. Hon. W. A. M.	St. Eloi
Edwards, Capt. A. C.	Loos
Edwards, Capt. A. N.	Ypres
Edwards, Lt. H. L. G.	Festubert
Egerton, Lt. A. G. E.	Loos
Egerton, Maj. G. A.	Ypres
Egerton-Warburton, Capt. J.	
Ethelston, Lt. H. W.	Neuve Chapelle
Evans-Freke, Lt.-Col. Hon. P. C.	Ypres
Faber, 2nd Lt. C. V.	Hooge
Fairbairn, Lt. G. E.	
Fardell, Lt. H. G. H.	Zonnebeke
Farmer, 2nd Lt. H. C. M.	Ypres
Farmer, Capt. H. G.	Loos
Farquhar, Lt.-Col. F. D.	St. Eloi
Fisher-Rowe, Lt.-Col. L. R.	Neuve Chapelle
Fletcher, 2nd Lt. W. G.	Bois Grenier
Forster, Capt. H.C.	Bellewarde Lake
Foster, 2nd Lt. A. C.	Neuve Chapelle
Fowler, Lt. G. G.	Loos
France-Hayhurst, Lt.-Col. F. C.	Richebourg-l'Avoué
Fremantle, 2nd Lt. T. F. H.	Bellewarde Farm
Garnett-Botfield, Lt. A. C. F.	Richebourg-l'Avoué
Gathorne-Hardy, Capt. A. C.	Loos
Gedge, 2nd Lt. C. B.	Loos
Gelderd-Somervell, 2nd Lt. R. F. C.	Neuve Chapelle
George, Capt. W. K.	La Bassée
Gibbs, Capt. E. L.	Ypres
Gladstone, Lt. W. G. C.	Laventie
Gledstanes, Capt. S. A.	St. Eloi
Godman, 2nd Lt. W. W. W.	Richebourg-l'Avoué
V.C. Gough, Brig.-Gen. Sir J. E.	Fauquissart
Grahame Stewart, 2nd Lt. J. C.	Loos
Green, Cpl. H. B.	Ypres
Gregory, Lt. G. F.	Loos
V.C. Grenfell, Capt. F. O.	Ypres
Grenfell, 2nd Lt. Hon. G. W.	Hooge
Grenfell, Capt. Hon. J. H. F.	Ypres
Gunter, Lt. F. J.	Hooge
Gwynne, 2nd Lt. R. T. S.	Le Touquet
Hamilton-Fletcher, 2nd Lt. G.	Givenchy
Hardy, Capt. R. M.	Hooge
Hargreaves, Capt. A. K.	Fromelles
Harrison, Maj. C. E.	Neuve Chapelle
Helyar, Capt. M. H.	Arras
Henderson, Capt. A. S.	
Henriques, 2nd Lt. P. B.	Ypres
Hoare, 2nd Lt. P. H. T.	Armentières
Hoare, Maj. V. R.	Ypres
Hobson, Lt. A. C.	Ypres
Hodgson, Capt. M. R. K.	Ypres
Hornung, 2nd Lt. A. O.	Ypres
Houstoun-Boswall, Capt. Sir G. R., Bt.	Loos
Howard, 2nd Lt. Hon. R. H. P.	Ypres
Hulse, Capt. Sir E. H. W., Bt.	Neuve Chapelle
Hulton-Harrop, Lt. H. de L.	
Huth, Capt. A. H.	Ypres
Inglis, Lt. J. A. C.	Neuve Chapelle
Ionides, Lt. A. C.	Ypres
Johnson, Bt. Maj. H. C.	Le Cateau
Johnston, Lt. G. S.	Hooge
Johnstone, 2nd Lt. J. A.	Bailleul
Keating, Lt. H. S.	La Bassée
Kekewich, Capt. A. St. J. M.	Loos
Kekewich, Capt. J.	Loos
King, Lt. N. W. R.	Ypres
Knott, Capt. H. B.	Bois Carré
Lawrence, Lt. M. E.	Cuinchy
Lawrence, 2nd Lt. O. J.	Festubert
Le Blanc-Smith, Lt. C. R.	Ypres

Lee Lee, 2nd Lt. L. C	
Legard, Lt. R. J.	Merville
Liebert, Maj. B. R.	Ypres
Lowry-Corry, Lt. F. R. H.	Ypres
Lumsden, Capt. B. N.	Ypres
Macculloch, Lt. S. H.	
McDonnell, Maj. Hon. Sir S. K.	Ypres
Maclachlan, Capt. K. D. M.	Ypres
Maclagan, Lt. G. S.	Pilckem Ridge
Makins, Capt. H.	Ypres
Marks, Capt. C. H.	St. Quentin
Marshall, Lt. F. G.	La Bassée
Marsham-Townshend, 2nd Lt. F.	Festubert
Martin, Lt. C. H. G.	Ypres
Maude, 2nd Lt. J. W. A.	Laventie
Meysey-Thompson, Capt. Hon. C. H. M.	Ypres
Middleton, Capt. W. A. A.	St. Julien
Mills, 2nd Lt. Hon. C. T.	Loos
Mitchell-Innes, Lt. G. R	Ypres
Mitford, Maj. Hon. C. B. O.	Ypres
Molineux-Montgomerie, Maj. G. F.	Loos
Monckton, Lt. G. V. F.	Cuinchy
Monk, Capt. G. P. de B.	Loos
Moon, 2nd Lt. B. O.	Festubert
Moulton, Lt. C. E.	Festubert
Mount, Capt. F.	Loos
Murray, 2nd Lt. C. William	Bellewarde Farm
Murray, Capt. R. A. C.	Neuve Chapelle
Murray-Smith, Lt. G.	Vermelles
Musgrave, Lt. T.	La Bassée
Nash, Capt. E. R.	Ypres
Nash, Capt. L. C.	Loos
Naylor, Lt. R. E.	Festubert
Neave, Maj. A.	Ypres
Newall, 2nd Lt. L.	
Newton, Capt. D. O. C.	Dickebusch
Nickalls, Brig.-Gen. N. T.	Loos
Northland, Capt. Visc.	Cuinchy
Nugent, Brig.-Gen. G. C.	La Bassée
Orde-Powlett, Lt. W. P.	Ypres
Osmond-Williams, Lt. O. T. D.	Loos
Parker, 2nd Lt. Cyril E.	Cuinchy
Parker, Capt. E. D.	Neuve Eglise
Penn, Capt. E. F.	Loos
Penn, 2nd Lt. G. M.	Ploegsteert
Perssé, 2nd Lt. R. A.	Cuinchy
Philipps, Capt. Hon. C. E. A.	Ypres
Phillipps, 2nd Lt. R. W.	Hulluch
Phillips, 2nd Lt. E. E. L.	Albert
Playfair, Capt. Hon. L. G. H. Lyon	Ypres
Pollock, Lt. M. V.	
Ponsonby, Capt. A. W. N.	Givenchy
Powell, 2nd Lt. R. H.	Richebourg-l'Avoué
Pratt, Lt. G. C. S.	Houplines
Pryce, Capt. H. B. Mostyn	St. Eloi
Pryor, Lt. R. S.	St. Julien
Radcliffe, Capt. J. D. H.	Hooge
Radclyffe, Lt.-Col. C. E.	Hulluch
Rawdon-Hastings, Capt. P. C. J. R.	Loos
Rawson, 2nd Lt. P. C.	Loos
Reynolds, Lt. J. E.	Gravenstafel
Richmond, Capt. H. C.	La Bassée
Riley, Capt. A. C.	Loos
Robertson-Ross, Capt. P. M.	Loos
Robinson, 2nd Lt. Hon. H. E. J.	Loos
Robinson, Maj. H. I.	Hohenzollern Redoubt
Robinson, 2nd Lt. R. F.	Hooge
Rolleston, 2nd Lt. F. L.	Armentières
Ross, Lt. W. M.	Neuve Chapelle
Rycroft, Capt. H. F.	
Samson, Capt. A. L.	Loos
Sandeman, Capt. G. A. C.	Ypres
Sartorius, Capt. E. F. F.	Neuve Chapelle
Scrimgeour, Lt. M.	Hooge
Scudamore, 2nd Lt. J.	Loos
Senhouse, 2nd Lt. O. W. Pocklington	Cambrin
Seymour, Lt. F.	Hooge
Shennan, Lt. D. F. F.	Ypres
Sim, Lt. H. A. C.	Fromelles
Skrine, Capt. H. L.	Hooge
Smallwood, Pte. A. P.	Ypres
Smith, 2nd Lt. C. J. Dudley	Givenchy
Smith, Lt. G. L. l.	
Smith, 2nd Lt. R.	Loos
Smith, Lt.-Col. W. R. Abel	Festubert
Somers-Smith, 2nd Lt. R. W.	Hooge
Sotheby, 2nd Lt. L. F. S.	Aubers Ridge
Spencer, Capt. H. M.	St. Julien
Stacpoole, Lt. G. E. G.	Ypres
Steele, Lt.-Col. G. F.	Hooge
Stracey, Capt. R. G.	Cuinchy
Sutton, Lt. H. J.	Loos
Swire, 2nd Lt. A. G.	
Tarver, Pte. P. E.	Neuve Chapelle
Tennant, 2nd Lt. C. A. R.	Aubers Ridge
Thesiger, Maj.-Gen. G. H.	Loos
Thorne, Capt. T. F. J. N.	Loos

Thornton, Lt. R. W.	Hooge	Wasbrough, 2nd Lt. W. L.	Loos
Thursby, Capt. A. D.	St. Eloi	Watney, Lt. W. H.	Fromelles
Timmis, 2nd Lt. R. S.	Bellewarde Lake	Wendover, Lt. Visc.	Ypres
Tower, Lt. C. C.	Loos	West, Capt. L. R. E.	Givenchy
Trefusis, Brig.-Gen. Hon. J. F. H.-S.-F.-		Williams, 2nd Lt. H. E. E.	Laventie
Trotter, 2nd Lt. K. S.	Ypres	Williams, Lt. R. A. W.	Ypres
Trotter, Capt. R. B.	Festubert	Willock, Capt. G. C. B.	Loos
Turton, Lt. E. S.	Ypres	Willyams, Sergt.-Maj. A. H. V.	Festubert
Twining, Capt. C. F. H.	Ypres	Wilson, Lt. C. F.	Ypres
Tylden-Pattenson, Lt. A. D.	Richebourg-St. Vaast	Wilson, Lt. D. C.	
		Wilson, Lt. R. E.	Hooge
Upton, Capt. Hon. E. E. M. J.	Rue-du-Bois	Wingfield, Capt. C. J. T. R.	Ypres
Vansittart, 2nd Lt. A. B.	Ypres	Winterton, 2nd Lt. W.	Loos
Wakeman, 2nd Lt. E. O. R.	Festubert	Wood, Capt. J. L.	Hooge
Warner, Lt. C. J.	Festubert	Wynter, Lt. C. D.	Loos

FRANCE, 1916

Aspinall, Lt.-Col. R. L.	Thiepval	Campion, Maj. E.	Ypres
Austen-Cartmell, Lt. A. J.	Vimy Ridge	Cazalet, 2nd Lt. E.	Ginchy
Austen-Cartmell, Lt. G. H.	Beaumont Hamel	Chapman, 2nd Lt. D. A. J.	The Somme
		Chattaway, 2nd Lt. P. S.	Thiepval
Bagot, 2nd Lt. E. L. H.	Ginchy	Chinnery, Lt. H. B.	Monchy-le-Preux
Bailey, 2nd Lt. A. Y.	Delville Wood	Cholmeley, Lt. H. L.	Beaumont Hamel
Bailie, Maj. T. M. D.	Ginchy	Cholmeley, 2nd Lt. H. V.	St. Jean
Baird, Capt. C. E.	Beaumont Hamel	Christy, 2nd Lt. B. R. F.	Lesbœufs
Ballance, Capt. L. A.	Flers	Christy, Lt. S. E. F.	Ypres
Bannatyne, Capt. J. F.	Merville	Clerke, Lt. F. W. T.	Lesbœufs
Barclay, Maj. G. W.	Ypres	Clive, Capt. Visc.	The Somme
Baring, Lt.-Col. Hon. G. V.	Martinpuich	Cockerell, 2nd Lt. A. P.	Mametz Wood
Barrington-Kennett, Maj. V. A.	Serre	Coles, Lt. A. N.	Delville Wood
Beech, Capt. R. C.	Lesbœufs	Combe, Lt. G. H. R.	The Ancre
Berridge, 2nd Lt. W. E.	Delville Wood	V.C. Congreve, Bt. Maj. W. La T.	
Bewicke-Copley, Capt. R. L. C.	Combles	Cooper, Sergt. H. A.	
Bibby, 2nd Lt. F. S.	High Wood	Corbett, Flight-Sub-Lt. Hon. A. C.	Maricourt L'Abbé
Birchall, Capt. E. V. D.	Pozières		
Bircham, Lt.-Col. H. F. W.	Pozières	Cubitt, Capt. H. A.	Flers
Boswell, Capt. W. G. K.		Cuninghame, Capt. A. K. S.	Lesbœufs
Bowlby, Lt. L. H. S.	Dickebusch	Cunliffe, Maj. Sir F. H. E., Bt.	The Somme
Bradshaw, Lt. R. E. K.		Dale, 2nd Lt. R. C.	Guillemont
Bradshaw, 2nd Lt. W. D.	Albert	Darley, 2nd Lt. D. J.	
Brassey, Lt.-Col. H. E.	Ovillers	Davies, Lt. R. H. S.	Boiselle
Brocklebank, Capt. T. G.	Maricourt	Deighton, Capt. G. W.	Ovillers
Buck, Lt. B. F.	Hamel	Dewhurst, Lt. G. C. L.	The Somme
Buller, Lt.-Col. H. C.	Sanctuary Wood	Dickens, Maj. C. C.	Leuze Wood
Burton, Lt. G. E. E.		Dilbéroglue, Lt. R. N.	Ginchy
Butterworth, Lt. G. S. K.	The Somme	Drury-Lowe, Capt. W. D.	
Buxton, Lt. H. F.		Dunn, 2nd Lt. J. H. M.	Pozières
Cairnes, Maj. A. B.	Ginchy	Edmonstone, Lt. W. G.	Ginchy
Campbell, Lt. D.	Cuinchy	Edwardes, Capt. G. D'A.	Mametz Wood
Campbell, Maj. M. I. M.	Guillemont	Edwards, 2nd Lt. G. O. C.	Contalmaison

Egerton, Capt. E. B.	Arras
Egerton-Green, Lt. C. S.	Loos
Ellicott, 2nd Lt. F. A. J.	Bernafay Wood
Ellis, Capt. F. B.	The Somme
Farmer, Lt. C. G. E.	The Somme
Farquhar, Maj. J. E. M.	Martinpuich
Fergusson, Lt. D. H. L.	Givenchy
Feversham, Lt.-Col. Earl of	The Somme
Filmer, Capt. Sir R. M., Bt.	Merville
Finlay, 2nd Lt. E. N. A.	Festubert
Fitton, Brig.-Gen. H. G.	Poperinghe
Frere, Lt. B. L. S.	Beaumont Hamel
Frere, 2nd Lt. E.	Vimy Ridge
Garth, L/ce-Cpl. H.	Thiepval
Garton, Capt. H. W.	The Somme
Gillies, 2nd Lt. H. G.	Serre
Gold, Lt. C. A.	Ovillers
Goodfellow, 2nd Lt. E. A. F.	Ypres
Goodford, Lt. C. J. H.	The Somme
Goschen, Capt. C. G.	Lesbœufs
Gough, Lt. H. S.	Ypres
Graham, Capt. A. C.	Ginchy
Grant, 2nd Lt. A. F. M.	Bailleul
Greenfield, Lt. R. W.	Le Transloy
Gregge-Hopwood, Capt. R. G.	
Gunnis, Capt. G. G.	Lesbœufs
Hall, Capt. F. G.	
Hall, Capt. P. S. B.	Ypres
Hammond-Chambers, Capt. H. B. B.	The Somme
Hargreaves, Capt. L. R.	Lesbœufs
Hartley, Lt. D'A. J. J.	Bazentin Wood
Heyworth, Brig.-Gen. F. J.	Ypres
Higgins, 2nd Lt. C. G.	Thiepval
Hills, 2nd Lt. C. H.	Delville Wood
Hoare, Capt. R. L.	Gommecourt
Holland, 2nd Lt. E.	Ginchy
Hopwood, Lt. R. H.	Bethune
Hudson, Lt. J. H.	
Hudson-Kinahan, Lt. D. D.	Ypres
Huntington, 2nd Lt. G. W.	
Impey, Lt. J. E.	St. Eloi
Jackson, Capt. B. R.	Ginchy
Johnstone, Capt. F. J. L.	High Wood
Joicey-Cecil, Lt. J. F. J.	Lesbœufs
Keele, Capt. C. A.	Poperinghe
Kelly, Lt.-Cr. F. S.	Beaucourt-sur-Ancre
Knott, Maj. J. L.	Fricourt
Lambart, Capt. G. E. O. F.	St. Eloi
Lane, Capt. G. R.	Guinchy
Lawrence, Capt. M. C.	The Somme
Lees, Lt. J. M.	Guillemont
Llangattock, Maj. Lord	The Somme
Lloyd, Capt. M. K. A.	The Somme
Lushington, Lt. S. E. J. C.	The Somme
Lynch, Lt.-Col. C. W. D.	Fricourt
McEwen, Lt. J. R. D.	Bullecourt
Mackenzie, Capt. A. K.	Ginchy
Macnaghten, 2nd Lt. Sir E. H., Bt.	Hamel
Madan, Lt. N. C.	Ypres
Marchant, 2nd Lt. F. G. W.	Flers
Master, Lt. G. G. O.	Bouzincourt
Matthews, Capt. M. L. W.	The Somme
Matthey, A.B., J. T.	
Meade, 2nd Lt. R. P.	The Somme
Monckton, 2nd Lt. C.	Mons-en-Chaussée
Moorsom, Lt. A. E.	The Somme
Morris, Lt.-Col. T. H. P.	Loos
Napier, Capt. L. R. M.	Pozières
Newton, Lt. C. H. F. A.	Ypres
Norbury, Lt. P. G.	The Somme
Norrie, 2nd Lt. G. S. M.	Goudecourt
Noyes, Capt. T. R. A. H.	Albert
Ord, Lt. O. R.	Lesbœufs
Orr-Ewing, Capt. E. P.	Ginchy
Parnell, Lt. Hon. W. A. D.	Lesbœufs
Parry-Crooke, Pte. L. W.	Delville Wood
Peake, Lt. R.	Bernafay Wood
Pease, Capt. C.	Martinpuich
Pease, Lt. R. H. Pike	Ginchy
Platt, Capt. H. E. A.	Hooge
Platt, Lt. J. R.	Ypres
Pollak, Lt. H. L.	Lesbœufs
Power, Lt. J. W.	Ginchy
Priestley, 2nd Lt. C. H.	Guillemont
Prior, Capt. E. F.	Delville Wood
Robertson, Capt. H. M.	Cambrai
Rouse-Boughton-Knight, Lt. T. A. G.	The Somme
Scott, Lt. S. M.	Ginchy
Shaw-Stewart, Lt. N.	
Sherlock, Capt. R. F.	Pozières
Sim, 2nd Lt. L. G. E.	Lesbœufs
Smith, Lt. G. Howard	Merville-St. Vaast
Soames, Maj. M. G.	Longueval
Somers-Smith, Capt. J. R.	Gommecourt
Southwell, Lt. E. H. L.	Flers
Stainton, Lt. W. A.	The Somme
Stanhope, Capt. Hon. R. P.	Flers
Stewart, Capt. W. A. L.	Lesbœufs
Stewart-Richardson, 2nd Lt. J. L.	Potijze
Struben, 2nd Lt. L. F.	Bapaume

Summers, Capt. A. S. M.	Bapaume
Summers, Capt. W. A.	Le Sars
Tennant, Lt. M.	Ginchy
Tennant, Capt. R. E.	Delville Wood
Thorpe, Maj. J. S.	The Somme
Tollemache, 2nd Lt. A. H. W.	St. Quentin
Treffry, 2nd Lt. D. K. de B.	Delville Wood
Trench, Lt. Hon. F. S.	Beaumont Hamel
Trotter, Lt.-Col. E. H.	Montauban
Tufnell, Capt. C. E.	Ginchy
Verelst, Capt. H. W.	Lesbœufs
Walpole, Capt. J. R.	Montauban
Ward, Lt. C. S.	Neuve-Chapelle
Wardley, Lt. G. C. N.	Albert
Warre-Cornish, Maj. G.	Flers
Webb, Capt. E. M.	Pozières
Weldon, Capt. G.	The Somme
Wernher, 2nd Lt. A. P.	Ginchy
Whately, Lt. R. H.	Hohenzollern Redoubt
Wilder, 2nd Lt. F.	Arras
Williams-Vaughan, 2nd Lt. J. C. A.	The Somme
Williamson, Lt. H. H. C.	The Somme
Wilmot-Sitwell, Lt. J. S.	Ypres
Wormald, Capt. G.	
Wright, 2nd Lt. E. G. E.	Ypres
Wynne, Lt. E. H. J.	Ginchy
Young-Herries, Capt. A. D.	

FRANCE, 1917

Aldersey, 2nd Lt. M.	Ypres
Allan, Flight-Sub-Lt. H.	
Anson, 2nd Lt. N. F. E.	The Yser
Armstrong, Capt. W. M.	Monchy
Astley, Coy.-Sergt.-Maj. Hon. J. J.	Ypres
Babington, 2nd Lt. R. V.	Langemarck
Banbury, Capt. W. M.	Ypres
Barclay, Lt. D. S.	Guillemont
Barne, Capt. S.	Arras
Bibby, Lt. J. Pengelly	Langemarck
Blackwood, Lt. H. S.	Cherissy
Blake, Capt. C. R.	Metz-en-Contare
Blewitt, Maj. A.	Audruicq
Bligh, Capt. J. F.	Ypres
Blyth, 2nd Lt. J. C.	Bailleul
Bowes-Lyon, Lt. G. P.	Fontaine-Notre-Dame
Brocklebank, 2nd Lt. R. R.	Bullecourt
Burnside, Capt. E. B. C.	Poelcapelle
Bush, Lt. H. G. de L.	Loos
Butcher, Capt. W. G. D.	Glencorse Wood
Butler-Stoney, Lt. T.	Boesinghe
Buxton, 2nd Lt. Hon. D. B. S.	Houthulst Forest
Cane, 2nd Lt. M.	Ypres
Cattley, Maj. C. F.	La Vacquerie
Cattley, Pte. H. P.	Albert
Chamberlain, Lt. N. G.	Cambrai
Chance, 2nd Lt. E. G. St. C.	Flesquières
Chapman, Pte. H.	Lens
Chitty, 2nd Lt. J. M.	Gonnelieu
Christie, 2nd Lt. P. N. J.	Gheluvelt
Cubitt, Lt. Hon. A. G.	Bourlon Wood
Davidson, Bt. Lt.-Col. N. R.	Langemarck
Denison, Maj. H.	Langemarck
Denman, Lt. R. C.	Gonnelieu
de Paravicini, Maj. J. M.	Masnières
Drewe, 2nd Lt. A.	Ypres
Drummond, 2nd Lt. R. C.	Bourlon Wood
Dunne, Lt. A. S.	Hargicourt
V.C. Dunville, 2nd Lt. J. S.	St. Quentin
Durant, Lt. N. H. C. F.	Gauzeaucourt
Dyer, Capt. Sir J. Swinnerton, Bt.	Ypres
Egerton, Capt. L. E. W.	Pilckem Ridge
Egerton-Green, Capt. J. W. E.	Langemarck
Eley, 2nd Lt. W. A. D.	Miraumont
Elliot, Lt. Hon. G. W. E.	Steenbeck
Farquhar, L/ce-Cpl. E. H. G.	Ypres
Farquhar, Lt. R.	Ypres
Fiennes, Capt. J. E.	Arras
Fleming, Maj. V.	Guillemont
Gartside-Tippinge, Lt. F.	Passchendaele
Gosling, Brig.-Gen. C.	Arras
Greer, Lt.-Col. E. B.	Boesinghe
Gregge-Hopwood, Maj. E. B. G.	Boesinghe
Gregson-Ellis, Capt. R. G.	
Gunther, 2nd Lt. N. O. F.	Monchy-le-Preux
Guy, Capt. C. G.	
Hall-Watt, 2nd Lt. R.	Passchendaele
Hammond, Capt. R. W.	Zuydecoote
Harvey-James, Capt. A. K.	Loos
Helme, Lt. G. M.	Passchendaele
Helme, Lt. R. B.	Villers Faucon
Henty, Maj. G. H.	Gonnelieu
Hermon, Lt.-Col. E. W.	Arras
Hext, 2nd Lt. T. M.	Oppy

Hills, Lt. W. F. W.	Arras
Holt, 2nd Lt. G. V.	Pilckem Ridge
Hope, Lt.-Col. G. E.	Nieuport
Hope-Wallace, Lt. J.	Wancourt
Horner, Lt. E. W.	Noyelles
Horsfall, Capt. R. E.	Vacquerie
Hubbard, Lt. B. J.	Gonnelieu
Hudson, Lt. A. J. B.	Messines
Huntsman, Capt. B. C.	Le Vergiuer
Jackson, 2nd Lt. P. A. D.	Ypres
James, Lt. G. C. B.	Cambrai
Johnson, Lt. R. L.	Ypres
Kay-Shuttleworth, Capt. Hon. L. U.	Vimy Ridge
Keppel, Lt. Hon. A. E. G. A.	Westhoek
Kerr, 2nd Lt. H. G.	Lens
Kindersley, 2nd Lt. L. N.	Bourlon Wood
Kinnaird, Lt. Hon. A. M.	Fontaine-Notre-Dame
Kirby, Capt. A. G.	
Laurie, Lt. W. W.	
Law, Lt. C. J.	
Lawson-Johnston, Lt. A. McW.	St. Pierre-Vaast
Lee, Capt. N. E.	Stirling Castle
Leggatt, 2nd Lt. L. C.	Pilckem Ridge
Leighton, Maj. J. B. T.	
Leveson Gower, Lt. R. C. G. G.	Boesinghe
Levett, 2nd Lt. R. W. B.	Loupard Wood
Loyd, Capt. A. T.	Zillebeke
Loyd, Lt. R. P.	Gonnelieu
Lubbock, Capt. Hon. E. F. P.	Ypres
MacBrayne, 2nd Lt. D. C. H.	Vitry
MacGregor, 2nd Lt. R.	Ypres
Maclachlan, Brig.-Gen. R. C.	Locre
Macneill, Capt. A. D.	Elverdinghe
Martin, Lt. W. G.	Sailly Sallise
Maude, 2nd Lt. G. H. F.	Arras
Messervy, Capt. E. D.	Ypres
Mitchison, Lt. W. A.	Ypres
Murray, Capt. W. R. C.	Loos
Napier, Lt. R. G. C.	Passchendaele
Newall, Lt. N.	
Nickalls, Lt. H. Q.	Nieuport
Noble, 2nd Lt. M. A. P.	Ypres
Ormrod, Capt. L. M.	
Parker, Lt. W. L. O.	Mametz
Philips, 2nd Lt. M. H.	Passchendaele
Pickering, Lt.-Col. F. A. U.	
Pixley, Capt. J. N. F.	Houthulst Forest
Pixley, Capt. R. G. H.	Gouey
Platt, Capt. L. S.	Vitry-en-Artois
Portal, Capt. O. S.	Rœux
Pretor-Pinney, Lt.-Col. C. F.	Arras
Prideaux, Capt. G. A.	Cléry
Pye-Smith, Lt. P. H. G.	Arras
Rawstorne, Capt. T. G.	Pilckem Ridge
Rhys-Davids, Lt. A. P. F.	Wœuvres
Samuda, Maj. C. M. A.	Ypres
Samuel, Lt. G. G.	Messines
Samuelson, Lt. G. B. F.	Fontaine-Notre-Dame
Shaw-Stewart, Lt.-Cr. P. H.	
Shepherd-Cross, Maj. C. H. S.	Ypres
Sillem, 2nd Lt. S. C.	Lille
Steel, Lt. A. I.	Langemarck
Stronge, Lt. J. M.	Passchendaele
Studholme, 2nd Lt. P. F. W.	Gheluvelt
Synge, Lt. A. F.	Bourlon Wood
Tarratt, 2nd Lt. D. McN. F.	Poelcapelle
Taylor, Lt. G. R. M. S.	Wieltje
Taylor, Lt. G. W.	
Tennant, 2nd Lt. H.	Péronne
Thompson, Lt. H. C. St. J.	Gauzeaucourt
Todd, Lt. A. G. E.	Arras
Toulmin, Lt. P. M.	Villers Faucon
Tyser, 2nd Lt. H. E.	Arras
Vane-Tempest, Lt. C. S.	Ligny-en-Cambresis
Venables-Llewelyn, Capt. J. L. Dillwyn-	Boesinghe
Wallington, Capt. G. S.	Langemarck
Walrond, Capt. V.	Arras
Ward, Capt. F. W.	Poelcapelle
Wasey, Capt. C. W. C.	The Somme
Webster, 2nd Lt. G. V. G. A.	Boesinghe
White, Lt. R. J. S.	Vimy Ridge
Wilson, Capt. H. H.	Monchy

FRANCE, 1918

Abbey, Lt. N. R.	Forest of Nieppe
Acland-Troyte, Lt-Col. H. L.	Venant
Amory, Capt. L. Heathcoat	Bayonvillers
Arnott, Capt. J.	Warfusée
Arthur, Maj. J.	Dunkirk
Bainbrigge, 2nd Lt. P. G.	Gauzeaucourt
Balfour, Capt. J.	Arras
Belhaven, Lt.-Col. Master of	Rochelieu

Name	Place
Boscawen, Maj. Hon. G. E.	
Bowman, L/ce-Cpl. A. W.	Valenciennes
Brassey, 2nd Lt. G. C.	St. Leger
Brooke, Maj. W. J.	St. Eloi
Broughton-Adderley, 2nd Lt. P. H.	
Carter, 2nd Lt. J. S.	Flesquières
Carter, Capt. R. T.	
Chapman, Lt. M.	Muris
Charlesworth, Capt. F. R.	Roussoy
Chisenhale-Marsh, Capt. A. H.	Wytschaete
Clive, Capt. P. A.	Bacquoy
Close, Lt. B. S.	Canal du Nord
Coles, Capt. J. H.	Wytschaete
Colfox, 2nd Lt. T. D.	Bethune
Coote, Lt. C. G. E.	Vermand
Creasy, Lt. R. L.	Cambrai
Crichton-Browne, Capt. C. H. V.	Salines
Cross, Lt. R. C.	Arras
Crosse, 2nd Lt. E. A. W.	Canal du Nord
Crossman, Lt. R. D.	Cambrai
Cubitt, Lt. Hon. W. H.	Ham
Curtis, 2nd Lt. J. S.	
Darley, Lt.-Col. J. E. C.	Moreuil Ridge
Dawson-Greene, 2nd Lt. C. J.	Arras
Denison, 2nd Lt. W. F. E.	Amiens
Dilbéroglue, Lt. A	Domart
Dundas, Lt. H. L. N.	Canal du Nord
Eaton, Lt. G. H.	Quierzy
Egerton, Lt. P. de M. W.	Brancoucourt Farm
V.C. Elliott-Cooper, Lt.-Col. N. B.	
Farquhar, Capt. Sir W. R. F., Bt.	Lens
Ferguson, Lt. V. J.	Sailly-le-Sec
Field, Lt. R. G.	Hamel
Follett, Brig.-Gen. G. B. S.	Flesquières
Foster, Lt. C. F.	Vaire
Gamble, Lt. R. D.	Moyenville
Garton, 2nd Lt. E. C.	Arras
Gladstone, 2nd Lt. W. H.	Havrincourt
Glentworth, Capt. Visc.	Etaing
Godsal, Maj. W. H.	Villar-Charbonelle
Grant, 2nd Lt. A.	Canal du Nord
Greenall, Capt. J. E.	Near Amiens
Greville, Lt. G. G. F.	Bertrancourt
V.C. Gribble, Capt. J. R.	Beaumetz
Gull, Capt. F. W. L.	Achiet-le-grand
Gunther, 2nd Lt. G. R.	Preux-le-Sar
Hambro, 2nd Lt. P.	
Hanbury, Maj. E. R	St. Quentin
Hardwicke, Lt.-Col. P. E.	Monchy-le-Preux
Hargreaves, 2nd Lt. S. J.	Gezaincourt
Harmsworth, Capt. Hon. H. A. V. St. G.	Cambrai
Harrison, Capt. B. C.	Rouvroy
Hatfeild, Capt. C. E.	Cambrai
Hay, Lt. C. E. E.	
Heywood, Maj. A. G. P.	Courcelette
Hill, Lt. R. A. G.	Ostend
Hobhouse, Capt. P. E.	Benay
Holland-Martin, 2nd Lt. E. G. R.	Cuy
Honeywill, 2nd Lt. S. R.	Cambrai
Howard, Capt. J. B.	Albert
Hughes, Lt. T. McK.	
Hunter, Lt. M.	Bernafay Wood
Jameson, Lt. J. B.	Amiens
Keating, Lt. H. F. A.	Forest of Nieppe
Lacaita, Capt. F. C.	Hamel
Lacon, Capt. S. J. B.	Ypres
Lascelles, 2nd Lt. G. E.	Pargny
Latham, Capt. S. G.	
Lee, Lt. M. P. E.	The Somme
Lees, Maj. E. B.	Albert
Leveson Gower, Capt. W. G. G.	Awoingt
Littledale, Lt. W. J.	Bapaume
Lubbock, Lt. Hon. H. F. P.	Arras
Lyon, Lt. F. C.	La Couronne
Macalpine-Downie, Lt.-Col. J. R.	Ham
Maclachlan, Brig.-Gen. A. F. C.	St. Quentin
Malcolm, Lt. P.	Mory-St.-Léger
Messervy, Capt. G.	Romilly
Mitchell, Lt. C. R. G.	Hangard
Myers, Sergt. K.	Lens
Noel, Lt. T. C.	
Nolan, Lt. P. J.	
Ogilvy, Lt. W. W.	Jussy
Osborne, 2nd Lt. B. R.	Warginer-le-Petit
Parsons, Capt. A. G.	Kemmel Hill
Peyton, Capt. H. S. C.	Morchain
Pitman, Capt. A. F. E.	Tenebrielen
Powell, Capt. E. I.	Villers Faucon
Powell, 2nd Lt. W. E. G. P. W.	
Ralli, Lt. L. P.	Avesnes
Reid, Capt. S. K.	Soissons
Rice, Capt. J. A. Talbot	Bois des Essarts
Ridout, 2nd Lt. G. A. E.	Hesbécourt
Ritchie, 2nd Lt. H. D.	Canal du Nord
Rosse, Maj. Earl of	Festubert
St. Aubyn, Maj. M. J.	Jussy

Saumarez, Capt. R. S.	Lechelle	Trelawny, Lt. H. W.	Beaurain
Settle, Lt.-Col. R. H. N.	Clèry	Upjohn, Lt. W. M.	St. Leger
Simpson, Lt. O. L. D. M.	Poperinghe	Walpole, Lt. H. S.	Arras
Squirl, Lt. M. E.	Berlaimont	Warren, Maj. R. D.	Ypres
Stephenson, Maj. D. C.	St. Quentin	Watson, 2nd Lt. Sir J., Bt.	Sussy
Stewart, Lt.-Col. W. N.	Épêhy	Willink, Capt. G. O. W.	Lamotte
Stuart-Wortley, Lt.-Col. J.		Wodehouse, 2nd Lt. Hon. E.	
Sturt, Capt. Hon. G. P. M. N.	Voisnes	Wood, Lt.-Col. R. B.	Courcelles
Tennyson, Capt. Hon. A. A.	Fleury	Woodhouse, Capt. L. M.	Grevillers
Thynne, Lt.-Col. Lord A. G.	Bethune	Wright, 2nd Lt. A. H. N.	Eterpigny
Tilney, Maj. L. A.	Dourges		

GALLIPOLI

Ainger, 2nd Lt. T. E.
Anstice, Lt. J. S. R.
Boxall, Capt. C. L.
Chapman, Capt. W. H.
Cherry, Sub-Lt. L. A.
Churchill, Maj. W. M.
Clement, Capt. S. R.
Draper, Capt. R. F.
Hall, 2nd Lt. J. E. K.
Hornby, 2nd Lt. W. R.
Hornsby, 2nd Lt. R. L. W.
Kennaway, Lt. A. L.
Learmonth, Capt. N. J. C. Livingstone
Lee, Brig.-Gen. N.
Lees, Lt. Sir T. E. K., Bt.
Legge, Capt. Hon. G.
Lister, Lt. Hon. C. A.
Loring, Capt. W.
McNeile, Lt.-Col. J.
Merivale, 2nd Lt. J. L.
Moseley, 2nd Lt. H. G. J.
Mundey, Lt. L. C.
Paton, Capt. G. A. L.
Quilter, Lt.-Col. J. A. C.
Romanes, Lt. E. G. R.
Sandbach, Maj. W.
Sartoris, Lt. C. F.
Scudamore, Lt. J. V.
Sheppard, Lt.-Col. S. G.
Stephenson, Capt. E. S.
Whitaker, Sub-Lt. H. J. I.
Williams, Pte. J. N.
Winterbottom, Capt. D. D.

PALESTINE, EGYPT, AND SINAI

Albright, Maj. M. C.	Huj	Kekewich, Maj. H. L.	Gaza
Aldersey, Capt. H.	Palestine	Lloyd-Baker, Capt. M. G.	Sinai
Anderson, Lt. R. G.	Rumani	Loder, Capt. R. E.	Gaza
Bailey, Lt. R. N. M.	Palestine	Middleton, 2nd Lt. E.	Agagia
Birkbeck, Capt. G. W.	Gaza	Mitchell, Lt. R. W.	Sheria, Palestine
Bonsor, Capt. M. C.	Jerusalem	Primrose, Capt. Hon. N. J. A.	Hill of Gezer
Chester, Capt. H. K.	Gaza	Quenington, Lt. Visc.	Katia, Sinai
de Knoop, Capt. J. J. J.	Hod el Bahein	Renton, Capt. A. J.	Jaffa
de Rutzen, Lt. Baron	Katia, Sinai	Richardson, Capt. A. T. L.	Gaza
Dunlop, 2nd Lt. A. H.	Palestine	Sandbach, Capt. G. R.	Palestine
Elcho, Capt. Lord	Katia, Sinai	Seely, Capt. C. G.	Gaza
Fletcher, Lt. H. W.	Gaza	Somerville, 2nd Lt. M. A.	Wadi Kanah
Glazebrook, Maj. P. K.	Birah	Sprigg, Capt. H. A. G.	El Kefr
Harter, 2nd Lt. J. C. F.	Palestine	Thomas, Lt. W. H.	Gaza
Helme, Capt. T. H.	Es-Salt	Wiggin, Capt. G. R.	Oghratina
Hodgson, Capt. C. B. M.	Palestine	Wright, Maj. R.	El Tahta
Jaffray, Lt. Sir J. H., Bt.	Oghratina	Wroughton, Maj. P. M. N.	Palestine
Kekewich, Capt. G.	Palestine		

MESOPOTAMIA

Alington, 2nd Lt. G. H.	Shumram	Harvey, Brig.-Gen. W. J. St. J.	
Caldwell, Lt. J. H.	Daur		Kut-el-Amara
Campbell, 2nd Lt. I.	Sheikh Saad	Howard, Maj. B. H.	Dujailah Ridout
Finlay, 2nd Lt. E. L.		Marchant, Lt. H. S.	Sheikh Saad
Foljambe, Bt. Maj. Hon. J. C. W. S.		Mewburn, Capt. S. W. R.	Kut-el-Amara
	Kut-el-Amara	Prothero, Lt. R. J.	The Lesser Zab
Goschen, 2nd Lt. Hon. G. J.	Sheikh Saad	Simpson, Maj. R. V.	Kut-el-Amara
		Woodhouse, Lt. R. C. H.	Orah

EAST AFRICA

Buller, Trooper F. E.
Drummond, Trooper F. J.
Eckstein, Lt. L. A.

Gibbs, Trooper N. M.
Greswolde-Williams, Lt. F. H. J.
Sandbach, Capt. H. H.

MISCELLANEOUS

Acland-Hood, Midshipman C. A. J.		Powell, Sub-Lt. O. P.	The Baltic
	Jutland	Ralli, 2nd Lt. E. J.	Air Raid, London
Durnford, Capt. R. C.	Persia	Schack-Sommer, Lt. G.	Galicia
Elsmie, Lt.-Col. G. E. D.	Kohat, India	Scott, Maj. J. M. C.	Balkans
Hunter, Capt. T. V.	Camazzole, Italy	Settrington, Lt. Lord	Archangel
Kesteven, Capt. Lord		Winterbottom, Maj. G.	Balkans
s.s. "Mercian," Mediterranean		Wollaston, Lt.-Col. F. H. A.	
Knowles, Lt. R. A. L.	Balkans		Air Raid, London
Middleton, Capt. F.	Sahil, Persia	Wormald, Capt. G.	Balkans

DROWNED

Ashmore, Lt. G. W. P.		St. Aubyn, Lt.-Col. Hon. E. S.	s.s. "Persia"
	s.s. "Transylvania"	Salomons, Capt. D. R. H. P.	
Lees, 2nd Lt. J.	s.s. "Falaba"		H.M.S. "Hythe"
Mullens, Sub-Lt. C. J. A.	Dunkirk		

FROM THE STAFF OF ETON COLLEGE

Mason, Lt. E.   Fromelles

It is regretted that this list is imperfect, and the Compiler asks for information which shall complete it, so that the Libro d'Oro may be accurate

SOME CORRECTIONS OF THE ETON WAR LIST

In the following entries make the alterations indicated

Allfrey, B. H., for T.D. put A.A.S.
Alston, F. G., add C.M.G.
Arbuthnot, R. G. U., "k. accid."
Babington, G., after Capt. insert N. Somerset Yeomanry.
Baird, A. W. F., strike out Australian Imp. Force.
Bankes, R. W., add S.A.D. before P.V.B.
Barker, H. A., strike out late Pte. R.A.M.C.
Blacklock, C. A., add K.R.R.C. in brackets after Maj.-Gen.
Borton, A. E., Bt. Lt.-Col. Black Watch, and Brig.-Gen. R.A.F.
Chance, E. G. St. C. (k. 27.9.18).
Chapman, H., after (t. Maj.) add between commas "discharged medically unfit."
Chinnery, E. F., "k. accid."
Cole, J. J. B., add (F).
Corkran, C. E., add C.B.
Coster-Edwards, J. F., for Derbyshire put Denbighshire.
Darell (in 4 entries), not Darrell.
de Falbe, C. F. G. W., Herts Yeomanry, att. Tank Corps, and Staff.
Eastwood, F. M. (k. 29.10.14).
Egerton, G. A., for 9th put 19th.
Egerton-Warburton, G., for H.E.W.T. put H.F.W.T.
Elliot, F. B., for O.B.E. put C.B.E.
Farquhar, E. H. G., after 2nd Lt. add between commas "discharged medically unfit."
Fergusson, N. M., add w.
Fitton, H. G., for Warwickshire put Berkshire.
Fletcher, Sir E. L., add C.B.E. (F).
Fraser, M. H. This entry to be rubricated.
Furse, Sir W. T., for 1881 put 1880.
Gascoigne, F. R. T. T., add Col. (Appendix).
Graham, A. C., add Gallipoli and w.

Greenwell, E. E. This entry to be rubricated.
Hardwick, P. E., for d. put d.w.
Harrison, J. F., for 1906 put 1900.
Henderson, I. H. D., "k. accid."
Lawson-Walton, J. E. H. This entry to be rubricated.
Lloyd, M. E. (k. 21.10.14).
Logan, C., for J.M.E. put J.H.M.
Loring, W., for D.S.M. put D.C.M.
Loyd, R. L., add O.B.E.
Maude, G. H. F., for The Buffs put E. Surrey Regt.
Maxsted, H. R., not Maxted.
Mellor, J. S. P., for Lt. put Capt.
Milner, E., before H.W.M. insert J.L.J.
Murray, K. R., for Bedfordshire put Wiltshire.
Noel, T. C. This entry not to be rubricated. Cancel brackets and their contents.
Norman, A. M. B., add France.
Paget, Lord V. W., add M.C.
Parker, R. F., add M.B.E.
Philip, W. T., not Phillip (Ruhleben).
Pilkington, F. C., for Canadian L.H. put Corps Mounted Troops.
Primrose, Hon. N. J. A., add Palestine.
Rawlins, E. C. D., for 1903 put 1901, add (F), and strike out France.
Richards, O. W., for R.A.M.C. put A.M.S.
Ruspoli, Don E. M. B. G., add M.C.
Scott-Hopkins, C., add (Hopkins at Eton).
Smith, G. L. I. for Granville L. I.
Stern, Sir A. G. for A. G.
Stock, J. E. K., 1900 for 1901.
Stronge, J. M., for R. Fusiliers put R. Irish Fusiliers.
Tailby, G. W. A., add "the late" (d. 22.12.16).
Thomson, A. G., for Thompson, A. G.
Tillard, T. A., "k. accid."
Trench, C. S. M., for R. Fusiliers put Leinster Regt.
Wardley, G. C. N. (d.w. 24.7.16).

White, J. H. B., 2nd Lt. Manchester Regt., late A.B., R.N.V.R., instead of particulars given.
Wilberforce, Sir H. W. for H. W., and add K.B.E.
Wilder, H. A. J., add w. (Appendix).
Williams, E. G., "k. accid."
Wilson, Sir H. F. M., for Gallipoli put Black Sea.
Wood, N. J., add late Trooper Ceylon Mounted Rifles, and Staff. India.
Worsley, Lord, Capt. R.H.G.
Wright, F. E. F., for 1901 put 1900.
Wyndham, Hon. H. A., for Intell. Off. put Lt.-Col.

Alterations of minor importance will be made in the book which is being written on vellum by Mr. Graily Hewitt for the Memorial Chapel.

The new names and corrections are so printed that they may be inserted in the Final Edition of the War List. Expense prohibits the publication of a further edition of the Eton War List, but a second edition of the supplement may be procured from me on payment of 2s. 6d. This supplement gives the exact places where those whose death was due to enemy action were killed or received a fatal wound.

Please put "Eton War List" on the outside of any communication.

E. L. Vaughan,
    The Marches,
        Willowbrook,
            Eton.

ETON WAR LIST

The following names are to be added to those contained in the Final Edition published on 4 June 1921

1890	Allfrey, H. C., Capt. R.F.A. France	T.D.
1872	Anstruther, C. F. St. C., M.V.O., D.S.O. (Anstruther-Thomson at Eton), Col. Staff	F.St.J.T.
1876	Anstruther, C. J. (Anstruther-Thomson at Eton), Maj. Res. Regt. of Cav.	F.W.C.
1877	Anstruther-Gray, W., Lt.-Col. empld. Scottish Horse	C.C.J.
1889	Candy, C. D. C., O.B.E., Capt. (t. Maj.) Remount Service. N. Russia	T.D.
1905	Cantrell-Hubbersty, E. de B., Lt. Lancashire Fusiliers. France	E.L.V.
1917	Couzens, R. W. H., 2nd Lt. R.E. Signals. France	K.S.
1884	Craven, Earl of, O.B.E. (F) Capt. Staff. France, Balkans, Egypt, Italy	A.C.J.
1905	Cust, R. B. Purey, D.S.O., M.C., Maj. R.F.A., w. 2, m. 3. France	H.F.W.T.
1908	Drexel, J. A., Lt.-Col. U.S. Air Service, late Sergent, Section Aéronautique, French Army. France	R.S.de H.
1886	Fenwick, E. G., Maj. Remount Service	E.H.
1917	Ferguson, A. H., 2nd Lt., late Trooper, 1st Life Gds.	A.B.R.
1877	Foster, Sir W. J., Bart., Col. Staff	H.S., G.R.D, J.P.C.
1887	Fremantle, S. H., C.S.I., C.I.E., Lt.-Col. India Defence Force. India	K.S.
1916	Garnett, P. N. H., 2nd Lt. 10th R. Hussars. France	A.E.C.
1905	Hodgson-Roberts, F. C., Lt. Res. Reg. of Cav., att. R. Scots Greys, late Trooper 19th Hussars. France	H.F.W.T.
1897	Hubbard, J. F., O.B.E., Lt. Grenadier Gds., empld. Lt.-Col. Staff, m. Egypt	H.W.M.
1892	Labouchere, C. E., Capt. Sp. List. France	K.S.
1901	Lacon, H. R. D., Lt. Canadian Artillery. France	J.H.M.H.
1904	Litton, M. V. (Lichtenstadt at Eton), 2nd Lt., late Pte., Middlesex Regt. France	A.C.A., R.S.de H.

1864	Mascall-Thompson, C. (Thompson at Eton), Capt. R.A.S.C. (d. 21.1.16)	J.W.H.
1894	Maxwell, R., Lt. R. Scots, and Staff. France	S.A.D.
1892	Morley, Earl of (Visc. Boringdon at Eton), Capt. R. 1st Devon Yeomanry, and Staff. France, Italy	W.D.
1881	Noel, H. C., Capt. (t. Maj.) Norfolk Yeomanry, empld. M.G.C. France	H.W.M.
1881	Rawlinson, A., C.M.G., D.S.O., C.B.E., Lt.-Col. R.G.A., and Staff, late Lt.-Cr. R.N.V.R. France, Balkans, Mesopotamia, S. Russia	F.W.C.
1876	Sandbach, S., Capt. R. Defence Corps	F.E.D.
1903	Scholfield, R. B., Capt. K.R.R.C. France	F.H.R.
1904	Selwyn, Rev. E. G., C.F., m. Italy	K.S.
1875	Shrewsbury and Talbot, Earl of, K.C.V.O. (Visc. Ingestre at Eton), Maj. Remount Service, and Staff	E.W.
1917	Slade, G. P., 2nd Lt. R.E. Signals. France	K.S.
1911	Stephenson, W. R. S., 2nd Lt. 11th Hussars. France	H.de H.
1917	Verrall, G. T., Lt. R.A.F. France	K.S.
1911	Wakefield, H. B., Lt. R.A.F. Italy	R.S.K.
1906	Wellesley, E. V. C. W., the late, M.C., Maj. R.E., w., m. 2. France (k. accid. in Ireland, 2.10.16)	K.S.
1886	Wethered, W. P., the late, Capt. Suffolk Regt. (d. 18.10.17)	J.C.
1905	Wigan, Sir R. G., Bart. (F) 2nd Lt. R.A.S.C. France	J.H.M.H.
1877	Wolley-Dod, A. G., Maj. Canadian E.F. France	C.W.D., H.S., J.H.M.

Appendix

1880	Jebb, G. S. W., Church Army. Egypt, Palestine	H.D.

Interned at Ruhleben

1903	Fellowes, Capt. Hon. R. A. (also interned at Schloss Celle)	R.A.H.M., L.S.R.B.
1902	Thynne, R. C. S.	C.L., H.F.W.T.

LIST OF ETONIANS WHO FOUGHT IN THE GREAT WAR MCMXIV – MCMXIX

Lightning Source UK Ltd.
Milton Keynes UK
13 August 2010

158340UK00001B/56/P